CHRISTIAN LIFE AND WORSHIP

I am the Vine; you are the Branches.

CHRISTIAN LIFE
AND
WORSHIP

REV. GERALD ELLARD, S.J., Ph.D.

PROFESSOR OF LITURGY

ST. MARY'S COLLEGE, ST. MARYS, KANSAS

Illustrations by
ADÉ DE BETHUNE

THE BRUCE PUBLISHING COMPANY
MILWAUKEE

IMPRIMI POTEST:

P. A. BROOKS
Praepositus Provincialis, Prov. Missourianae, S.J.

NIHIL OBSTAT:

JOHN A. SCHULIEN, S.T.D.
Censor librorum

IMPRIMATUR:

✠ ALBERTUS G. MEYER
Archiepiscopus Milwauchiensis

July 31, 1956

The nihil obstat and imprimatur are official declarations that
a book or pamphlet are free of doctrinal or moral error. No
implication is contained therein that those who have granted
the nihil obstat and imprimatur agree with the contents,
opinions or statements expressed.

Revised and Enlarged, 1950, 1953, 1956

(18/60)

1139339

TO THE CATHOLIC COLLEGIANS OF AMERICA

MEN AND WOMEN

OF IDEALS, AND ARDOR, AND TRAINING

FOR LEADERSHIP,

INTO WHOSE HANDS THE CAUSE OF CHRIST

IN AMERICA PASSES,

THIS BOOK IS AFFECTIONATELY

DEDICATED

ACKNOWLEDGMENT

The quotations from the *Collectio Rituum* (Milwaukee: Bruce, 1954) are made with the kind permission of His Excellency, the Most Reverend Edwin V. O'Hara, chairman of the Episcopal Committee, Confraternity of Christian Doctrine.

AUTHOR'S FOREWORD

THE truths, whereby it is intended that all men should attain salvation, and come to the knowledge that alone can make them happy, were entrusted by Christ to His Church with the bidding, "Keep the deposit." In preserving this faith safe and undiminished, the Church knows how, in every age and in the presence of the most diverse world conditions, to set out her precious doctrines in the manner best calculated, then and there, to win favor and credence. Everywhere and always she has been able to inspire men even to sell all things in order to purchase this pearl of great price. The Church is ever ready to meet the needs of the day, as one of her great sons phrased it, by teaching after a new manner, yet without ever teaching new things.

With each year it becomes increasingly clear that in our age the "new manner" in which Catholicism is being presented, both to its own adherents and to the world at large, is through her social organization and mission. As in course of time an outmoded social order collapses, the Church prays to be allowed to rebuild it on the Christian principles of justice and charity. Thus the multiple social relationships of Christians to one another and to non-Christians are being studied from every angle, and inculcated with every means modern civilization furnishes for the spread of truth. Now, the doctrine most capable of supplying a complete synthesis of the social implications of Christianity is that of "the Mystical Body of Christ." It is thus coming about that this very doctrine is at the present moment fast attracting the special attention of Catholics in their religious thinking.

Again, the corporate worship of the Church, not as a body of incidental knowledge, but as a living system of social sanctification, furnishes in turn the ideal presentation of the Mystical Body. In a masterful analysis of "Catholicism in the Nineteenth Century and at the Beginning of the Twentieth," an English author finds that all the special manifestations of Catholicism at present "fall under a general heading; namely, the corporate activity of the Church as the Mystical Body and renovator of society." In speaking of our Eucharistic worship, he goes on:

> Moreover, all that has been said so far about the social mission of
> the Church reaches its apogee here. The visible unity of the Church is
> manifested and defined in the liturgy of the Redemptive sacrifice, the
> social unity in Communion and the theological interpretation of this
> corporate life in the doctrine of the Mystical Body and sanctifying
> grace. . . .
> The whole trend of the prayer and behavior of the Church [now-
> adays] is dictated by the image called up by Christ of the vine and
> the vine-branches, toward that unit of the Head with the members,
> which has always been the secret of the Church, but is now being
> increasingly realized and manifested.[1]

Keeping pace with this growing realization of recent years, our educa-
tional curricula, from elementary grades to the universities and seminaries, are rapidly undergoing revision to include formal study of the
Mystical Body as mirrored in corporate worship. Moreover, in that
happiest token of a cultural growth among us, adult education, the
subject of worship plays an ever increasing part in the work of study
clubs, lecture groups, evidence guilds, round-table discussions, radio
broadcasts, and the like. This widespread study of the liturgy does not
aim, as do so many similar movements, at keeping abreast of an interesting, modern, intellectual development: it has the deep spiritual purpose
of enabling one to share more intelligently and more fruitfully in the
service of corporate worship in which our lives are necessarily lived.

But here is a striking fact, illustrative of the basic oneness of the whole
Catholic life. While studying and reducing to practice the social implications of corporate *worship,* we find we thus possess ourselves of the key
to so many modern problems of corporate *work*. Press reports constantly
testify that numerous local, regional, or national Catholic organizations,
formed to wrestle with the most varied problems, social or economic,
literary or artistic, all find in this study of the liturgy the source of their
proper motivation, the solution in large measure of their several problems.
The masterful historical syntheses of Christopher Dawson have made
clear, how in the past "every culture is a religion culture": this development of our own day furnishes an example that *our* culture is a religion
culture, and that the integrating element of culture is cult.

---

[1] M. C. D'Arcy, *The Life of the Church* (New York: Sheed & Ward, 1932), pp. 320–22.

Thus while studying the liturgy in order to worship God more perfectly, we find we have come to know at close range, and find our places
in, and play our several personal roles in, the Mystical Body at Prayer.
In this light it is then possible to function as members "knit and compacted" into the same Body at external work, for which the modern name
is Catholic Action. These ideas are set out with cameo sharpness in the
epigrammatic words of our Supreme Pontiff: "What our age needs is
communal prayer," and "The first element of Catholic Action is prayer."
This study of the Mystical Body is the special apprehension of Catholicism proper to the twentieth century.

That this book may be a more serviceable tool for study-club groups,
evidence guilds, and similar organizations, it will be found to contain
abundant supplementary material. Besides a select bibliography, there
will be found short reading lists in every chapter. Also certain allied
subjects for discussion or further private reading along the lines of the
chapter topics are there suggested. Lastly, the chapters themselves are
terminated by some bit of documentation from original sources. In selecting these, as will be seen at a glance, the author's preferences have run
steadily to the precious heirlooms of primitive Christianity. Several
reasons have guided the writer here. There is, first, the universal and
unfailing charm evoked by everything connected with the Church of the
Apostles and the Martyrs. Again, the temper of the Christian life, result-
ing from the widespread consciousness of the social mission of the
Church — the ideal aimed at in this book — finds its finest exemplar
in the lives of the first Christian centuries. Lastly, if any group of men,
then surely, as Cardinal Newman said, "the primitive Christians are to
be trusted as witnesses of the genius of the Gospel system."

It will be noted that the New Testament quotations are cited, throughout, from the new and superior Westminster Version, now for the most
part in print. Thus, passages long familiar in the Douay wordings are
here found couched in somewhat different terms; but the superior in-
telligibility and the freshness of the Westminster renderings are ample
warrants for adopting the newer translation. Longer citations are, as a
rule, here broken into sense-lines, the advantages of which arrangement
are so patent as to need no explanation.

The final and pleasant task remains of acknowledging assistance
received while preparing the materials for this book. Almost every page

has benefited by the discriminating touch of a brother, G. Augustine Ellard, S.J., Professor of Mystical Theology in St. Louis University. Permission to reproduce copyrighted matter was unstintingly given by many authors and publishers of America and Europe, as the frequent acknowledgments throughout the book will testify.

No small gratification was experienced when the publication of this book under the Religion and Culture aegis was arranged. That initial satisfaction, I am happy to state, has constantly increased, thanks to the wholehearted cooperation of the General Editor and the personnel of The Bruce Publishing Company. Their efforts enhance the value of the work.

May it find a warm welcome, and may it have its own share in forming Christ in the Christian of today!

GERALD ELLARD, S.J., PH.D.

The Presentation of Our Lady, 1933,
St. Mary's College, St. Marys, Kansas

PREFACE TO THE FIRST REVISED EDITION

SO CORDIAL was the welcome accorded this book seven years ago that its many known deficiencies have been a matter of acute embarrassment to me ever since. Minor inaccuracies and other blemishes were removed in successive printings, but the publication of this revision, long planned, has by force of circumstances been deferred to the present. Doubtless the delay has excellently served its purpose, for I saw the margins of my own classroom copy of the book gradually acquire scores of notations, many of them elaborated by the book's friends far and near. In particular the late scholar and apostle, August F. Schinner, D.D., sometime bishop of Spokane, spared himself no trouble to enhance the value of this work. By a happy inspiration, too, teachers across the country sent me the written criticisms and impressions of their classes. Most pupils and many teachers found the opening chapters of the first edition unmanageable, and these have been entirely recast now with a view of obviating the former difficulties. Apart from that, the changes introduced in revision have scarcely modified the original outlines. We trust they will be found to make for greater clarity and a more cogent documentation. In this connection one might note that in the former edition source readings were chosen almost exclusively from primitive Christian times: some students felt that documentation in a similar strain and running through the centuries right down to our own times would provide a stronger brief. Lastly, it was felt good in this edition to take more direct cognizance of the current American scene in the matters of active participation in corporate worship and the motivation of Catholic Action. The publisher is fortunate in having secured the services of Miss Bethune whose talent has lovingly translated the message of the script into noble and graphic beauty. The exacting tasks of seeing this through the press have been greatly lightened for me by the labors of Reverend Gilbert C. Peterson, S.J.

No book that has the things of God for its theme can be in any sense finished or complete, for, as the son of Sirach said long since,

> We shall say much and yet shall want words,
> but the sum of all our words is
> He is ALL.

Such as it is, may He deign to use it to His greater glory, and to the manifesting in America of an ensign for peoples near and far!

GERALD ELLARD, S.J., PH.D.

St. Marys, Kansas
The Manifestation (Epiphany)
of our Lord, January 6, 1940

The way this book has stood the wear and tear of time may probably augur its further usefulness. In a national survey of college Religion texts made some years ago, this one, among a hundred books, stood behind but two in the number of college-adoptions. A Minnesota college has organized its Religion Department under the name of this volume, and a Green Bay bank carries a checking-account called Literature For Christian Life and Worship. I have, as a souvenir from a Rochester, New York, youth rally, a lapel-button reading "Let's be Christocrats," a word with which the book concludes. Trifles in themselves, these latter facts disclose that, under God, the book has proved a serviceable tool. Of course, it could be a much better one.

I did not suspect when the book was planned as showing the Mystical Body of Christ engaged in worship that Pope Pius XII would give us masterful encyclicals on just those two themes in 1943 and 1947 respectively. These papal directives did not entail material changes in this work, but still no book upon this theme could pretend to be up-to-date that did not take account of this doctrinal and pastoral guidance of Christ's Vicar. Within the framework of the volume the encyclicals (and other new materials) have been cited as opportunity afforded, but in the chapters dealing directly with the Mass, that on the liturgy is quoted verbatim and at length. This was all the easier to do for Canon Smith's excellent translations, published by the Catholic Truth Society, and cited here with their permissions. The work thus gains immeasurably in authority and in relevance, and so should be a finer instrument in hand. God continue to prosper it!

GERALD ELLARD, S.J., PH.D.

Easter Sunday, April 9, 1950

CONTENTS

CONTENTS

fellowship with, and sense of responsibility toward, other Christians: the unifying concepts of Christ-life and Christ-work: nobility and dignity of working for Christ as "Christocrats."

CHRISTIAN LIFE AND WORSHIP

CHRISTIAN LIFE AND WORSHIP

Chapter I

ADULT CATHOLICISM AND A SECRET

With milk I fed you,
not with solid food,
for you were not yet strong enough (I Cor. iii,2).

MOST of us had as little to do with our becoming Catholics as with our being born into a given family, or holding citizenship in our nation. Early in our reasoning years we simply learned of these existing relationships. Just as naturally as we were taught to cherish parents and family in a unique manner, or to foster patriotism for our native land, so with equal spontaneity we grew into an attachment for Catholicism, as the dwelling place, so to speak, of God among men. In our earliest years we were grounded in its basic teachings, and this preliminary training was yearly expanded, somewhat like the annual rings of a tree's growth, in that each embodied the previous circuit and widened it ever so little all around. At adolescence we had learned, as we thought, all there was to know about the truths of faith, and had been inducted into the practice of its ordinary acts proper to our years. We were urged to hold steadfast to those teachings, and to be faithful to the practices learned. That is the training suitable to childhood. Like so much early training, it was largely a matter of storing the memory with truths that would only slowly and gradually take real root in the understanding, and so be a sufficient aid to the will. It is no one's fault that this childhood apprehension of religion, like childhood apprehension of anything else, is not deep: it is measured to the growing child. It is not meant to be the complete, but merely the preliminary part of one's religious education. The process of further education is, of course, largely a matter of using the known data in new associations and rela-

1

tionships. Higher mathematics studied in maturity can never dispense with the multiplication tables learned by rote in childhood, but in the matter of new associations goes far beyond any use of those tables possible to childhood. There is likewise what we may justly call the Catholicism studied in maturity, or, simply, adult Catholicism, which in corresponding fashion exceeds the shallows of the immature mind. Unfortunately few Catholics attain this mature understanding of their religion, because, in proportion to the full membership of the Church, so very few have the opportunity, as adults, to pursue this study in systematic, organized fashion. It is generally conceded that little systematic knowledge on the adult level is acquired by listening to sermons, even for a lifetime. For, to the majority of their hearers the preachers on Sundays could always say with St. Paul:

> We have much to say,
> and it is difficult to expound it . . .
> For whereas by this time ye ought to be teachers,
> ye still need someone to teach you
> the simplest elements of the oracles of God,
> and ye have become such that ye need milk,

Heb. v,11–14   and not solid food.

But as collegians we are in the singularly privileged position of being able to

> pass over the initial teachings concerning Christ,

Heb, vi,1   and press on to their full development.

What the Apostle in the same context calls the strong meat of fully developed doctrine can now enlarge the adolescent's apperception of revealed Truth:

> When I was a child,
> I spoke as a child,
> I felt as a child,
> I thought as a child,
> now that I am become man,

I Cor. xiii,11,12   I have made an end of childish ways.

Elements of Christianity. It is not easy to characterize briefly and accurately this "elementary Catholicism" as distinguished from
the breadth and length and height and depth

which St. Paul challenged his adult converts to explore. Perhaps it can
be done by saying that the former is like a fair knowledge of Catholicism
derived exclusively from the *Gospels* of *Matthew, Mark,* and *Luke* and
the latter to a knowledge of Catholicism as mirrored also in *The Acts
of the Apostles,* the *Epistles,* and *St. John's Gospel.* The first three
Gospels, written roughly around the year 50, may be called a triple
transcript of the preaching in which the *simplest elements* about Christ   Heb. v,12
are given the chief emphasis. They show a Teacher, who speaks with
authority from God, announcing truths of a future Church; they show
a Saviour of tenderness and matchless sympathy for men, who died on
a cross for man's salvation and the remission of our sins. *The Acts of
the Apostles* picture Catholicism springing into existence in Pentecostal
fire and spreading through that Circle of Lands on the shores of the
Mediterranean, which the ancients called their universe. The *Epistles*
of the New Testament, unlike the *Gospels of Matthew, Mark,* and *Luke,*
are not the first elements of Christianity, but are addressed to those
who have heard the Gospels. They are subsequent teachings and applications of Christianity. They came only when the elements, called milk
by the Apostle, had prepared their hearers for a maturer presentation
of the Good Tidings. Taking the full content of the former revelations
for granted, they pass on to an *inner penetration* of the Sermon on the
Mount, the Parables, and the Kingdom. Nothing in the early records
is ever in least degree contravened or cast aside, but a luxuriant unfolding of inner verities replaces external features and detached historical
facts. Those Gospels are a doorway, and St. Paul leads us over the
threshold into the house of God on earth.

An Apostle's Great Secret. There is in St. Paul an inner, deeper
knowledge of Catholicism, as we said, of which the more superficial
Catholic may have scarcely an inkling. To neophytes, who were just a
little wearied of their first elements, and longed for further knowledge,
he could write:

> Among the [spiritually] *mature*
>   we do speak of a wisdom . . .
>   *the* wisdom of God [embodied] in a *mystery* . . .   I Cor. ii,6
> [Heretofore] I could not speak to you as spiritual men,
>   but . . . as babes in Christ . . .   I Cor. iii,1

To quote Saint Paul
is to requote Jesus Christ.
(Saint John Chrysostom)

Here and elsewhere St. Paul speaks of a great "secret" entrusted to him. By divine guidance he emphatically preached to the growing churches a doctrine which was *not* emphasized in Matthew, Mark, and Luke. But Paul's secret shared the fate of so many secrets, in that it speedily became public. Indeed, his secret was not intended to be held back longer; as it was, the world had waited centuries for it:

> To establish you in *my* gospel,
> and in the preaching about Jesus Christ,
> in accordance with *His revelation of that mystery*
> *which in ages past was kept secret,*
> but now hath been made manifest.   Rom. xvi,25,26

This passage in *Colossians* gives a summary formulation of the content of the secret:

> Now I rejoice in my sufferings on your behalf,
> and make up in my flesh
> what is lacking to the sufferings of Christ,
> on behalf of *His Body, which is the Church,*
> whereof I am become a minister.
> Such [is indeed] the command of God
> given me in *your* regard,
> to utter the *full* word of God *touching the mystery*
> which hath been hidden from former ages and generations,
> but it hath now been made manifest to His saints . . .
> to whom God hath willed to make known
> what is the wealth of the glory
> of this *mystery*
> for the *Gentiles,*
> *which is Christ [dwelling] in you.*   Col. i,24–28

The "secret," the new "Gospel," the new "revelation," is that Christ dwells in the members of His Church, vivifying it into a living body. In brief, *Christ dwells in us.*

Secret Becomes Sacrament and Mystery. When translators rendered St. Paul's *Letters* into Latin, they sometimes put "sacrament" for his secret, and sometimes "mystery." Each term brings out a part of his meaning; together they lay bare the secret, on which, as he reminds us, his special emphasis was laid by divine guidance. If we substitute these two words in the passage from *Colossians* given just above, St. Paul's thought is this: *Christ dwells within His Church making us a living body, and this is a great mystery, and this is a great sacrament.* Any Catholic, asked to define "mystery," would answer readily enough that it is a truth of revelation partly understandable by man, but in part beyond our limited comprehension. We still subscribe to the definition quoted by Father Gruden from St. John Chrysostom, enunciated fifteen hundred years ago: "We call a mystery that of which one aspect is seen and the other aspect is believed."[1] "Sacrament," too, has a meaning every child knows by heart: a visible sign, instituted by Christ, to give [invisible] grace. The seven Sacraments have in current usage so exclusively appropriated that word to themselves that it is now not applied to anything else. But St. Paul called the Church a sacrament. Surely the Church, which contains all the Sacraments, may very justly and accurately be called a sort of Super-Sacrament. No reality on earth more eminently fulfills the definition of being a visible sign, instituted by Christ, to confer grace. Well, then, to sum up: The Catholic Church is revealed to us as a living body, and this is a "mystery": That is, one aspect of the Church is seen, the other unseen; one aspect is understood; the other remains mysterious. And Catholicism is revealed to us as a "sacrament," a divinely instituted sign of invisible grace. With the mention of grace we come closer to the full measure of adult Catholicism.

In Epis. I ad Cor. Hom. VII

Eph. v,32

Life and Light and St. John. When the nascent Catholic Church had assimilated with divine help, and over a period of about forty years,

> things hard to understand [naturally],
> as our beloved brother Paul . . . hath written to you,
> in virtue of the wisdom given him,

II Pet. iii,16

the time was ripe for the final revealed formulation, that of St. John's *Gospel,* written that *our joy might be full!*

I John i,4

---

[1] J. C. Gruden, *The Mystical Christ* (St. Louis: Herder, 1936), p. 59.

That which was from the beginning . . .
    that which we beheld,
    and our hands handled,
    in regard of the WORD of LIFE: I John i,1–3
    In Him was LIFE,
and the LIFE was the LIGHT of men . . .
    Of His fulness we have all received,
    and grace on grace.   John i,4–16

Life, light, and grace in Christ: St. John portrays on one and the same canvas the first elements of the earlier Gospels, that is, the Christ of history, and the fuller developments of St. Paul, that is, the Christ of "mystery," where everything is dominated by the indwelling within us of the LIFE of God:

The glory which Thou hast given Me,
    I have given them,
    that they may be one,
      as We are one,
      I in them,
    and Thou in Me,
that they may be perfected in unity . . .
    in order that *the love*
wherewith Thou hast loved Me,
    may be in them,
    and I in them.   John xvii,23–26

This love, wherewith the Father loved the Son, is, as we shall see, the Person of the Holy Ghost. If St. Paul stresses chiefly that the Church is the Body of Christ, St. John further discloses that within that Body Catholics have in some way a share in God-life. These two doctrines are the hallmarks of adult Catholicism. Collegiate study of religion can begin in no better way than by a first grappling with them.

Christ of History, Christ of Mystery. All Catholics are taught to say the *Apostles' Creed* daily, but the "catechism" Catholic, as we may call him, repeats the statements of the *Creed* about Christ without going beyond the synoptists' history, or penetrating into the mystery. His birth, passion, death, resurrection, ascension into heaven, and future coming as Judge, state this Catholic's faith in Christ's redeeming function. To the mature Catholic, Christ is all that and besides is the Word Incarnate extended to the whole Catholic Church, making this a living, mysterious body, in which He lives, and grows, and attains fulfillment. Besides being King and Lord, Divine Exemplar, Christ is within us, sanctifying us and uniting us to the Father through the working of the Holy Spirit. Listen to St. Augustine, and see how the great Bishop of Hippo expands the *first elements* of the Creed:

Heb. vi,1

> Our Lord Jesus Christ is as one whole perfect Man, both Head and Body: We acknowledge the Head in that Man, who was born of the Virgin Mary, suffered under Pontius Pilate, was buried, arose from the dead, ascended into Heaven, sitteth at the right hand of the Father, whence we wait His coming as Judge of the living and the dead. This is the Head of the Church . . . Christ's Body, of which Christ is the Head.

In Ps. XC, Serm. II

Few have phrased this central doctrine of adult Catholicism as felicitously as Father D'Arcy in the words:

> The heart of the Christian mystery is this, that the Christ, who was both God and man, has determined to extend His life from the terrain of Galilee and Jerusalem to the ends of the earth, and His span of days from thirty odd years to the end of time; and He is to bear the same relation, as far as that is possible, to human individuals which His divine nature bore to His own body and soul. There is one fundamental difference, of course; His own soul and body had no human personality, whereas we, no matter how close we live in the divine life, remain persons, able to say: "no longer I but Thou!"[2]

I Cor. iii,23   **Ye Are Christ's.** We are Catholics. How did we become so? The answers given to that question might be an index of our understanding of adult Catholicism. One might conceivably compare becoming a Catholic with joining a club, or fraternity, or social grouping. That is simplicity itself: Some idea is proposed, accepted, this acceptance signified in simple fashion, as a payment, or signature, and the matter is accomplished. But in becoming a Catholic, one does not accept, one *is accepted:*

---

[2]M. C. D'Arcy, *The Life of the Church* (New York: Sheed and Ward, 1933), p. 19.

Ye have not chosen Me,
but I have chosen you.   John xv,16

Another might suggest that becoming a Catholic is like becoming a
naturalized citizen, which is a much more difficult matter. St. Paul calls
his converts newly enfranchised citizens:

Ye were at that time Christless . . .
But now ye are no longer strangers and foreigners,
but ye are fellow-citizens of the saints.   Eph. ii,13,19

The context of this quotation might possibly suggest yet another answer,
that being accepted as a Catholic is like being named to membership in
what we call the official family of the President:

Ye are . . . members of the household of God.   Eph. ii,19

Even so, membership in some capacity in a large official household is far
from the same as being *adopted* legally and socially into the President's
family circle. Well, every Catholic knows that our Baptism effects in us
a *sonship of adoption*. In brief, one who has studied adult Catholicism,   Eph. i,5
would be inclined to say: "One does not 'join' Catholicism: *Christ takes
hold of a man and implants him into Himself,* and he is then a Catholic.
Henceforth he lives in permanent, personal, *vital* relationship with
Christ." Baptism is a rite, as we shall see, whereby man is embodied into
Christ. Once baptized into Christ's Body, his life is supposed to be a   I Cor. xii,13
constant growing into Christ:

Thus we shall be no longer children . . .
Rather we shall hold the truth in charity,
and *grow in all things into Him*
Who is the Head, Christ.   Eph. iv,14,15
Unto the building up of the Body of Christ,
till we all attain . . .
to the full knowledge of the Son of God,
to the perfect man,
the full measure of the stature of Christ.   Eph. iv,12,13

This corporate Catholicism of maturity will be studied in this book, but
not so much directly, as by the indirect avenue leading through the acts
of corporate worship.

Summary. Much deeper than in the "catechism" religion of childhood and adolescence, the Catholic Church is revealed to the mature mind as a mysterious Super-Sacrament, as it were, which Holy Writ calls a body, the soul of which is the Holy Spirit.

First-Century Source Material

(From "Letter of Pope Clement I" to the Church of Corinth on the occasion of schism in about the year 90.)

The great cannot exist without the small, nor the small without the great; there is a certain mixture among them all, and herein lies the advantage. Let us take our body; the head is nothing without the feet, likewise the feet are nothing without the head; the smallest members of our body are necessary and valuable to the whole body, but all work together and are united in a common subjection to preserve the whole body (xxxvii).

. . . Why are there strife and passion and divisions and schisms and war among you? Or have we not one God, and one Christ and one Spirit of grace poured out upon us? And is there not one calling in Christ? Why do you divide and tear asunder the members of Christ, and raise up strife against our own body, and reach such a pitch of madness as to forget that we are members one of another? . . . Your schism has turned aside many, and has cast many into discouragement, many to doubt, all of us to grief; and your sedition continues (xlvi).

Eph. iv,4–6

Take up the *Epistle* of the blessed Paul the Apostle. What did he first write to you at the beginning of his preaching? With true inspiration he charged you concerning himself and Cephas and Apollos, because even then you had made yourselves partisans. But that partisanship entailed less guilt upon you; for you were partisans of Apostles of high reputation, and of a man approved by them. But now consider who they are who have perverted you, and have lessened the respect due to your famous love for the brethren. It is a shameful report, beloved, extremely shameful, and unworthy of your training in Christ, that on account of one or two persons the steadfast and ancient church of the Corinthians is being disloyal to the presbyters . . . (xlvii).

Let him who has love for Christ, perform the commandments of Christ.

Who is able to explain the bond of the love of God? Who is sufficient to tell the greatness of its beauty? The height to which love lifts us is not to be expressed. Love unites us to God. "Love covereth a multitude of sins." Love beareth all things, is long suffering in all things. There is I Cor. xiii,4–7 nothing base, nothing haughty in love; love admits no schism, love makes no sedition, love does all things in concord. In love were all the elect of God made perfect. Without love is nothing well pleasing to God. In love did the Master receive us; for the sake of the love which He had toward us did Jesus Christ our Lord give His Blood by the will of God for us, and His Flesh for our flesh, and His life for our lives . . . (xlviii).

Topics for Further Discussion:

In the first three Gospels the word *Christ* (literally "anointed" and used as the equivalent of the Hebrew *Messiah*) is an adjective denoting a title, while in St. Paul and in St. John's Gospel it is used as a proper name. In the light of what we have said, do you see any significance in this fact?

The miracle of the loaves and the fishes is the only incident of the Public Life recorded in the first three Gospels (Matt. xvi, Mark vi, Luke ix) and *repeated* by St. John (vi). Try to assign a good reason for this singular fact.

In this chapter we have used the word *sacrament* in a wide sense: find three Postcommunion Prayers in your missal in which the word is used in the same broad sense.

St. Ambrose wrote a treatise with the title, *The Sacrament of the Incarnation of the Lord:* in what sense does he use the word *sacrament?*

A famous Cardinal, Berulle, once wrote, "Christ is Himself the major Sacrament." What does he mean by this?

Readings:

K. Adam, *The Son of God* (New York: Sheed and Ward, 1934), "The Sources for the Life of Jesus," pp. 49–86; "The Mental Stature of Jesus," pp. 87–133; "The Interior Life of Jesus," pp. 134–156.

R. H. Benson, *Christ in the Church* (St. Louis: Herder, 1913), "Introductory," pp. 3–34.

M. C. D'Arcy, ed., *The Life of the Church* (New York: Sheed and Ward, 1932), "The Faith of the Disciples," pp. 63–92.

R. Guardini, *The Church and the Catholic* (New York: Sheed and Ward, 1935), "The Awakening of the Church in the Soul," pp. 11–31.

C. Lattey, *The Atonement, Papers Read at the Summer School of Catholic Studies, Cambridge, 1931* (New York: Sheed and Ward, 1932), "In St. Paul's Epistles," pp. 47–81.

W. J. McGarry, *Paul and the Crucified* (New York: America Press, 1939), "We Preach Christ Crucified," pp. 29–69.

E. Mersch–J. R. Kelly, *The Whole Christ* (Milwaukee: Bruce, 1938), "St. John — Jesus Our Life," pp. 165–181; "St. John — Our Divine Life," pp. 182–195.

E. Mersch–D. F. Ryan, *Morality and the Mystical Body* (New York: Kenedy, 1939), "Religion, Christianity, Catholicism," pp. 3–18; "Christianity," pp. 19–37; "Catholicism," pp. 38–60.

E. I. Watkin, *The Catholic Centre* (New York: Sheed and Ward, 1939), "Liturgy, the Expression of the Catholic Centre," pp. 1–26.

Chapter II

CATHOLICISM IS CHRIST BEING FULFILLED

Unto the building up
of the body of Christ (Eph. iv,12).

WHEN God pitched His tent among men in the Person of His Son, as St. John phrased it in Greek, He proceeded to John i,14 make the great revelation spoken of in the preceding pages, and to establish, as the channel of salvation, an imperishable society Matt. xvi,18 which He called a Church. Recruits to this society, after freely accepting the revelation whole and entire, would be inducted by baptismal rites. Matt. xxviii,20 This society was often styled a kingdom, the kingdom of God in mankind, as in the Old Testament the Jewish people were called God's Kingdom. Another common metaphor of the Ancient Dispensation found more sparing use by Christ, that wherein the new union of God and man was likened to marriage. That the society would perforce live among Matt. ix,15 enemies was pictured in terms of a field sown by Christ with wheat and oversown with enemy cockle. That the original sowing would nevertheless Matt. xiii enjoy a vast, natural development was foretold by the comparison of a mustard seed, smallest of seeds, growing into a great tree. That from Matt. xiii small beginnings the new society would enliven and vitalize mankind as a whole was predicted in the figure of a handful of leaven fermenting the entire mass. That in some real manner Christ, even after His ascent Matt. xiii,33 into heaven, would abide within His kingdom all days was promised in several connections; as, that He would be with His teachers; would be Matt. xxviii,20 with even two or three gathered in His Name; that *He* would be fed and Matt. xviii,20 clothed and comforted in His needy brethren. Not Christ alone, but also Matt. xxv,40 the Holy Spirit, the Paraclete, whom the Father would send at Christ's behest, was to abide with the Church permanently and bring to its mind all those things once said by Christ Himself. On the occasion on which John xiv,26 He instituted the Holy Eucharist, at least, Christ used language that

13

Saul, Saul, why dost thou persecute Me?

clearly indicated an identity of life and of fruitfulness between Himself
and His disciples:

> I am the Vine,
> ye the branches;
> he that abideth in Me,
> and I in him,
> the same beareth much fruit.   John xv,5

To establish this society Christ died and rose from the dead. Thus, taken   John x,11-18
comprehensively, Christ founded a visible society wherein man is taken
possession of by the Father, in Christ, through the instrumentality of
the Holy Ghost. To the fiercely separatist Jew, the revelation of Christ
could, and to some extent did at first, appear to sanction and promote
separatism, of salvation for the Jew and not for the Gentile.

An Apostle for the Gentiles. Among the most hostile opponents
of the new Way, as Catholicism was first called, was Saul, Pharisee
among Pharisees. At home and abroad he harried Christians in utter
fury. Once, while on such an errand, on the highroad to Damascus, at
midday, he saw a light brighter than the sun, whereat he and his associates fell to the ground. He tells the story:

> I heard a voice saying to me in the Hebrew tongue,
> "Saul, Saul, why dost thou persecute Me?
> It is hard for thee to kick against the goad."
And I said: "Who art Thou, Lord?"
> And the Lord said: "I am Jesus, Whom thou dost persecute.
> But arise, and stand upon thy feet;
> for to this purpose have I appeared to thee,
> that I should appoint thee minister and witness
>   both of what thou hast seen
>   and to what thou shalt yet see of Me,
> delivering thee from the people and from the gentiles,
> unto whom I am sending thee,
>   to open their eyes,
> that they should turn from darkness to light
>   and from the power of Satan unto God,
> thus to receive forgiveness of their sins,
> and a portion with those sanctified by faith in Me."   Acts xxvi,14-18

Saul (the future Paul) rose up, a Pharisee turned inside out, as has been
said, the Apostle of the Gentiles.

Gal. i,11 **"The Gospel Preached by Me."** Years later, when the time came to fulfill what was specifically *his* mission to the Gentiles, that is, both to bring them into the Church, and to win acceptance for them from the separatist Jewish Christians, Paul showed how well he had studied his problem. What he had seen in the dazzling light near Damascus was the supreme fact of Jesus of Nazareth claiming identification with His persecuted Church; what he was to see in subsequent revelations in Arabia, whither he had retired, was the full content of the Christian revelation.

> The gospel preached by me
>   is no gospel of man,
>   nor did I receive or learn it from man,
>   but by revelation from Jesus Christ.

Gal. i,11,12

In dealing with the Gentiles, Paul knew and used the metaphors of the Kingdom, of marriage, of the sown field, of the leaven in the dough, but his preference was all for expressions which emphasized an identity of life between Christ and Christian, as when he spoke of the Roman converts as fruitful because engrafted into Christ. In framing his message to the Greco-Romans, Paul would speak in terms of their culture as clearly as he could. Thus, no one of the Hellenic world would be ignorant of the famous fable of Aesop:

I Cor. vi,9
Eph. v,23
I Cor. iii,9
I Cor. v,7

Rom. xi,24

THE STOMACH AND THE MEMBERS

One fine day it occurred to the members of the body that they were doing all the work, while the stomach was getting all the food. So they held a meeting, and after a long discussion, decided to strike, until the stomach should take its proper share of the work. So for a day or two, the hands refused to take the food, the mouth refused to receive it, and the teeth had no work to do. But after a day or two the members began to find that they themselves were not in a very active condition: the hands could hardly move, and the mouth was all parched and dry, while the legs were unable to support the rest. So thus they found that even the stomach in its dull, quiet way was doing necessary work for the body, and that all must work together or the body will go to pieces.[1]

Aesop's Fables

Every Roman citizen would know how the telling of that very fable

---

[1] *The Harvard Classics, XVII, Folk-Lore and Fable* (New York: Collier & Son, 1909), p. 22.

had eased a serious crisis in Roman history, when the plebs had seceded to the Sacred Mount. Xenophon, among the Greeks, had applied the analogue, Cicero among the Latins. Besides, applying the fable to the citizens and the State was merely a figurative way of expressing what Plato had taught in his *Republic*, that the State is but a man magnified. Although the Church is a far higher kind of society than the State, St. Paul found here apt data for casting the ancient analogue into a formulation of Catholicism. As a result, in simple, graphic terms the sublime mystery of the Christian man possessed and vitalized by the Father, in Christ, through the Holy Ghost, glows forever enshrined in the Inspired Writing in terms of the head and members. The Hellenes of Galatia, of Colossae, of Ephesus, of Philippi, of Corinth, of Rome were taught by Paul that the Catholic Church is a Person, a vast collective personality, the Head of which is Christ, the body of which complements Christ by giving Him Catholics as members.

Livy, ii,32
Xenophon, *Mem.*, II, iii,18
Cicero, *De Offic.*, III, v,22
Plato, *Republic*
Gal. iii,20
Col. iii,11
Eph. ii,13
Phil. i,21
Rom. xii,4
I Cor. xii,12

> He [the Father] hath subjected all things
>   beneath His [Christ's] feet,
>   and hath given Him for supreme Head to the Church,
>   which is His body,
> the fulness of Him Who is wholly fulfilled in all.

Eph. i,22,23

"Ye Are the Body of Christ." Before further analysis of the thought of the Apostle, it will help not a little to study his phraseology, so to speak, in his most detailed exposition of this concept. It will be noted that he improves the occasion to inculcate contentment with one's station in the Church:

I Cor. xii,27

> For as the body is one
> and hath many members,
> and all the members of the body,
>   many as they are,
>   form one body,
> so also [it is with] Christ.

> For in one Spirit
> all we, whether Jews or Greeks,
>   whether slaves or free,
>   were baptized into one body:
> and we were all given to drink of one Spirit.

Now the body is not one member, but many.

If the foot say,
"Because I am not a hand, I am not of the body,"
not for all that doth it cease to be of the body.

And if the ear say,
"Because I am not an eye, I am not of the body,"
not for all that doth it cease to be of the body.

If the body were all eye,
where would be the sense of hearing?
If it were all hearing,
where would be the sense of smell?

As it is, God hath set each several member of the body
according as He willed.

And if they were all a single member,
where would be the body?

But, as it is, there are many members,
yet one single body.

And the eye cannot say to the hand,
"I have no need of thee";
or again the head to the feet,
"I have no need of thee."

Nay, much rather, those members of the body
which seem to be weaker
are [still] necessary,
and those which we deem less honorable in the body,
we surround with special honor.

[Yea], God hath so compounded the body
as to give special honor where it is lacking,
that there may be no schism in the body,
but that the members may have common care for each other.

And if one member suffereth,
all the members suffer therewith;

> if a member be honored,
> all the members rejoice therewith.

> Now ye are [together] the body of Christ,
> and severally His members.

I Cor. xii,12–27

A Body Which Is a Church. Such Bible passages are the seed-bed of the Church's teaching on this subject, on which in 1943 Pope Pius XII published an encyclical. The first pages of that letter are like a sketch of the whole, and they are set out herewith. But to read only that opening sketch would be like reading the superscription on the envelope, and then not reading the letter inside! The introductory draft, however, will provide ample material for our immediate attention. "The doctrine of the *Col. i,24* Mystical Body of Christ, which is the Church, a doctrine received originally from the lips of the Redeemer himself," says His Holiness, "and making manifest the inestimable boon of our most intimate union with so august a Head, has a surpassing splendor which commends it to the meditation of all those who are moved by the divine Spirit, and with the light which it sheds upon their minds, it is a powerful stimulus to the salutary conduct which it enjoins. We accordingly consider it our duty to address you on the subject . . . , developing and explaining especially those aspects of it which concern the Church militant." *Mystical Body*

Corporate Fall — Corporate Redemption. "As we begin to consider this doctrine we recall the words of the Apostle, 'Where sin abounded, grace did more abound.' We all know that the father of the *Rom. v,20* whole human race was by God constituted in such an exalted state that together with the life of this earth he would have transmitted to posterity also the supernatural life of heavenly grace. But after Adam's unhappy fall the whole of mankind, infected by the hereditary stain, forfeited its participation in the divine nature and we all became children of wrath. *II Pet. i,4* Nevertheless, the God of mercies 'so loved the world as to give His only- *Eph. ii,3* begotten Son,' and with that same divine love the Word of the eternal *John iii,16* Father took to Himself of the race of Adam a human nature — innocent, however, and without stain — so that from the new and heavenly Adam the grace of the Holy Spirit might flow into all the children of the first parent. These, having been deprived of the divine adoptive sonship through the sin of the first man, would now, through the Incarnation of the Word, become brethren according to the flesh of the only-begotten Son of God, and so receive the power to become sons of God. And *John i,12* therefore Jesus Christ on the Cross not only compensated the outraged justice of the eternal Father, but also merited for us, His kindred, an unspeakable abundance of graces."

Mystical Body

The Church, the Grace-Channel. The Pope goes on to say: "These graces He might Himself, had He so chosen, have bestowed directly upon the human race; but He willed to do this by means of a visible Church in which men would be united, and through which they would all in some sort co-operate with Him in distributing the divine fruits of Redemption. As the Word of God vouchsafed to use our nature to redeem men by His pains and torments, in a somewhat similar way He makes use of His Church throughout the ages to perpetuate the work He had begun. And so to describe this true Church of Christ — which is the Holy, Catholic, Apostolic, Roman Church — there is no name more noble, more excellent, none more divine, than 'the mystical Body of Jesus Christ,' a name which blossoms like a flower from numerous passages of the Sacred Scriptures, and the writings of the Fathers."

*Vat. Coun.,
prol.,1*

Mystical Body

One, Undivided, Visible Body. "That the Church is a body we find asserted again and again in the Sacred Scriptures. 'Christ,' says the Apostle, 'is the Head of the Body, the Church.' Now if the Church is a body it must be something one and undivided, according to the statement of St. Paul: 'Being many, we are one body in Christ.' And not only must it be one and undivided, but it must also be something concrete and visible, as our predecessor of happy memory Leo XIII says in his Encyclical *Statis cognitum*: 'By the very fact of being a body the Church is visible.' It is therefore an aberration from divine truth to represent the Church as something intangible and invisible. . . ."

Col. i,18

Rom. xii,5

June 29, 1896

Mystical Body

Memberly Self-Help. "But a body requires a number of members so connected that they help one another. And, in fact, as in our mortal organism when one member suffers the others suffer with it, and the healthy members come to the assistance of those that are ailing, so in the Church individual members do not live only for themselves; they also help their fellow-members, all co-operating with one another for their mutual support and for the constant growth of the whole body."

Mystical Body

Organically Compacted. "Moreover, just as in nature a body does not consist of an indiscriminate heap of members, but must be provided with organs, that is, with members not having the same function, yet properly co-ordinated, so the Church for this special reason merits to

be called a body, because it results from a suitable disposition and co-
herent union of parts, and is provided with members different from one
another but harmoniously compacted. It is thus that the Apostle
describes the Church: 'As in one body we have many members, but all
the members have not the same office; so we, being many, are one body
in Christ; and every one members one of another.' "   *Rom. xii,4*

Clergy, Religious, the Laity. "But it must not be supposed," the
Holy Father states, "that this co-ordinated, or organic, structure of the
Church is confined exclusively to the grades of the hierarchy. . . . It is
certainly true that those who possess the sacred power in this Body must
be considered primary and principal members, since it is through them
that the divine Redeemer himself has willed the functions of Christ as
teacher, king, and priest to endure throughout the ages. But when the
Fathers of the Church mention the ministries of this Body, its grades,
professions, states, orders, and offices, they rightly have in mind not only
persons in sacred orders, but also all those who have embraced the evangel-
ical counsels . . . ; also those who, though living in the world, actively de-
vote themselves to spiritual or corporal works of mercy; and also those
who are joined in chaste wedlock. Indeed, it is to be observed, especially in
present circumstances, that fathers and mothers and godparents, and
particularly those among the laity who co-operate with the ecclesiastical
hierarchy in spreading the kingdom of the divine Redeemer, hold an
honored though often an obscure place in the Christian society, and that
they, too, are able, with the inspiration and help of God, to attain the
highest degree of sanctity, which, as Jesus Christ has promised, will
never be wanting in His Church."   *Mystical Body*

The Sacramental Life-Stream. "The human body, finally, has its
own means for fostering the life, health, and growth of itself and of each
of its members. And the Saviour of the human race in His infinite goodness has in like manner admirably equipped His mystical Body by en-
dowing it with the SACRAMENTS, making available for its members a
progressive series of graces to sustain them from the cradle to their last
breath, and abundantly providing also for the social needs of the whole
Body. By BAPTISM those who have been born to this mortal life are regenerated from the death of sin and made members of the Church, and
also invested with a special character which makes them able and fit to
receive the other Sacraments. The chrism of CONFIRMATION gives believers new strength so that they may strenuously guard and defend

Mother Church and the faith which they have received from her. The Sacrament of PENANCE offers a saving remedy to members of the Church who have fallen into sin, and this not only for the sake of their own salvation, but also in order that their fellow-members may be saved from the danger of contagion, and receive instead an example and an incentive to virtue. Nor is this all; in the sacred EUCHARIST the faithful are nourished and fortified at a common banquet, and by an ineffable and divine bond united with one another and with the divine Head of the whole Body. And when at last they are mortally ill, loving Mother Church is at their side with the Sacrament of EXTREME UNCTION, and although, God so willing, she does not always thereby restore health to the body, she nevertheless applies a supernatural balm to the wounded soul, so providing new citizens for heaven and heavenly intercessors for *Mystical Body* herself, who will enjoy the divine goodness for all eternity."

With Social Helps as Well. The papal letter goes on: "For the social needs of the Church Christ has also provided in a particular way by two other Sacraments which He instituted. The Sacrament of MATRIMONY, in which the parties become the ministers of grace to each other, ensures the regular numerical increase of the Christian community, and, what is more important, the proper and religious education of the offspring, the lack of which would constitute a grave menace to the mystical Body. And HOLY ORDERS, finally, consecrates to the perpetual service of God those who are destined to offer the Eucharistic Victim, to nourish the flock of the faithful with the Bread of the Angels and with the food of doctrine, to guide them with the divine command- ments and counsels, and to fortify them by their other supernatural *Mystical Body* functions. . . ."

Conditions of Membership. "Only those are to be accounted really members of the Church," says Pius XII in a most important passage, "who have been regenerated in the waters of Baptism and profess the true faith, and have not cut themselves off from the structure of the Body by their own unhappy act or been severed therefrom, for very grave crimes, by the legitimate authority. 'For in one Spirit,' says the Apostle, I Cor. xii,13 'were we all baptized into one body, whether Jews or Gentiles, whether bond or free.' Hence, as in the true community of the faithful there is Eph. iv,4 but one Body, one Spirit, one Lord, and one Baptism, so there can also be only one faith: and therefore whoever refuses to hear the Church must, Matt. xviii,17 as the Lord commanded, be considered as the heathen and publican. It

follows that those who are divided from one another in faith or government cannot be living in the one Body so described, and by its one divine
Spirit."   *Mystical Body*

Sinners Not Excluded. A factor that has often proved puzzling,
the relation of the sinner to the Body, is handled with precision and
clarity in our context: "But the fact that the Body of the Church bears
the august name of Christ must not lead anyone to suppose that, also
during this time of its earthly pilgrimage, its membership is restricted to
those who are eminent in sanctity, or that it is composed only of those
whom God has predestined to eternal beatitude. For it is in keeping with
the infinite mercy of our Saviour that He does not here refuse a place in   Matt. xi,11
His mystical Body to those whom He formerly admitted to His table.   Mark ii,16
Schism, heresy, or apostasy are such of their very nature that they sever   Luke xv,2
a man from the Body of the Church; but not every sin, even the most
grievous, is of such a kind. Nor does all life depart from those who,
though by sin they have lost charity and divine grace and are consequently no longer capable of a supernatural reward, nevertheless retain
Christian faith and hope, and, illumined by heavenly light, are
moved by the inner promptings and stirrings of the Holy Spirit to
conceive a salutary fear and be urged to prayer and repentance of
their sin."   *Mystical Body*

Summary. "No greater glory, no greater dignity," writes Pius XII
toward the *end* of the long letter whose *beginning* we have read, "no
honor more sublime, can be conceived than that of belonging to the Holy,
Catholic, Apostolic, and Roman Church, wherein we become members
of this venerable Body, and are governed by this one august Head,
filled with the one divine Spirit, and nourished during this earthly exile
with one doctrine and with the one Bread of angels, until at last we
come to enjoy in heaven one everlasting happiness."

Second-Century Source Material

(*In his great work*, FALSE WISDOM UNMASKED AND REFUTED, *St. Irenaeus is
arguing against Gnostics [the "Wise"], who held that nothing
corporeal is holy or can be saved.*)

He [Christ] recapitulated in Himself the long history of men, sum-
ming up and giving us salvation, in order that we might receive again
in Christ Jesus that which we had long lost in Adam . . . (III, 18, 1).

No Father before Augustine,
no Theologian after him
has treated this mystical unity
so profoundly.   (Karl Adam)

Those who say that He was only a man, the son of Joseph, remain and die in the slavery of the first disobedience; they are not united to the Word of God the Father, nor do they receive freedom from the Son, according to His words:

> If the Son shall make you free,
> you shall be free indeed.   John viii,36

But since they know not the Emmanuel born of the Virgin, they are deprived of His gift, which is eternal life ... (III, 19, 1).

Some do not receive the gift of adoption, because they sneer at the pure Incarnation and birth of the Word of God. They rob man of his ascent to God and remain ungrateful to the Word of God who became incarnate for their sakes. For this is why the Word of God is man, and this is why the Son of God became the Son of Man, that man might possess the Word, receive adoption, and become the son of God....

God willed to be born, to be with us, to descend into the lower regions of the earth in order to find the lost sheep that is His own creature; He willed to ascend into heaven, to present to the Father this man that He had found, and to offer in Himself the first-fruits of man's resurrection. As the Head is risen from the dead, so the rest of the body of every man will rise again when the penalty of disobedience shall have been paid. This body will be united again by joints and sinews; it will be strengthened by a divine growth, and every member will have his own proper place in the body. There are many mansions in the Father's house, since there are many members in the body (III, 19, 3).

Topics for Further Discussion:

St. Paul appeals to the doctrine of the mystical body as motive in inculcating many moral virtues, as:

a) Fellowship in the Holy Eucharist (I Cor. x,14–22);
b) Fraternal "memberly" union (Eph. iv,4; Col. iii,15);
c) Love of husbands for wives (Eph. v,22–32);
d) Contentment with inferior lot (I Cor. xii,4–11);
e) Commiseration with others' suffering (I Cor. xii,26);
f) Rejoicing in good fortune of others (I Cor. xii,26);
g) Truthfulness (Eph. iv,25);
h) Modesty of demeanor (Rom. xii,4–11);
i) Chastity (I Cor. vi,15–19);
j) Supernatural equality of sexes (Gal. iii,28);

k) Union of Gentile and Jew (Eph. ii,19; Gal. iii,28);
l) Union of peoples of all races (Col. iii,9–11);
m) Union of all social classes (Gal. iii,28; Col. iii,9–11).

Readings:

Pope Pius XII, *On the Mystical Body of Jesus Christ:* Encyclical Letter, June 29, 1943: translated by Canon G. D. Smith (London: CTS, 1948), cited with permission.

K. Adam, *The Spirit of Catholicism* (New York: Macmillan, 1929), "The Church, the Body of Christ," pp. 31–45.

———— *St. Augustine* (New York: Sheed and Ward, 1932), pp. 39–56.

M. E. Boylan, *The Mystical Body* (Westminster: Newman, 1948), "In Christ," pp. 57–68.

L. F. Cervantes, *That You May Live* (St. Paul: Guild Press, 1945), "Christ to Paul," pp. 13–33.

Father Cuthbert, *God and the Supernatural* (New York: Longmans, Green, 1920); E. I. Watkin, "The Church as the Mystical Body of Christ," pp. 235–276.

A. Goodier, *The Inner Life of the Catholic* (New York: Longmans, Green, 1933), "Life in Jesus Christ," pp. 43–75.

C. Grimaud–J. F. Newcomb, *One Only Christ* (New York: Benziger, 1939), " 'Our' Union with the Head," pp. 39–55.

J. C. Gruden, *The Mystical Christ* (St. Louis: Herder, 1936), "The Mystical Body of Christ," pp. 27–63.

R. Guardini, *The Church and the Catholic* (New York: Sheed and Ward, 1935), "The Fellowship of the Liturgy," pp. 141–149.

D. A. Lord, *Our Part in the Mystical Body* (St. Louis: Queen's Work, 1935), "The Astounding Truth," pp. 13–34; "The Sublime Figure," pp. 66–76.

C. Marmion, *Christ, the Life of the Soul* (St. Louis: Herder, 1923), "The Church the Mystical Body of Christ," pp. 85–98.

W. J. McGarry, *Paul and the Crucified* (New York: America Press, 1939), "The Mystical Body of Christ," pp. 208–256.

E. Mersch–J. R. Kelly, *The Whole Christ* (Milwaukee: Bruce, 1938), "The Mystical Christ in Paul's Preaching," pp. 85–102; *passim.*

E. Mersch–D. F. Ryan, *Morality and the Mystical Body* (New York: Kenedy, 1939), "The Mystical Body and Contemporary Humanity," pp. 161–178.

E. Myers, "The Mystical Body of Christ," *The Teaching of the Catholic Church* (New York: Macmillan, 1949), II, pp. 659–690.

M. Perkins, *Speaking of How to Pray* (New York: Sheed & Ward, 1944), "The Church Which Is His Body," pp. 48–65.

R. Plus, *God within Us* (New York: Kenedy, 1924), "Grace and Our Possible Relations with God within Us," pp. 73–122.

H. Pope, *The Church, Papers Read at the Summer School of Catholic Studies,* ed. C. Lattey (St. Louis: Herder, 1928), "The Mystical Body of Christ," pp. 57–90.

F. Prat, *The Theology of St. Paul* (London: Burns, Oates and Washbourne, 1926–27), I, "The Church, the Mystical Body of Christ," pp. 300–308; II, "The Mystical Body, Foundation of Morality," pp. 285–288.

M. J. Scheeben–C. Vollert, *The Mysteries of Christianity* (St. Louis: Herder,

1946), "Position Occupied by the God-Man With Reference to the Human Race," pp. 364–389.

F. J. Sheed, *Theology and Sanity* (New York: Sheed & Ward, 1946), "The Mystical Body of Christ," pp. 266–279.

A. Tanquerey, *The Spiritual Life* (Tournai: Desclée, 1930), "Jesus the Head of a Mystical Body," etc., pp. 75–99.

C. J. Woolen, *Christ in His Mystical Body* (Westminster: Newman, 1948), "The Mystic Sacrifice," pp. 58–64.

Chapter III

GOD-LIFE SHARED WITH MAN

In Him dwelleth all the fulness
of the Godhead corporally:
and ye are filled [therewith]
in Him Who is the Head (Col. ii,9,10).

THERE are insects, science assures us, whose life span is but a single day. It makes us marvel that birth, growth, the complicated processes of reproduction, senescence, and, after an allotted period, death itself could all be crowded into the space of twenty-four hours. In comparison to the length and more especially to the *depth* of man's mortal existence that of such an insect seems as nothing. Man's life as compared to God's is even at greater disadvantage than the insect's beside man's. For the insect and the man are both in the range of the finite, and both *can* be measured in the same terms. St. Bonaventure says that such is the reality of God's Being that ours by comparison is nothing. But man's *natural* life is not, and never was, the whole story. Man was created in God's image and likeness precisely with a view *to being lifted up by the grant of a share in God's own life itself.* Man's natural life is intended to serve only as the foundation, the substratum, of a second and incomparably higher *kind* of life, to be planted thereon by an act of God. We are accustomed to call the former, familiar living of man *natural* inasmuch as it corresponds to man's created *nature;* but because the second kind of life, the "superimposed life," the sharing in God-life, *altogether exceeds the capacities of any creature,* we are accustomed to call it *grace* (Latin for *gift*), as if one would say simply THE GIFT. Now, the words, *gift* or *grace,* do not directly suggest *life,* dynamic being and acting and growing with God-life, and so there is need of studying the supernatural reality we call grace in its primary meaning of God-life, rather than in its secondary characteristic of *something gratuitously conferred.* And as soon as we speak of grace in terms of *life,* we

28

find we are back in the mystic body system, too. It was in terms of this body that the Fathers of the Council of Trent defined the acquisition and functioning of grace:

> . . . Jesus Christ Himself as the Head [imparting life] to the members, and as the Vine [vivifying] the branches, ceaselessly communicates a life-force to those justified [i.e., to those who are in the state of grace], and this life-force always precedes, accompanies and follows their good works, and without it these could in no way be pleasing to God or worthy of merit. . . .

Eph. iv, 15

John xv, 5

Sess. vi

God-Life at the Source. The Ancient of Days from eternity called Himself, "I am who am." He is the uncreated, self-subsistent Spirit, whose Wisdom, Power, and Goodness knew no imaginable limitations. Such are God's perfections, too, that He, the one God, has a triple Personality. The Father has the Divine Nature; the Son has the same Nature, and likewise the Holy Spirit, but the *manner* in which each Divine Person has it is different, unique, and incommunicable. Contemplating the unfathomable depth of His own essence, the Father by an infinite act of the divine intelligence, knows Himself, expresses Himself to Himself, and thereby begets in intellectual generation a spotless Image of His Majesty. This Image is the Son, the Second Person of the Holy Trinity. With unspeakable and everlasting affection the Father regards the Beloved Son, and with no less affection the Son rejoices in the Father. From this never ceasing flow of love and love-for-love springs, as it were, a divine Fire, a Divine Love impersonate, and this is the Third Person of the Holy Trinity, whom we call the Holy Spirit (*Spiritus* = the *Breath* of the Father and the Son). Though we have no way of phrasing it which does not imply a difference in time or inferiority in perfection, we know that these incomparable processions of Godhead within God do not militate against perfect equality among the Three Divine Persons. These mutual and eternal relations of the Three Divine Persons to each other constitute the *life,* and the all-joyous *living,* and ineffable bliss of the Triune God. Infinite, pregnant Truth is ceaselessly contemplated, and beatifying Beauty enjoyed without cessation. "O happy Three-in-one," cries the Church in wondering adoration.

Dan. vii, 9

God-Life Overflowing. God was perfectly sufficient for His own boundless bliss, but *love feels that it must give* and give of itself. As if compelled by love God *had* to create: "There remains nothing for God,"

De Pot. q. ix, a.9 says St. Thomas, "than that external activity which we call creation." So God made creatures, on whom He might heap benefactions, to whom He might give of His perfections and of His own beatitude. Highest were the angels, noble spirits of intellect and will, who radiate outward from Divinity through nine grades of created being. "A little less than *Ps. viii,6* the angels" God made man, who shares intelligence and free will with the celestial spirits, but is nonetheless immersed in corporeal nature. Man thus links in himself the immortal world of the spiritual and the mortal one of the flesh. Below man are the myriad forms of non-rational animal life and non-sentient vegetative life, and inorganic being devoid of life. These lower realms do not concern us here. Both angels and men are so made *naturally* that they can be made over, "built upon," *supernaturally:* Their finite nature and highest endowments were such that they could be raised or elevated by God Himself and made capable of sharing God-life, at least in its divine operations. To understand this elevation we must realize that there is question not merely of sharing *a* knowledge or *a* love of God, but of participating in *God's way of knowing, God's way of loving;* even, of sharing God's *act* of knowing, and God's *act* of loving. Thus, to characterize God's *kind* of knowledge, as compared with ours, it is enough for our present purpose to recall that, while we *derive* knowledge through sense pictures of objects, etc., God contemplates infinite Truth without any *medium of knowledge.* That *way* of knowing is natural only to God, not natural to any creatable nature. Now, in elevating man, or angel, to that condition wherein he is able to share *that* Act of knowing with Himself, God must divinize, or deify, the created nature at least to some extent. Thus, if in daily life we met a speaking *Mickey Mouse* we should know that, along with the rational function of speech, it had received enough rational nature on which to ground that function. So, St. Peter did not hesitate to say that we may

II Pet. i,4   become partakers of the divine nature.

St. John used the same argument, that sharing an Act proper only to God, argues in us a certain sharing in God-nature as well:

> We shall be like to Him
> *because* we shall see Him as He is.

I John iii,2

Old Adam — New Adam. This great GIFT of a new, supernatural life was given as a *seed capable of developing* into the intimate sharing of God's highest activity in heaven, God's generative knowing, God's vital union in love. It was entrusted to our race in Adam, who was to hand it on to his progeny, even as he transmitted our physical or natural life. But everyone knows the sequel of Adam's fall, and our sad losses therein. His recreancy cost us heavily, for he lost for us as well as for himself the nice poise and balance of the various elements of human nature, lost his freedom from sickness and pain, his bodily immortality, and, worse than all else, lost the humanly irretrievable germ of God-life. Man after Adam sank into savagery, barbarism, idolatry, and was called by St. Augustine "a mass of sin." To restore the God-life, there was need of a new Adam. God's answer is the Incarnation.

Atonement and At-one-ment. The Word, by whom all things were made, the well-beloved Son, who possessed the God-life in all its pleni-tude, wedded our nature to His own in a personal union so close that thenceforth *He* existed *in two natures.* The humanity of Christ, body and soul, intellect and will, was indissolubly assumed to the Second Person of the Holy Trinity:

John i,3
John i,14
John i,16

> He is the Head of the body, the Church . . .
> *in Him*
> it hath pleased the Father
> that all fulness should dwell
> and *through Him*
> to reconcile all things to Himself.

Col. i,9,10

To that sacred humanity in which

> dwells the fulness of the Godhead corporally

Col. ii,9

God communicated the plenitude of deity, to ennoble it, to consecrate it, to adorn it with the uncreated Life of God. This is called Christ's *personal* endowment. Over and above that, the same humanity was filled with the plenitude of created, communicable riches of grace needed to make all men

> gracious in the Well-Beloved.

Eph. i,6

This is the fullness of Christ as Head of the Body, the Church. By His redeeming death Christ merited a *share of that grace* for us, so that our baptism into Him effects in us a *finite, created reproduction of the just-*

ness of God. St. Paul speaks in the first person, but he speaks for all who are *in Christ*:

Phil. iii,9

> my justness . . . which is . . . in Christ,
> that justness which cometh from God.

In the very next verse the Apostle speaks, in one of those Pauline words impossible of translation, of becoming of *one and the same nature* with
Phil. iii,10 Christ in His death. The Tridentine Fathers, who specified this justness as "the justice of God, not that whereby He is just Himself, but that
Sess. vii whereby He maketh us just," follow the Apostle in affirming that this great GIFT is given to His members, by Christ, through the indwelling of the Holy Spirit:

> Know ye not that your bodies are members of Christ? . . .
> Know ye not that your body is the temple of the Holy Spirit
>   Who is within you,
I Cor. vi,15–20   Whom ye have from God?

Gal. vi,15 The *effects* of this *new* life of the *new* creature in Christ cannot be summarily described more graphically than by the Apostle:

> If, then, any man be in Christ,
>   he is a *new creature:*
>   the former things have passed away:
II Cor. v,17   behold, I make all things *new*.

Eph. iii,8 **"Unsearchable Riches."** Our yearnings and dreams for fullness of life, for a role commensurate with the talents and vital forces we feel surging within us — these rainbow dreams will never be realized during
Gal. v,24 our mortal lives. The "flesh" is marked for its "crucifixion." By ineluctable destiny our talents, forces, and capacities will never in this life get their full chance *to live*. They are not created for so small a theater. Instead the task assigned us is to develop, even in the squirrel-cage smallness of everyday existence, that

I John iii,9   seed of God abiding in [us].

John x,10 For out of that seed grows *the more abundant life*, wherein nothing less than

> the depth of the riches
> and of the wisdom
Rom. xi,33   and of the knowledge of God

Christ dwells in us

THE BLESSED TRINITY

indwelling ~ elevating ~ energizing ~ divinizing man

	External Graces		
Supernatural Order	SUPER-NATURE →	SUPER-FACULTIES →	SUPER-ACTIVITY →
	Sanctifying grace	Faith Hope Charity — Seven Gifts of H.G.	Prompting grace Helping grace
			growing →
			ASSIMIL-ATION → God-like
			TO GOD → HAPPINESS

	External Things		
Natural Order	HUMAN NATURE	FACULTIES	ACTIVITY
	Soul →	Intellect | Will →	Stimu-lation | Reac-tion →

is to be the scope and field of our keen searching and our joy. Now, even our sluggard spirits are tireless in searching for truth: God beholds in His nature inexhaustible depths of clearest Truth. Our purblind wills cleave to whatever seems good to us: God enjoys from all eternity the serenest possession of endless goodness. The smallest, broken fragment of beauty, how it delights and ennobles and elevates man! How shall one picture God's fruition of limitless, all-embracing beauty? The enjoyment of this bliss is, so to speak, the lifework of God. Not less is the destiny given man in the mystic body. What if one's capacity to live the fullest life on earth go unrealized? The day-by-day growth in knowledge of God, and the loyal performance of daily duties, *internally fit us* for the fullest living of the God-life in Heaven. 11139339

> Filled with the knowledge of God's will
> and all wisdom and spiritual insight.
> Thus may ye walk worthily of the Lord . . .
> being fruitful in all good works
> and increasing in the full knowledge of God . . .
> joyfully rendering thanks to the Father,
> Who hath *fitted us*
> for *our portion*
> of the inheritance of the saints in light.   Col. i,9–14

Two students, one of whom is only *naturally* alive, the other a Catholic *also supernaturally alive,* have a chemistry assignment to study under the common stimulus of a class quiz. But the student supernaturally alive has the additional stimulus of thereby serving God. For the first it is merely a matter of studying chemistry. In the case of the second the act of studying proceeds also from a vital principle *supernaturalized* by sanctifying grace, and is "stepped up" by special helping acts of God (actual graces), so that the very act by which chemistry is being assimilated, aids in the deepening and expanding of the God-life in the student. Any and every act performed in Christ, or "in grace," is a further divinization of the member of Christ, "since Jesus Christ Himself . . . Council of Trent ceaselessly imparts a life force," as was seen above.

A Difficulty. Before going on to survey the plane of the super-life, it is well to take cognizance of a *difficulty* which inevitably arises about taking this Scriptural language literally. In a Christian there is no visible manifestation of any vital change or transformation wrought within. The difference between him and an unbaptized person is not externally visible. But, if a living being must act, as is said, only in accord with its own *kind* of life, should there not be some external signs of this immeasurable elevation of nature? The complete answer to this difficulty must take account of two factors. First, that the supernatural life is *only embryonic* or latent in man *now,* to become fully operative at his "entrance" into heaven. Thus, the highest supernatural faculty, that of seeing God, is latent in us now, much the same as the gift of speech and other gifts are for a time latent or inoperative in young children. A more important phase of the problem, however, is the wholly *spiritual* nature of the realities here in question. The super-life and all that pertains to it is altogether spiritual, and completely escapes the senses. It is taken wholly on faith, just as the difference between a consecrated and a non-consecrated host. But mere inability to understand fully what one is or has in no way lessens the inheritance: a king's child has the presumptive rights and prerogatives of a king, though as yet he knows of them only imperfectly.

Life-Principle Superimposed. This chart will illustrate the *status* or *plane of the supernatural* life, with its own faculties, aspirations, and goal. Human nature, or the man-life, with all its faculties and powers remaining quite intact, receives by "being ingrafted into Christ" a super-nature, which permeates, and elevates, and assimilates human nature to the divine, without abolishing anything of it. The man-life is thus raised to heights and possibilities otherwise as far beyond it as the power of speech to a statue. Grace is often called a super-soul, a term quite intelligible in the light of what has been said. But it is more accurate to speak of this super-life as a real likeness of the life of God, produced by God within the human soul. Like every vital principle, it is a positive power, an operative force. It brings with it super-faculties, in virtue of which man is enabled to walk in what St. Paul calls newness of life.

Super-Faculties in Act. The chief among these super-faculties, the infused virtues of *faith, hope,* and *charity,* harmoniously cooperate with man's intellect and will, so that *all combine* in the production of a supernatural act. This act is now evaluated by God in the light of the vital principle producing it, and since this is *principally* the Christ-life streaming through the Christian, the act takes on a worth and value as of Christ, or as of the Godhead itself. A supernatural act is an *act-in-Christ.* Thus the Christian, as a brilliant modern apologist has it,

Rom. xi,17–24

gains the value of Him with whom he is incorporate, and his actions, more than intertwined with Christ's, truly "Christ-ed," have Christ's value before God. Such is the Christian mystery. If a man be incorporate with Christ, God, looking down upon His Son, sees that man within Him; looking on the man, He sees Christ. When Christ praises God, I in Him am offering that praise; when Christ offers Himself to God, He offers me in Himself, I Him in myself, and myself in Him.[1]

Living Temples of God. Let us revert here to a circumstance but lightly touched upon above. There is with grace an *accompanying* phenomenon far more sublime than anything that has been said of grace itself. *Grace is always accompanied* in the Christian soul by an intimate, *personal presence of the three Divine Persons.*

> We will come to him,
> and make Our abode with him,   John xiv,23

said Christ in reference to the Christian. This indwelling of God in the soul, His being "at home" in the Christian, is usually attributed to the Person of the Holy Spirit, in His character of Sanctifier and Personal Love. Thus, the Holy Spirit is given to us, who makes of our bodies living   Eph. v,5
temples, who helps us pray because we do not know how to pray as we   I Cor. iii,16
ought, and, in a word, the Holy Spirit becomes for us a Paraclete, our   Rom. viii,26
Helper, our Comforter.

Let us draw out the notion one step farther. If God is in us, then He acts in us. Now the *inner* life of God is the enjoyment, as we said, of the endless wonders of the All-Holy Trinity, and His *exterior* life is the governance of the universe. These two orders of action, taken together, make up the infinite, all-embracing Act of God. The Christian can assure himself that, as he is a permanent temple of the living God, so too does this infinite all-embracing Act go forward within him, through him, with him so that *his* every least action is caught up and associated with the very life of God. St. Paul spoke to the Athenians of a God in whom we move and live and are; with equal truth can the Christian speak of   Acts xvii,28
God who moves and lives and is in him. Even in this probation period the Christian enjoys unfathomable depths of *life.*

Summary. Man was created with a view to a supernatural elevation by which he should share the divine life. After his fall, his sins may be

---

[1] C. C. Martindale, *The Faith of the Roman Church* (London: Methuen, 1927), p. 89,

forgiven, his super-nature restored, and his sharing by communication in God-life effected by contact with Christ in His mystic body. Christ pours the Holy Spirit upon His members, who, besides dwelling in them, effects in their souls a created reflection or reproduction of the God-life. This God-life within us is ordinarily called sanctifying grace. By Christian living this God-germ develops, and thereby fits man to enter more and more into and live by the life of God in heaven. There is no question, of course, of pantheism, or becoming God, for we retain our personalities and natures, though these are really "divinized" by cooption into God-life.

It is no longer I that live,
but Christ that liveth in me.

Gal. ii,20

Third-Century Source Material

(How Christians at Carthage reacted when some Numidian Christians were enslaved. A Letter of St. Cyprian.)

Cyprian to Januarius, Maximus, Proculus, Victor, Modianus, Nemesian, Nampulus, and Honoratus, Greeting:

With the greatest distress of spirit and not without tears have we read, dearest brothers, the letters which your solicitude has sent us about the captivity of our brothers and sisters. Who would not feel sorrow in such misfortunes, or who would not reckon the sorrow of his brother *his own* sorrow, since the Apostle saith:

If one member suffereth,
all the members suffer therewith,
and if one member be honored,
all the members rejoice therewith,

I Cor. xii,26

and in another place:

II Cor. xi,29   Who is weak, and I am not weak?

Hence to us here and now the captivity of our brethren must be reckoned our own captivity, and the sorrow of those in danger our own sorrow, since in our union we are only one body. Not alone love but even the duty of faith urges and impels us to redeem the members, the brethren. For the Apostle again saith:

Know ye not that you are the temple of God,
and that the Spirit of God dwells in you?

I Cor. iii,16

So that even if our love were not strong enough to rescue the brethren, we should in that case consider that it is the temples of God which are held captive. We dare not refuse, and, forgetful of sympathy, suffer it that temples of God be held in captivity, but with all the forces at our command must we strive and quickly bring it about that by our good offices we serve Christ our Judge and the Lord our God. For since the Apostle saith:

> All of you who were baptized into Christ,
>   have put on Christ, Gal. iii,27

we must see Christ in our captive brethren, and rescue Him from the danger of captivity who rescued us from the danger of death. . . .

All this has your letter made us consider and pierced us with sorrow. Therefore have all promptly and willingly gathered alms for our brethren. . . . For when the Lord says in His Gospel:

> I was sick and ye visited Me, Matt. xxv,36

shall He now with much greater reward say to our almsgiving: "I was in prison and you have redeemed Me"? And as He elsewhere saith:

> I was in prison and ye came unto Me, Matt. xxv,36

of how much more worth will it not be on the Last Day, when we shall receive our reward from the Lord, to hear Him say: "I was in the prison of captivity, lay chained and handcuffed among barbarians, and from that prison of slavery ye have bought Me My freedom."

And finally we thank you that you permit us to share your sorrow with you, and to have part in this good and necessary labor of love. . . . We hereby send you a hundred thousand sestercii [about $5,000], which were collected by the donations of our clergy and laity of our church, in which by God's mercy I am bishop. Apply this money there as your diligence suggests.

Lastly, we trust that in future no such misfortune overtake you, that our brethren, protected by God's power, be not again visited by such dangers. But if, for a testing of our faith and love something similar again befalls, do not delay in informing us by letter. Be assured that our church and the whole community here earnestly prays it may not happen, but if it does happen, know that we shall willingly raise alms. And that you may aid with your prayers our brothers and sisters, who have freely

contributed to this gift of love, I have subjoined the names of all. . . .
May you fare well ever in the Lord, and forget us not.

Topics for Further Discussion:

Entrance into heaven adds nothing fundamentally new to one's supernatural faculties, but merely releases the inhibitions now attaching to some of them.

It is not *natural,* but *supernatural,* for the angels to see God.

The super-life communicated to man is an incomparably higher kind of life than the natural life of an angel that has missed his destined supernaturalization.

The oldest extant Christian sermon (*II Clement*) embodies this idea: "Let us choose to belong to the Church of life, that we may be saved. You are not ignorant, I think, that the living Church is the body of Christ."

Why would the Church, in Newman's phrase, "rather save the soul of one single wild bandit of Calabria . . . than draw a hundred lines of railroad through the length of Italy"?

Readings:

G. H. Joyce, *The Catholic Doctrine of Grace* (London: Burns, Oates & Washbourne, 1930), "Sanctifying Grace," pp. 1–48; "Acquisition of," pp. 119–141.

E. Leen, *The Holy Ghost* (New York: Sheed and Ward, 1937), "Born of Water and the Holy Ghost," pp. 241–264.

D. A. Lord, *Our Part in the Mystical Body* (St. Louis: Queen's Work, 1935), "Bridging the Chasm," pp. 35–48; "How is This Done?" pp. 77–90.

V. Many–A. Talbot, *Marvels of Grace* (Milwaukee: Bruce, 1934), "Excellence of Sanctifying Grace," pp. 1–15.

C. C. Martindale, "Man and His Destiny," *The Teaching of the Catholic Church* (New York: Macmillan, 1949), I, pp. 286–319.

J. V. Matthews, *With the Help of Thy Grace* (Westminster: Newman, 1944), "What is Actual Grace?" pp. 20–36.

M. Perkins, *Speaking of How to Pray* (New York: Sheed & Ward, 1944), "In Whom We Have Redemption," pp. 36–47.

R. Plus, *In Christ Jesus* (New York: Benziger, 1923): "The Fact of Our Incorporation with Jesus Christ," pp. 1–11; "Jesus Makes Us Divine through His Spirit," pp. 36–42.

J. Pohle, "Grace, II, Sanctifying Grace," CE.[2]

M. J. Scheeben–C. Vollert, *The Mysteries of Christianity* (St. Louis: Herder, 1946), "Second Significance of the God-Man . . . Communication of Divine Life," pp. 389–395.

F. J. Sheed, *Theology and Sanity* (New York: Sheed & Ward, 1946), "Natural and Supernatural Equipment of Adam," pp. 148–153; "Life in the Body," pp. 280–288; "The Life of Grace," pp. 347–363.

F. J. Sheen, *The Life of All Living* (New York: Century, 1929), "What is Life?" pp. 1–39.

A. Tanquerey, *The Spiritual Life* (Tournai: Desclée, 1930), "The Nature of the Christian Life," pp. 44–70.

E. Towers, "Sanctifying Grace," *The Teaching of the Catholic Church* (New York: Macmillan, 1949), I, pp. 549–583.

---

[2] The *Catholic Encyclopedia* is cited under this symbol.

Chapter IV

A LITURGIST FITTED TO OUR NEEDS

Now to crown what we have said:
such a High Priest we have . . .
at the right hand . . . of Majesty . . .
as Liturgist of the sanctuary (Heb. viii,1,2,
Greek).

NOT least among the doctrines to which adult Catholicism invites us to give the best study of which we are capable is that of the continuous role of Christ as Head of the Mystical Body. Among the new facts that emerge in this connection is that the New Testament in its original Greek speaks of Christ as a Liturgist, and of His work as a liturgy in which we have part. The word *liturgy* had not Heb. viii,2,6 won acceptance in our language when the older Scripture versions were made, and it is still usually rendered by a synonym in the English versions of the Inspired Writings. We here indicate some of the meanings of the word *liturgy* because it is a term so much to the fore at present, and well repays a little investigation. This is especially true of the Pauline meaning in which it has now become current. In classical Greek liturgy (λειτουργία) meant any public work or office or benefaction by an individual on behalf of the commonwealth, whether this was paying the chorus of a municipal opera, or furnishing the army with a span of horses. It was *something done by one from which the whole society profited*. Religion was conceived in such social terms by the ancients, that any act around the temples, down to the humble task of sweeping up, was a liturgy. Any act of worship of God profited the entire community, it was rightly conceived. When the Old Testament was rendered into Greek by the so-called Seventy Scholars, they chose the word *liturgy* to designate the services of the Jewish Temple. In the same sense the word greets us on the threshold of the New Testament, as when St. Luke wrote of Zachary that when the days of his *liturgy* were completed,

Luke i,23 he departed to his home.

The first occasion we know of on which the term is applied to Christian worship happens to be that memorable for the ordination of SS. Paul and Barnabas:

At Antioch,

in the church which was there,

as they were performing the *liturgy* to the Lord . . .

the Holy Spirit said:

"Set apart for Me Barnabas and Saul

Acts xiii,2 unto the work to which I have called them."

But under the hand of St. Paul, who spoke with irresistible predilection in terms of our corporate union with Christ, the word takes on its truest Christian meaning. To the members Christ is the Head in worship as in all else beside, and so Christ in us and through us becomes *the* Worshiper, *the* Liturgist. We in Him and through Him worship along with Him, and so have part in His liturgy, whereof He is High Priest and Mediator. Let us add to an already long paragraph a somewhat full quotation of Paul's triumphant phrases on the matchless perfection of Christ's Priesthood:

He, because He remaineth forever,

hath an unchangeable priesthood,

wherefore He can at all times save those

who *approach God through Him.*

Such was the High Priest fitted for our needs —

holy, guileless, undefiled,

set apart from sinners,

and made higher than the heavens . . .

Heb. vii,24–28 one Who is *Son, forever perfect.* . . .

Now to crown what we have said:

such a High Priest we have . . .

Who hath His seat at the right hand

of the throne of Majesty in heaven

as Liturgist of the sanctuary,

and of the true "tabernacle, which the Lord,"

and not man, "hath set up" . . .

He hath attained to a *liturgy*

so much the more excellent,

as the testament is better,

Heb. viii,1–6 whereof He is Mediator.

Eternal High Priest. One of the most precious gifts we received from the hands of Pope Pius XI is the Encyclical Letter *On the Catholic Priesthood* (1935). But that document was surpassed in sweep and significance by the subsequent Encyclicals, *On the Mystical Body of Jesus Christ* (1943), and the specifically liturgical one, *On Christian Worship* (1947) of Pope Pius XII. In all of these adult Catholicism is portrayed as the whole Mystical Body worshiping God, the members in vital union with their Head: "The sacred liturgy, then, is the public worship which our Redeemer, the Head of the Church, offers to the heavenly Father, and which the community of Christ's faithful pays its Founder, and through Him to the Eternal Father: briefly, it is the whole public worship of the Mystical Body of Jesus Christ, Head and members." In particular shall we ponder the papal teaching that "the Mass being offered by the Mediator between God and men is to be regarded as the act of the whole Mystical Body." *Christian Worship*

Religion Requires Priesthood. The very mention of priesthood calls up the cognate idea of public worship. Then, too, there arises the thought of sacrifice, which is both the highest office of worship and the chief function of the priest. Of these several concepts more detailed exposition will be found in subsequent chapters; rudimentary, rule-of-thumb definitions will answer present purposes. *Religion,* as one of the basic tendencies of human nature, is found among all peoples, throughout all ages of man's history. It is *man's recognition of his dependence* upon some superior Being. Man feels naturally constrained to give external and social expression to this feeling of submission, hence there arise at once organized and public acts of worship. Through the hands of persons designated to act for all, homage is paid the superior Being, be this by formal address, by extending the arms, lifting up the eyes, bowing the body to the ground, or by a hundred other actions suggestive of submission. Upon analysis, this recognition of dependence upon a superior Being carries with it the concept that one's very life is owing to Him. In consequence, man feels prompted to acknowledge this *complete* dependence upon God, who has given him all, even life, by giving something in return, by making God a Return-Gift which stands for man himself. This is sacrifice, and by universal consent, it is the foremost act of worship. To offer homage, and especially *the* homage of sacrifice, *priests* are chosen to act as society's representatives, the go-betweens, the ambassadors between man and God. Obviously society's first concern in selecting and accrediting a representative is to find one who is *sinless,* or at least as sinless as may be, lest he draw down wrath in place of benediction. Again, since *worship* involves recognizing the *relative worth* of Creator to creature, there is need of one with the closest approximation to a limitless knowledge of God. God is to be worshiped, King David sang,

Ps. cl,2   according to the multitude of His Greatness.

But our needs exceed our human capacities. Where could be found a son of Adam *either* sinless *or* possessed of anything like an adequate knowledge of God's Sovereignty or Sanctity, Loving-Kindness or Mercifulness? What mere man was at all capable of mediating between mankind and the Godhead?

Christ, the Bridge-Builder. The most important group of pagan priests of ancient Rome were called *pontifices,* literally bridge-builders. Whether this was, as Varro and Cicero and others believed, because these priests supervised the building of and kept in repair an important bridge across the Tiber, or for some other reason lost in the remoteness of history, no one knows for certain. But by whatever strange process it came about that the name *bridge-builder* was reserved for the highest rank of the priesthood, a name more expressive of the real nature of the priestly office could hardly be found. There is perhaps no better way to study the priestly character of the Redeemer, and the priestly character of the Christian body, than by focusing attention on Christ as One who builds a bridge between God and men.

But why is it necessary to speak of the priesthood, or of *Christ as a Priest?* Because the Fall was an act of *irreligion;* the supernatural order was lost by a deliberate refusal of homage, the homage of obedience, to God: hence, the Redemption will be in first instance an act of *religion;* the supernatural order will be recovered by a deliberate rendering of homage, the homage of obedience, to God. This was to be no private, personal undertaking, but the public act of an accredited representative of mankind. It was to be no inferior act of homage, but the highest possible expression of worship, the worship of sacrifice. This meant that a priest was necessary. The Redeemer was a Prophet and a King, but He *must* be pre-eminently a *Priest.*

Christ's Perfect Priesthood. The absolutely *unique perfection* of Christ's Priesthood becomes evident forthwith. None could really bridge the abyss between God and man but a Person who was God, equal to the Father from all eternity, and yet man, "tried in every way like ourselves, short of sin." Hence, in the very act of the Incarnation the Divinity anointed, as with the chrism of priestly ordination, the human flesh it assumed. Jesus, Son of Mary and Son of God, was therefore called the *Christ*, the *Anointed One*. He, the Head of mankind, came into the world to repair the primal refusal of worship. This He would do by offering the sacrificial gift that was hardest of all to make, the voluntary sacrifice of His own life. The Anointed One of God `Heb. iv,15`

> loved [you]
> and delivered Himself up for you,
> an offering and sacrifice of sweet savor to God. `Eph. v,2`

Clearly only a Person in whom Divinity and humanity meet and fuse into one can be a real Mediator. Listen to St. Augustine inculcate this in his preaching:

> Christ is the "Mediator between God and men," because He is God with the Father, and because He is man with men. Man is not a mediator with respect to the Divinity, God is not a mediator with respect to humanity. Behold the Mediator: the Divinity without the humanity [he repeats] is not the Mediator, nor is the humanity without the Divinity, but, between the Divinity alone and the humanity alone, the Mediator is the human Divinity and the Divine Humanity of Christ. `Serm. 47`

"Designated by God as High Priest." Before proceeding to the analysis of Christ's priestly function, it will clear the ground to take a second cursory view of Christ's *qualifications* as a possible Mediator. Of the two requirements already mentioned, there is scarce need to recall His absolute sinlessness (did He not challenge His enemies to point to *any* sin in His life?), and His Wisdom incarnate. What St. Augustine justly insists upon in the passage quoted is that Christ *unites in His Person the two natures* of which He was to be Mediator. St. Paul put it: `Heb. v,10` `John viii,46`

> It behooved Him
> on account of Whom all things are,
> and through Whom all things are,
> when He was bringing many sons to glory . . .
> it behooved Him to be made like unto "His brethren"
> in all respects
> that He might become a merciful and faithful High Priest. `Heb. ii,10–18`

Of Christ's *vocation* (being called) to the priesthood the Apostle is no less clear and emphatic:

> None taketh to himself the honor,
> but one who hath been called by God, as was Aaron.
> So, too, Christ did not appoint Himself
> the honor of becoming High Priest,
> but He Who said to Him:
> "Thou art My Son . . . "
> as He elsewhere saith:

Heb. v,4–6   "Thou art a Priest forever."

But let us see the Priest in act, in that act for which He was made High Priest, the offering of sacrifice:

> Every priest . . . is appointed
> as representative of men
> in the things that refer to God,

Heb. v,1   that he may offer gifts and sacrifices for sin.

Christ's Perfect Sacrifice. Every Catholic knows how at the Last Supper Christ offered His life to the Father as a *sacrifice* and *sin-offering* for our redemption — and at the same time inaugurated a visible priesthood for the continuance of this new, this one *true*, sacrifice. The sacrificial offering made in the Cenacle was actually fulfilled later on the cross, when Christ voluntarily gave up His life. On the altar of the cross His Body was given for us; His Blood copiously ratified the new and eternal testament. The New Man as Priest had made His sacrifice.

But every sacrificial gift offered to God is made with the hope that God will accept it and even give some *sign* of His divine good pleasure. In Christ's sacrifice there could be no question but that the sacrifice would be most acceptable, since it had been agreed upon beforehand. But the divine good pleasure was wondrously shown to all mankind when God

> raised Jesus our Lord from the dead,
> who "was delivered up for our offenses,"

Rom. iv,25   and rose again for our justification.

Apoc. v,12 This divine glorification of "the Lamb that was slain" was confirmed in a still more striking manner, if possible, when God lifted up our human nature in Christ to His eternal throne, and allowed Him to prove

GOD

IS WORSHIPED CONJOINTLY BY

CHRIST (head)

and the CHRISTIANS (members)

whose

ADORATION–THANKSGIVING–PETITION–REPARATION

is expressed in offices of

PRAYER : SANCTIFYING RITES : SACRIFICE

SACRAMENTS ~SACRAMENTALS

– publicly –

by means of

speech – posture – symbols

in consecrated manner and setting

the efficacy of His sacrifice by sending thence the Pentecostal Spirit of Love upon His people, His brothers by adoption, purchased by His Blood, and incorporated into His Mystical Body.

> He humbled Himself by obedience unto death,
>   yea, unto death upon a cross.
> Wherefore God hath exalted Him above the highest,
>   and hath bestowed on Him THE NAME
>   which is above every name.

Phil. ii,8,9

> In Him we have redemption through His blood,
>   the forgiveness of our transgressions. . . .
> It was the purpose of His [the Father's] good pleasure —
> a dispensation to be realized in the fulness of time —
>   to bring all things [as] to a Head in Christ.

Eph. i,8–10

Christ's Priesthood Perpetuated. But the final drama of Redemption was accomplished in a few hours: the sanctification of the whole race of Christians, *that* is a greater work of Christ, and that goes on and on, and will do so, as long as the world lasts. It will be found that this is no less a distinctly priestly work on Christ's part. For He came to act as Priest not only at the Redemption, or to show man how he was henceforth to worship God in spirit and in truth in the new dispensation, but *Christ as Head of the Mystical Body was to be henceforth and forever the High Priest of mankind, the one and only.*

John iv,23

> He became
> for all who obey Him
> the Author of eternal salvation,
> designated by God as High Priest: . . .
>   for this, then,
> is He the *Mediator* of the new testament.
>   [And just as] there is [but] one God,
> [so there is] one Mediator also between God and man,
>   Himself man, Christ Jesus.

Heb. v,10

Heb. ix,15

I Tim. ii,5

The entire process of Christian sanctification, which is called in Holy Writ the building up of the [Mystical] Body of Christ, is thus a distinctly *sacerdotal function.* The vast structure of the world-wide Mystical Body, resting everywhere upon a priestly hierarchy of Pope and bishops and priests, is the divinely instituted sphere of Christ's priestly activity.

Eph. iv,12

Priesthood

Confirmation

Baptism

Wherever we have Christians there also are to be found Christ's priestly representatives, His agents in the performance of priestly functions. As far as the work of sanctification is concerned, pontiff and bishops and priests are but so many visible expressions of the tireless, invisible work of the great Bridge-Builder "accomplishing the work God gave Him to do."

John xvii,4

That the words of the visible priests are the moral acts of Christ is illustrated by the forms "*I* baptize, *I* confirm, *I* absolve, this is *My* Body, *My* Blood." Christ and His minister are a moral unit, to their joint act Christ contributes the efficacy, the priest its visibility.

Christ's Priesthood Extended. There is another and very inspiriting phase of this subject; namely, *the priestly character of the Christian race.* From previous considerations we know that Christians are most intimately associated with, assimilated to, Christ. They are, so to speak, Christ-men; their lives are hid in Christ, they act in Him and through Him, and in them and through them Christ lives and acts. This being so, we should expect that Christ would associate the Christian with His chief prerogative — His priestly character. This is indeed what happens. St. Peter calls the general body of the Christians "a chosen race, a royal priesthood," and St. John twice praises Christ because He has made us priests of God.

I Pet. ii,9
Apoc. i,6; iv,10

Priesthood of the Laity. Of course, those initiated into Holy Orders are priests of Christ, but can it be true that *all Christians,* as such, men and women, are in some true sense *priests?* As will be further explained elsewhere, and particularly when dealing with baptism, it is a traditional tenet of the Catholic faith that every baptized person shares in the priesthood of Christ. "By reason of their baptism (says Pius XII) Christians are in the Mystical Body and become by a common title members of Christ the Priest; by the 'character' that is graven upon their souls they are appointed to the worship of God, and therefore, according to their condition, they share in the priesthood of Christ Himself." St. Irenaeus, a glorious martyr of Lyons (d. 202), says: "All the just have a priestly ordination." St. Chrysostom, the Mouth of Gold, echoes the same thought in the formula, "You were made a priest at baptism." St. Jerome calls baptism "the priesthood of the laity," and in his famous *City of God,* St. Augustine speaks as follows: "Just as we call all *Christians* because of the mystic chrism, so we call *all priests,* because they are *members of the one Priest.*"

Adv. Haer. VIII,3
Hom. 3 in II Cor.
C. Lucif. IV

xx,10

Thus, in urging us to practice reparation to the Most Sacred Heart, Pope Pius XI adduces this priesthood of the laity as the objective basis for the value of *our* acts-in-Christ. The pontiff says in part (Douay):

The Apostle admonished us that "bearing about in our body the mortification of Jesus" and "buried together with Him by Baptism II Cor. iv,10 unto death," not only should we "crucify our flesh with the vices and Rom. vi,4 concupiscences," "flying the corruption of that concupiscence which is Gal. v,24 in the world," but also that the "life of Jesus be made manifest in our II Pet. i,4 bodies," and, having become partakers in His holy and eternal priest- II Cor. iv,10 hood we should offer up "gifts and sacrifices for sins." For not only Heb. v,1 are they partakers in the mysteries of this priesthood, and in the duty of offering sacrifices and satisfaction to God, who have been appointed by Jesus Christ the High Priest as the ministers of such sacrifices, to offer God "a clean oblation in every place from the rising of the sun even to the going down," but *also those Christians called, and rightly* Mal. i,10 *so,* by the Prince of the Apostles, *"a chosen generation, a kingly priest-* *hood,"* who are to offer "sacrifices for sin" not only for themselves but I Pet. ii,9 for all mankind, and *this in much the same way as every priest* and Heb. v,1 "high priest taken from among men is ordained for men in the things that appertain to God."[1]   Heb. v,1

Threefold "Character." As members of the one Priest, then, all Christians are with Him engaged in the priestly worship of God, and so are stamped with the seal of the priestly order. This is the sacramental seal imprinted at baptism (and at confirmation). St. Thomas Aquinas speaks of this common priesthood of the faithful in these terms:

Each of the faithful is deputed, to receive or to bestow on others, things pertaining to the worship of God. . . . Now the whole rite of the Christian religion is derived from Christ's Priesthood. Consequently it is clear that the sacramental character is specially the seal of Christ, to whose figure the faithful are likened by reason of their sacramental characters [of baptism and confirmation], which are nothing else than certain participations of Christ's Priesthood, flowing from Christ *S.T. III Q. lxiii,* Himself.   *a.*3

Through this general priesthood of the laity we are all associated with the uniquely perfect priestly worship of God by the one High Priest. All real worship of God is "through Him," through Christ our Lord, Rom. xi,26 as the concluding formula of our prayer never ceases to repeat. Ours is thus the precious opportunity to be

---

[1] Encyclical, *Reparation Due to the Sacred Heart,* May 8, 1928.

as living stones,
built up into a spiritual house,
to be a holy priesthood,
to offer spiritual sacrifices

I Pet. ii,5,6   well pleasing to God through Jesus Christ.

We are thus at all times enabled to share in the earth-wide, heaven-wide worship of God in the Person of the one true Priest, through whom earth and sky, men and angels, and all created things worship the uncreated God.

We called Christ a Bridge-Builder. Of similar content is a saying of Christ Himself, who one day spoke to Nathaniel of a great thing people were to witness, the great Ladder 'twixt earth and sky:

Ye shall see the heavens standing open,
and the angels of God ascending and descending

John i,51   upon the Son of Man.

This Ladder of the skies is the priestly mediation of Jesus Christ, who

can at all times save those
who approach God through Him,

Heb. vii,25   since He liveth to make intercession for them.

Summary. Since, in God's Providence, the irreligion of the Fall was to be atoned for by a perfect act of religious homage, a sacrifice, it was necessary that Christ be for mankind a Liturgist supreme. This office of His is eternal, and is now exercised through Christians associated in several degrees with Himself in the unique Priesthood of the New Law.

Fourth-Century Source Material

(Niceta of Remesiana, author of Te Deum: Sermon Extract)

. . . You will find in David's psalms everything that can help edify and console men and women of every class and age. Children will find milk for their minds; boys, material to praise God; youths, correction for their ways; young men, a model to follow; and old men, food for prayer. Women can learn modesty. Orphans will find David a father; widows, a vindicator; the poor, a protector; strangers, a guardian. Rulers and magistrates learn lessons in fear. A psalm consoles the sad, tempers the joyous, calms the angry, comforts the poor, and stirs the conscience of the rich. A psalm offers medicine for all who will receive it — including even the sinner, to whom it brings the cure of holy penitence and tears. . . .

God is revealed and idols are scorned; faith is accepted and infidelity rejected; justice is recommended and injustice forbidden; mercy is praised and cruelty blamed; truth is demanded and lies are condemned; guilt is accused and innocence commended; pride is cast down and humility exalted; patience is preached; the banner of peace is unfurled; protection from enemies is prayed for; vindication is promised; confident hope is fostered.

And what is more than all the rest, the Mysteries of Christ are sung. The Incarnation is clearly indicated, and, even more so, His rejection by an ungrateful people and His welcome among the Gentiles. The miracles of the Lord are sung; His venerable passion is depicted; His glorious Resurrection made clear; and mention is made of His sitting at the right hand of the Father. In addition to all this the coming of the Lord in a cloud of glory is declared, and His terrible judgement of the living and the dead. Need more be said? — Quoted with permission from *Writings of Niceta of Remesiana* (Fathers of the Church, Inc.) .

Topics for Further Discussion:

That in some ecclesiastical documents the Blessed Virgin is called a priest: the unique sense in which this is true of her, and the common sense in which it is true of every baptized woman.

The gross exaggeration of what Tertullian said as a heretic: "Are we not likewise priests and are we not doing all the priest does?" (*Exhor. Cast.* vii.)

Why Catholics ceased speaking of the priesthood of the laity at the time of the Reformation.

The differences in popular participation in our public worship which the spread of the consciousness of the priesthood of the laity will evoke.

Why the concept of the priesthood of the laity is well adapted to raise, and not lower, the laity's esteem of the clergy.

Readings:

Pope Pius XII, *On the Mystical Body of Jesus Christ:* Encyclical Letter, June 29, 1943: translated by Canon G. D. Smith (London: CTS, 1948).

――― *Christian Worship:* Encyclical Letter, Nov. 20, 1947: translated by Canon G. D. Smith (London: CTS, 1949).

K. Adam, *Christ Our Brother* (New York: Macmillan, 1931), "Christ's Redeeming Work," pp. 111–144.

E. Burke, "The Priestliness of God's People," *The Sacramental Way* (New York: Sheed & Ward, 1948), pp. 41–51.

M. C. D'Arcy, "Jesus Christ, Priest and Redeemer," *The Teachings of the Catholic Church* (New York: Macmillan, 1949), I, pp. 477–512.

——— *The Mass and the Redemption* (London: Burns, Oates & Washbourne, 1926), "The Sacrifice of the Mass," pp. 58–76.

C. Grimaud–J. F. Newcomb, *One Only Christ* (New York: Benziger, 1939), "Priests with Christ," pp. 153–158.

J. A. Jungmann, *Liturgical Worship* (New York: Pustet, 1941), "In Whom the Liturgy Is Reposed," pp. 30–46.

C. Lattey, *The Atonement, Papers Read at the Summer School of Catholic Studies, Cambridge, 1926* (St. Louis, Herder, 1928), "The Principle of Solidarity," pp. 70–81.

D. A. Lord, *Our Part in the Mystical Body* (St. Louis: Queen's Work, 1935), "Royal Priests," pp. 138–147.

E. Mersch–D. F. Ryan, *Morality and the Mystical Body* (New York: Kenedy, 1939), "All Priests in the Unique Priest," pp. 138–160.

F. Prat, *The Theology of St. Paul* (London: Burns, Oates & Washbourne, 1927), II, "The Redeeming Mission," pp. 161–179.

J. Wilhelm, "Mediator, Christ as," *CE.*

Chapter V

THE SOUL NATURALLY LITURGICAL

From one man He hath made
the whole human race
to dwell upon the entire face of the earth . . .
that they should seek God (Acts xvii,26,27).

ONE of the great enigmas for the historians of the future will be the fact that millions of men of our once Christian civilization of the period, say, 1750–1930, sought happiness in *irreligion.* However regrettable may be the continuous drifting farther from clear beliefs to an indefinite theism, on through a still vaguer "religion of nature," into positive disbelief, which was the singular misfortune of this large group, *that* does not constitute the problem for the historian. Other peoples have had Catholicity and have it no longer. But the ages to come will ponder over the phenomenon, here met with for the first time in human annals, of a widespread and deliberate attempt to build a culture without the underlying foundation of a cult of some divinity, however false. The most advanced civilizations and the least advanced, the records of ancient Egypt, Persia, and Greece, those of Oriental Mohammedanism of old or of Hinduism of today, all these are at one with the records of the so-called primitives just emerging from savagery, in showing that man everywhere knows *his nature demands a recognition of God.* The soul of man is naturally liturgical; he must worship God, must even worship Him socially, if he is to be true to himself. It makes one smile now to read of how the ancient pagans railed at what they considered the *impiety* of the early Christians, because these had, so they thought, no public worship, and especially, no altar of sacrifice. "Why their mighty effort to hide and shroud whatever it is they worship, since things honest ever like the open day . . . ? Why have they *no altars, no temples, no images?*" How those same ancient pagans would have scoffed, provided *Octavius,* x,2 amazement did not render them speechless, had they been given a glimpse of the irreligion of the modern "enlightened" and "emancipated" man. And, on his side, the religious "liberal" of the nineteenth and opening twentieth century looked down from immeasurable heights of sophistication on the natural reverence and pious folly of the ancients. Peter Wust trenchantly answers their charge:

"They prayed to Zeus and Poseidon and to a multiplicity of gods, and that was folly." Of course it was folly; but the *actual prayer* itself was not folly. On the contrary, it was the ancients' supreme act of childlike wisdom. Their whole life was fashioned and hallowed to a liturgy, and from thence it derived its sheer greatness and its monumental quality, and that character of sacredness before which even today we still feel ourselves obliged to linger in reverence.[1]

Now that the world of cultless culture, built on sand and tumbled down by a crash in Wall Street, lies about us in ruins, the illusion of self-sufficiency, not to say, self-worship, has been dispelled. Modern man begins to realize that even for material well-being he needs God and the worship of God.

Modern Religiosity. But in the era just closed man's inborn hunger and thirst for God, and man's awful weariness of inescapable guilt, has fed itself on scraps and crumbs of information about religions, and speculation about "religious experiences." Witness the constantly recurring phenomenon of modern life, not only in America but elsewhere, that, when anyone has achieved eminence in any line of work, he is asked to expound his views on religion. Newspaper editors illustrate something similar in allotting the most conspicuous places in the papers to items concerning religion. Magazines constantly furnish their readers with articles on religion of the "Why-I-am-a ——" sort, since people who have but the faintest interest in other phases of cultural or social life, and no interest at all, it may be, in *living* a religion, avidly read minute accounts of the religions of even the most primitive savages. What the world's remotest barbarian thinks about religion seems to concern the whole world. Why is this, if not because the tendency which prompts religious worship is a vital bond making all men brothers? Religion is the business of life. A manual of Christian conduct of about the year 260 says in fact: "Pursue your trades therefore as a work of superfluity, for

---

[1] P. Wust, "The Crisis in the West," *Essays in Order* (New York: Macmillan, 1931), pp. 99, 100.

your sustenance, but *let your true work be religion.*" The modern capi- *Didas. Apos.* xiii talist of America may actually realize as little as the pagan primitives the reason of his interest in religion, but so long as he is a man, he has a nature planned and built and fashioned for religion. Man is made *to seek for God.* Less desirable and indeed erroneous manifestations of the same basic tendency are shown in the widespread influence of superstition, which is the first step toward the baleful realm of magic, or the attempt to compel and control by spells preternatural or supernatural forces. Newman was convinced that "they who are not superstitious without the Gospel, will not be religious with it."

Man Made for God. Suppose we attempt a brief analysis of man's religious impulse. On the one hand, the Creator could not fashion a race of creatures *not destined to magnify His own glory;* on the other, this Creator in His boundless goodness actually created man to share His own life and beatitude. Things being so, God *had* to implant deep in the very roots of man's nature a thirst unquenchable except at the Fountain of Life itself. "Thou hast made us, O Lord, for Thee," St. Augustine addresses God in a famous passage, "and our heart shall find no rest until it rest in Thee." However incompletely man may know God, if he *Conf.* I be true to the deepest impulse of nature, he will seek and grope for Him. Man constantly tries to put himself into communication with the Divinity.

Written in Human Heart. Because this tendency is universal among men, it is not necessary in seeking a true and clear concept of religion to open Holy Writ and read what God has revealed on the subject. There, of course, one finds what might be called a religion let down from heaven, the whole matter disclosed by Divine Wisdom Itself. But as far as all the basic notions are concerned, one can turn to the history of mankind, ancient or modern, civilized or savage, and find (with varying degrees of clarity and completion, to be sure), the same, single religious sentiment incarnate from age to age *in the very heart of man.* Man groping his way toward God possesses himself of exactly the same fundamental religious notions as God was pleased to reveal to His chosen people. St. Paul appealed to this very fact in addressing the Romans:

> For when the Gentiles, who by nature have not the Law,
>   fulfil the requirements of the Law,

> these . . . are a law unto themselves,
> *showing as they do*
> *the demands of the Law to be written in their hearts;*
> and an approving conscience beareth them out,
> amid the debate of thoughts that accuse or defend.

Rom. ii,14,15

Creed, Code, Cult. A developed religion, then, whether directly revealed by God, or the fruit of man's own effort

> in discerning and contemplating
> in God's visible works
> His invisible attributes,
> His everlasting power and divinity,

Rom. i,19

as St. Paul put it, embodies three elements, a *creed,* a *code,* and a *cult.* There is, first of all, a series of beliefs touching the divine origin of the world, and the divine origin and destiny of mankind. Moreover, these are beliefs, which, it is held, man is not at liberty to reject. The second element concerns conduct: Here it is agreed generally that certain norms of morality are imposed upon man with the sanction of the Deity. The third constituent deals with the regulation of communications between men and the Divinity. It consists in a system of rites and practices calculated to promote individual and social contact with the Deity. This is the elaborated and finished definition of religion. Let us look at this definition in the making, by quickly examining the psychological stages of its formation.

Dependence and Gratitude. When we analyze religious phenomena, we find these implications. At the bottom of all religious sentiment is man's explicit or implicit *recognition of his dependence* upon a Divinity. Whether this be in the full, clear light of the revelation of Sinai, "I am the Lord thy God," or in the sufficient, if indirect, light of deduction, man feels the selfsame urge:

Exod. xx,2

> Come, let us bow down and fall prostrate . . .
> For He is the Lord our God,
> And we are people of His pasture,
> the sheep of His hand.

Ps. xciv

Coincident with this recognition that the world and his own being are owing to God, man feels a prompting of *gratitude:* he says in substance "Let us praise the Lord *because He is good.*"

Ps. cv,1

O Lord, our God,
   How wonderful is Thy Name
   In all the earth!
For Thy glory is exalted above the heavens. . . .

If I look on the heavens,
   The work of Thy hands,
   And on the moons and the stars which Thou hast made. . . .

What is man that Thou shouldst remember him?
   Or the son of man that Thou shouldst visit him?

[Yet] Thou hast placed him over the works
   of Thy hands,
All things hast Thou put beneath his feet.   Ps. viii

Love and Contrition. The very knowledge of God's goodness or lovableness shows man that his *happiness* will *consist* largely in having *God for his friend.* He is moved to adhere closely to God lest he cut himself off from this all-lovable Goodness. Logically man surrenders himself to God. To Him who gives him all, and who, he sees, is the source of his happiness, man gives himself in return. He feels that the closer he binds himself to God, the more liberal will God be in accepting him and treating him as a friend. Man therefore prays and proposes to remain ever acceptable to God.

   I love the Lord,
      Because He hath heard my prayerful voice;

   Because He hath bent to me His ear;
      I will cry out [unto Him] all my life long . . .

   I will walk in God's pleasure
      In the land of the living.   Ps. cxiv

These relationships are those of a sinless creature with his Creator. But, alas! mankind inherits from Adam the heavy *consciousness of guilt.* Therefore his religion from the outset has necessarily included another note, the necessity of placating this good God now justly estranged by man's wrongdoing.

   Out of the depths I cry to Thee, Lord!

If Thou, Lord, shouldst retain sin,
O Lord, who could stand?

My soul hopeth for the Lord
More than watchers for the morning.

For with the Lord is loving kindness
And plenteous redemption is with Him,

And He will ransom Israel
From all its sin.

Ps. cxxix

Need of Ceremonial. These fundamental religious concepts which we have been sketching — adoration, thanksgiving, petition, and propitiation — are in themselves *predominantly intellectual*. Theoretically speaking, a relationship based on them might be established between any single individual and the Divinity without enlisting the service of any bodily organs or operations. But "such is the nature of men," says the Council of Trent, "that, without external helps, he cannot easily be raised to the meditation of divine things." If men were all spirit, like the angels, and *if each lived in isolation apart,* they *could* so serve God. But, in the first place, man has his complex corporeal structure, so closely linked to his spiritual powers, that when he thinks, his *imagination,* his bodily *emotions,* and his nervous system, all to some extent come into play. The more intense his mental operations, the more necessary also it becomes for him to give *corporeal expression* to them in some way. Spontaneously and irresistibly, therefore, with the recognition of God's dominion over him, man feels urged to bow down, to kneel, to prostrate himself before this sovereign Lord. At the very sight of God's numberless gifts to him, arises a desire to make a gift in return:

Sess. xxii,c.5

How shall I make return to God,
For all His gifts to me?

Ps. cxv

(The answer to this question, which we will consider farther on, is: "I will offer Thee a sacrifice.") Similarly, there is the natural impulse to accompany a prayer of petition by raising the eyes toward heaven, by holding out our hands as if to receive divine favors, and by other gestures. The consciousness of guilt expresses itself in natural tokens of sorrow, such as beating the breast, which is the home, as it were, of the guilty heart. In this way man does not hesitate to employ any word or tone,

any gesture or posture, fire or water, light or darkness, oil or incense, or
any object about him as an aid in expressing his religious sentiment, just
as in the political sphere citizens employ and honor a flag or other emblem
to "personify" the country, and the like. On a moment's reflection it is
seen how inextricably interwoven psychologically are creed and code and
cult. Clearly, an inner, invisible worship is not enough for man.

Religion Essentially Social. Then there is another element of
religion only hinted at thus far. Just as man is a compound of body and
soul, and uses both to express himself suitably, so he is inevitably from
birth until death a *unit in a social system.* He lives in constant and manifold relationships with his fellows, in the family, as well as in civic,
political, and communal entities of numerous kinds. His instincts and
impulses are social: the Emperor Marcus Aurelius phrased this thought
in saying, "We are made for social action; to oppose one another is   *Thoughts,* ii,1
contrary to nature." *Religion,* therefore, *imposes* not only individual
self-dedication to God, but *social self-dedication* to Him also. "This
duty," says Pope Pius XII, "obliges men primarily as individuals; but
the whole community of mankind, linked together by social bonds, is
bound by it also, because the community, too, is dependent upon God's
supreme authority."

Sacrifice, the Crown of Worship. "Divine worship," repeats the
Pope, "is a duty for human society as such, and not only for individuals;
and how can religion be social unless it, too, has its external bonds and
signs?" This outward symbol is all the more necessary when worship is
communal and not individual. Thus it came about that in almost all
religions *sacrifice,* the public rendering of a gift to God, is considered
the *highest, most perfect* expression of worship. The paramount importance of the idea of sacrifice demands that we have clear and exact
notions about it. From its universality among men it has been argued that
it belongs to the natural law itself. Thus St. Thomas says: "At all times   *S.T.* ii, Q. lxxxv,
and among all nations there has always been the offering of sacrifices.   *a.*1
Now, that which is observed by all is seemingly natural. Therefore the
offering of sacrifice is of the natural law." The Council of Trent says
pithily: "The nature of man *requires* sacrificial worship."   *Sess.* xxii,c.1

Sacrifice is defined as *the public rendering to God through the hands
of a priest of some visible gift that symbolizes a giving of one's self to
Him.* It involves adoration of God as supreme Lord: it ought to include
both thanksgiving for former favors and petitions for further ones; lastly,

A pagan altar
made into the pedestal
for a Christian altar

when sin has intervened between God and man, the sacrificial gift likewise expresses an intention and attitude of reparation.

Food-Offerings, Blood-Offerings. Obviously any visible gift may serve the purpose of sacrifice. But since *sacrifice is symbolic of complete self-dedication,* foodstuffs, as the sustenance of life, have been the customary objects of oblation. Sheaves of freshly cut grain, flour, bread, grapes, wine, all manner of food-offerings, have been laid upon the sacrificial altar. The bloody sacrifice, also so common, is directly connected with the consciousness of guilt. "Without the *shedding of blood* there is no pardon" was a commonplace among the ancients, *because* "the wages of sin is death." Guilt-laden mankind felt that only a vicarious blood-letting could adequately express his sentiments of contrition.   Heb. ix,22   Rom. vi,23

Altar, God's Agent. This formal gift-offering requires, of course, that it be accepted by God, unless the whole process is to fail of its object. From this fact arises in sacrificial ritual the importance of the altar, considered as invested with God's holiness, a visible *representative of God,* as it were, to receive in His place and stead the sacrificial gift.

Altar Becomes Banquet Table. But with the gift once offered on the altar and accepted, is the sacrifice concluded? Strictly speaking, it is. Yet, following upon their sacrifice, men have always sought some special *token of the divine acceptance,* even some *divine largess* in return. This has led to the sacrificial banquet. Man considers himself invited to sit down as God's table-guest, and to partake of the (now sanctified) sacrificial food-offering. Here is the symbol of God's good pleasure in the offering. In the sacrificial banquet the fruit of the sacrifice is gathered.

Christianity a Perfect Religion. Nothing has been said in this analysis of worship that is specifically Christian, or even that applies exclusively to the revealed religion of the Old Testament. Is Christianity also a compound of creed and code and cult? Is it a religion of external actions and rites? Is it essentially social and communal, like the imperfect natural religions we have been studying? Has it that perfection of all religions, public and sacrificial worship? There is among speculative theologians a school of thought which maintains the proposition, that *even if* man had committed no sin, Christ would nevertheless have been born. One of the reasons alleged in support of this view is the claim that *only in a God-man as Priest* can *perfect worship* be rendered to God. The mediator must necessarily reach to both extremes, even as the bridge must touch both shores if one is to pass over it. Without committing ourselves unreservedly to this hypothetical case, it will become clear in subsequent chapters that in the present order of things perfect worship of God is had, and had only, through

I Tim. ii,5	the one Mediator of God and men . . .
Col. i,18	the Head of the Body the Church . . .
Heb. vii,25	Jesus Christ always living to make intercession for us.

Summary. Since man was fashioned to find happiness in the enjoyment of God, his religious impulse, quite independently of "civilization," is spontaneous and fairly uniform. Dependence upon God the sovereign Lord, gratitude toward Him as the great Benefactor, love for Him as the Source of endless Goodness, and sorrow for having offended against a God so good — these are the basic concepts of religion. These convictions of a soul naturally liturgical naturally find expression in external and corporate worship, the highest form of which is called a sacrifice. Herein gifts as symbols of self-dedication are offered to God at the hands of a priest, and later received back from God with His blessings at a sacrificial meal. Christianity, because it has a God-Man as Priest, is the one perfect religion.

Fifth-Century Source Material
(St. Augustine on the Communism of the Mystic Body:
COMMENTARY OF PSALM CXXX,6.)

The eye seeth, and heareth not; the ear heareth, and seeth not; the hand worketh, but it neither heareth nor seeth; the foot walketh, but it heareth not, nor seeth, nor doth what the hand doth. But if there be health in one body, and the members contend not against one another, the ear seeth in the eye, the eye heareth in the ear; nor can it be objected to the ear that it seeth not, so as to say to it: You are nothing, you are inferior; can you see and discern colors, as the eye doth? For the ear answereth from the peace of the body and saith: I am where the eye is, I am in that body; in myself I see not, in that wherewith I exist I see. So when the ear saith, My eye seeth; the eye saith, My ear heareth; and eyes and ears say, Our hands work for us; the hands say, The eyes and the ears see and hear for us; the eyes and the ears and hands say, The feet walk for us; while all members do their work in one body, if there be health therein and the members be in concord, they rejoice, and rejoice with one another. But if there be any trouble in any member, they forsake not one another, but suffer with one another. . . . Thus, then, brethren, whosoever in the body of Christ cannot restore the dead to life, let him not seek this power, but let him seek that he may not be at discord in the body; just as there might be discord if the ear should seek to see. . . . When therefore a man who is progressing heareth this, as it were a calumny cast in his teeth by ignorant heathens, by men who know not what they speak of, in the sodality of the body of Christ let him answer and say: Thou who sayest, thou art not righteous because thou dost not work miracles, thou couldst also say to the ear, thou are not in the body, for thou seest not. You, he saith, should do that which Peter did. But Peter did it for me also, since I am in that body, wherein Peter wrought it. In him, from whom I am not divided, I can do what he can. In that I can do less, he suffereth together with me; and in that he can do more, I rejoice with him. The Lord Himself cried from on high on behalf of His body, "Saul, Saul, why dost thou persecute Me?" and no Acts ix,4 man was touching Him. But the head cried from Heaven for the body suffering on earth. — Quoted with permission from Przywara-Martindale, *An Augustine Synthesis,* New York: Sheed and Ward, 1936, pp. 255, 256.

Topics for Further Discussion:

The psychological impossibility of atheism or skepticism as a spontaneous attitude toward religion.

That false religions, because they are in some ways *false, cannot* provide a complete system of self-sanctification.

Strange aberrations of the impulse to offer sacrifice that come to light even in our times.

Your answer to one who says: "I worship God best in solitude, communing with nature."

Your answer to one who would say: "Paganism with all its hideous savagery is superior to Protestantism."

The desire to please God as voiced by a Persian pagan hymn:

How can I please Thee, Thou wise Lord? Full well I know that I am not good as it behooves me. This, I lament, O Lord. Vouchsafe me Thine aid as a friend to a friend. Teach me to merit bliss by a good heart. . . . O ye Spirits of wisdom and righteousness, your will will I accomplish. This is the resolve of my thought and my soul.

How an Egyptian pagan would like to stand at his final reckoning:

He must be able to say on the Day of Judgment in the presence of the Lord of truth: "Lo, I come before Thee. I have eschewed sin against Thee. I have not sinned against men, I have afflicted no man. . . . I have not cursed God, and have done nothing that is abominable in the sight of the heavenly ones. I have not slandered the servant to his lord, have suffered no man to hunger, have made no man to weep, have done no murder nor procured it to be done, have hurt no man, have not enlarged the corn measure, have done no deed of violence."

A Babylonian pagan's Act of Contrition:

(After a lengthy catalogue of sins was set before the penitent seeking quiet of conscience.) . . . In respect of all the evil whereby he hath disregarded his god and goddess. . . . It is searched out, it is searched out — now therefore may it be cancelled, Thou Judge, Shamash. Blot it out, O Marduk, compassionate Lord. Blot it out, Thou God of the sinner. Blot it out, Thou God of the evildoer.

A Roman pagan's treaty oath as sealed by sacrifice:

The Roman envoy to the inhabitants of Alba, as he slew the sacrificial victim: "If we are the first to violate with evil intent the treaty which we have publicly concluded, then, do Thou, Diespater, smite the Roman people as I now smite this sacrificial victim." — Quoted with permission from O. Karrer's *Religions of Mankind*, New York: Sheed and Ward, 1936.

Readings:

C. F. Aiken, "Religion," *CE.*

L. de Grandmaison, *Lectures on the History of Religions* (St. Louis: Herder, 1910), I, "The Study of Religion," pp. 1–28.

—— *Personal Religion* (New York: Sheed and Ward, 1929), "Piety," pp. 19–36.

C. C. Martindale, "Man and His Destiny," *The Teaching of the Catholic Church* (New York: Macmillan, 1949), I, pp. 286–319.

J. Pohle, "Sacrifice," *CE.*

W. Schmidt, S.V.D.–J. J. Baierl, *Primitive Revelation* (St. Louis: Herder, 1939), "Sacrifice," pp. 144–146.

A. D. Sertillanges, *The Church* (New York: Benziger, 1922), "Religious Feeling in General," pp. 1–6; "Necessity and Permanence of Religious Feeling," pp. 7–12; "Religious Feeling and Christianity," pp. 13–19; "Social Character of Religious Feeling," pp. 27–38; "Social Character of Christianity," pp. 39–44.

M. de la Taille, *The Mystery of Faith, an Outline* (New York: Sheed and Ward, 1930), "Sacrifice," pp. 3–10.

Chapter VI

"THE SOUL NATURALLY CHRISTIAN"

He that hath the Son,
hath the life;
he that hath not the Son of God,
hath not the life (I John v,11,12)

IN THE summer or autumn of the year 197, Tertullian of Carthage, then a rather recent convert from paganism, addressed to the provincial governors of the Roman Empire his *Defense of Christianity.* Referring in that work to certain words of a pagan judge, Tertullian used the expression: "Behold the testimony of a soul naturally Christian." *Apol.* xvii We see what store he set by his happy phrase since he wrote an appendix to his *Defense* merely to enlarge upon this thought. In his immediate context Tertullian really meant no more than that pagans, by spontaneous exclamations and ordinary modes of speech, often unconsciously betray a correct, *natural* knowledge of God, a belief in His unity and sanctity, and in the life of man with God beyond the grave. Suppose in borrowing Tertullian's words we broaden their original meaning and say: In God's present economy, every man is naturally Christian in the sense that only by becoming Christian can he begin to enjoy a full life. Only the elevating and transforming effects of grace fully release the possibilities of the human heart.

Catholicity Allows Full Homage. We do not in our turn intend here to launch upon a *Defense of Christianity.* Remaining well within the framework of our theme; namely, worship in its relationships to social life, we seek merely to indicate what Tertullian saw, what every instructed Catholic clearly recognizes, that the *sacramental* and *sacrificial system of the Church* puts perfect purpose and poise and order into the restless religious and liturgical yearning of the *nature of man* as we know him. It alone imparts the *supernatural life* in a complete system of sanctification, wherein all life's needs and aspirations are met so superabundantly. It alone allows an expression, perfect from every point of view, of man's humble homage; it alone brings to actual accomplishment man's longing to put himself into communication with, to unite himself with, God. Only Catholicity gives full play to the needs of bodily as well as spiritual homage, of corporate as well as individual homage, enabling society to enlist in its worship color and sound and fabric, lights and incense, oil and water, bread and wine.

"**Spoils of Paganism?**" A charge against Catholicity that never seems to grow outmoded, since it is still being repeated, after having done periodic service since early patristic times, is that she uses in her worship, besides an altar of sacrifice, lights, oil, processions, images, and other ceremonial objects very much like those used by pagan religions long ago. The external features of Catholic worship are thus said to be spoils of paganism. Well, that the false religions used these things does not mean that the things themselves are false. A true understanding of the nature of man dictated those expressions of man's true religious impulse. Christianity is not ashamed to use in the service of the true God the forms suited to man's nature, even though these were formerly used in paying divine homage to idols. To Faustus St. Augustine admits readily: "There can be no religion, true or false, without external ceremonial. . . . We *have* some things in common with the Gentiles, but our purpose is different." "Because we once worshiped idols, is that a reason," asks St. Jerome pointedly, "why we should not worship God, for fear of seeming to address Him with an honor like that which was paid to idols?" Moreover, so sure is the Church of Christ of her inherent power to sanctify all creation, that she stands ready to appropriate existing rites and customs. A classic instance is furnished by the example of St. Gregory the Wonder-Worker, who, on his appointment to the diocese of Pontus, found only seventeen Christians there. His biographer, St. Gregory of Nyssa, narrates and interprets with praise how he set about hallowing existing religious usages dear to the populace:

Contra Faustum, xix,11; xx,23 Cf. Epis. 103, 18

C. Vigilant. viii

> After revisiting the country round about, he increased the devotion of the people everywhere by instituting festive meetings in honor of those who had fought for the faith. The bodies of the Martyrs were distributed in different places, and the people assembled and made merry, as the year came 'round, holding festival in their honor. This indeed was a proof of his great wisdom . . . for, perceiving that the childish and untrained populace were retained in their idolatrous error

Saint Gregory

by creature comforts, in order that what was of first importance should at any rate be secured to them, *viz.,* that they should *look to God in place of their vain rites,* he allowed them to be merry, jovial and gay at the monuments of the holy Martyrs, as if their behavior would in time undergo a spontaneous change into greater seriousness and strictness, since faith would lead them to it; *which has actually been the happy issue in that population.*

Vit. Thaum.
xxvii

That short passage might almost stand as a summary of *The History of Christ's Influence upon Creation:* Incorporation into the Mystical Body hallowed rational nature, while irrational nature is in some way sanctified by contact.

An Understanding of Mankind. The non-Catholic world often regards Catholicity as a gloomy system of superstition, based on fear and allied with magic, a sort of melancholia weighted with a sense of sin; in short, something quite at cross purposes with healthy human nature. The facts of the case are just the other way around. It is Christianity which has a sane and healthy, a bold and confident, a sympathizing and dignifying appreciation of our human nature and of the world we live in. Deeper, too, than all intellectual convictions, Christians have a new vital principle within them:

> He that hath the Son,
> hath the life;
> he that hath not the Son of God,
> hath not the life.

I John v,11–12

Spirit-World and Sense-World Wedded. Long had men thirsted to know the Living God. If He

> had by many partial revelations
> and in various ways
> spoken of old to the Jews

Heb. i,1

still, to the vast majority of men, He was quite unknown. Then squarely and fully to satisfy this natural longing of men concerning Himself, God disclosed Himself to all mankind in the Person of His Son incarnate in human flesh. The Dweller in light inaccessible was made visible in the familiar lineaments of human nature. Heretofore the nature and attributes of God were capable of only the faintest comprehensions; now, as the Word of life, God dwelt among men so that

I Tim. vi,16

> their eyes could see,
> their ears hear,
> their hands handle Him.   I John i,1

Redemption was accomplished by *God-in-the-flesh;* in keeping with that dispensation, the Wisdom of God established a religion in which *things of the spirit* are constantly linked with *things of sense.* God will communicate His own absolutely spiritual life to man — but in a manner not wholly spiritual. God will catch up fallen humanity — but as by the cords of the New Adam, that is, by sensible, material objects and forms and symbols. This is one thing which makes Christianity so pre-eminently suited to human nature.

The New Birth. In His redeeming work Christ offered man the supernatural life. But He laid down as a condition of its bestowal a sensible rite, which He called a *new birth,* or *birth from above.* This new   John iii,2 birth was to effect an interior renewal, the removal of original sin; to be, as it were, a birth into the grace-world. Therefore Christ chose that the new birth should be effected and exteriorly signified by washing with water or dipping into water. Thus man is *christened,* or made a sharer of the divine life through incorporation into Christ. The actuality is tremendously important; small wonder, then, that the rite becomes gradually invested with natural signs to express its importance. Christ means "Anointed," so the new member of Christ is actually anointed; the ablution removes all trace of sin from the soul, so the neophyte is robed in a white garment: the rebirth imparts a new and higher life within, so in the hands of the newly born is placed a bright and shining light.

The Strengthening Spirit. This new Christian,

> begotten anew,
> not from perishable,
> but from imperishable seed,   I Pet. i,23

can never be unbaptized, can never be de-Christianized. But he can *kill the divine life* within him by a deliberate violation of God's law in a serious matter. He carries his treasure in a vessel no stronger than a human will. Now the new life within must grow and unfold; hence, the human will must be *guarded* and *strengthened,* given a permanent *set* sufficient to meet all the dangers of the way. This spiritual effect will be achieved by giving the Christian a divine Helper, the Holy Spirit, with

His abundant gifts and graces. By anointing the body with oil the athletes of olden times sought to obtain litheness and suppleness for the Olympic and other games. Again, in the realm of spiritual things, the imposition of the hand of a sacred personage on the head of another signified the transferring of invisible force to such a one. These two sensible actions were, by Christ, made the external signs of the abiding communication of divine strength to the Christian in the Sacrament of Confirmation.

"Our Daily Bread." For the inner, *supernatural life* to unfold to its highest possibilities, and to recover the losses of everyday life, it must needs have *nourishment, sustenance*. Therefore, under the signs of bread and wine, received as food and drink, the Christian is enabled to unite himself immediately and most intimately with the Godhead dwelling in the Body and Blood of Christ.

> He that eateth My Flesh
>   and drinketh My Blood
> hath everlasting life,
> and I will raise him up on the last day.
>
> For My Flesh is food indeed,
> and My Blood is drink indeed.
>
> He that eateth My Flesh
>   and drinketh My Blood
> abideth in Me, and I in him.
>
> As the living Father hath sent Me,
>   and as I live of the Father,
>   so he that eateth Me,
>   he also shall live of Me.
>
> This is the bread that came down from heaven,
>   not as the fathers ate and died:
>   he that eateth this bread shall live forever.

John vi,54–58

How this everyday sustenance of the supernatural within us is linked up with the natural impulse to sacrifice and to partake of a sacrificial banquet, needs no further explanation just now.

A Cordial of Bittersweet. In man's natural life come sicknesses, slight or grave, to be a passing inconvenience or to completely prostrate and paralyze him as the case may be. So the *life of God-within-us* can be lamed by slight strokes of malice, or killed outright by serious and deliberate sin. These contingencies are provided for in the *medicinal rites of penance,* to the healing of which are joined effectual comfort and strength. Here, too, the Catholic has always known what the modern research in mental hygiene now brings out so clearly, that from the purely natural point of view, the institution of confession answers a real and deep-seated need of human nature.

Social Obligations and Helps. Baptism admits one to Christianity; confirmation affords mature strength; Holy Eucharist keeps Christians as living, growing, functioning members of the Mystical Body. Penance is a medicine to counteract sin's poisons. There are other sacraments for other special crises in the full and normal supernatural life of the individual. The prompting *to marry* arises from the conviction that founding a family is a fuller, completer human existence. But the life of man and woman in marriage requires, for its success, mutual fidelity and a deep, never-failing love. Obligations so fearsome in their scope make marriage a grave step. Christian couples receive the supernatural helps needed to be faithful in these obligations because Christ has made their mutual promises a divinely instituted sacrament.

Troops of children to supply ever new members for the increase of the Mystical Body are assured by matrimony. Priests to effect the *spiritual parenthood* of sacramental administration in the same Mystical Body are guaranteed by the sacrament of holy orders. The priestly calling, if hedged by strict obligations, imparts tremendous powers. How much, therefore, in keeping with the far-reaching congruity of the whole sacramental system is all the stately ritual that surrounds the investing of the chosen candidate as deacon, priest, or bishop.

Strength at the Last. The hour of death, so universally dreaded, is in some ways the most serious crisis in human existence. Body and soul wrenched apart, the disembodied spirit is sent out into a world of which it has no sensible knowledge. Because this hour is the last wherein the use of human freedom can determine the weal or woe of the unending future, it becomes extremely critical for the Christian. This need was foreseen and provided for by Christ in the sacrament of the *last anointing.* As the symbol of this special sacramental *healing* and soothing *comfort* He appropriately chose *anointing with oil,* one of the commonest instruments of therapy in the ancient East.

Grace-World Well Planned. Such is the sacramental system, that series of sense-symbols, instituted to act as channels of the super-life circulating in the Mystical Body. By this system Catholics are, everywhere and always, both *living* a supernatural life and expressing their religious sentiment in a progressively *sanctifying worship of God.* The scheme is complete in *seven* sacraments: if there were but six, some human need would be unprovided for; if eight, there would be needless overlapping and duplication. *The Catechism of the Council of Trent,* in speaking of the number of the Sacraments, says:

> In order to exist, to preserve existence, and to contribute to his own and the public good, seven things seem necessary to man: To be born, to grow, to be nurtured, to be cured when sick, when weak to be strengthened; as far as regards the public welfare, to have magistrates invested with authority to govern, and to perpetuate himself and his species by legitimate offspring. Now, since it is quite clear that all these things are sufficiently analogous to that life by which the soul lives to God, we discover in them a reason to account for the number of the Sacraments.

II, I, Q. xv

The Crown of Sacrifice. Far reaching as these sacramental rites are, so completely in agreement and harmony with human nature, they would still, did they not include a sacrifice, fall far short of answering man's religious needs. To offer God gifts in a formal, social way, and as tokens of self-dedication is, after all, the *foremost expression of religion.* "Sacrifice," says St. Thomas, "expresses the right relation of the soul to God: the right relation of the soul to God implies man's recognition that all he has comes from God as from the first beginning, and man's direction of all to God as to the last end." A religious system without sacrifice would be inadequate and incomplete. But in Christianity, important as all other rites may be, they but radiate from the altar of the Christian Sacrifice.

S. T. I, II. Q. cii, a.3

In oft-repeated catechetical formulas all Catholics have heard such expressions as: the Mass is a real sacrifice; it is the renewal of the sacrifice of the cross; *the Priest* at Mass and the Victim are the same as on the cross; namely, Christ; the Mass is like the cross all over again, only in an unbloody manner; on the cross our Redemption was accomplished, in the Mass the fruits of it are applied, etc. But because we live in an atmosphere so thoroughly irreligious, the *concept of sacrificial worship* has lost its sharpness and clarity. Often in calling the Mass a sacrifice, one uses a conventional phrase conveying little meaning. To freshen this idea, let us ask two questions: What is meant by saying that *Christ's death* was a sacrifice? What is meant by saying that the Mass is the *Christian's sacrifice?* Detailed analysis will follow later.

Christ "Gave" Himself. Sacrifice, we remember, is the public rendering to God through the hands of a priest of some visible gift which symbolizes a giving of one's self to Him. Now the *Man-God*, as *representative* of the whole human race, and in accordance with an agreement arrived at in the august councils of the Holy Trinity, *offered* as gift *His own life's Blood* (to be shed by executioners into whose hands He voluntarily gave Himself). The offering was made at the Last Supper; the saving Blood was poured out upon the cross of Calvary. From creation onward this was the single sacrificial Gift wholly pleasing to God, and it effected mankind's Redemption, as we know. The Mass repeats as a perpetual memorial the offering of the supper room as consummated on the cross. In every Mass the peerless Gift, as slain, is presented once more to the Father, this Gift which is the Head of the Mystical Body, the Church. By reason of our incorporation, the Gift becomes ours, becomes, in a way, ourselves. St. Thomas has it: "As the Head and the members are, as it were, one mystical person, so the *satisfaction* of Christ *belongs to* all the faithful as to His members." In another passage he says more briefly: "The satisfaction of Christ has its effect in us as far as we are concorporated in Him."

Sup. Q. xiii,a.2

Q. xlix,a.3 ad 3

We "Give" Christ and Ourselves. But have Christians no *personal gift* to offer at Mass by way of expressing their own internal sacrificial attitude of mind? If not, the great tomes of the Fathers, and the teachings of the Church for centuries are rendered meaningless. Meaningless, too, would be the canons of Church councils which anathematized such as wished to be present at Mass without contributing the sacrificial elements. The gift-offering of *bread and wine* (or their equivalent), *as symbol* and sign *of personal and social consecration* to the divine service, *that* is the individual Christian's part in the great sacrificial cycle. These petty, insignificant oblations of our bread and wine become in the divine dispensation changed into the one, great Gift, the Body and Blood of Christ; they are accepted by the Father in an odor of sweetness, and thus sanctified, they are returned to us as food at the supper table of the Lord, Holy Communion. At every Mass there must be self-immola-

Serm. 55,3

Dial. iv,59

De Ador. in Spir. et Ver., I,11

De Civ. Dei, x,20

tion. St. Leo the Great speaks of "the oblation of our human nature"; St. Gregory the Great refers to the "necessity at Mass of imitating what we re-enact, and so making to God the sacrifice of our hearts." In the same strain St. Cyril of Alexandria said: "In our sacrifices [of bread and wine] we sacrifice our own souls in an image and offer them to God." Let St. Augustine's terse phrase close the patristic consensus: "[The Church] being the body of Him, the Head, learns to offer herself through Him."

"**Incredible Cogency of Mass.**" The truth outlined in the fore-going paragraphs is expressed with vigor and clarity in the lines here quoted:

> When a man is "in Christ," forthwith He and Christ are vitally united, and Christ offers Himself and His Christian in Himself, and the man offers Christ and himself in vital unity, and God, looking upon Mass, sees both His Son and those who are "in one" with Him. Hence you cannot but perceive the incredible cogency of Mass. It is a gift that God cannot resist: the priest, and the layman too, since there is solidarity between them, have omnipotence in their hands. Mass is an act — not a prayer recited, not a ceremony contemplated, but the supreme act of history unequaled in the world.[1]

Summary. As a composite of body and soul, man must use both in any satisfactory system of worship. Catholicity ideally meets this ele-mental demand, since it provides not only fullness of revelation in a God-man, but an entire system of worship on this "incarnational" plane, the constant union of sense-objects with sanctifying processes, a system which provides in sacramentals, sacraments, and Sacrifice the fullest possible satisfaction of the religious promptings of human nature.

Sixth-Century Source Material

(St. Gregory the Great, who was one of the most influential popes the Church has ever had, writes on the Mass and the Mystic Body.)

At the beginning of this work [*Moralia*], in discussing the unity of head and body, we were careful to indicate in advance how close is its bond of love, since the Lord still suffers many things in His body, that is ourselves, and His body, the Church, is even now glorified in its Head; namely, the Lord, in Heaven. At this point the sufferings of that Head

---

[1]C. C. Martindale, *The Faith of the Roman Church* (London: Methuen, 1927), p. 115.

ought to be pointed out, so that it shall be clear how much He bears with in His body. For if our afflictions touched not our Head, He would in no wise cry out from Heaven on behalf of His agonizing members against the persecutor:

Saul, Saul, why dost thou persecute Me?   Acts ix,4

And if our pains were not His sufferings, Paul, converted and himself in torments, would never exclaim:

I . . . make up in my flesh
what is lacking to the sufferings of Christ. — Bk. III, ch. xii.   Col. i,24

*　　*　　*　　*　　*

We ought to immolate to God the daily sacrifice of our tears, the daily Offering of His flesh and blood. For this Offering peculiarly preserves the soul from eternal death and it renews for us in mysterious wise the death of the Sole-Begotten, who, although being risen from the dead, dieth no more, and death hath no more dominion over Him; yet, while   Rom. vi,9 in Himself He liveth immortal and incorruptible, for us He is immolated again in this mystery of the sacred Oblation. For it is His body that is there given, His flesh that is divided for the salvation of the people, His blood that is poured, no longer into the hands of unbelievers, but into the mouths of the faithful. For this let us ever estimate what this Sacrifice is for us, which for our absolution ever imitates the Passion of the Only-Begotten Son. For what one of the faithful can have any doubt that at the very hour of the Offering [Mass], at the word of the priest, the Heavens are opened, the choirs of angels are present at the Mystery of Jesus Christ, the lowest things are united to the highest, earthly things with the heavenly, and of the invisible and the visible there is made one?

But it is necessary that when we assist at the Sacrifice, we should by contrition of heart, sacrifice ourselves unto almighty God. For when we celebrate the mystery of our Lord's Passion, we ought to imitate what we do. Then it shall be a real sacrifice for us unto God, if we offer ourselves also to Him in Sacrifice. — *Dialogues*, ch. lvii, lix.

Topics for Further Discussion:

The myth, born of sixteenth-century polemics, of "primitive simplicity (barrenness) of Christian worship," in the sense that Christianity ever rejected cult acts because they appeal to the senses.

"It is only the Catholic Church that retains true worship," said Lactantius in the fourth century, and Pope Pius XI repeats his dictum with approval in the Encyclical on Promoting True Religious Unity (1928). What other religion has hallowed all the natural expressions of worship, a sacrificing priesthood, fixed ritual, hieratic use of music and art, nature symbols, and so forth?

The reasons for the widespread return at present to Catholic ritual and ceremonial by non-Catholic Christians and even by non-Christians.

"Mass — a solemn rite destined to take exclusive possession of mankind's religious consciousness." — *Walter Pater.*

How the Protestant endeavor to preserve Communion without sacrifice resulted in a tasteless "wafer," and an empty "cup," with no communicants.

The psychological necessity of confession as shown by the numberless "soul clinics," "psycho-therapy institutes," as well as the nonsacramental "confession" of some Protestant bodies.

Readings:

Father Cuthbert, *God and the Supernatural* (New York: Longmans, Green, 1920); C. C. Martindale, "The Sacramental System," pp. 277–305.

F. C. Kolbe, *The Four Mysteries of the Faith* (New York: Longmans, Green, 1926), "The Sacramental System," pp. 128–132.

C. C. Martindale, "The Sacramental System," *The Teaching of the Catholic Church* (New York: Macmillan, 1949), II, pp. 733–766.

M. J. Scheeben–C. Vollert, *The Mysteries of Christianity* (St. Louis: Herder, 1946), "The Inner Structure of the Individual Sacraments and Their Relation to One Another," pp. 572–584.

A. D. Sertillanges, *The Church* (New York: Benziger, 1922), "The General Idea of the Sacraments," pp. 135–140; "The General Idea of the Sacramentals," pp. 187–192.

F. J. Sheed, *Theology & Sanity* (New York: Sheed & Ward, 1946), "Dispensing the Gifts," pp. 247–265.

Chapter VII

"COMMUNIONISM" AND THE BOND OF WORSHIP

*They persevered in the teaching
of the Apostles,
and the fellowship,
the breaking of Bread and the prayers* (Acts ii,42).

WHEN Christ swallowed down death, that we might be the heirs of life everlasting — as the strong language of the Vulgate renders the original Greek — the Temple veil was rent from top to bottom, as a sign that the sacrificial worship of Israel was now fulfilled on the Cross. When the religion of Catholics was publicly inaugurated a few weeks later, new men, "Christ-men," suddenly appeared on the scene. Feeling themselves united to God by a Mediator, who was weak as themselves in human flesh but holy as God in the Spirit, this *new race*, as they called themselves and were called, was conspicuous for a sense of true manliness, of human dignity, liberty of spirit, a catholic, that is, a world-wide, all-embracing range of interest, and easy confidence of a triumphant future. But most of all they were marked off from Jew and Gentile alike by a sense of fellowship and mutual love. Their contemporaries charged many things against the Christ-men, but, as Tertullian sums up, "it is *mainly* the deeds of a love so noble that lead many to put a brand on us, 'See,' they say, 'how they love one another,' for they themselves are animated by a mutual hatred . . . and they are wroth with us, too, because we call each other brethren." Tert. *Apol.* xxxix
Again, a pagan could be quoted as saying: "They recognize each other by marks and signs, and love each other almost before they recognize." Min. Fel. *Oct.*ix
Thereby those pagans fulfilled to the letter prophetic words spoken by Christ, when He instituted the holy Eucharist:

By this shall all know that ye are My disciples,
if ye have love one for another.   John xiii,35

Glance back at the quotation from the *Acts* at the head of this paragraph, and note how St. Luke expands the "fellowship" with the appositional

Acts ii,42 phrases, "the breaking of Bread and the prayers." In his next little summation of expanding Catholicism, the Evangelist again signals out their mutual accord:

Acts iv,32 The multitude of believers were of one heart and soul.

When St. Paul came to speak of what we might call the effects of the Holy Eucharist, he used only that selfsame word of fellowship:

> The Cup of blessing, which we bless,
>   is it not fellowship in the Blood of Christ?
>
> The Bread which we break,
>   is it not *fellowship* in the Body of Christ?
>
> *We many are one bread, one body,*
I Cor. x,14–16 *for we all partake of the one Bread.*

And lest a modern reader miss the *connection* between this *fellowship* and the bond that cemented it, the *Eucharistic Bread,* Pope Leo XIII took pains to point it out: "If in the record of the Church it is deservedly reckoned to the credit of its first ages that *the multitude of the believers*
Acts iv,32 *had but one heart and one soul,* there can be no doubt that this was due
Mir. Car. to their common meetings at the divine Table." This fellowship fostered by common feeding on the Eucharistic Bread illustrates in practice what the Fathers of the Council of Trent were to define as dogma fifteen hundred years later, when heresy had challenged it: "He [Christ] wished this Sacrament to be a symbol of that one *body* of which He is the Head, and to which we are all united as members . . . in order that

I Cor. i,10   all speak the same thing,
Sess. XIII, c.2   thus ending the divisions among you."

The new race of "Christ-ed" men found in the Eucharist the symbolical expression, and the actual nourishing of their distinctive fellowship one with another.

"A Love-Feast." The Sacrifice was instituted at the close of an elaborate, Jewish ritual supper, and it is *in a supper-setting* that we find it first mentioned in the *Acts.* The name "breaking the Bread" was already stereotyped when St. Luke wrote the *Acts.*

Day by day they persevered
with one accord in the temple,
and breaking Bread at home,
they took food with joyful simplicity of heart.   Acts ii,46

This meal in common, of which we shall see St. Paul's picture below, was called *Agape*, a Love-Feast. One of the most charming features of dawning Christianity, it was, so to speak, too good to last. St. John Chrysostom calls it: "an occasion for practising charity, a means of alleviating poverty and of making wealth wiser, a grand spectacle of edification and a school of humility."

The *Acts* give only one clear picture of the Bread-Breaking. The scene is at Troas, not very far from Constantinople; the time, a Sunday evening of the spring of the year 57, "when we were assembled to break Bread." Paul was long a-preaching, so that a young man, Eutychus, Acts xx,7 began to nod, fell from his place on the window sill (it was the third story), and was picked up apparently dead. Paul went down, and after a bit assured them that Eutychus would revive. Then he returned to the assembly and "breaking Bread and tasting . . . so he departed." On Acts xx,11 this occasion, as far as one can judge, the Eucharist was not united with the Agape.

Abuses Rebuked by Paul. At Corinth, however, whither the Apostle was writing in the winter of 54–55, it was the custom to celebrate the Eucharistic Sacrifice in conjunction with the *Agape*. In the Apostle's absence disorders had crept in, disorders which grieved him sorely. The circle of the brethren was dividing into cliques; these groups, instead of sharing provisions with the community, consumed their own for themselves. Again, they did not wait for all to assemble; most serious of all, some so far forgot the sacred purpose of their common repast as to drink to excess. It is the rod of the pedagogue that Paul wields now:

In the first place I hear
that when you come together to church
there are divisions among you,
and in part I believe it.

For there must even be factions among you,
that those of tried virtue may become manifest
among you.

When you meet together, then,
it is not possible to eat the Lord's Supper;
for at the repast each one taketh first his own supper,
and one is hungry and another drinketh overmuch.

Have you not homes in which to eat and drink?
Or do you despise the house of God,
and put to shame the needy?

What am I to say to you?
   Am I to praise you?
In this I praise you not.

For I have received from the Lord,
as I have also delivered to you,
   that the Lord Jesus
on the night wherein He was being betrayed,
took bread, and giving thanks
   brake and said,
"This is My Body which [is being given] on your behalf;
   this do ye in remembrance of Me."

In like manner after the supper
   He took the cup saying,
"This cup is the new covenant in My Blood;
this do ye, as often as ye drink [thereof],
   in remembrance of Me."

For as often as you eat this Bread
   and drink of the Cup,
you proclaim the death of the Lord,
   until He come.

So that whoever eateth the Bread
or drinketh of the Cup unworthily,
   shall be guilty of the Body and the Blood of the Lord.

But let a man prove himself,
and so let him eat of the Bread,
   and drink of the Cup;
for he that eateth and drinketh
without distinguishing the Body [from other food],
   eateth and drinketh judgment to himself. . . .

clergy　clergy

choir　choir

women　men

lavabo

Sacristy　Sacristy

Wherefore, my brethren, when you come together for the repast,
   wait for one another.
If one is hungry, let him eat at home,
lest you meet together [only] for judgment.
The rest I shall set in order when I come.

I Cor. xi,17–34

Communal-Fellowship in Eucharistic Body. The Agape and the celebration of the Eucharistic Mysteries, never inseparably united to each other, were destined to be permanently dissociated later on, and the former love-feast is scarcely recognizable in our annual or semiannnal parish dinners or parish picnics. But to recall that dual assembly of primitive usage is to glimpse the secret of the martyr's ardor, or the force behind the conquering apostolate, in brief, the transforming power of Christ-in-humanity. A miscellaneous group of all ages and social ranks, but with the poor and slaves in the majority, makes its way after nightfall to the designated meeting place, usually the spacious home of a "brother" of wealth. Mingling freely and at perfect ease, they converse together until a signal marks the entry of the clergy. The account of the Mass then following we give from the *Apology* of St. Justin, Martyr, which portrays the developments of about the year 160. The language is necessarily somewhat general, since Justin is writing for pagans, but for all that we can readily trace our Mass of today in these unadorned lines. Justin died for his "witness" not long after writing this.

Sunday.	On the day called Sunday, all who live in cities or in the country gather together
Single sacrifice.	to one place,
Scripture lessons.	and the *Memoirs of the Apostles* or the writings of the prophets are read, as long as time permits;
Sermon.	then, when the reader has ceased, he who presides gives a verbal instruction, and exhorts us to imitate these good examples.
Prayer in common.	Then we all rise together and pray,
Offering of gifts.	and . . . when our prayer is ended, bread and wine and water are brought, and he who presides in like manner offers Eucharistic prayers and thanksgivings according to his ability, and the people assent saying, "Amen."
Canon improvised.	

Communion to all.	And there is a distribution to each one, and a sharing in the Eucharistic Elements,
Even to absent.	and to those who are absent a portion is sent by the deacons.
Free-will offerings for needy.	And they who are well-to-do, and willing, give what each thinks fit; what is collected is deposited with the president [bishop] who succors the orphans and widows, and those who, through sickness or any other cause, are in want, and those who are in bonds, and the strangers sojourning among us, and in a word, takes care of all who are in need.
The Lord's Day.	Sunday is the day on which we all hold our common assembly, because it is the first day, on which God made the world; and Jesus Christ our Saviour on the same day rose from the dead.
Eucharistic Presence.	And this food is called by us the Eucharist. . . . Not as common bread and common drink do we receive these, but . . . we have been taught that this Food . . . is the Flesh and Blood of that Jesus who was made flesh.

The custom at Rome of emphasizing the unity of Christians in *communion* by sending to those who were absent, particles of the Holy Eucharist is also described for us in a letter of this period by St. Irenaeus, later martyred at Lyons, France, and others.

Fellowship in Mystic Body. The Eucharistic Mysteries concluded, or quite independently of them, as the case might be, the Agape took place. "As with God Himself," says Tertullian, "a peculiar respect is shown to the lowly," in that places of honor were given to the widows, the poor, and the dependent. With prayer the feast was commenced, and *Apol.* **xxxix** so it closed with prayer. Each in turn had the happy task of voicing the corporate prayer, either in recitation or in song, in the words of Holy Writ, or in improvisation. The meal was a natural occasion for the presentation of guests and pilgrims from other communities, for the interchange of news from far and near, rumors of impending persecution, for the writing of the letters to those engaged in enforced

labor for conscience' sake, and so forth. At times there would be
the saddening news of some strife among the brethren. When differences of note arose locally, the bishop heard both sides and rendered
judgment. There is a charming injunction to a bishop to hold his
court on Mondays, since that allowed the entire week, if it were
needed, to reconcile the brethren, *before the Sunday Sacrifice*. The
extreme judgment was what we call excommunication nowadays, and
consisted "in the severance from us in prayer, in the assembly and in all
Tert. *Apol.* xxxix　sacred dealings." Alms were given of one's abundance, or of one's modest
competence, or of one's dearth: alms for the support of the dependent,
for the comfort of those in prison, for the decent burial of Catholic and
non-Catholic dead. It was the view of one moralist that "fasting is better
II Clem. xvi　than prayer, but the giving of alms is better than both." What we might
call a sociological feature of the assembly deserves note. This served
regularly as an employment bureau for Catholics out of work, and there
is even evidence that the Catholic community recognized the right of an
unemployed coreligionist to secure a position from the brotherhood in
Didache, xii,etc.　his own locality.

"Gathered from Four Winds." Among the most precious relics
in writing of the Apostolic Age is a little booklet called *The Teaching
of the Twelve Apostles,* which dates from the period 80–100. Several
of its passages mirror the essence of primitive Catholic piety, and all
of these show that the object of their passionate love was the *Church
gathered from the four winds and fed upon the Eucharist.* On Sunday
worship in general *The Teaching* prescribes:

> On the Lord's Day come together, breaking Bread, and celebrate the
> Eucharist, after confessing your transgressions, that your Sacrifice may
> be pure. But let none who has a quarrel with his fellow join in your
> meeting until they be reconciled, that your Sacrifice be not defiled. For
> this is that which was spoken by the Lord: "In every place and time
> offer Me a pure Sacrifice, for I am a great King," saith the Lord, "and
> My Name is wonderful among the heathen."[1]

Among the prayers suggested for the Christian assemblies, (which,
it is decreed, are reserved to the baptized only), we read:

> Now as regards the Eucharist, give thanks after this manner:
> First, for the Cup: We give Thee thanks, our Father,

---

[1]This is a citation from memory of Malachy's prophecy, i,11.

for the holy Vine of David, Thy servant,
   which Thou hast made known to us
     through Jesus, Thy Servant.
To Thee be the glory forever.

And for the Bread that is broken:
   We give thanks to Thee, our Father,
for the LIFE and knowledge Thou hast made known to us
   through Jesus, Thy Servant.
To Thee be the glory forever.

And as this Bread was [once] *scattered over the mountains,*
   and having been gathered together, became one,
    so let Thy Church be gathered together
     from the ends of the earth,
      into Thy Kingdom:
for Thine is the glory and the power through Jesus Christ forever. ix

Now after being filled, give thanks after this manner:
   We thank Thee, holy Father, for Thy holy Name,
   which Thou hast caused to dwell in our hearts,
and for the knowledge and faith and immortality
   which Thou hast made known to us
    through Jesus Thy Servant.
To Thee be the glory forever.

Thou, O almighty Sovereign,
   didst make all things for Thy sake,
Thou gavest food and drink to man, for enjoyment,
   that they might give thanks to Thee.
But to us Thou didst freely give
   spiritual Food and Drink and eternal LIFE,
    through Thy Servant.
Before all things we give thanks to Thee that Thou art mighty.
   To Thee be the glory forever.

Remember, O Lord, Thy Church;
   to deliver her from all evil
   and to perfect her in Thy love.
   And gather her together from the four winds,
sanctified for Thy Kingdom which Thou didst prepare for her.
   For Thine is the power and the glory forever.   xi,1–5

I Clem. xlvi,5–7 **"Why Tear the Members of Christ?"** To the people of Corinth
St. Paul found it good to write in the year 55 his most detailed treatment of the body of Christ. Forty years later that flourishing church
was thrown into violent disturbance by the opposition of a small faction
to the hierarchy. The pope then reigning was the glorious Clement I, a
martyr-to-be, who undertook by letter to compose this schism. After a
wistful sketch of the ideal fellowship Corinth had been, famous alike
for orthodoxy and a whole litany of virtues, Clement deplores the effect
of schism in language that rings familiar:

> Let us take our body: the head is nothing without the feet, likewise
> the feet are nothing without the head; the smallest members of our
> body are necessary and valuable to the whole body, but all work to-
Ibid. xxviii,5   > gether and are united in common subjection to preserve the whole body.
> Why are there strifes and passions and divisions and schisms and
> war among you? Or have we not one God, and one Christ, and one
Eph. iv,4–6   > Spirit of grace poured out upon us? Is there not one calling in Christ?
> Why do you divide and tear asunder the members of Christ, and
> raise up strife against our own body, and reach such a pitch of madness
> as to forget we are members of one another?
Rom. xii,5   > Take up the *Epistle* of the blessed Paul the Apostle . . .

I Cor. xiii So Clement goes on to paraphrase the Apostle's golden lyric of love,
as we have seen at the end of Chapter I, and bespeaks return of love to
I Clem. xlix,6 Him "who gave His Flesh for our flesh, His life for our lives." Thus
"adult Catholics" of long ago knew that, antecedent to any personal
preferences, they actually formed a body, and *therefore* their determination to foster union, and *therefore* their fellowship in the Eucharist, the
I Cor. xi,17 eating of which made them all a unity. We learn no more of that trouble
at Corinth, so it is likely that this papal quoting of *First Corinthians*
restored harmony to the City of the Twin Seas.

"Branches of the Cross, Members of the Son." A few years subsequent to the events just spoken of, the Catholic world was filled with
the brilliant glory of the martyrdom of St. Ignatius of Antioch, who was
St. Peter's second successor as bishop of that great city. He was taken
from Antioch to Rome to be exposed to the beasts in the capital. En route
he wrote seven letters to churches and churchmen in the neighborhood.
The faith in Asia Minor was just then threatened by heretical teachers,
so that the burden of these celebrated and impassioned letters is always

the same, the unity of the Church, which is identical with the *unity of Christ*. To Ignatius Christians are "branches of the Cross, by which *Trall.* xi through His Passion He calls you who are His members." This unity of the members is the fruit of praying together, praying around one altar, *Eph.* v,2 and breaking one Bread, professing the same faith, abiding in concord, *Eph.* xx,2 and obeying the hierarchy that "the Father may recognize . . . that you are members of His Son." To the Christians of Smyrna Ignatius *Eph.* iv,2 pens this passage, in which (incidentally) the expression "*Catholic Church*" occurs for the first time:

> Let no one do anything pertaining to the Church without the bishop. Let that be considered a valid Eucharist which is *celebrated by the bishop,* or by one whom he appoints. Wherever the bishop appears, let the congregation attend; just as wherever Jesus Christ is, there is the Catholic Church. It is not lawful either to baptize or *to hold the Agape* *Smyr.* viii,1,2 *without the bishop.*

In addressing the churches of Philadelphia, in Asia Minor, and Ephesus, the future martyr writes respectively:

> Be careful to have [only] *one Eucharist* for there is *one Flesh* of our Lord Jesus Christ, and *one cup* for union in His Blood, *one altar,* as there is one bishop with the presbyters and the deacons, my fellow servants, in order that whatever you do, you may do it according to *Phil.* iv God.
>
> If Jesus Christ permits me . . . in a second despatch [letter] . . . I will instruct you concerning the dispensation of the new man Jesus Christ . . . dealing with His faith and His love, His suffering and His resurrection . . . so that you obey the bishop and the priests with an undisturbed mind, *breaking one Bread,* which is the medicine of immortality, the antidote that we should not die, but live forever in *Eph.* xx,1.2 Jesus Christ.

"Wheat of God." To St. Ignatius the Holy Eucharist was not alone the bond of union among Christians, but the instrument of personal sanctification. Fearing that the Christians at Rome would seek to prevent his martyrdom, he begs them to give up such thoughts:

> I am the wheat of God, and I must be ground by the teeth of lions that I may become the pure bread of Christ. . . . I have no pleasure *Rom.* iv,1 in the food of corruption or in the delights of this life. I desire the

Rom. vii,3
Bread of God, which is the Flesh of Jesus Christ, who was of the seed of David, and for drink I desire His Blood, which is incorruptible love.

A Bishop's Prayer, a Bishop's Epitaph. If there is an aura of holiness upon the persons of martyrs-to-be, an indefinable fascination attaches to glimpses into their minds and souls. Here is the *catholic* prayer of a bishop arrested at the age of eighty-six. Polycarp, Bishop of Smyrna, ordered food and drink set before the soldiery sent to arrest him (it was just at nightfall), and in turn asked the favor of praying a little. "To this they assented," runs the story of his martyrdom, "and he stood and prayed . . . so that for two hours he could not be silent . . . *remembering all who had ever even come his way, both small and great, high and low, and the whole Catholic Church throughout the world.*" St. Polycarp died by fire in the arena of Smyrna in 155.

Mart. Poly. vii, viii

This chapter could scarcely close more appropriately than by reproducing one more voice from this distant past, a metrical message written for his tombstone by Bishop Abercius of Hierapolis, in Phrygia, about the year 180. Before reading what a Christian bishop thought proper to inscribe upon his tomb even in those days of persecution, let us recall what a wealth of Christian thought is contained in the Greek word for *fish*. As a five-letter acrostic, 'ι-χ-θ-ύ-ς, it yields the initial letters of the Greek words meaning "Jesus Christ, Son of God, Saviour." A symbol so simple and noncommittal in itself, and yet pregnant with such depth of meaning to the initiated, was bound to serve as a watchword in a thousand different contexts. Abercius' uses of the word are easily understood.

> Citizen of a distinguished town,
> This sepulcher I have living made
> That I may sometime lay my body here.
> Abercius is my name, disciple of a Shepherd,
> Who feeds His flocks o'er mountains and o'er plains;
> Whose eyes see all, who taught me words of life.
> He sent me Romewards sovereign majesty to see.
> To see a queen in golden robe and golden sandals shod.
> People everywhere I saw stamped with a gleaming seal.
> In Syria's plains and all her cities, Nisibis beyond Euphrates.
> Brethren everywhere I found, for I was following Paul.
> Faith before me, the FISH she always served me,
> A huge FISH from the fountain, which the chaste Virgin caught.

And this she gives her friends to eat forever and for aye.
Delicious wine she has too, which she serves with bread. . . .

Summary. Besides being our Sacrifice, the holy Eucharist symbolizes
and effects our truest fellowship. Apostolic teaching, the testimony of
pagan adversaries, the writings of the apologists, letters, social customs,
prayers, both public and private, and an epitaph are here adduced to
show that the early Christians were vividly conscious of their social
fellowship as based on their common sharing in the Eucharist.

Seventh-Century Source Material
*(If St. Ildephonse of Toledo in this instruction to newly baptized, of about 657,
passes lightly over transubstantiation, he is crystal clear on the Eucharist
as the bond of Christians.)*

What you see is to the senses bread and a chalice, but what your faith
dictates is this: the bread is the Body of Christ, the chalice [contains]
His Blood. That is quickly said, and may perchance suffice for faith,
but faith desires instruction. . . . You may say to me: "You have
commanded us to believe, but explain it that we may believe." Or such a
thought as this can arise in someone's mind: "We know whence our Lord
Jesus Christ received His Flesh, from the Virgin Mary. Suckled as an
Infant, He was nourished, grew, came to youth, suffered persecution at
the hands of the Jews, was hung on the wood, killed, buried. On the
third day He rose again, and when He chose, ascended into heaven, took
His Body thither, from whence He shall come to judge the living and
the dead, and there He now sits at the Father's right. How is the bread
His Body, or how is that His Blood which the chalice holds? These
things, brethren, are for this reason called Sacraments, because in them
one thing is seen and another thing is understood. That which is seen has
bodily [material] appearance; what is understood has spiritual profit.
If you wish, therefore, to understand the Body of Christ, listen to the
Apostle saying to the faithful:

You are the body of Christ and severally His members.   I Cor. xii,27

If you are the body of Christ and severally His members, this mystery is
placed on the altar of the Lord; you have received this mystery of yourselves, and have responded *Amen* to that which you are. Be a member of
Christ that your *Amen* be true. Therefore in the bread let us offer nothing as of our own; let us hear the same Apostle saying:

We many are one bread, one body.

Understand and rejoice. We many are unity, love, the truth of the flesh, one bread, one body." — *Lib. de Cogn. Bap.*, c. xxxvii.

Topics for Further Discussion:

The spread of Catholicism was the greatest *revolution* this world has ever known — yet it was accomplished by love.

Anyone may sign himself with the sign of the cross, may say "Amen" and sing "Alleluia," may present himself for baptism, visit churches and help to build them. The only thing which distinguishes the children of God from the children of the devil is love. — *St. Augustine.*

"The Eucharist is what makes men men." — *G. K. Chesterton.*

"The early Christians met constantly to support one another"; the probability of their being able to draw the same support from our assemblies, should persecution break over us.

"The Faithful gather at sacred shrines that they may draw piety thence . . . *by actually participating* in the venerated mysteries and in her public and solemn prayers." — *Pius XI.*

Some reasons for supposing that Catholics of today as a body lack the social-mindedness of the early Church.

That Christian worship, and Eucharistic worship in particular, still offers abundant remedies for the present situation.

Ways in which zealous lay-leadership can make parish organizations, and the parishes themselves real *Agapae*, centers of love.

Readings:

F. Cabrol, *The Prayer of the Early Christians* (New York: Benziger, 1930); "The Eucharist — The Mass," pp. 14–27.

———— *Liturgical Prayer, Its History and Spirit* (New York: Kenedy, 1922); "Primitive Christian Assemblies," pp. 54–61; "Mass at Rome at Beginning of the Third Century," pp. 62–79.

———— *The Mass, Its Doctrine and Its History* (New York: Kenedy, no date), pp. 9–18.

A. Fortescue, *The Mass, A Study of the Roman Liturgy* (New York: Longmans, Green, 1937); "The Eucharist in the First Three Centuries," pp. 1–75.

J. C. Hedley, *The Holy Eucharist* (New York: Longmans, Green, 1907); "The Mass as a Liturgy," pp. 173–195.

P. Parsch–F. C. Eckhoff, *The Liturgy of the Mass* (St. Louis: Herder, 1936), "Historical Development," pp. 16–38.

J. de Puniet, *The Mass, Its Origin and History* (London: Burns, Oates and Washbourne, 1931); "The Synaxis of the Apostolic Fathers," pp. 40–53; "The Earliest Witness to the Roman Use," pp. 54–66.

Chapter VIII

THE SACRIFICIAL CALENDAR

Some of them
God made high and great days,
and some of them
He put in the number of ordinary days
(Ecclus. xxxiii, 10).

I
N CIVIL life we are so accustomed to the prevalence of *our* calendar,
as we say, almost everywhere, that any observance of a New Year,
other than January 1, strikes us as strangely unreal. Our calendar,
called the Gregorian, after Pope Gregory XIII who reformed it in
the late sixteenth century, though now so universally adopted, is merely
one of many systems in use at different times with which to mark and
calculate the progress of time as measured by the solar system. Nor is
our civil year merely a norm for *measuring* time: such is man's desire to
preserve the memory of past events by attaching them to definite dates
that the year becomes a table of annual commemorations of major hap-
penings of former years. Every year thus furnishes a condensed *record*
of the great historic past.

Church Year. However universal the Gregorian calendar may be in
the civil life of Christian civilization, still we are accustomed to another
calendar in our worship: Sunday for Sunday the "date" of the day in
the ecclesiastical year is announced in our churches according to our
Catholic calendar of worship, which we call the Church Year. The Church
Year and the civil correspond in length, but the whole period of twelve
months is laid out by the Church in a seasonal arrangement adapted to
the measuring of time in its relationship to worship. Such a year in any
religious system, pagan, Jewish, Protestant, or Catholic, besides being a
unit of cyclic advance, will present a commemorative summary of God's
relationships with the religious group in question. In European museums
one can still see large marble tablets engraved with the "worship year,"

so to speak, of this or that pagan deity. In Holy Writ the book called Ecclesiasticus records how, for the Jews primarily, but for all men by implication, this "worship year" is of divine institution:

> Why doth one day excel another,
>   and one light another,
>   and one year another,
> when all come of the sun?

By the knowledge of the Lord they were distinguished . . .

> And He ordered the seasons,
>   and holidays of them,
> and in them they celebrated festivals . . .

> Some of them
> God made high and great days,
>   and some of them
> He put in the number of ordinary days.

Ecclus. xxxiii, 7–10

So we are not at all surprised that the Church of Christ, the fulfillment of *all* imperfect religions, has *its* year of worship, high and great days alternating with ordinary ones. Taken together the days of the Church Year will give a summary of God's relationships with men through their Mediator Christ. And such is the solidarity of human living, that the full sweep of God's relationships with mankind through Christ, even in the case of any single individual, must reach back even to Adam and must look forward even to the resurrection of the body at Christ's second coming. Thus the Church year sums up the record of the Old Dispensation, when men looked forward to Christ, portrays the period of Christ's mortal life, runs through the twenty centuries of our New Dispensation with all men either actually or potentially living as members of Christ, and lastly points ahead to the final consummation and end of mortal living.

Supernatural Pedagogy. Some of the Greek Fathers delighted in calling Christ our "Pedagogue," and one might well begin a study of the Church Year as an institution of supernatural pedagogy. One of the marked characteristics of our worship, especially in the Roman Rite, is this, that while the Mass remains ever the same, it is, week for week, and day for day, given a different tone and setting by being brought into rhythmic relationship with definite historical events, or doctrines, or persons. Sundays, the Lord's days, have all a common aspect, but because of the Scripture readings and prayers proper to each, no two strike exactly the same note, or, one might say, have exactly the same function to perform. Weekdays are generally anniversary commemorations of the saints, men and women who in their manifold ways have signalized themselves in living the Christian life. From time to time occur the great festal commemorations of the epochal events attending our redemption, the celebration of which *inculcates the doctrine* itself, according to an age-old axiom the Church never wearies of citing: "Let the law of praying confirm that of believing." This basic function of feasts in teaching the truths of faith was luminously described by Pope Pius XI at the institution of the Feast of Jesus Christ King: *Cf. Quas primas, 1925*

> For imbuing the people with the faith and leading them by faith to the interior joys of life, the annual celebrations of the sacred mysteries are far more efficacious than even the most weighty documents of ecclesiastical teaching. As a rule these latter reach only the few and the more learned, whereas the former impress and teach all the faithful. The one means, We may say, speaks but once; the other speaks every year and forever. The one touches the mind only; the other effectively appeals to mind and heart, that is, to the whole man. Since man consists of body and soul he should be so moved and interested as to drink in divine doctrines more abundantly through the variety and beauty of the sacred rites, and, converting these into vigor and blood, make them serve him for progress in the spiritual life. *Quas primas*

St. Thomas speaks of the layman's obligation of *explicitly* professing faith in the mysteries of which the Church celebrates feasts, whereas an implicit belief is sufficient for doctrines not so celebrated. Since such feasts have multiplied through the centuries, according to that standard the faith of the twentieth-century layman is much more explicit than it was in St. Thomas' age, just as it was more explicit then than in patristic or apostolic times. Thus, through successive ages are the dogmas of our faith more and more explicitly proposed for our belief. *De Veritate, Q. xiv, a.xi,6*

Prismatic Worship. The round of the Church's feasts is didactic, but for a far higher purpose than the mere imparting of religious information. Worship is primarily for the sake of God, not primarily for the sake of man; but the quality or excellence of our worship, that is to say,

5th Sunday

4th Sunday

3rd Sunday

2nd Sunday

Low Sunday

EASTER S.

Palm Sunday

Passion Sun.

Lætare Sun.

3rd Sunday

2nd Sunday

Ember days

1st Sunday

Ash Wed.

Quinquage-
sima

Sexagesima

Septuagesi-
ma

6th Sunday

5th Sunday

4th Sunday

3rd Sunday

2nd Sunday

1st Sunday

S. aft. Xmas

4th Sunday

Ember days

3rd Sunday

2nd Sunday

PASCHAL

─LENT─

SEPT.

XMAS

TIME

EPIPHANY

ADVENT

Annunci-
ation
St. Joseph

Purification
B.V.M.

Circumcision

Nativity

Christmas

East

MAR

APR

FEB

JAN

MA

PENTECOST
Ember days
Trinity Sun.
Corpus Xti.
2nd Sunday
Sacr. Heart
3rd Sunday
4th Sunday
5th Sunday
6th Sunday
7th Sunday
8th Sunday
9th Sunday
10th Sunday
11th Sunday
12th Sunday
13th Sunday
14th Sunday
15th Sunday
16th Sunday
17th Sunday
18th Sunday
19th Sunday
20th Sunday
21st Sunday
22nd Sunday
23rd Sunday

ME

TIME - AFTER - PENTECOST

TIME - AFTER - PENTECOST

John Bapt.
Peter and Paul

JUL
AUG
SEP
OCT

Assump-
tion B.V.M.

Ember days

Christ the
King
All Saints
All Souls

its capacity for glorifying God, since He wishes to be served by our free and intelligent acts, largely depends upon the measure in which we *understand Christianity*. As we see and interpret and apply to ourselves the doctrines of Christ in the work of building up Christian characters, in that degree are we individually enabled to serve Christianity. Now, this mission of Christianity, to promote the glorification of God and the sanctification of souls, is achieved principally through the Sacrifice of Christ, offered once in a bloody manner on the Cross, and renewed in every Mass. The work of sanctifying Christians is therefore summed up in the two words, "Cross" and "Mass." This whole redemptive process is, moreover, the all-embracing lesson each individual must learn and make his own. To enable us more easily to grasp this vast synthesis of truth, the Church Year acts as a refracting prism interposed between the Mass and ourselves. Section by section of Christ's work, the outstanding events of His life long ago, and as continued now in His brethren, are spread out for our separate study and assimilation. During Advent we summarily recall the centuries of the old Dispensation when salvation was by believing in Christ-that-was-to-come. From Christmas until Ascension we study Christ-in-the-flesh. Successively and quickly the first appearance of Christ, His infancy, childhood, the periods of obscurity and public teaching, the incidents of the sacred Passion and Resurrection and final triumphant Ascent into heaven pass before us with their sanctifying graces and blessings. From Pentecost until the end of the Church Year we are studying Christ-in-His-Church, and our own places therein.

Cycles and Units. The Church Year, like the civil year, consists of weeks and seasons; unlike the civil, it is made up of *two concomitant cycles* of feasts and observances. Of these the first relates to God and the mysteries of Redemption; it is called the *dominical* (Lord's) *cycle*. Of the feasts of this cycle, some, like Christmas and Epiphany, are "fixed," that is, they always fall on the same date, while many others, like Easter and Pentecost are "movable" because they can occur on any date within a certain interval. The second series of feasts comprises those of the Blessed Virgin Mary, the Apostles, martyrs, and other saints, and is known as the *sanctoral cycle*. Most feasts of the sanctoral cycle are fixed; hence, there is no special complexity attaching to it. Moreover, these feasts have essentially the same function; they magnify God, "who is wondrous in [us] His holy temples." They demonstrate, "since we

Ps. lxvii,36

have such a cloud of witnesses about us," that the Christian life is cap- Heb. xii,1
able of heroic success at every age and in all walks of life. With this brief
mention we may dismiss the sanctoral cycle and turn to the more complex
dominical one.

The *week*, as such, is a Jewish contribution to civilization, one based
directly on the divine command of a Sabbath rest. By the time of Christ
the week had become common in the Greco-Roman world; in fact, our
names of the weekdays are the old Teuton equivalents of their Latin
names. The Jewish Christians at first continued to frequent the synagogues on the Sabbath, but in memory of Christ's Resurrection observed
the first day of the week as the *Lord's day,* the day of sacrificial worship.
When the final break with the synagogue came, the Sabbath observance
disappeared among Christians.

At the opening of *each of* the four seasons, certain days of fasting are
observed, called *Ember Days* (Old English, *ymbren,* period). With the
Ember Days were sometimes connected observances *pertaining* to harvest-
ing the summer grain, the autumn vintage, the winter yield of olives.
Ember Days were long of great importance, because they were reserved
for a higher kind of harvest, the ordination of the Church's ministers;
to the rank and file of Catholics nowadays they should always serve as
penitential consecrations of each new season.

Christ Walking Through the Year. In his masterly Encyclical on
Christian Worship Pope Pius XII gives us a detailed and very moving
instruction on the Church Year, as Christ, Head of the Mystical Body,
walking through the year with us, His members. His Holiness treats
first of the feasts of Christ, and then of those of the saints, and their
Queen, Mary. We feel we can do no better than by listening carefully
to this papal instruction:

The Head in the Members. "All the year round the celebration
of the Eucharistic Sacrifice and the recitation of the Divine Office revolve,
as it were, about the Person of Jesus Christ; the cycle being so contrived
as to be wholly dominated by our Saviour in the mysteries of His humiliation, His redemptive work, and His triumph.

"In thus reminding the faithful of these mysteries of Jesus Christ the
sacred liturgy seeks to make them share them in such a way that the
Divine Head of the Mystical Body lives by His perfect holiness in each
of His members. Each Christian soul should be like an altar on which
the various phases of the Sacrifice offered by the High Priest are as it
were re-enacted: the sorrows and tears that remit and expiate sin; the

prayer rising up to heaven to God; the self-sacrifice and self-immolation, eager, generous, whole-hearted; the intimate union whereby we commit ourselves and all that is ours to God and find our rest in Him: 'The essence of religion is to imitate Him whom you worship.'

St. August., City of God, 8,17

For Our Imitation. "Conformably with this scheme and purpose whereby the liturgy at fixed times sets the life of Jesus Christ before us for our meditation, the Church holds up examples for our imitation and exhibits the treasures of holiness that we must make our own; for what the voice sings the heart must believe, and what the heart believes, private and public conduct must reflect.

"During Advent the Church reminds us of the sins we have unhappily committed; she exhorts us, by curbing our passions and by the use of voluntary mortifications, to reflect devoutly and recollect ourselves, and to be moved by the fervent desire to return to God, who alone by His grace can deliver us from the stain of sin and from its dreadful consequences.

"On the anniversary of the birthday of the Redeemer she invites us to return in spirit to the cave of Bethlehem, and there learn that it is necessary for us to be born again and thoroughly reform ourselves; and this happens only when we come into close and vital touch with the Word of God Incarnate and receive a share of His divine nature, to which we have been elevated.

"On the feast of the Epiphany she reminds us how all nations have been called to the Christian faith, and desires us to thank God daily for so great a benefit; to seek the living and true God with earnest faith, to reach a deep and devout understanding of supernatural things, and to love silence and meditation in order that we may more easily perceive and obtain the gifts of heaven.

Dying With Our Head. "At Septuagesima and during Lent our Mother the Church urges us again and again to meditate upon our unhappy condition, to make a powerful effort to amend our lives, to detest our sins above all things and get rid of them by prayer and penance; for it is by continual prayer and repentance for our sins that we obtain God's help, without which all our works are of no avail.

"During the sacred time at which the bitter Passion of Jesus Christ is commemorated by the liturgy, the Church invites us to Calvary, that we may follow in the bloody footsteps of the divine Redeemer, with Him willingly take up the Cross, reproduce in ourselves His sentiments of propitiation and expiation, and all die together with Him.

Rising Also With Him. "At Easter, when we commemorate the triumph of Christ, our hearts are filled with joy; and we ought to reflect deeply that we also have to rise again with our Redeemer — to rise from a life of coldness and indifference to a life of greater fervour and holiness, giving ourselves generously to God, and forgetting this unhappy earth to seek only after the things of heaven: 'Risen, then, with Christ, you must lift up your thoughts above . . . you must be heavenly-minded.' *Col. iii,2*

"And at Pentecost the Church urges us, both by her teaching and by her action, to be responsive to the action of the Holy Spirit. He longs to fill our hearts with divine charity, in order that we may more and more eagerly advance in the path of virtue, and may become holy as Christ our Lord and His heavenly Father are holy.

Whose Mystical Members We Are. "The Liturgical year is therefore a magnificent hymn of praise offered by the Christian family through Jesus, its perpetual advocate, to the heavenly Father. But it also demands that we should strive seriously and systematically to increase in our knowledge and praise of our divine Redeemer; it requires of us also an earnest and powerful effort and unremitting practice, that we may imitate the mysteries of His life, and follow willingly in the way of His sufferings, and so at last share His glory and everlasting happiness. . . .

"The sacred liturgy puts Christ before us whole and entire, in all the phases of His life: the Christ who is the Word of the eternal Father, who is born of the Virgin Mother of God, who teaches us truth, who heals the sick and consoles the afflicted, who suffers, and dies; and who then triumphs over death by His resurrection, and from His throne in the glory of heaven sends down upon us the Spirit, the Paraclete, to live for ever in His Church. 'What Jesus Christ was yesterday, and is today, He remains for ever.' And the liturgy presents Christ to us not *Heb. xiii,8* only as an example to imitate but as a teacher for us to believe, as a shepherd for us to follow, as the advocate who saves us, as the source of our holiness, and as the Mystical Head whose living members we are and whose life we live.

Christ in Us by Mysteries. "And because His cruel sufferings constitute the mystery from which our salvation chiefly springs, it is in keeping with the Catholic faith that the Passion should be emphasized; indeed it is the center of our worship, because it is what the Eucharistic Sacrifice daily represents and re-enacts, and because all the Sacraments are closely linked with the Cross.

"Therefore the liturgical year, animated throughout by the devotion of the Church, is no cold and lifeless representation of past events, no mere historical record. It is Christ Himself, living on in His Church, and still pursuing that path of boundless mercy which, 'going about Acts x,38 and doing good,' He began to tread during His life on earth. This He did in order that the souls of men might come into contact with His mysteries and, so to speak, live by them. . . . The Doctors of the Church tell us that the mysteries of Christ's life are at the same time most excellent models of virtue for us to imitate and also sources of divine grace for us by reason of the merits and intercession of the Redeemer. They live on in their effects in us, since each of them is, according to its nature and in its own way, the cause of our salvation.

Unto Fullness of Life. "It is to be remembered, too, that our loving Mother the Church, in proposing the mysteries of our Redeemer to us for our contemplation, also prays that her children may receive the supernatural gifts which, by the power of Christ, will fill them with the spirit of those same mysteries. By His inspiration and grace it becomes possible for us, through our own co-operation, to receive into ourselves the sort of life-giving energy that branches receive from the tree and members from the Head; and we thus become able gradually and Eph. iv,13 laboriously to attain to that 'maturity which is proportioned to the completed growth of Christ.'

Lesser Members, Great Models. "Besides the mysteries of Jesus Christ, the feasts of the Saints in heaven are also celebrated in the course of the liturgical year. This celebration is indeed of a lower order, yet here too the aim of the Church is always to set models before the faithful which may lead them to cultivate in themselves the virtues of the divine Redeemer.

"In the virtues of the Saints the virtue of Jesus Christ is variously reflected, and we must imitate them as they imitated Christ. In some we see apostolic zeal, in others an heroic fortitude that shrank not from the shedding of their blood; in some a constant watchfulness in expectation of the Redeemer, in others a virginal purity of soul and the gracious modesty of Christian humility; and in all a burning love of God and their neighbor. All these gems of holiness are set before our eyes by the *Missal,* liturgy that we may gaze upon them with profit to our souls and that Com. MM. 'rejoicing in their merits we may be set on fire by their example.' Thus we must observe 'innocence in simplicity, harmony in charity, modesty in humility, diligence in administraton, vigilance in helping those who labor, mercy in assisting the poor, constancy in defending the truth, and strictness in self-discipline; so that in all good works we may follow their example. These are the footsteps which the Saints, on their way back to their heavenly country, have left behind them, so that following in their path we may share their joys.' And in order that our senses also may be stimulated to salutary purpose the Church desires images of the Saints to be exposed in our churches, always to the end that 'we may imitate the virtues of those whose images we revere.' St. Bede, Hom. 70, *All Saints*

Missal, St. J. Damas.

Above Saint and Seraphim. "There is a further reason why the faithful ought to pay honor to the Saints in heaven, and that is in order to beg their help, so that 'taking joy in their praise we may find succour in their patronage.' This is why the liturgy contains so many formulas for us to use in invoking the intercession of the Saints. St. Bernard, Ser. 11, *All Saints*

"Among the holy citizens of heaven the Virgin Mother of God receives honour of a special kind. By reason of her God-given function her life is most closely interwoven with the mysteries of Jesus Christ; and assuredly no one better or more closely followed in the footsteps of the Word Incarnate, no one enjoys greater favour or influence with the Sacred Heart of the Son of God, and through It with the heavenly Father. She is holier than Cherubim and Seraphim, and enjoys greater glory than all the heavenly citizens, because she is 'full of grace,' because she is the Mother of God, and because by her blessed child-bearing she gave us the Redeemer. She is 'Mother of mercy, our life, our sweetness, and our hope,' and therefore let us all cry to her 'mourning and weeping in this vale of tears,' and with confidence commit ourselves entirely to her patronage. She became our Mother while the divine Redeemer was offering the sacrifice of Himself; and therefore, by this title too, we are her children. She teaches us all the virtues; she gives us her Son and, with Him, all the helps we need; for God 'has willed us to have everything through Mary.' *Salve Regina*

St. Bernard, *In Nat. B.V.M.,* 7

Mothering Love. "Along this path of the liturgy which year by year opens out before us, under the sanctifying influence of the Church, helped by the assistance and example of the Saints, and especially of the Immaculate Virgin Mary, 'let us come forward with sincere hearts in the full assurance of the faith, our guilty consciences purified by sprinkling, our bodies washed clean in hallowed water,' to 'the great Priest,' that we may live with Him and with Him be enabled to 'reach that inner sanctuary beyond the veil,' there to honor the heavenly Father for all eternity." Heb. x,22 Heb. x,21

Christian Worship

Summary. The Church Year is designed to further divine worship by focusing attention on the manifold truths of Christianity, and to assist in Christian character building by proposing doctrines linked with examples of how others have already lived them. Of its two cycles, the sanctoral presents saints' anniversaries, the dominical includes the Sundays and the feasts relating to God and Redemption. The whole dominical cycle evolved from the celebration of Easter; that of the saints from a desire to perpetuate their memory after the manner of the mortuary banquets of the ancients.

Eighth-Century Source Material

(How Villagers of France Began the Seasons of the Year: From *Abbot Angilbert's* RITUAL OF THE ABBEY OF ST-RIQUIER.)

For the Greater Litanies [three days before Ascension] let the cross-bearers and processions of the [seven] nearby parishes convene at St-Riquier, namely, . . . and gather before the church of the Nativity, where, the prayer being said, let the crosses be arranged in orderly fashion on either side. The populace shall be drawn up in good order at the gate of Blessed Michael the Archangel, the men on the north, the women on the south.

Then the monks with the choir of the church of St-Riquier shall issue from the church and proceed in this order: First, three with holy-water vessels shall pass out through the above-mentioned gate of St. Michael, then three with smoking thuribles and incense. Then come the seven crosses, the one in the center being that of the Holy Redeemer. These are followed by the great reliquary of the same [church]; on the right of which let there be three priests with lesser reliquaries, and the same on the left. Behind shall follow seven deacons and seven subdeacons, and acolytes, exorcists, lectors and door-keepers, seven of each. Then the monks, seven by seven. We prescribe this marching in seven so that we shall show forth in our work the sevenfold grace of the Holy Spirit: and, besides, so many monks, walking in twos or threes, would be [a line] almost a mile long. Then let the lay boys' choir [of the abbey school] come next with its seven long floating banners in the breeze. Behind these are the noblemen, chosen by the provost or dean, seven by seven; then let the noblewomen observe the same order. Then come the seven crosses [of the neighboring parishes] above-mentioned. Let these be followed by the boys and girls who can sing the *Lord's Prayer* and the *Creed* and such other things as by the help of Our Lord we have caused them to be taught. These are to be followed by the leading citizens of the place, men and women; next the mixed populace, such old and feeble as are able to walk, and these, like the rest, in sevens. Lastly let such of the old and feeble as cannot walk close up the procession on horseback. Arranged in this order, on the first day, let them go through the monastery court by the public road, and circle the wall, going out by the south gate and returning by the north.

The musical program shall be so disposed that when they first go out they shall sing the antiphon: *Exsurge, Domine, adiuva nos.* After the customary prayer is said they file out and all begin the *Exclamemus omnes ad Dominum,* which is followed by three other [antiphons], namely: *Iniquitates nostrae, Domine, multiplicatae sunt; Exaudi nos, Domine;* and *Domine, non est alius Deus praeter te,* until they are beyond the gates. Then let the brethren [monks] sing their psalms in alternate verses, but the boys' choir, and such others as can, sing the *Apostles' Creed,* then after a pause, the *Creed of Constantinople,* then the *Athanasian Creed,* then the *Lord's Prayer.* After this the *General Litany,* which stands at the head of our book, then let the boys' school sing the *Acclamations* for the good estate of all Christendom. When this is finished, let the monks leave off their psalms, and sing along with the boys the several *Litanies,* the Gallic, then the Italian, lastly the Roman. The village boys and girls who have no learning are to have help in joining in from the scholars and the young gentlemen, so that after all they may be able to join in the singing. Thus those behind and ahead, hearing these things, will give thanks to Almighty God.

Care must be taken that everything will be so timed that the items here prescribed be finished when they re-enter the monastery, so that then all may join in the *Te Deum laudamus, te Dominum confitemur,* which they shall complete in alternate verses. If it should happen that they finish too soon, let them sing *Kyrie eleison* and *Christe eleison* until they get to the church of the Nativity. Thus throughout and in all things and by all God shall be praised and honor accorded the Name of our Lord Jesus Christ, who is blessed forever. Amen.

[The ritual goes on to prescribe for the orderly arrangement at Mass after this first day's procession, and ends this section by laying out different routes through the seven villages for the second and third days' marches.]

Topics for Further Discussion:

In the Ages of Faith civil life and civilization itself rested largely upon the sacrificial calendar, "living from festival to festival."

Subsidiary but eloquent ways in which the Church emphasizes the spirit of feasts or seasons; color of sacrificial vestments, use or absence of flowers, incense, number of lights, organ music, use of veils, etc.

The Divine Office in the offices of the saints begins by setting up Christ as the King of the state of life of the saint of the day, King of martyrs, King of confessors, King of virgins, etc.

The practical meaning, as applied to the Church Year, of the expression "Living with the Church."

Ways in which a school year might be organized into liturgical focal points.

Ways consonant with our modern mode of life of giving greater individual and corporate expression to the "spirit of the several ecclesiastical seasons."

Readings:

Pope Pius XII, *Christian Worship:* Encyclical Letter, Nov. 20, 1947: translated by Canon G. D. Smith (London: CTS, 1949), *passim.*

F. Cabrol, *Liturgical Prayer, Its History and Spirit* (Westminster: Newman, 1950); "The Christian Day," pp. 137–151; "The Christian Week," pp. 152–154; "The Christian Year," pp. 155–169.

––––––– *The Prayer of the Early Christians* (London: Burns, Oates and Washbourne, 1930); "The Cult of the Martyrs, of the Blessed Virgin, the Angels and the Saints," pp. 125–131.

––––––– *The Year's Liturgy* (London: Burns, Oates and Washbourne, I, 1938), *passim.*

O. Haering, *Living with the Church, A Handbook of Instruction in the Liturgy of the Church Year* (New York: Benziger, 1930). (For high-school use.)

B. Laukemper, "The Year of Our Lord," *The Sacramental Way* (New York: Sheed & Ward, 1948), pp. 151–164.

A. Loehr, *The Year of Our Lord* (New York: Kenedy, 1937); *passim.*

M. S. MacMahon, *Liturgical Catechism* (Dublin: Gill and Son, 1926); "The Liturgical Year," pp. 193 sqq.

C. Marmion, *Our Way and Our Life.* An abridged edition of *Christ in His Mysteries* (St. Louis: Herder, 1927).

C. C. Martindale, *The Mind of the Missal* (New York: Sheed and Ward, 1929); "The Year of Mass," pp. 21–206.

T. Müller, *Our Children's Year of Grace* (St. Louis: Pio Decimo, 1943): domestic applications of the Church Year.

J. Rickaby, *The Ecclesiastical Year,* "My Bookcase" series (New York: Wagner, 1927).

A. Tanquerey, *The Spiritual Life* (Tournai: Desclée, 1930); "The Three Ways and the Liturgical Cycle," pp. 741–750.

H. Thurston, "Calendar, Christian," *CE.*

Grailville (Loveland, Ohio), occasional booklets as manuals for celebrating phases of the Church Year: *Advent, Ember Days, Candlemas, Epiphany, Holy Spring, Lenten Sundays, Thanksgiving,* etc.

Chapter IX

THE SETTING OF THE SACRIFICE

We have an altar
from which they are not entitled to eat
who serve the Tabernacle (Heb. xiii,10).

A PAGEANT of progress twenty centuries old is unfolded for us yearly in the Church's sacrificial calendar, and it is a drama in which we see a beneficent Providence constantly enriching man's original capital. If it is true that one of man's fundamental reverences is for the memory of his forbears, what a triumph of Christian solidarity to see ourselves full in this stream of historical worship that links us directly with every Christian that ever lived, or ever shall! In our prayers and rites we reach back through the long Middle Ages, past the Church of the martyrs, even to the Temple and the Synagogue. Christian worship has its historical side, as well as its hyper-historical side, if one may so express it. We have studied Christian worship from the hyper-historical side, the single, changeless service of God in the Person of our Head and Mediator, Himself a man, Christ Jesus. Historically, and in the members I Tim. ii,5 of the Mystical Body, there is the one, holy, Catholic, and Apostolic worship, a vast collection of rites and forms, prayers and thoughts, to which *every civilization and culture,* every race and people, Semite and Syrian, Greek and Roman, Goth and Frank, Celt and Saxon, *have made their own contributions.* In sharing in the present-day Christian Sacrifice anywhere in the world we are thereby caught up not alone with Christ's worship before the Ancient of Days in heaven, but we are carrying forward thoughts and sentiments and rites of all the Christian peoples of our past. Even a superficial knowledge of this fact adds immensely to our appreciation of what may be called the depth of Christian worship.

Thus, some knowledge of the different types of piety manifested by the several Christian peoples and by successive ages in the Church is a necessary condition to understand the ceremonies and rites we now possess.

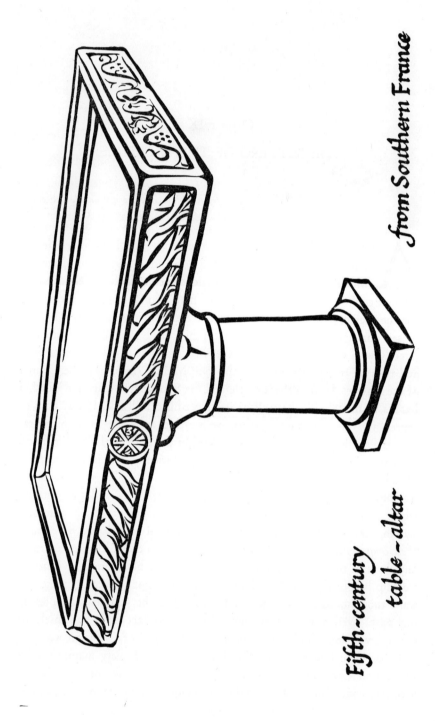

Fifth~century
table~altar

from Southern France

For ritual is merely the external expression of the religious sentiment within; and the manifestations of this religious sentiment according to circumstances of time and place may vary widely, though doctrines remain ever the same. This fact is nowhere more clearly in evidence than in the history of the sacrificial altar, to which our attention is now naturally drawn.

God's Representative. Let us begin with a dogmatic consideration, the purpose or function of an altar. The altar receives the sacrificial gift offered to God. It acts as God's agent. It is viewed, therefore, as a sort of representation of the Godhead. It is considered as clothed with God's Majesty, God's Sanctity, even as an ambassador carries the majesty of his sovereign or government. As such the altar is incomparably greater than any merely human gift laid upon it. This truth was driven home vigorously by Christ in speaking to the Jews:

> Ye blind,
> which then is greater,
> the gift, or the altar that halloweth the gift?

Matt. xxiii,19

The House of Sacrifice. The home of the Christian altar is the Christian church. In earliest times the small number of Christians made it possible to celebrate their Sacrifice in private dwellings, a use to which the homes of the better classes were well adapted. But long before the persecutions were over we find the Christians in both East and West in possession of their own church buildings. Not long before the Edict of Toleration a pagan historian, Porphyrius, complains how "the Christians, rivaling the construction of our temples, build vast edifices where they assemble for prayer." Only two years after the same edict, as we learn from St. Optatus, Rome possessed more than forty basilicas. In structure these were simply adaptations of the larger private dwellings of the day. Large, rectangular structures, they had a semicircular, domed apse at the front end raised by steps a little above the level of the nave. In the crown of this apse was an elevated and ornamented throne, the *cathedra,* or bishop's chair, which was flanked on both sides by a row of seats running all around the wall of the apse. From this seat, as St. Augustine said of the bishops, "we can see [you] enter and depart."

Ap. Macar. Magn. iv,22

Ennar. in Ps. cxxvi,3

Table-Altars. At the edge of the apse in the center was a small table, hung (during the Sacrifice) with some precious stuff, and overspread with a linen cloth. This was the primitive Christian altar, the only type of altar known among "the brethren" until about the middle of the ninth century. This altar might be wood, or, from about 350 on, of stone, or even plated with gold and gem incrusted. St. Jerome (died 420) speaks of seeing such altars in the East. Constantine gave St. Peter's basilica, which he erected, a silver altar figured with gold and four hundred gems. Nothing was allowed to be placed upon the altar but the bread and wine, the sacrificial gifts, and for a while at the beginning of Mass the book of the Gospels, this last because it was regarded as representing Christ, and enthroned, therefore, on the altar.

Ciborium or Baldaquin. A modification of this primitive setting, which in the long run had great consequences, dates from Constantine himself. It was the erection over the altar of a permanent, domical baldaquin, or *ciborium* it was then called, resting on four columns. This had at first a practical purpose, which in the West proved passing, but in the East lasts to this day. The religious sentiment of the fourth century felt that the action of sacrifice and even the altar were too holy not to be screened from the public gaze, and so were veiled from the public. The first baldaquin was a vast affair of silver topped with gold, given by Constantine to the Lateran basilica. By and by the impulse to veil the altar disappeared in the West, and then the merely decorative possibilities of the baldaquin were gradually realized. On great days flowers and garlands wreathed the columns, a circle of many lights was suspended by chains over the table, and in similar fashion gold crowns and crosses lent adornment to the "table of the Lord," yet without violating its sacred character by contact. All in all the baldaquin proved a highly satisfactory fixture and was in use for a full five hundred years. But it will be noted that every advance in enlarging or decorating the baldaquin detracted further from the bishop's throne, and put barriers, even if of silver and gold, between the body of the people and the sacred ministers.

I Cor. x,21

Priest's Position at Altar. It is often made a matter of objection to Catholic worship that the officiating minister, priest or bishop, sacrifices and conducts services generally with his back to the people. Non-Catholic objectors, who know something of the great Roman basilicas, can even find in this fact an argument of "corruption," since the papal altars, they point out, are erected so that the celebrant faces the people. Well, to begin with, it is more logical that the officiant, as spokesman of the other worshipers, should stand at their head, and they behind him, as he addresses their common homage to God. Too, there is a reason based on a once common historical consideration that taken by itself would weigh lightly with us nowadays. The early Christians, who were so keenly expectant of Christ's second coming to judge mankind, always prayed with eyes to the East, facing the orient from whence

He shall rise and visit us from on high. Luke i,78

If the church building had its entrance façade at the East end, the officiant faced toward the congregation (*they*, then, at times during the service, faced away from him!) at worship. Outside of Italy the more common arrangement was that the Church had its altar at the eastern end, and in that arrangement the relative positions of priest and people were the ones common to us now. It is only custom, not prescription, that dictates that the altar be located as we know it, with the priest facing away from the congregation. The rubrics of the missal still contain this direction, as an aid to the celebrant in accommodating himself to whatever arrangement he finds:

> When the altar is erected eastwards and towards the people, since he is already facing them, the priest does not turn his back to the altar when he is about to say; *Dominus vobiscum, Orate Fratres, Ite missa est,* or when he gives the blessing. But he kisses the altar in the center, extends and rejoins his hands, as directed above, and gives the salutation and the blessing. *Rit. Cel.* v,3

Altar and Relic Shrine. The *Acts* of the martyrdom of St. Lucian, who was martyred on January 7, 312, at Nicomedia, preserve a beautiful instance of Mass offered on the altar of the living breast of a martyr-to-be. It had been arranged that Lucian once more offer the mystic Sacrifice before complementing It with his own bloody one, but when the time came he lay perforce on his back, his feet being fastened in the stocks. So the sacred elements were laid upon a pall upon his breast, and with assistants supporting his head and hands, he sacrificed in that fashion and broke the Bread of everlasting life. But in those ages of persecution *Ruinart,* III, 182 prior to Constantine we know of no relics in direct connection with the altars, but the structure of the catacombs itself allowed a Mass on a martyr's anniversary to be celebrated near, or even upon, the tomb itself. In the fourth century, the first of official freedom, *permanent altars* began to be erected at famous tombs, those of SS. Peter and Paul being among the first such known. Within a century this custom of an altar at the martyr's tomb was common everywhere. Devotion to the martyrs found expression in lavishly adorning these shrines; *ex voto* offerings, in token of favors received, further enriched them. In the turbulent times of the barbarian invasions these numerous shrines were choicest prizes for plunder, all the more so, since the tombs were outside the cities and utterly defenseless. In the case of Rome, for instance, it was seldom that the barbarians actually penetrated into the city, but again and again, they swept up to its gates and they did plunder the Roman catacombs at will. As most of the barbarians were themselves Arian Christians, they felt a special joy in possessing themselves of the relics of famous martyrs. In 537 the Goths thus violated many of the holiest graves: the trampling Lombards in 756 worked such awful havoc in the catacombs that Pope Paul I in 761 resolved upon the wholesale transfer of the bodies of all known martyrs to the crypts of the Roman churches. Besides tombs in the crypts, graves were dug in the pavement of the churches, and even in the stone footing of the altar-tables.

A Barrier of Relics. This work of transferring the martyr's relics, interrupted more than once, was spread over a full century, 761–855. Solemn "translation" processions "with hymns and spiritual songs" were almost a daily feature of Roman life at that time. Now this period 761–855 just coincides with the real greatness of the Carolingian dynasty, the princes of which, accompanied by numerous ecclesiastics, were so frequently visitors at Rome. Seeing the Romans every day enriching their churches with the relics of the martyrs, these Frankish bishops and abbots began to think of their own faraway churches and sought *to secure relics for them.* At that time it was felt unseemly to divide the body of a martyr, so that a reliquary was the shape and size of a coffin, and usually larger because ornamented with metal plating finely wrought. Such relic cases were now taken over the Alps in great triumphant processions and were, with great fanfare and solemnity, installed — where? In hidden, out-of-the-way crypts? Not at all. They were put where they would be most conspicuous, *at the altar.* Now the other local churches, which possessed founders' or martyrs' relics, hastily disinterred them, made costly shrines, and set them on display. As it happened, a great many churches were rebuilding then, as a consequence of the Norse raids, and so it was not long before enterprising churches far and near had new and strange-looking altars.

Relic Shrines Upon the Altar. These churches of the North, unlike those of Rome and Italy, were for the most part orientated in the traditional manner, so that the priest, facing the East, had his back to the people. Here there was no need of passing behind the altar, nothing therefore to prevent the relic shrine or chest being set upon a platform behind the altar, at right angles to it, so that the end of the shrine would rest *upon the altar itself*. "Let nothing be placed upon the altar," runs a famous Frankish decree of this date, "*except* reliquaries of the saints, or perchance the four holy Gospels of God, or a pyxis with the Body of our Lord." Here the age-old sanctity of the altar was silently invaded, a fact which itself testifies to a change in religious sentiment.

Subsequent Development. The first consequence of the new arrangement was that the altars now had a fixed front, quite independently of the old idea of facing eastward. It was no longer possible to stand at the altar except opposite the relic shrine. The throne, too, was now invisible. This resulted before long in setting the throne at the side, and the shrine and altar back against the wall, where the throne had been. Again, the new setting, throwing the emphasis on the relic shrine and not on the table as formerly, made the baldaquin hard to handle. It was first moved back over the relics and then discarded generally. With the passing of the baldaquin the way was opened to putting *upon* the altar the cross, candles, flowers, and other objects of adornment, all of which were formerly suspended from the baldaquin or its columns. This necessitated additional space, and so steps, shelves one might almost say, were constructed for these accessories at the sides. In the vast churches of the Middle Ages this departure alone provided unlimited possibilities for decorative superstructures. Lastly, a small, square altar looked incongruous in conjunction with such large relic shrines. Thus, as the altars little by little grew taller, they also became longer in proportion.

The Tabernacle Introduced. Nothing has been said in the foregoing paragraphs about what is now regarded as the central feature of the altar, the tabernacle. *The altars then had no tabernacles.* The whole realm of non-sacrificial worship of the Eucharist was beginning to manifest itself only in the eleventh and twelfth centuries. Moreover, even after this type of devotion developed and was spread rapidly (as a consequence of the establishment of the feast and public procession of Corpus Christi in the thirteenth century), there was still no need of a tabernacle *at the altar,* because the new devotion was non-sacrificial. There was need, indeed, to remove the Blessed Sacrament, which had hitherto been kept in some inconspicuous place, to some sort of tabernacle, where it could be publicly "visited," worshiped, prayed to. But since people did not communicate more than a few times a year, at the great feasts, there was not yet need of a tabernacle at the altar itself, and the first tabernacle took various forms, such as a silver dove suspended in plain sight somewhere, or a specially constructed Sacrament house against the wall, or a grill opening in a pillar. The practice of frequent Communion began to spread again in a noticeable way in the late sixteenth century. Throughout the following century this was one of the most noted characteristics of the Catholic revival. The twentieth century brings us in this matter "the fullness of time," since we are now once more in the spirit of the early Church. "Let the faithful be exhorted frequently, even daily, to partake of the Eucharistic Bread, and when present at Mass . . . to communicate sacramentally," runs the text of the current legislation. The restoration of frequent Communion has given us our modern tabernacle.

Canon 863

Table-Altars Once More. How this advance in religious sentiment is at present affecting the construction of our altars becomes more evident every year. The more conscious emphasis now directed to the sacrificial Gift is reflected in fashioning the altar which receives that Gift. Modern adaptations of the old table-altar are becoming common. In some localities the closer fellowship now felt in worship is bringing in a free-standing altar, sometimes even with the celebrant facing the people.

Sacred Vestments. The ministers at the Sacrifice wear garments such as we now see nowhere else. These are modifications of the ordinary civil dress of the late Empire, say of the fourth century. Some of the priestly vestments are garments properly so called, others are insignia of office. A few paragraphs on this sacrificial vesture may well conclude the present topic.

Amice. In the order in which the vestments are put on, the first is a white, rectangular linen cloth put upon the shoulders and wrapped about the neck. This vestment is called an *amice* (*amicta*). It is a survival of the customary neckerchief or *scarf* of the ancients; by the older authors it is often called "the protection of the voice." Originally meant to serve purely practical purposes, to cover the neck, and to protect the other vestments from the hair, the amice became a very conspicuous item in the Middle Ages, when it was decorated with a wide, rich band of embroidery and allowed to show outside the other garments. Up to a certain point in the Mass, it was even worn over the head, a usage that survives still in some monastic Orders. With the disappearance of this rich ornamentation, the amice went back to its original, humbler form.

Alb. In the whole of the ancient Roman Empire of the fourth century the customary body-garment of both sexes and all classes was a sleeved *tunic* reaching well below the knees and caught at the waist with a girdle. It was of white linen. Later a short tunic became commoner in civil life, but churchmen kept to the longer form in their official functions. This old tunic lives on in our *alb* (Latin for *white*). Like the amice, the alb was often adorned with rich embroidery attached to the wrists, to the lower parts, or to the hem. The use of lace on the alb is a modern departure from tradition, and destined, it would seem, to disappear before long.

Tunic and Dalmatic. The decorated outer vestment worn by the subdeacon, called a *tunic,* as well as the (now) identical vesture of the deacon, called a *dalmatic,* are in origin outer tunics, with shorter, wider sleeves, and shorter body. The dalmatic is so called because this style of highly ornamented tunic came from Dalmatia.

Maniple. The *maniple,* a band of colored, decorated fabric laid across the left forearm, is a relic of a *handkerchief* carried as an emblem of office by Roman officials. The consul carried such a ceremonial handkerchief and with it gave the signals for the opening of games and other functions. In the first detailed description of a Roman Mass we have, the Pope's handkerchief is used to give the signal to begin Mass. The maniple was formerly made of linen, and by reason of its humble origin was called a *sudarium,* a sweatcloth, or because carried in the hand, a *manual.* Until about the year 1000 this clerical emblem of office was carried in the hand (usually the left); then began the custom of wearing it upon the wrist or forearm. When that happened, its original purpose was lost sight of, and instead of white linen, it was made of a colored and ornamented fabric.

Stole. Quite a different mark of the clerical order is what is now called a *stole* (a Greek word for garment in general). This was in ancient times called the *orarium* (literally, the mouth-cloth). How it was that a long, flowing band, slung over one or both shoulders and hanging loosely about the body, and originally destined for such humble purposes, should have become a highly prized symbol of the clerical order, remains in the present stage of our knowledge an unanswerable question. Old mosaics and pictures show the stole worn in many different ways, even as now it is worn in distinctive ways by bishop and priest and deacon respectively.

Chasuble. The most conspicuous of the sacrificial garments is the *chasuble,* as we say, from the Latin *casula,* a little house; so called, said St. Isidore of Seville, because it covered the whole man. It is a modified form of the ancient *paenula,* a cone-shaped outer garment, reaching down, more or less, the full length of the body all around, and provided with an opening and hood for the head. Designed for protection against all weathers in traveling, it finally became the ordinary outdoor garment for all wear, even replacing the toga of the high officials. At Rome it continued to be the ordinary outer garment for both sexes and all classes until the end of the sixth century or later. Thus everyone in a Roman church then wore a chasuble. St. Augustine speaks of it as the clothing of even the poor, but of course, it could be something very fine, and only a generation or so later St. Fulgentius will not have a colored chasuble because he thought that something for wealthy people. But Fulgentius was a monk and wore his monk's robe at the altar. In the new European nations the chasuble was at first the ordinary garment of clerical attire for church, street, and domestic uses. In the course of time it became reserved for priests and later still, for priests at the time of Mass only.

Not Now a "Little House." The ordinary chasuble of today represents a very *truncated* form of the ample "little house" of former ages. The garment, to allow freedom to the hands, had to be caught up over the forearms. Even in classical antiquity the chasuble was often cut somewhat shorter at the sides to facilitate freer movement. As long as pliable silk, the prescribed material for this vestment, continued to be used in making it, there was no great need of radical altering, but it was another thing entirely when stiff brocaded velvets, themselves heavily embroidered, began to be substituted for the silk. Then it was necessary to *cut* and *trim* away all that should have folded. The nadir of the trimming process was reached in the eighteenth century, when the attenuated vestment of today made its appearance. Since that day a gradual reversion to the traditional garment has been making itself felt. This movement will probably be slow in progressing, because it depends in last instance upon the slow-growing, inner religious sentiment, to which all change in external features of worship corresponds.

Summary. The Christian Sacrifice has its setting in a building adapted from the private homes of classical antiquity. In the twenty centuries of Christianity its altar has undergone many accidental modifications of size and structure, all of which are instructive reflexes of changing modes of religious thought. In the priestly vestments of today the civil dress of the late Empire lives on, hallowed by the religious associations of all the Christian past.

Ninth-Century Source Material

(From Walafrid Strabo's precious work, ON THE ORIGINS AND DEVELOPMENTS OF USES PERTAINING TO WORSHIP.)

Altars were erected to the Lord, as we read, by Noah, Abraham, Isaac, and Jacob, while Moses was the first to erect a Tabernacle for the sons of Israel freed from the Egyptian servitude. This he did in the desert of Sinai, and according to plans made known by heaven. Afterwards, when the same Jews had long dwelt in the Land of Promise . . . Solomon at great outlay erected and adorned that marvelous Temple of Jerusalem. In both Tabernacle and Temple were placed the Ark of the Covenant, and altars with their vessels, and the manifold other appurtenances corresponding to the religion of that time . . . (Ch. I).

Afterwards came the day when worshipers in spirit and in truth (John iv) began to adore the Father spiritually, and not locally only in Jerusalem or on the mountain of Samaria, when the doctrine of salvation was sent out unto all peoples. The faithful then began to search out "clean" places, and such as were removed from the noise and business of carnal affairs, in which they might offer "clean" prayers, and the holy Mysteries, and celebrate the comforts of mutual edification. . . . Not only were new houses erected for prayer, but even pagan temples, their unclean cults and idols being swept clean away, were changed into churches of God (Ch. III).

And because the diversity of idolatrous worship had built temples in different manners, the faithful of that age were at no great pains as to

Classical Antecedents

Greek charioteer
in girded tunic
(alb)

greek boy
in wide-sleeved ungirt tunic
(dalmatic)

Roman sailor with
amice (neck cloth)
and chasuble

Chasuble serves goatherd as a little house

Roman father and son in chasubles over
banded tunics

Mercury in chasuble

Roman consul wearing
tunics and stole and
holding maniple

what direction the houses of prayer faced, provided only that the omnipresent God, Creator of all things, be worshiped and adored where the filth of demons had been removed. Of course the learned will say that we ought to face the East in worshiping (and in fact this is a fitting and salutary institution) . . . (Ch. IV).

[To those prompted to give "unclean" money for the construction or ornamentation of churches, Walafrid addresses strong words:]

It is to these the Saviour saith:

> Woe to you,
>   scribes and Pharisees, hypocrites;
>   because ye tithe mint and dill and cummin,
> and ye have neglected the weightier things of the Law,
>   justice and mercy and faith.

Matt. xxiii,23

We do not say this to blame the devotion of those who build and adorn churches, but to show that almsgiving to the needy is to be preferred. As Blessed Jerome says: "It is a mere external observance to have the wall bright with gold, while Christ at the entrance suffers from hunger and nakedness." And when He comes in judgment, He will not ask if we have built churches, but whether we have done good to His least brethren . . . (Ch. XIV).

Matt. xxv

Nothing could be found more appropriate than these Species for showing forth the union between Head and members. Because, as the bread is one body made of multiple grains of wheat moistened with water, and the wine is pressed from many grapes, so the body of Christ is filled up by the unified multiplicity of the faithful [saints] . . . (Ch. XVI).

The hour of celebrating Mass varies according to the rank of the solemnity. Sometimes Mass is offered in the forenoon, sometimes about three in the afternoon, or again at sundown, at times, even at night . . . (Ch. XXIII).

The vessels in which our Sacraments are prepared and consecrated are chalices and patens. . . . Boniface, martyr and bishop, when asked if it were lawful to consecrate in wooden chalices, replied: "Formerly priests of gold consecrated in wooden chalices, now priests 'of wood' use golden chalices."

Pope Sylvester established that the Sacrifice should be offered, neither on silk, nor a shabby cloth, but only on clean linen "born" of the earth. . . . The sacred vestments have developed by gradual stages to the ornamentation of the present day. At first priests offered Mass in every-day garments. . . . Stephen, the twenty-fourth pope, prescribed that priests and deacons should not use sacred vestments when engaged in profane occupations, but only in church. And Pope Sylvester ordained that deacons should wear dalmatics in church. . . . And others made still other additions to the sacred vestments, either by way of imitating what ancient priests had worn, or to express some mystical significance (Ch. XXIV).

Topics for Further Discussion:

The entire altar-table is ideally one piece of natural stone, containing a "sepulcher" of relics of martyrs, and resting on stone supports: only such an altar is a "fixed" or "permanent" altar.

If made of any other material, provision must be made for the location of an altar-stone (containing relics). Technically, only this altar-stone is the pre-scribed altar: it is known as a portable altar.

Altars are by prescription consecrated by a bishop, or, in some cases, a prelate of lower rank designated for the purpose by the bishop.

Altars lose their consecration by being cracked seriously, by any damage to the "sepulcher," etc., and in such cases must be reconsecrated after being repaired.

The latest American altars are reverting to the simple table type: cf. photo-graphs in *Liturgical Arts* (quarterly).

Advantages from the social point of view of the free-standing altar, at which the sacrificing priest faces the people.

Readings:

D. Attwater, "Vestments of the Western Church," *Thought*, II (1927–28), pp. 98–113.

E. Bishop, *Liturgica Historica, Papers on the Liturgy and Religious Life of the Western Church* (Oxford: Clarendon, 1918); "The Christian Altar," pp. 20–38.

J. Braun, "Vestments in Western Europe," *CE*.

H. E. Collins, *The Church Edifice and Its Appointments* (Westminster: New-man, 1946); "Altar," pp. 43–69; "Sacred Vestments," pp. 167–174.

M. M. Hassett, "Altar, History of the Christian," *CE*.

H. Lucas, *Holy Mass, the Eucharistic Sacrifice and the Roman Liturgy* (St. Louis: Herder, 1914); I, "The Christian Altar," pp. 14–23.

J. B. O'Connell, *Church Building and Furnishing: the Church's Way* (Notre Dame Univ. Press, 1955), Part II, "The Altar," pp. 136–186; *passim*.

A. Roulin, *Vestments and Vesture* (Westminster: Newman, 1949); "The Chasuble (1): From the Beginning to the XIX Century," pp. 56–71; *passim*.

A. J. Schulte, "Altar (in the Liturgy)," *C.E.*

C. L. Souvay, "Altar (in the Greek Church)," *C.E.*

G. Webb, *The Liturgical Altar* (Westminster: Newman, 1949), *passim*.

Chapter X

HIGH MASS WITH ST. GREGORY THE GREAT

The cup of blessing, which we bless,
is it not fellowship in the Blood of Christ?
(I Cor. xi,26.)

WHEN Alaric and his Visigothic hosts sacked and pillaged Rome in the summer of 410, the national pride of the Romans was cut to the quick. In the provinces no less than in the city, Christians as well as pagans were amazed and dumbfounded to see the Eternal City, "the mistress of the world," violated and plundered by the hands of barbarians. It was not long before the still remaining adherents of paganism raised the cry, "This happened because Rome turned from her ancient gods to adopt Christianity!" This charge drew from St. Augustine, then bishop of an African town, the greatest of all his works, *The City of God.*

After refuting the old calumny that pagan worship was necessary for temporal happiness or prosperity, Augustine passes to a positive defense of Christianity, which he calls in Scriptural language "The City of God." In his tenth book he deals at length with the true nature of worship, of sacrifice, and in particular of the sanctifying value of the Sacrifice of the Mystical Body. We find him here forcibly restating the language of the New Testament, and its earliest exponents, as already summarily reviewed in these pages. Here we shall allow ourselves only a short quotation from his thought. He says:

> We owe [God] that worship which the Greeks call *latria*, both in external symbols and in our own selves, for we are all His temple . . . our hearts elevated to Him are His altars; His only Son is the Priest by whom we are made pleasing to Him.
>
> The whole ransomed city, that is, *the Church and the communion of saints, forms the universal sacrifice* offered to God by the High Priest,

Chap. iv

122

who in His passion gave up His life that we might become the Body of so great a Head. . . . This is the Christian's Sacrifice: we being many are one Body with Christ, as the Church in the Sacrament of the Altar, so well known to the faithful, wherein is shown that in that oblation *the Church is offered.* Chap. vi

This entire part of *The City of God* is the classic presentation of what full Christian worship implies.

Gregory the Great and Our Worship. It may, therefore, come as a surprise to learn that all through the Middle Ages people called *St. Gregory the Great* (pope, 590–604), "the Father of Christian Worship." This was because that great pontiff, who so uniquely embodied the Roman genius for organization, revised the Roman worship of his day with a result so satisfactory that Rome has kept to it ever since. What Augustine sketched in theory in the early fifth century, Gregory at the end of the sixth reduced to perfect practice. It happens that we possess a detailed account of a papal feast-day Mass of an age not long after Gregory's, and scholars agree that, barring a detail here and there, it shows us Gregory's own Mass. On reading this ancient sketch of Gregory's Mass, one does not wonder that the Church for more than thirteen hundred years has regarded it as the most perfect expression of her Eucharistic worship ever realized. The full *sacrificial consciousness* on the part of the worshipers there had its counterpart in the chief fruit of their worship, an ennobling *sense of the Christian solidarity.*

Approaching the Station. On great days the Roman Mass was a "stational" affair, that is, a papal Mass in some particular church of the city designated beforehand, to which clergy and people of the whole city came. At meeting places in each of the seven ecclesiastical "wards" the populace assembled, where with a prayer they fell in behind the Christian standard, the cross, and set off in processions for the station. There they found, ranged along the bench of the apse, to right and left respectively of the papal throne, the seven suburban bishops and the city's twenty-five pastors. Numerous monks would be already there, probably reciting, or singing, their psalms, and there would be found soldiers from the Roman garrisons. Meanwhile from the Lateran palace a striking procession would be approaching. Carrying sacred vessels and vestments, came various minor clerics on foot; on horseback rode deacons and subdeacons (one from each of the seven regions), the papal chancellor, and notaries. In a second troop rode the Pontiff attended by his major-domo, his sacristan, and his almoner. Dismounting at the entrance, all vested in the sacristies, located in front of the main entrance to the basilica. Their ceremonial garment was the chasuble, in cut and shape the same as in civil life, but of finer texture and adornment, and now beginning to take on a sacred character because these particularly fine specimens were reserved for the sacred functions. Two choirs of singers would already be in place on either side at the front, with the men standing behind the boys. A sub-deacon, attended by an acolyte, would enter and "place the Gospel-book honorably upon the altar." When all was ready, a subdeacon, carrying as a badge of authority the Pope's ceremonial handkerchief, the maniple, would give notice to the choir to begin the chant. The Introit, a Psalm with a short refrain intercalated between the verses, thereupon began, and the great procession moved into the basilica.

ROMAN CONSUL WITH OFFICIAL HANDKERCHIEF
The priest's *maniple* is a development of the official handkerchief, an insignia of office, with which high Roman officials opened and closed games, sessions, etc.

Torches of Honor. When high magistrates of Rome entered their courts, they were preceded by attendants carrying *torches,* and a *brasier* of coals, for relighting the torches should these be extinguished. St. John the Evangelist no doubt often saw such processions, and memories of them may have subconsciously shaped his vision in the *Apocalypse* of Apoc. ii,1 "the One who walked in the midst of the seven golden lamps." Be that as it may, the Pontiff is now preceded by seven acolytes each bearing a gold or silver candlestick, by the seven deacons, and the seven subdeacons, one of whom holds a fuming censer.

Beginning the Mass. As the imposing procession approached the presbytery, the acolytes separated, three on one side and four on the other, to allow those behind to pass up through their midst. Then the subdeacons would do the same, and at the foot of the altar the deacons likewise. As the Pope proceeded to the altar, two acolytes approached, carrying a casket in which a fragment of the consecrated Species from a

GROUP OF CLERICS VESTED

The clerics, vested in alb, stole, tunic, and chasuble carry maniples in right or left hand indifferently. (From a ninth-century Bible Codex.)

former Mass was preserved. The Pontiff would inspect, and, presumably with a bow, salute, the Sacred Species. Also with a bow he saluted the altar, and prayed silently for a moment. Thereupon he made the sign of the cross on his forehead, gave the kiss of peace to one of the suburban bishops, to the archpriest, and to the seven deacons. Then he motioned the precentor to end the Introit Psalm. While awaiting its conclusion, he would kneel for a few moments in prayer. During the interval the deacons had approached the altar two by two and kissed its extremities. The Pontiff now ascended, kissed the Gospels and then the altar. Thereupon he went to his throne, where he stood facing eastward, away from the people. The choirs continued singing the *Kyrie* alternately until a signal was given them to stop. Turning to the assembly, the Pontiff would now intone *Gloria in excelsis Deo* (Glory be to God on high), and at once face eastward again while this was being sung throughout by the chanters. Again turning, the Pontiff saluted the throng with *"Peace be with you,"* and intoned the short Collect prayer. This over, he would seat himself and motion to the bishops and priests to do the same.

The Scripture Lessons. A subdeacon appointed beforehand now went without accompaniment or ceremony into a pulpit and read the Epistle. When he descended, a singer went up and chanted a Psalm, to the several verses of which the entire congregation answered with a short, simple refrain, as, for instance, *Alleluia.* The chanting of the Gospel was, so far as external ceremonials is concerned, the high point of the entire function. In much the same manner as now, with lights and incense, a procession moved to a second pulpit on the opposite side, where the deacon chanted the sacred message. At its close, the Gospel-book was kissed by everyone in the presbytery.

Bringing the Gifts. Two deacons now approached the altar, one of them holding a cloth. This "he lays on the right side of the altar, throwing the other end of it to the second deacon in order to spread it." The choir again began a Psalm, the verses of which were again marked off by some simple refrain. The Pope now went down with his attendants to receive the offerings of the people. The men come on the north side, the women on the south, carrying their gifts, little loaves of bread, and little flagons of wine. The bread they put directly into the hands of the Pontiff, and it was then put upon a cloth held by attendants. The wine was poured into a great, two-handled chalice, from which, when filled, it was poured into large bowls carried by acolytes. Everyone in the congregation would make an offering to express his or her participation in the common Sacrifice, and to symbolize in these gifts the dedication of their lives to Almighty God and to Christian ideals. It was the privilege of the choir boys, who were for the most part orphans, to offer the water that was required for the sacrifice.

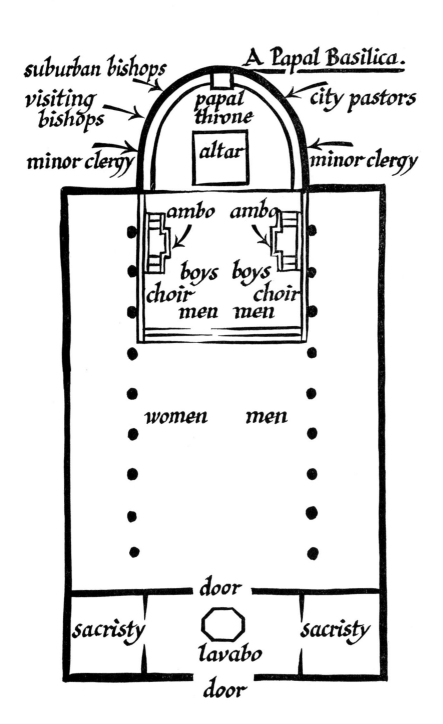

A Papal Basilica.

suburban bishops
visiting bishops
minor clergy

papal throne
altar

city pastors
minor clergy

ambo ambo

boys choir men
boys choir men

women men

door
sacristy
lavabo
sacristy
door

After receiving the offerings, the celebrant returned to his throne and washed his hands. The archdeacon meanwhile arranged some of the loaves upon the altar. Next, the offerings of the clerics were received, rank by rank. The chalice was placed upon the altar and water added to it. The Pontiff approached the altar and received his own oblation, two small loaves brought for this purpose from the Lateran. The signal was then given to end the Psalmody.

Dedicating Self Through Gifts. With the heaped-up altar between himself and his flock, and with the attendant bishops, priests, the minor clerics ranged in order about him, while all bowed deeply in reverence, the Pontiff recited in an audible voice the prayer now called the Silent Prayer. This brief prayer varied from day to day, but it always echoed the thought that the gifts now laid upon the altar represented the persons who had made them. In direct, concise form, the wish was expressed that in return for these gifts, God would deign to grant some blessing in return. For instance, the prayer that follows was said each year by Gregory on the Tuesday of Passion Week:

O God, our Lord, who in these objects especially, which Thou hast created for the support of our weakness, hast commanded gifts to be offered; grant, we beseech Thee, that they may become the support of the present life, and a symbol of life everlasting. Through Jesus Christ, Thy Son our Lord.

Another train of thought, which often recurs in these Offertory-prayers, and also dates from St. Gregory at the latest, is this; we repeat it on the seventh Sunday after Pentecost:

O God, who hast enacted one perfect Sacrifice in place of all the victims that were under the Old Law, receive this Sacrifice offered by Thy devout servants, and sanctify it as Thou didst sanctify the offerings of Abel, that *what they have severally offered to the honor of Thy Majesty, may avail them all unto salvation.* Through, etc.

A Sacrifice of Thanksgiving. The Pontiff raised his voice to chant the final words: "Through endless ages of ages." The subdeacons stood erect to respond, "Amen." Then as now *Sursum corda* (Lift up your hearts), and *Gratias agamus* (Let us give thanks to the Lord our God), led up to the Preface, which, then as now, was followed by the *Sanctus*, at the singing of which all again bowed the head profoundly. The most noticeable difference between a High Mass of the sixth century and our own of today was the manner of praying during the Canon. The *Sanctus* over, the celebrant alone stood erect and began the Canon. While up to this point there had been constant movement and chant, now the Act progressed in comparative quiet, while all bowed profoundly. There was thus the same profound sense of deepest reverence before God during the entire period of the Canon as marks, in our Mass, the fleeting moment of consecration. No bell, or incensation, or elevation gave external sign of that moment when the transubstantiation changed the poor gifts of bread and wine into the supreme Gift of the Body and Blood of Christ. The people merely knew when the Pontiff raised his voice once more, that this change had been effected, and the perfect Gift ritually offered before God's Majesty. The Pontiff would call upon the people to signify their common assent to this sacrificial Action by joining in the "Amen." The sacrificial ritual was here complete.

A Portion for the Absent. The Pontiff now returned to his throne to say, as a special preparation for Communion, the *Our Father,* and a subsequent short prayer. The remnant of the consecrated Species from a former Mass, held all the while on a paten by an acolyte, was now dropped into the chalice. This was done to symbolize the oneness of the Christian Sacrifice, and this same idea lies behind another action that followed. If any of the priests of the city happened to be absent from the stational Mass, *a portion of the Eucharist* was broken off, one of the Pope's own oblations being used for this purpose, to be sent to the absentee as a token of union. The Eucharist means *fellowship* in Christ above all else. After the actions just described, the time and place of the next "station" would be announced by the archdeacon as: "Tomorrow the station will be at the Basilica of St. Peter, the chief of the Apostles." To this the people responded, "Thanks be to God."

Breaking the Bread. The general *breaking of the Bread* was an impressive ceremonial preparation for Communion. Acolytes, carrying the Bread in little linen bags around their necks, passed up and down the presbytery, allowing bishops and priests to take the Bread. At a signal from the Pontiff, all would join with him in breaking the Bread in unison. It was then returned to the altar, for distribution at the sacrificial Banquet which followed forthwith. The Pope communicated himself at his throne, the archdeacon supporting the Chalice, of which the Pontiff partook.

Then the bishops and higher clergy came before the Pope to receive in their hands the species of Bread, while at the altar a bishop proferred them the Chalice. The singers once more intoned a Psalm with a fixed refrain after every verse. The people came forward as before, called now to the Table of God as guests, to receive as from His hand the visible token and pledge of the acceptance of their gifts.

A ninth-century legendary touch in the biography of St. Gregory depicts how closely gift and Return-Gift might be psychologically related: A noble woman was said to have smiled as Gregory was about to communicate her; whereupon he passed her by, and asked afterwards the explanation of such levity: "Why, you said 'The Body of the Lord,' and I recognized It for a bit of my own baking."

Bk. iv,10

On the palm of the right hand of the communicant the Pontiff laid the Bread, and the archdeacon offered each in turn the Cup of fellowship in the Blood of Christ. The Communion of the lower clerics followed upon that of the people.

The Fruit of Union. After the Communion the celebrant went to the altar to say the prayer now called "Postcommunion." This links up in a brief compass the thought of the Sacrament just received and the fruits of that Sacrament to be perceived in a better living of the Christian life. The following short form still keeps its place in St. Gregory's Mass Book, on the Saturday before Laetare Sunday:

> We beseech Thee, Almighty God, that we may ever be numbered among *His members,* in whose Body and Blood we have communicated. Through the same Jesus Christ Thy Son our Lord.

The Gregorian Postcommunion we say now on the sixth Sunday after Epiphany runs:

> Fed as we have been, O Lord, on heavenly delights, we pray Thee that we may ever have a longing for the same *by which we truly live.* Through Jesus Christ Thy Son.

These last words re-echo a celebrated passage of St. Augustine in which he says. "O sign of unity! O bond of charity! Whosoever would live, hath here where to live, hath here whereof to live. Let him come, let him believe; let him be incorporated, that he may be enlivened. Let him not shrink from the *whole* into which *the members* are compacted together. . . . Let him cleave to the body, let him live to God by God."

Hom. xxvi in Ioan.

Recessional. After the Postcommunion the deacon sang: *Ite missa est* (Go, it is the time of dismissal), to which the entire congregation responded: "Thanks be to God." Whereat the long procession, swelled this time by the monks and the soldiers, formed and marched down the basilica, the Pontiff bestowing blessings as he went.

A Reflection. In this sketch of High Mass in St. Gregory's day we realize that the substantial rites have changed but little. But everyone will also realize that the intervening centuries have brought a profound difference in the general attitude of the congregation toward those rites at the altar. Then everyone, high or low, publicly *expressed* his or her *individual homage in a social, public gift-offering,* and similarly everyone high or low felt prompted by an enlightened self-interest, so to speak, to partake of God's *Return-Gift,* Communion.

How forcibly did not this rite portray the fellowship of the Church, and its corporate spirit! By reason of the general obscuring of the sacrificial consciousness, Christians of the present day are much poorer than those of Gregory's time. True, the Sacrifice is essentially the same, and is *in a measure* profitable to us by its own intrinsic value, however we may lack what a modern phrase would call "sacrificial-mindedness." But inasmuch as our service of God must be reasoning and intelligent, we shall share in the unspeakable riches of the Eucharist all the more as we penetrate its social and sacrificial character. That is the task of twentieth-century Christianity.

Summary. In two important respects social participation in Eucharistic worship has diminished since the end of the sixth century; first, the individual worshipers no longer make a personal gift-offering of the sacrificial elements, and second, the reception of Communion is not now regarded as a necessary adjunct of assistance at the Sacrifice.

Tenth-Century Source Material

(Our better-informed age may improve a little on the faulty history but not on the faith or piety of Remigius of Auxerre in his work: on the celebration and meaning of the mass.*)*

Mass is celebrated in memory of the Passion of Christ. He Himself, in giving them His Body and Blood, bade the Apostles, "Do this in memory of Me" (Luke xxxi,19), that is, in memory of My Passion. As if He should say, what I have suffered for your salvation, do you recall, and take pains to do the same thing for the weal of yourselves and yours. Peter is said to have been the first to celebrate this Sacrifice, at Antioch, using (in that beginning of the faith) only three prayers, beginning at that place [in the Canon] where it is said: *Hanc igitur oblationem*. . . .

First of all the antiphon at the introit is said. Now "antiphon" is a Greek word, of which the Latin equivalent is "reciprocal," two singing alternately, the one after the other in order. The Greeks are reputed to have invented this mode of singing. This antiphon is called "at the introit [entrance]," because through it we enter the divine mystery, as one enters through the doorway into the interior part of the house. . . .

The chanter beginning *Kyrie, eleison*, the candles are arranged by an acolyte in a row from south to north, thus showing forth in what order the Lord Almighty had mercy on the world. [*R. was writing near the then "North Pole" of European civilization.*] . . . The Latins sing in Greek, "Kyrie, eleison," and the Greeks in Latin . . . that we may show ourselves as one people, and that both races believe in one God. Kyrie, Lord, eleison, have mercy, *Christe,* eleison, that is, Thou who art anointed, not with visible oil, but with the plenitude of the Godhead, have mercy, for *chrism* is anointing.

Then the priest begins *Gloria in excelsis Deo,* the hymn sung by the angels at the birth of the Saviour, and later completed, as it were, by Blessed Hilary of Poitiers, and after the manner of the angels, to show that we worship the same Lord on earth whom the angels venerate in Heaven. . . .

Thereupon the priest says *Dominus vobiscum,* greeting the people and praying that the Lord be with them, as He deigned to say by the Prophet, II Cor. vi,16   "I will dwell amongst them" and the rest, and as the Saviour said to His Matt. xxviii,20   disciples, "Behold I am with you." This salutation is not of human composition, but is taken as used by the authority of Sacred Scripture, where one often reads it both in the singular and plural forms. . . .

Then he says *Oremus,* inviting the people to pray with him. . . . There follows the *Collect,* so called from the act of collecting . . . because from many words one prayer is gathered up. . . .

After the recitation of the Gospel, the priest again greets the people, praying that the words they have heard of the Lord may be strengthened in their hearts, and inviting them to pray, saying *Oremus.* And although in our rite this Collect between the Gospel and the Offertory is no longer said, it is retained by the Greeks. Our custom may be understood in this manner: that the people is enjoined to make its offering, and the offerers should make their intention, that their oblations be pleasing to the Lord. . . .

Then follows the Offertory itself, which derives its name from the circumstance that the people present their gifts. . . . Meanwhile the priest receives the gifts of the people, that he who stands as mediator between God and the people, may present their prayers and wishes to the Lord. In this offering water is mixed with the wine. Christ is signified in the wine, the people in the water. If wine were to be offered without water it would signify that the Passion of Christ had not benefited the human race; but if water without wine, it would mean the man could have been redeemed without Christ's Passion. . . .

The *thanks* which it is fitting for us to offer are to be rendered through our Lord Jesus Christ, who is Mediator between God and us, and High-priest of highpriests. . . .

Cum quibus et nostras voces, and so forth. The voices of the angels hymn their Maker in the very ecstasy of intuitive contemplation. What should be the character of *our* voices, that we beg to be admitted, that is introduced, into the angelic choirs before the Face of God? . . . Our *words* do not carry our voices unto the inmost ears of God, but *our desires do,* and because the heavenly city is peopled by angels and men, the holy Church, which is to be joined with them in Heaven, and carry on with them the praises of God, the Church is right, I say, in even now praising God with those very same voices on earth with which the holy angels sing in paradise. . . .

Topics for Further Discussion:

Advantages to society now lost to us, derived by the Christians of St. Gregory's day from their type of Mass celebration.

Limited ways and means by which popular participation in the public functions of the Church can be reproduced in collegiate and parish services.

"In order that the faithful may participate more actively in divine worship Gregorian chant in that which pertains to the people must be given back to them." — *Pius XI.*

"Do not pray at Mass, pray the Mass." — *Pius X.*

The so-called Dialogue Mass, or *Missa Recitata,* and its advantages.

The justice of the saying, "Ceremonial is to public worship as the body to the soul."

The suitability of the materials in this chapter for a Mass pageant of medieval civilization.

The possibility of dramatic representation of modern American youth presenting in symbolic tokens their lives of work and play.

Readings:

C. F. Atchley, *Ordo Romanus Primus,* Text, Translation, Notes (London, 1905).

E. Bishop, *Liturgica Historica, Papers on the Liturgy and Religious Life of the Western Church* (Oxford: Clarendon, 1918); "The Genius of the Roman Rite," pp. 1–19.

L. Duchesne, *Christian Worship, Its Origin and Evolution* (New York: Macmillan, 1923); "The Roman Mass," pp. 161–188.

A. Fortescue, *The Mass, A Study of the Roman Liturgy* (New York: Longmans, Green, 1937); "The Mass since Gregory I," pp. 172–177.

J. A. Jungmann, *The Sacrifice of the Church* (Collegeville: Lit. Press, 1957), "The Celebration of Sunday and the Life of the Church," pp. 24–45.

J. Kramp, *Live the Mass* (St. Paul: Cat. Guild, 1954), "A Papal Mass in the Eighth Century," pp. 220–239.

J. de Puniet, *The Mass, Its Origin and History* (London: Burns, Oates and Washbourne, 1931); "The Setting of the Roman Mass in the Time of St. Gregory the Great," etc., pp. 81–95, sqq.

Chapter XI

SACRIFICIAL-MINDEDNESS PARTLY LOST — AND FOUND

Take ye and eat (Matt. xxvi,26).

REFERENCE has been made several times in these pages to the gradual but profound changes affecting the religious outlook of succeeding ages. In particular a good deal of the sacrificial and Eucharistic atmosphere of the early Church seems remote from us, not only in time, but in concept and feeling. A little puzzled, we ask ourselves how it could be that, while the faith in the Eucharist remained quite unchanged, the Christian mentality toward it could undergo far-reaching changes. How did it come about that *we* are inclined to regard attendance at Mass as an irksome duty, while it was originally considered as the exercise of the *supreme right* of the Christian man and woman? Or how was it that the Church was forced to make a matter of law binding under mortal sin the annual reception of Communion, when once men and women, and usually even infant children, communicated at every Mass, and privately in their homes when there was no Mass?

Why Piety Changed. These questions are partly answered by saying, "The piety of the people grew cold and formal, and so these changes resulted." Besides being incomplete, such an explanation is partly incorrect, since there has never been a lack of seraphic saints in the Church. The full truth of the matter must take account of the fact that in the course of time the piety of the people gradually grew *different*. There is no more important or instructive chapter in the Church's inner history than the beginning of this very process, whereby what is pre-eminently the sacrament of love and union, became invested with attributes of dread and fear. What is really at stake here is the concept of Christ as the *Bridge-Builder*, the very notion of mediatorial worship of God *through* the New Man, His Son.

Daily Communion, the Common Thing. In the first centuries, Christ's unique position as Mediator of the New Law was the focal point of the Glad Tidings of Salvation. Therein men found an unfailing source of individual strength and peace and "confident access unto God." The Eucharistic Food united them with God through Christ, and so it was eagerly and ardently eaten on rising every morning. Even though Mass was, as a rule, celebrated but once or twice a week in the earliest ages, Christians kept the Eucharist in their homes and communicated themselves at their morning prayer. Tertullian, in urging upon women not to marry pagans, speaks of the misunderstandings inevitably to arise out of the fact that the pagan husbands will know, but not understand, what it is they eat on rising. The words of St. Hippolytus of Rome, about 225, speak volumes by implication: "Let each of the faithful hasten, before eating any other food, to partake of the Eucharist . . . and let each be solicitous lest any unbeliever share of it, or that a mouse or any other animal touch it, or that any of it fall [to the ground] and perish."

Eph. iii,12

Ad Ux. ii,5

Apos. Trad. lxxvii–viii

A SECOND-CENTURY EUCHARISTIC FRESCO
A symbolic representation of the Holy Eucharist, the fish supporting a basket of bread and glass of wine. (Crypt of Lucina, Catacomb of Callistus.)

Carried in Wicker Baskets. In inveighing against the pagan theaters, at least one preacher spoke of the shamelessness of Christians appearing at them "as they return from the Sacrifice, carrying the Eucharist, as is customary." In the mural decorations of the catacombs a frequent theme is that of a fish bearing on its back a basket of small loaves, among which one can discern a glass vessel of wine. The fish, of course, stood for Christ, as was explained previously, and the loaves and wine were unquestionably the Eucharistic Species. The Christians were constantly

De Spectac., v

taught to interpret the words, "Give us this day our daily bread," as referring primarily to the Food that had become Christ's Body in their public Sacrifice of thanksgiving. If there is one thing that stands out clearly in the meager records of early Christianity, it is this popular hunger and thirst for the Eucharist as affording "confident access unto God."

The Bridge Broken — or Unused. This primitive attitude lasted unchanged until, at the turn of the fourth century, Arianism appeared in the Orient, fiercely denying the divinity of the Word, and hence of Christ. In the ensuing struggle, one of the wildest and bitterest of the Church's long history, every move made by Arians to insist on the humanity of Christ was parried by a counterstroke of the Catholics emphasizing His divinity. In this process many an old prayer expressive of Christ's *mediation,* now deemed *capable* of an Arian interpretation, was changed so as to bring out with unequivocal clarity Christ's divine nature equal with the Father's. Thus, an old form of the common doxology, "Glory to the Father, *through* the Son . . ." was altered to "Glory to the Father, *and* to the Son. . . ." When the violence of this storm had passed, the Oriental Churches had developed a quite different *attitude toward Christ.* Arians no longer worshiped God *mediatorially* through Christ, for to them Christ was a mere man; Christians, by focusing all attention on the divine nature of Christ, were also losing the *practical consciousness* of His office of Bridge-Builder. "Now Christ no longer stands by man's side, as the representative of mankind, and no longer as *the* man, Christ Jesus, and the First-born of His brethren, offers the Sacrifice of mankind to the Triune God. He has, so to speak, crossed over, and is now by God's side, and Himself is the awful and unapproachable God."[1]

Origin of "Cultual" Dread. Within a generation this new attitude brought about epoch-making consequences in the primitive outlook toward the Eucharist. It surrounded both Sacrifice and Communion with a *sense of awe and dread.* Thus, within twenty years of the condemnation of Arianism, we find a Council at Antioch (341), and one at Sardica, in Thrace (343), threatening to cut off Christians from the Church because they had begun *to abstain from the reception of Communion at public worship.* The famous *Catechetical Instructions* of St.

---

[1] K. Adam, *Christ Our Brother* (New York: Macmillan, 1931), p. 49.

Cyril of Jerusalem date from the year 348: In them the period of the Canon of the Mass is called "that most awful hour." This "awfulness" is a note that will echo louder and louder in the preaching of subsequent ages: The Holy Eucharist was in the East fast becoming "the dread Mysteries," at the celebration of which the Christians were bid to stand "in fear and dread." For the reception of the "awful Body" preachers were beginning to find that no preparation really sufficed, and they began attaching hard and oftentimes insupportable *conditions* to the reception of Communion. So swift were matters moving in the East that at the end of the century, St. John Chrysostom complains at Constantinople:

> In vain is the daily Sacrifice, in vain do we stand before the altar, and there is no one to partake: Everyone that partaketh not of the Mysteries is standing here in shameless effrontery. . . .

But almost the next words on the lips of this strict preacher were hardly adapted to bring the people in numbers to the Communion Table.

> These things I say to you, not to induce you to come in any which way, but that you should render yourselves worthy to partake. . . . It is sincerity and purity of soul. With these approach at all times, *without them, never!*

Hom. iii in Ephes.

Jerome's Influence. The great St. Jerome was a Roman by training, but at this time he had long been a resident in the East, and he was imbued with these Eastern ideas. He was more than once asked by correspondents if they should communicate daily "as the Roman and Spanish churches do." In his replies Jerome *"neither praises nor blames the Roman custom,"* but for the rest, "let his questioners follow the usages of their localities," that is, let them abstain from Communion, if that be the local usage. Moreover, St. Jerome found, as he thought, Scriptural reasons for supporting the hard conditions that were then being attached to the reception of Communion. When we recall that Jerome's authority in matters of Scripture was supreme, it is clear that his influence tended to accelerate the common abstention from Communion.

West Feels Cultual Dread. Before very long this new spirit had penetrated into the West, partly through the spread of Arianism, but probably more by reason of the pilgrimages to the Holy Places. A council at Saragossa, Spain, in 381, found it necessary to excommunicate those who received the consecrated Bread into their hands as usual *but*

refrained from eating it. How the new ideas filtering in from the East Mansi iii,634
were being combated in the West is clearly shown in many contemporary
documents. Probably no passage so briefly and so cogently states the
whole case as the lines quoted below. They are from a little treatise *On
the Sacraments* written somewhere in the north of Italy during the episcopacy of the great St. Ambrose at Milan. Some scholars consider them
as a stenographic report of Ambrose's sermons.

> *Give us this day our daily bread.* As often as Christ's Blood is shed
> (it is shed for the remission of sin), I ought daily to receive Him; for
> since I continually sin, as continually should I drink of His
> medicine.
> For if it is *daily* Bread, *why do you receive it but annually, as the
> Greeks are wont to do?* Receive daily what will daily help you. So live
> that you may be fit to receive daily. *He who is unfit for daily Com-
> munion is equally unfit to receive but once a year.*

St. Augustine in Africa, St. Hilary of Poitiers, France, St. Zeno of
Verona, Italy, and other great pastors of this time were protecting their
local churches from the new spirit. How one's own attitude may be
misinterpreted is well illustrated by an incident in the life of St. Augustine. On being asked by a certain correspondent just what the spirit of
the Church in this matter of frequent Communion was, Augustine composed a very gracious answer in which he set down the customs of various
churches.

> Some receive the Body and Blood of the Lord every day; others on
> certain days only; in some places no day passes on which the Sacrifice
> is not offered; in others on Saturday and Sunday only, in others on
> Sunday only.

Augustine goes on to offer a kindly interpretation for those who received
seldom as well as to commend those who received daily. The one party
resembles Zachaeus of the Gospel, who received our Lord rejoicing into Luke xix,6
his house; the other is likened to the centurion, who thought himself Matt. viii,6
unworthy of that honor. Unfortunately, at a later date, this letter was
quoted and requoted as showing Augustine's approval of a rare reception
of Communion.

The Barbarian Invasions. When matters stood thus, the fifth century ushered in the barbarian invasions. In a generation the whole of
the Western Empire, barring the city of Rome, and a few such "islands,"

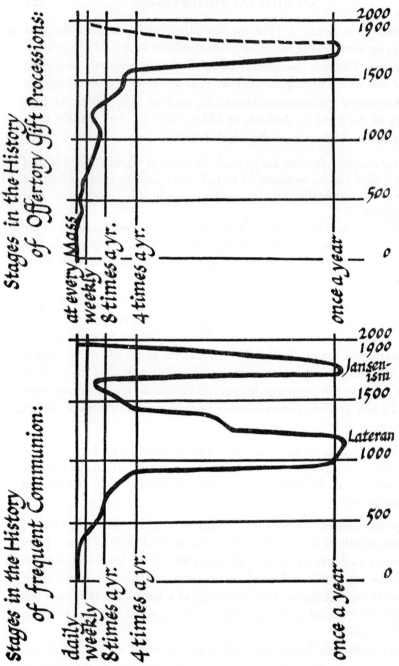

Stages in the History
of frequent Communion:

daily
weekly
8 times a yr.
4 times a yr.

2000
1900

1500
Jansen-ism

Lateran
1000

500

0

once a year

Stages in the History
of Offertory Gift Processions:

at every Mass
weekly
8 times a yr.
4 times a yr.

2000
1900

1500

1000

500

0

once a year

This graph, of course, is only a rough approximation: it would be impossible for lack of materials to represent the case with complete accuracy. But these tables are based on several careful studies, and are, no doubt, correct in the main. The dotted line indicates that the relation of coin-offerings to the sacrifice is not generally known.

was overrun by semicivilized people, who were fanatical, if ignorant, Arians. The work of winning them to Catholicity lasted over a century. It should not, therefore, be very surprising that when the new nations arose, they were pretty generally imbued with the "fear-and-dread" attitude toward the Holy Eucharist.

The Losses Heavy. The result was, that with the exception of Rome and a few such centers of the old traditions, Communion was ceasing to be in the minds of the people the *Return-Gift* of the Sacrifice. This led to the obscuring of the popular notion of sacrifice and sacrificial worship. Fast fading, too, was the concept of the Eucharist as the Christians' bond of union. Suppose we here sketch the main stages in this obscuring of the sacrificial concept by noting the gradual disappearance of the Offertory procession, that solemn external act by which the people's sacrificial purpose was expressed.

One of the first manifestations of the spirit of dread and fear in Eucharistic worship, as we saw, was that whereby people received the Species in their hands as before *but did not communicate*. In other words, they still offered their own sacrificial gifts, but they *hesitated to accept the Return-Gift of God*. Since the individual's offering of a gift is, after all, the very basis of the whole sacrificial system of worship, this idea would naturally persist even a long time after a feeling of unworthiness had constrained the worshiper not to accept God's Gift in return. But by the time Communion had come to be received only three or four times a year, several ominous phenomena make a simultaneous appearance.

Sunday Mass, an Obligation. In place of the early Christians' eagerness to be present at the Sacrifice, lest their absence should *"cause the Body of Christ to be short a member,"* Christians now had to be *Didascalia* xiii compelled by a *precept under sin* to assist at Mass. Again, preachers now felt it necessary to tell the people that they must not leave the church *after the sermon,* but that Catholic worship was really the Sacrifice. Lastly, from this time on the people are being urged and urged with endless repetition to make the bread-and-wine offerings at the altar. The first traces of positive legislation on all these points are found in the south of France, where, just then, the spirit of the Orient had entered by way of the monasticism imported from the East. The precept of assistance at Sunday Mass, and particularly that of making sacrificial offerings, was destined to echo wearily through the acts of Church councils for centuries.

Gift-Processions Repeatedly Enjoined. These first conciliar enactments had some temporary effect in checking the disastrous decline
of the sacrificial concept. But at the end of the sixth century, which was
at Rome just the golden age of St. Gregory the Great, we find these
decrees being reaffirmed in new French councils. Throughout the seventh,
eighth, and ninth centuries these canons are enjoined again and again, a
clear sign that, despite all efforts, pastors could not bring their people to
maintain the Offertory procession. When things had reached the pass
when *men* no longer brought gifts, it was urged upon their *womenfolk*
to make the offerings for themselves and their male relatives.

In this whole matter one must *not* think of these offerings as made
for the support of the churches or clergy. *That* type of offering was
being made, and generously. What is here in question wholly concerns
sacrificial gifts, the visible tokens of self-dedication publicly offered to
God and in the transubstantiation linked up with the self-oblation of
Christ upon the cross.

Communion Ever Rarer. But along with these repeated urgings to
continue the sacrificial gifts, there were parallel enactments surrounding
the reception of the Eucharist with conditions which made it extremely
difficult for people living in the world. The two tendencies develop side
by side. Communion comes to be regarded as a spiritual reward to be
won at great cost on the three or four principal feasts, and the gift procession dwindles until it is no more a public, social affair, but an occasional sight, a relic come down from times long past.

Unleavened Bread Adds New Difficulty. In the period 800–1000
the use of *unleavened bread* at the altar was spreading throughout the
West. This was a further hindrance to the bringing of gifts, for now
ordinary table bread would no longer serve for the offering. About the
year 1200 money first began to be brought to the altar as a substitute for
the old gifts of bread and wine. For a time this made the gift-procession
easier, and in places helped to restore it for a while.

Yearly Communion Obligatory. By this date the reverential awe
surrounding the reception of Communion had brought it about that even
the greatest saints, and whole religious orders in the first fervor of their
foundation, communicated only three or four times a year. Many people
living in the world put off Communion for years at a time. In the face
of these conditions, the Lateran Council in 1215 enjoined the annual

Easter Communion under pain of excommunication (the penalty of excommunication has since been removed). The same Council spoke of priests "who celebrate Mass only three or four times a year."

Opinions of Theologians. This was the age of the great theologians, and it is interesting to see how they face the question of frequent Communion. St. Thomas sees too clearly to doubt the *lawfulness* of frequent or even daily Communion, but finds that "in the case of the majority of men there are so many obstacles to the [requisite] devotion . . . [that] it is not praiseworthy to receive this Sacrament daily." His celebrated *S.T. III. Q. lxxx, a.10* contemporary, St. Bonaventure, leaves the burden of final decision to another, but clearly indicates on what strict principles the judgment would rest.

> Should one receive Communion frequently? If one finds oneself in the state of the primitive Church, one should: but if you find yourself in the state of the Church in its last stage, namely cold and sluggish, you should go rarely; if in a middle state, one should go from time to *In IV Sent. Dist.* time, and sometimes stay away to learn reverence, and sometimes go *xii, punct. ii,* to be inflamed with love. *a.2, q.2*

This age reached the lowest point in the history of the Eucharist as Communion. But let us not forget that the same age witnessed a deep and widespread enthusiasm for the Blessed Sacrament in non-sacrificial forms of devotion. It was St. Thomas who composed the marvelous hymns and Office for the Feast of Corpus Christi then recently instituted. Stamped with the spirit of the age, the newer forms of devotion were non-mediatorial in character: practically speaking, they leave the Blessed Trinity as such quite out of consideration.

End of Gift-Processions. As one approaches the sixteenth century, the Offertory procession becomes rarer and rarer. Whereas, at the beginning of the fifteenth century, synods could still prescribe eight such processional gift-offerings of money annually, by the end of that century they could enjoin no more than four. Then came the religious upheavals of the sixteenth century. *Except in the Alpine villages* the gift-processions now disappeared. In our day a few faint traces of the old usage remain as ceremonies on certain high occasions. When a bishop is consecrated, for example, he makes an offering of two candles, two miniature barrels of wine, and two loaves of bread. At a papal Mass for a canonization, and at a priest's ordination Mass, there is likewise a gift-offering made at the altar. In some rural districts of Germany a gift-procession of money-offerings is made at funerals, but these offerings are for *other* Masses, not for the one being celebrated. In the Cathedral of Milan on a few feast days ten old men and ten old women, clad in garments of an age long past, present gifts of bread and wine at the altar. "The faithful assisting at Mass," says Pope Pius XII, "sometimes — *in ancient times more frequently* . . . present bread and wine to the sacred ministers in order that it may become the Body and Blood of Christ."

Christian Worship

Turn of the Tide. As the gift-procession tapered off toward disappearance, the restoration of Communion as something *to be received* slowly progressed. In this matter as in others the pontificate of Innocent III (1198–1216) was a turning point in history. After the Lateran Council under his presidency had prescribed the reception of Communion once annually as a minimum, the ideal of more and more frequent, even daily, Communion, again came to the fore. St. Catherine of Siena, one of the most influential women the church has known, was with papal approval a daily communicant. Particularly in Italy and in the sphere of the Spanish Dominicans the frequentation of the Holy Table was slowly spreading. Thus a Eucharistic springtime, as far as the reception of Communion was concerned, was under way before the outbreak of the sixteenth-century Protestant revolts. In the face of that great apostasy this preaching was continued with renewed zeal. The members of the newer religious institutes, the Theatines, the Capuchins, the Oratorians, and the Jesuits brought this movement to the masses, so that, as was said of St. Philip Neri's church at Rome, "every morning looked like Easterday." St. Ignatius Loyola's *Book of the Spiritual Exercises,* than which in God's Providence there was scarcely a more timely instrument in effecting the Catholic Counter-Reform, embodied certain rules for enabling one "to follow as we ought the true mind of the Militant Church." Conspicuous among these was the injunction: "To praise . . . the reception of the Most Holy Sacrament once a year, and much more every month, and *much better every week.*" The full mind of the Saint in this matter was manifested in a letter to a Spanish nun in 1543:

. . . As to communicating every day, let us recall that in the primitive Church all communicated daily, and from that time to this there is no order or writing of our holy mother, the Church, or of her holy doctors, scholastic or positive, forbidding those whose devotion so prompts them, to receive Communion every day. Then, too, the blessed St. Augustine says that he neither praises nor blames those who communicate daily, adding elsewhere that he exhorts all to communicate every Sunday. In another passage, speaking of the most blessed Body of Christ Our Lord, he says: "This is daily Bread: live therefore in such wise as to be able to receive it daily."

All this being so, even if there were not at hand so many indications of good, and so many wholesome motions of grace, there is the criterium of the testimony of a good conscience: To wit, if you are persuaded, first of all, that it is licit in Our Lord, *since you are free from known mortal sins or what you may regard as such;* then, if you judge that your soul is advanced and inflamed by love of your Creator and Lord; then, if communicating with such an intention, and finding out by experience that this sacred and celestial Food gives you nourishment, peace of soul, and lastly, if persevering in this practice, you advance in God's greater service, worship and glory, then, *without any doubt it is allowed and it is the better thing for you to receive Communion every day.*   *Mon. Ign. Ep. 73*

Council of Trent. With half or more of its entire membership lost through defections, the Militant Church mustered its spiritual forces in the great Council of Trent (1545–63), wherein the whole economy of salvation was reaffirmed, original and personal sin, justification, the Sacraments, etc. Of the Tridentine definitions three points only need concern us just now. First of all, *justification,* described as "the translation from that state wherein man is born a child of the first Adam to the state of grace and of the adoption of the sons of God through the second Adam, Jesus Christ," gives the "new man" *vital contact* with the   Col. i,12
life-force of Christ,

. . . since Jesus Christ Himself, as the Head [acting] on the mem-   Eph. iv,15
bers, and as the Vine [vivifying] the branches, ceaselessly communi-   John xv,5
cates a life-force to the justified, and this life-force always precedes,   *Sess. vi, 1547*
accompanies and follows their every good action.

Again, in speaking of the reasons that prompted Christ to institute the Sacrament of the Altar, the conciliar Fathers touch this same note of social solidarity:

He [Christ] wished [this Sacrament] . . . to be a symbol of that

I Cor. xi,3
Sess. xiii, 1551 one body whereof He is the head, and to which He would fain have us as members united by the closest bond of faith, hope and charity.

Most pertinent to our present consideration is Trent's handling of the Mass, and the relation of Communion to integral sacrificial worship. The *true doctrine*, the *ultimate goal*, and the *temporary, regretful acquiescence* in current customs are all clearly expressed in this paragraph:

> The sacred and most holy Synod would fain indeed that, *at each Mass, the faithful* who are present *should communicate*, not only in spiritual desire, but also by the sacramental participation of the Eucharist, that thereby a more abundant fruit may be derived to them from this most holy Sacrifice: but not, therefore, if this be not always done, does it condemn, as private and unlawful, but approves of, and therefore commends those Masses in which the priest alone communicates sacramentally; since those Masses ought also to be considered as truly common; partly because the people communicate spiritually thereat; partly also because they are celebrated by a public minister of the Church, not for himself only, but for all the faithful who
Sess. xxii, 1562 belong to the body of Christ.

To interpret its own decrees, the Council of Trent ordered that an official commentary, the so-called *Catechism of the Council of Trent* (published 1566), be put into the hands of all priests. This most authoritative document mirrors the program of the Catholic Counter-Reform for the restoration of the reception of Communion. Thus, we read:

THE CHURCH DESIRES THE FAITHFUL TO COMMUNICATE DAILY

> Let not the faithful imagine that it is enough to receive the Body of the Lord once a year only, in obedience to the decree of the Church. They should approach oftener; but whether monthly, weekly, or daily, cannot be decided by any fixed universal rule. St. Augustine, however, lays down a most certain norm: *Live in such manner as to be able to*
II, Euch. a.14 *receive every day.*

Thus, the Church was engaged with the restoration of Communion: it was hoped, and we see this hope realized in our own day, that time would effect the popular recovery of full sacrificial-mindedness, the mediatorial position of Christ, and the internal relation of Communion *as a part of Mass.*

Blight of Jansenism. Hardly had the primitive attitude toward the Eucharist begun to take possession of the collective consciousness of Europe, when a backwash of the spirit of exaggerated awe again swept over Christendom. This was the application to the Eucharist of Jansenist ultra-rigorist views, and was brought to a head by the publication of a treatise *On Frequent Communion* by Anthony Arnault in 1643. By an unhappy alliance Jansenism became linked with State polity in France and subsequently in other Bourbon courts, such as Spain and Portugal. Almost two centuries elapsed before this corrosive element could be entirely eliminated. In that long and sometimes very bitter conflict progress toward daily Communion as the goal for all Catholics marked slow advancement.

Pope Leo XIII. In our modern age events move more rapidly, even in the realm of the spiritual realities here in question. In 1902 the great Pope Leo XIII published an encyclical letter on the Most Holy Eucharist. This gave the *coup de grace* to the Jansenist position:

> Away then with the widespread but most mischievous error . . . that the reception of the Eucharist is in a manner reserved for those narrow-minded persons (as they are deemed) who rid themselves of the cares of the world in order to find rest in some kind of professedly religious life. For this gift, than which nothing can be more excellent, or more conducive to salvation, is offered to all those, whatever their office or dignity may be, who wish — as every one ought to wish — to foster in themselves that life of divine grace whose goal is the attainment of the life of blessedness with God.   *Mirae caritatis*

No message from Pope Leo went far in its unfolding without deploring "frequent disturbances and strife between class and class: arrogance, oppression, fraud on the part of the more powerful: misery, envy and *Ibid.* turbulence among the poor." The Vicar of Christ was persuaded that against such evils it is vain to seek remedies in legislation, or any device of merely human prudence. But the remedy was to be the social appreciation of the Eucharist:

> All of which is confirmed by the declaration of the Council of Trent that Christ left the Eucharist in His Church "as a symbol of that unity and charity whereby He would have all Christians mutually joined and united . . . a symbol of that one body of which He is Himself the Head, and to which He would have us, as members, attached by the

Sess. xiii   closest bonds of faith, hope, and charity." The same idea had been expressed by St. Paul when he wrote:

I Cor. x,17
> We many are one bread, one body,
> for we all partake of the one Bread.

Very beautiful and joyful too is the spectacle of Christian brotherhood and social equality which is afforded when men of all conditions, gentle and simple, rich and poor, learned and unlearned, gather round the holy altar, all sharing alike in this heavenly banquet. And if in the records of the Church it is deservedly reckoned to the special credit of Acts iv,32   its first ages that the multitude of believers were of one heart and soul, there can be no shadow of doubt that this immense blessing was due to their frequent meetings at the divine table; for we find it recorded of them:

Acts ii,42
> They persevered in the teaching of the Apostles
> and the fellowship,
> the breaking of Bread and the prayers.

Leo's determination "to bend all our efforts to that point, that the fre-
Mirae caritatis quent use of the Eucharist be widely revived among Catholic peoples," soon issued in the decrees of Pius X, 1905, that all Catholics, the world over, of every condition and walk of life, provided only they have a right intention and be *free from known mortal sin,* must be allowed to communicate when present at Mass. Indeed under Pius X, as a subsequent chapter will disclose more in detail, the papal program was broadened out to include the *most active possible participation in the Mass,* of which communicating is but the main feature. Under Pope Pius XI the movement has reached full circle, when the advocacy of integral Eucharistic worship begins by dedication of self to God in the symbol of the sacrificial-gift. Centuries had elapsed since the Father of Christendom addressed to all his children such a message as this from the Encyclical On Reparation to the Sacred Heart:

> The more our oblation and sacrifice of self resemble the sacrifice of Christ, in other words the more perfect the immolation of our self, and of our passions . . . the more abundant are the fruits of propitiation and expiation which we receive for ourselves and others. . . . To this most august Eucharistic Sacrifice *ministers and faithful must join the offering of themselves* as victims "living, holy, well-pleasing to

God." Therefore St. Cyprian did not hesitate to say: "The Sacrifice Rom. xii,1
of Our Savior *is not celebrated with the requisite sanctity if our own* Ep. lxiii
offering and our sacrifice of self *do not correspond* with His Passion." *Mis. Redemptor,*
1928

Summary. As a consequence of the widespread Arian heresy, Christians in their worship so emphasized the divinity of Christ, that His position as Bridge-Builder, between God and men, so far as piety is concerned, was popularly obscured. The resultant relationship induced feelings of awe and dread, which began by keeping people away from Communion, and ended by obscuring the very concept of sacrificial worship. In the Catholic revival of modern times the old ideas are being rapidly recovered.

Eleventh-Century Source Material
(Although repeating the familiar teaching of the Eucharist as the bond of the mystical Body, Peter Damian does not urge the reception of Communion in this passage from his book, THE LORD BE WITH YOU.)

The Sacrifice Offered on Our Altars is That of Women Alike and Men. That is the reason why, in the very celebration of the Mass, is said: *"Be mindful, O Lord, of Thy servants and handmaids,"* and, as is added shortly "for whom we offer, OR who offer up to Thee, this sacrifice of praise." These words clearly show that the Sacrifice of praise is offered by *all* the faithful, not men only, but women also, although it is seen to be offered by one priest in a special manner. What he holds in his hands presenting unto God, that the whole multitude of the faithful by their devout intentions commends and offers. This is further shown again when it is said, "We therefore beseech Thee, O Lord, graciously to accept this oblation of our servitude *and that* of Thy whole family." It is as clear as light in these words that the Sacrifice put on our holy altars by the priest is the joint gift of the entire family of God.

The Apostle openly declares this unity of the Church, when he says, "We many are one body, one Bread." So great is the unity of the Church I Cor. x,17 in Christ, that the bread of the Body of Christ is one throughout the whole world, and one is the chalice of His Blood. For just as the Divinity of the Word is one, which fills the universe, so, even though the Body is consecrated in different places and on many days, there is but one Body of Christ. And as the bread and wine are really changed into the Body of Christ, so all who worthily receive It in the Church, become beyond all doubt the one body of Christ, as He Himself saith:

He that eateth My Flesh
and drinketh My Blood,
the same abides in Me,
and I in him.

John vi,57

If therefore we are all one body of Christ, and, although we seem to be separated by corporeal appearances, we cannot be separated from one another, as long as we remain in Him. There is no disadvantage that I see in abiding always in this symbol of individual unity, and one and all holding the common custom of the Church. For when I alone speak the common words of the Church, I show myself to be one with her, and testify that the Spirit really abides in me. And if I am truly her member, it is but proper that I promote the well-being of my "whole."

Topics for Further Discussion:

As the temptations surrounding youth today are more evident and alluring than since the ages of paganism, so, too, are the sacramental helps of the Church.

Since all Christians are to be urged to communicate daily, the moral responsibility of collegiate-trained lay people in this matter.

The dogmatic and social values of reviving the thought connection between the offering made at Mass and intrinsic participation in the Sacrifice.

The effects of Pius X's recommendations in America, where older people in certain localities object to (*a*) children receiving Communion before the age of twelve; (*b*) frequent, especially daily, Communion for lay people. What arguments could be adduced, besides the Pontiff's pronouncements, to make them change their attitude?

Readings:

K. Adam, *Christ Our Brother* (New York: Macmillan, 1931); "Through Christ Our Lord."

G. Dix, *A Detection of Aumbries* (Westminster: Dacre, 1942), "Reverence for the Reserved Sacrament," pp. 42–68: The author is an Anglican.

J. B. Ferreres, *The Decree on Daily Communion* (St. Louis: Herder, 1910), "Historical Sketch," pp. 34–102.

J. C. Hedley, *The Holy Eucharist* (New York: Longmans, Green, 1907); "On Frequent Communion," pp. 129–146.

J. C. Husslein, "Communion in the Early Church," *The Ecclesiastical Review* (81), 1929, pp. 491–509.

J. A. Jungmann, *The Sacrifice of the Church* (Collegeville: Lit. Press, 1957), III, "Jeopardy," pp. 46–62; "Phases," pp. 64–71.

E. King, "Holy Communion in the Early Church," *The Month* (108), 1906, pp. 1–13.

J. Kramp, *Live the Mass* (St. Paul: Cat. Guild, 1954), "The History of Eucharistic Adoration," pp. 302–333.

——— *The Liturgical Sacrifice of the New Law* (St. Louis: Herder, 1926); "The Notion of Sacrifice and Christian Holiness," pp. 201–214.

Chapter XII

ANTE-MASS, A TIMELY AND A TIMELESS
FUNCTION

Jesus went about the whole of Galilee,
teaching in the synagogues (Matt. iv,23).

A T THE head of the Roman Mass Book there has been printed
since 1634 a Bull of Pope Urban VIII which begins, "If there
is one thing in human life absolutely divine, one thing that the
citizens of Heaven might envy, if envy were consistent with their state,
it is the holy Sacrifice of the Mass. . . . Accordingly, the more must
men endeavor to hold a privilege so great in becoming honor and reverence." "It is therefore important," says Pius XII's recent letter, "for
all the faithful to understand that it is their duty and highest privilege
to take part in the Eucharistic Sacrifice." This must now be completed
by a brief study of the august rite as we possess it today, after nineteen
centuries of such universal and frequent use.

The Name "Mass." The first circumstance that attracts attention
concerns the name now so common in modern languages, the *Mass.*
This term illustrates how factors, trivial and inconsequential in themselves, may come to have far-reaching effects. The Christian Sacrifice,
like all public functions, has a formal opening and a formal ending.
The formal ending, in imitation of the Jewish synagogue rites, took the
form of a ceremonial dismissal, or leave to depart, proclaimed by the
officiating ministers. At a certain point the announcement was made from
the altar, as indeed it is still so made, *Ite, missa est* (Go, this is the
dismissal). *Missa* here is low Latin for *missio,* sending away or dismissal.
Again, when adherents of the Jewish religion, or pagans or those preparing for baptism, were present at a service of prayer and instruction,
which was to be followed by the Sacrifice, all these had to be dismissed
before the sacrificial Action began. Thus, a conspicuous element of the
rite was *this* dismissal also. People began before long to refer to the

Christian
Worship

151

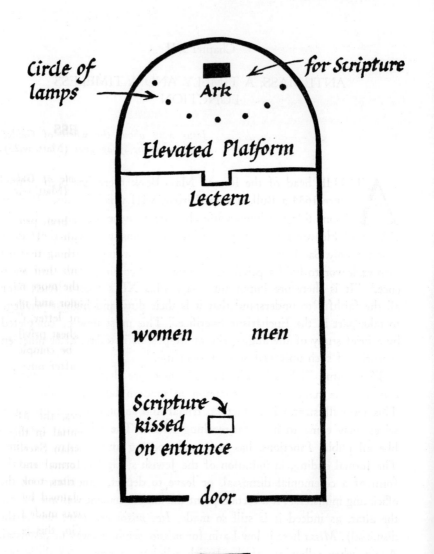

Plan of a Synagogue.

Circle of lamps

for Scripture

Ark

Elevated Platform

Lectern

women   men

Scripture kissed on entrance

door

water

whole rite in both cases as the *Missa,* the Dismissal of the Catechumens and the Dismissal of the Faithful. In popular speech, this term was soon synonymous with the more formal designations of the Sacrifice. From *missa* are derived our English word "Mass," and cognate terms in the other modern languages.

Types of Worship in the Mass. The next feature to be noted is that our Mass of today represents the union or combination of two types of worship, the non-sacrificial and the sacrificial. Just as the Jews had sacrificial worship only in the Temple of Jerusalem, but non-sacrificial worship in countless synagogues everywhere, so in the primitive Church there was a clear-cut distinction between sacrificial and non-sacrificial worship. True, the Christian Sacrifice was not limited to Jerusalem, or any other place, but it was, from the outset, limited to certain days, and very strictly limited to Christians only. On the contrary, non-Christians were admitted to, and by all honest arts of persuasion urged to attend, the more frequent Christian gatherings for instruction and prayer in common. In course of time the custom grew of having the Sacrifice immediately after the non-sacrificial rites. The old forms of non-sacrificial worship are preserved, abbreviated, it is true, but in no way substantially changed, in the first part of our Mass. We call it, for that reason, the Ante-Mass, or the Fore-Mass, or the Mass of the Catechumens, that is, the rites which people preparing for Baptism were allowed to attend. Since catechumens have disappeared as a class, perhaps the Ante-Mass were better styled the Mass of the Learners. At any rate, by prayer and Scripture readings we can always learn better how to attune ourselves for the Sacrifice impending.

The Synagogues of Israel. Since the Jews not resident at Jerusalem could participate in the Temple rites very seldom, the local synagogue was in great measure the *focal point of their religious,* civil, and national *life.* With the civil or juridical position of the synagogue we are not now concerned: our interest is its worship. It had become a tradition that the synagogue should be built on the highest spot in the community, and that it should outrank all other structures in dignity. Circumstances permitting, it was built facing eastward. On completion the new synagogue was ceremoniously consecrated to the purposes of worship. Within, at the end opposite the entrance, was the Ark, wherein the Sacred Scrip-

CHART SHOWING HOW OUR ANTE-MASS IS THE SYNAGOGUE SERVICE SLIGHTLY AMPLIFIED

Jewish Synagogue	New Testament	Apostolic Times	Roman Missal
1.	1.	1. "Come together after confessing your transgressions."—*Teaching* (80).	1. Preparatory prayers: A. Psalm. *Judica* — Judge me. B. *Confiteor* — I confess.
2.	2.	2.	2. Ascending the altar *Aufer* — Take away.
3.	3.	3.	3. Priest kissing altar *Oramus te* — We beseech.
4.	4.	4.	4. *Introit* — Antiphon and verse.
5.	5.	5.	5. *Kyrie* — Lord, have mercy.
6.	6.	6.	6. *Gloria* — Glory be to God.
7. Opening prayers, standing facing place of sacrifice.	7.	7.	7. *Collect* — prayer standing facing East.
8. First Lesson — Moses.	8. "Moses . . . in the synagogues being read every sabbath" (*Acts xv,21*).	8. [Or] "the writings of the prophets are read as long as time permits." — *St. Justin* (150).	8. First Scripture Lesson Epistle (usually).
9. First Psalm chant.	9. "Teach and admonish one another, and in Psalms, hymns and spiritual canticles sing in your heart" (*Col. iii,16*).	9. "Saying they had been accustomed to assemble on a fixed day before daylight and sing by turns a hymn to Christ as a god," — *Letter of Pliny to Trajan* (112).	9. Chanting of Gradual Psalm.
10. Second Lesson — Prophet.	10. "Prophets, which are read every Sabbath" (*Acts xiii,27*).	10.	10 [Lesson formerly here now dropped.]
11. Second Psalm — chant.	11.	11.	11. Alleluia verse.
12.	12.	12.	12. Preparation for Gospel. A. *Munda cor* — Cleanse. B. *Dominus sit* — May the Lord.

13.	13.	13. "The Memoirs of the Apostles are read." — *St. Justin.*	13. Scripture Lesson — The holy Gospel.
14. Sermon by someone invited to preach.	14. "The presidents of the synagogues sent word to them saying: 'Brethren, if ye have any words of exhortation unto the people, speak'" (*Acts xiii,15*).	14. "When the reader has ceased, the president orally admonishes and exhorts us to imitate these excellent things." — *St. Justin.*	14. Sermon.
15.	15.	15.	15. *Credo* — I Believe.
16. Great intercession for needs of each group in community.	16. "I urge that petitions, prayers, intercessions, thanksgivings be made on behalf of all men" (*II Tim. ii,1*).	16. "We rise . . ., and offer prayers . . . making earnest prayers in common for ourselves . . ., and for all others everywhere." — *St. Justin.*	16. *Oremus* — Let us pray. [These prayers are now omitted. They were like the series we say on Good Friday.]
17. Solemn Blessing.	17.	17.	17. Blessing now given at end of Mass.
18. Prayer for peace and union (kiss).	18. "Greet ye one another with the kiss of charity" (*I Pet. ii,14*).	18. "We salute one another with a kiss when we conclude our prayers." — *St. Justin.*	18. Kiss of peace now given before Communion.
19. Almsgiving, gifts of money and in kind.	19. "Concerning the collection for the saints [at Jerusalem]. . . Upon the first day of [every] week let each one of you put by whatever he may well spare" (*I Cor. xvi,1*).	19. "They who are well-to-do and willing give what each thinks fit." — *St. Justin.*	19. Almsgiving now united with Offertory oblation.
20. Dismissal.	20.	20.	20. Dismissal of catechumens formerly took place.

tures were kept. This Ark might take many forms, from a simple niche in the wall, to an elaborate chest set upon a dais. Before the Ark one or more lamps burned constantly. Upon a raised platform near the Ark, or on the same platform, was a lectern, at which the Scriptures were read, and a chair for the preacher. Seats were ranged all about, those in front for the "presidents of the synagogue" and their associates, the elders. The seats for the populace were so disposed that the men and women occupied separate sections.

Acts xiii,15

Service of Prayer and Sacred Reading. In such synagogues, on the Sabbath all the Jews came together. Before entering they purified their hands; after entering they kissed a copy of some portion of the Scriptures set upon a stand near the entrance for that purpose. The services opened with common prayers, led by a "ruler"; these prayers were said standing, and facing toward Jerusalem, the place of sacrifice, after which all sat down to listen to the Scriptures. Seven designated readers were attached to the staff of the synagogue, and since several passages were to be read, they took turn and turn about at the lectern. Or, the president or officiant might invite a stranger, or one he wished to honor, to take this charge. Passages from the Books of Moses, or the Law, as they were called collectively, alternated with corresponding readings from the Prophets. As the sacred scrolls were replaced in the Ark, some of David's prayer-poems, the Psalms, were sung. A precentor sang a verse in solo, and the congregation answered the alternate ones. This mode of antiphonal singing still in use among us, was used by the Babylonians and many Eastern peoples. Besides the Psalms and Scriptural canticles, hymns were also used on occasion.

The Scriptures Expounded. The Scripture passages read had now to be expounded to the people. Here, too, the synagogue service lent itself to a certain variety and promoted social unification, since anyone might be invited to preach or address words of exhortation to the assembly. The sermon was followed by a series of short prayers, cast in the form of blessings on behalf of all the classes of the people, and their several needs. Thus, the priests, the doctors, and scribes, and the young students of the Law, the rulers of the synagogue, the elders, and the congregation in general, were in turn prayed for. Those who gave oil for the lamps before the Ark, those who gave hospitality to strangers, also to the poor, the aged, the sick, in fact all ranks and classes of the community were commended to God, the voice of the rabbi being supported by the "Amens" of the people. After a final blessing for the peace and union of the congregation, the worshipers were dismissed. At some undetermined point in the rite, alms were collected for the needy.

The Christian "Synagogue" Service. A careful scrutiny of the chart of pages 156, 157 shows how the old *Jewish synagogue service is reproduced* in our Ante-Mass. The opening prayers, the Scripture lessons alternating with psalmody, the sermon, all, despite the long ages since Church and Synagogue have parted company, are preserved in a manner a Jew would instantly recognize. In addition, we now find in our Ante-Mass some few distinctly Christian features at the beginning. Again, toward the end, and as a result of combining this non-sacrificial rite with the more important sacrificial one, certain elements of the Jewish rites have been transposed to positions within the Christian Sacrifice proper.

Only one important item of the synagogue ritual has now quite disappeared; that is the long, litany-like intercession for all the classes of society. As late, however, as the time of St. Augustine (fifth century), these prayers were still to be found in the Ante-Mass. His letters have several accounts of them. Infidels were prayed for, the Jews, the catechumens, the several ranks of the clergy, and the whole Church of God. The series of such prayers we now say publicly only on Good Friday is, in all likelihood, the last relic of this Jewish rite, so eloquent in its appeal, but eventually abandoned for the sake of greater brevity.

Growth without Change. The surplus items in the column to the extreme right of the chart show at a glance the accretions to the Ante-Mass since it was taken over from the Synagogue. An examination of the individual items, as to their content and spirit, to which we now pass, will also disclose a remarkable fidelity to the structure and function of the original parts, however much in the course of centuries the actual message of some of the parts, particularly the chanted ones, may have become obscured. The Ante-Mass remains what the Synagogue Service was, the worship of public prayer, followed by an instruction drawn from Holy Writ. Thus, if the Ante-Mass carries forward usages that were historic even when Christ attended the synagogues, there is a constant timeliness in this message of divine love offered the creature by his Creator.

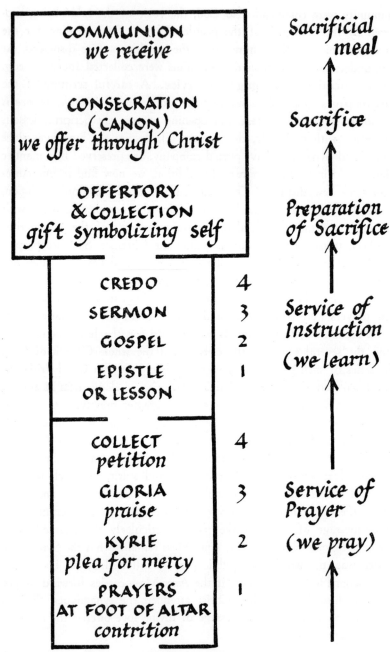

COMMUNION *we receive*		Sacrificial meal ↑
CONSECRATION (CANON) *we offer through Christ*		Sacrifice ↑
OFFERTORY & COLLECTION *gift symbolizing self*		Preparation of Sacrifice ↑
CREDO	4	Service of Instruction
SERMON	3	
GOSPEL	2	(we learn)
EPISTLE OR LESSON	1	↑
COLLECT *petition*	4	Service of Prayer
GLORIA *praise*	3	
KYRIE *plea for mercy*	2	(we pray)
PRAYERS AT FOOT OF ALTAR *contrition*	1	↑

—Adapted from Parsch-Eckhoff's *The Liturgy of the Mass,* by courtesy of B. Herder Book Company.

THE ORDINARY OF THE MASS: FIRST PART[1]

Prayers at the Foot of Altar

"Cleanse Me from Sin" (Ps. l,4). The preparatory prayers are an outgrowth of that sense of unworthiness felt by a priest approaching the altar of Sacrifice,

Since he is himself encompassed with weakness,
and because of it must make offerings for sin,
not merely on behalf of the people,
but *also for himself* (Heb. ii,3).

These prayers were originally the priest's private prayers of preparation, and were said in silence, or in whispered dialogue with his attendants, as he proceeded to the altar. Later they came to be regarded as part of the public rite. Psalm 42 recited here, expressed the longing of a priest, whom enemies (sins) have driven far from the Temple, as he recalls the enthusiastic joy of his youthful ministrations at God's altar.

That I may go to the altar of God!
    To God, who was the joy of my youth,
That I may praise Thee with the harp,
O God, my God!

Priest: In the name of the Father, and of the Son, and of the Holy Ghost. Amen.
I will go up to the altar of God.
Response: To God, the giver of youth and happiness.
P: O God, sustain my cause; give me redress against a race that knows no piety; save me from a treacherous foe and cruel.
R: Thou, O God, art my strength, why hast Thou cast me off? Why do I go mourning, with enemies pressing me hard?
P: The light of Thy countenance, the fulfillment of Thy promise, let these be my escort, bringing me safe to Thy holy mountain, to the tabernacles where Thou dwellest.
R: There will I go up to the altar of God, the giver of youth and happiness.
P: Thou art my God, with the harp I hymn Thy praise. Soul, why art thou downcast, why art thou all lament?
R: Wait for God's help; I will not cease to cry out in thankfulness: My champion and my God! (Ps. xlii,1–6.)
P: Glory to the Father, and to the Son, and to the Holy Ghost.
R: As it was in the beginning, is now, and ever shall be, world without end. Amen.

---

[1] The English version here quoted is from the *Daily Missal in Latin and English,* published by Sheed & Ward, New York, and Burns, Oates & Washbourne, London.

Rubrical directions are indicated by italic type, as well as short Scripture quotations within the prayers.

Psalm 42, as St. Ambrose describes for us, was used as a hymn sung by newly baptized Christians as they marched into Church for their First Communion Mass on Easter. It is not clear just how it came to be chosen by way of putting the priest into the proper frame of mind in which to approach the altar, but baptismal memories are the very best preparation in which to come to the Holy Eucharist, the fulfillment of that of which Baptism is but the pledge.

The *Confiteor* is an act of contrition, a mutual public confession of sin couched in general terms. This was a preliminary to sacrificial worship from the dawn of Christianity, as we saw in the *Teaching of the Twelve Apostles:* "On the Lord's Day come together, breaking Bread and celebrate the Eucharist, *after confessing your transgressions,* that your Sacrifice may be pure" (Chap. xiv). The *Confiteor,* as we have it, is one of the many variant forms current in past ages: even yet some of the old monastic Orders, like the Carthusians and the Dominicans, recite an older version of this prayer.

P: I will go up to the altar of God.
R: To God, the giver of youth and happiness.
The priest crosses himself, saying:
P: Our help is in the name of the Lord.
R: Who made heaven and earth.
Then he bows and says:
P: I confess to almighty God, etc.
R: May almighty God have mercy upon you, forgive you your sins, and bring you to everlasting life.
P: Amen.
The ministers repeat the Confession:
I confess to almighty God, to blessed Mary, ever-virgin, to blessed Michael the archangel, the blessed John the Baptist, to the holy Apostles Peter and Paul, and all the saints, and to you, father, that I have sinned exceedingly in thought, word, and deed; (*they strike their breasts three times saying*): through my fault, through my own fault, through my own most grievous fault. Therefore I beseech the blessed Mary, ever-virgin, blessed Michael the archangel, blessed John the Baptist, the holy Apostles Peter and Paul, all the saints, and you, father, to pray to the Lord our God for me.
P: May almighty God have mercy upon you, forgive you your sins, and bring you to everlasting life.
R: Amen.

(*Frankish*)

These ejaculatory prayers serve to illustrate how Christians of an older age constructed their prayers. They knew that Christ had known and loved the divinely inspired words of the Psalter, and so they combed the Psalter for expressions suited to their prayer-needs and linked them together in doublets, a verse, as we call it, answered by a response.

All cross themselves as the priest says:
P: May the almighty and merciful Lord grant us pardon, absolution, and remission of all our sins.
R: Amen.
(Frankish)
He bows his head and continues:
P: *Thou wilt relent, O God, and bring us life.*
R: *And thy people will rejoice in thee* (Ps. lxxxiv,78).
P: *Show us thy mercy, Lord.*
R: *And grant us thy salvation.*
P: *Lord, heed my prayer.*
R: *And let my cry be heard by thee* (Ps. ci,2).
P: *The Lord be with you* (Ruth ii,4).
R: *And with you.*
P: Let us pray.
(Frankish)

There is utilized here an old Roman Collect, which, written for Lent, continues the same train of thought as in the foregoing, namely, self-purification at approaching the altar.

The celebrant goes up to the altar, saying silently:
Take away from us our iniquities, we entreat thee, Lord, so that, with souls made clean, we may be counted worthy to enter the *Holy of Holies* (Exod. xxx,10): through Jesus Christ our Lord.
(Frankish adaptation of Roman prayer)

An important *difference in outlook* marks this prayer, in that the priest prays *in the singular number.* This is a relic of an era when Mass was often regarded as a private affair of the priest's.

Bowing down he says:
We pray thee, Lord, by the merits of thy saints whose relics are here (*he kisses the altar in the middle*), and of all the saints, that thou wilt deign to pardon all my sins. Amen.
(Frankish)

It is doubtless in imitation of the

At High Mass: Blessing of Incense.

prescription of the Old Law, that the High Priest must not approach the Holy of Holies without incense, that this use was introduced (Lev. xvi,12).

May He bless thee, in whose honor thou shalt burn. Amen.

(Frankish)

Entrance, Introit[2]

It will suffice to refer back to the description (at page 127) of St. Gregory's High Mass by way of recalling the very important dramatic function of the Entrance Chant, or Introit, now preserved in its barest outline. This element of Psalmody was introduced at Rome to add solemnity to the entrance of the ministers, and their "marching music" was given an accompaniment of song, choir alternating with choir, in such wise that a refrain was sung after *each verse* of the psalm, or psalms, required to fill up the interval of the entrance.

Antiphon (Psalm cix,4).
The Lord has sworn an oath there is no retracting, Thou art a priest for ever in the line of Melchisedech (Ps. cix,1). The voice of the Lord came to my master, Sit thou at my right hand. *V.* Glory to the Father, and to the Son, and to the Holy Ghost. *R.* As it was in the beginning, is now, and ever shall be, world without end. Amen.
(Antiphon repeated):
The Lord has sworn an oath there is no retracting, Thou art a priest for ever in the line of Melchisedech.

(Roman)

Kyrie

The Greek words betray the Hellenic source of this popular acclamation for mercy. Recent research has shown good reason for ascribing its relation to the Roman Mass to the time of Pope Gelasius (492–96). When Gregory I was pope (590–604), he introduced the *Christe, eleison.* Our precise three-three-three arrangement is a later modification.

P: Lord, have mercy.
R: Lord, have mercy.
P: Lord, have mercy.
R: Christ, have mercy.
P: Christ, have mercy.
R: Christ, have mercy.
P: Lord, have mercy.
R: Lord, have mercy.
P: Lord, have mercy.

(Greek)

Gloria

Those who have studied the *Gloria* find it is an enlargement of the message at Christ's nativity

Glory be to God on high, and on earth peace to men of good will. (Luke ii,4.) We praise thee

[2]The variable, or "proper," parts of the Mass are from the votive Mass of Our Lord Jesus Christ Eternal High Priest.

(Luke ii,4) by a marvelous array of old ejaculations and expressions drawn from New and Old Testament sources, and other documents of the most venerable Catholic antiquity. Such a text was, naturally, the product of evolution and addition, but by the fourth century it had reached, practically speaking, the finished form we now have. It was a morning hymn of Greek-speaking Christians, and, as such, was recommended by St. Athanasius to the consecrated virgins for their morning devotions (*De Virg.*).

At first the *Gloria* was a privilege of the pope at Christmas. Pope Symmachus (498–514) allowed it to be chanted on Sundays and martyrs' feasts. Later restrictions gradually fell away, until, about the twelfth century, the present custom of using it in all Masses of a joyous character was adopted.

we bless thee, we adore thee, we glorify thee, we give thee thanks for thy great glory. Lord God, heavenly King, God the almighty Father. Lord Jesus Christ, only-begotten Son. Lord God, Lamb of God, *Son of the Father* (II John 3), *who takest away the sins of the world* (John i,29), have mercy on us; thou who takest away the sins of the world, receive our prayer; thou *who sittest at the right hand of the Father* (Col. iii,3), have mercy on us. For *thou alone* art the Holy One. Thou alone art Lord. Thou, Jesus Christ, *art the Most High* (Ps. lxxxii,19), with the Holy Ghost, in the glory of God the Father. Amen.

(*Greek*)

Salutation

Turning towards the people, the priest says:
P: The Lord be with you.
R: And with you.

Collect

This prayer, which fulfills the all-important function of sounding the worship-motif of the feast or occasion, preserves in its name a link with a vanished usage, the stational Mass. For this the Romans met in one church, called "church of the assembly or *Collecta*," and then marched to the church of the Mass. Before setting

O God, who to glorify thy sovereign power and for the salvation of mankind didst ordain Thy only-begotten Son a high priest for ever, grant that those whom He has chosen to be *His ministers and the stewards of His mysteries* (I Cor. iv,1) may be found *faithful* in the office committed to them: through the same Lord Jesus Christ out, a prayer was said, *Oratio ad collectam*. Later on, the prayer itself came to be known by the name of *Collecta*. Almost invariably these prayers are addressed to God the Father, who is approached *through* our Mediator, His Son.

Thy Son, our Lord, who is God, living and reigning with Thee in the unity of the Holy Spirit, for ever and ever.

R: Amen.

Lesson

Scripture reading was of the very essence of the Synagogue service, and St. Luke gives us a graphic description of how Christ one Sabbath read and expounded Holy Writ for His townsmen of Nazareth.

He writes:

He came to Nazareth,
where He had been brought up;
and according to His custom
He entered the synagogue
upon the Sabbath day and rose
to read.

And the volume of the Prophet Isaiah was handed to Him.

And He opened the volume and *found the place*

where was written:

The Spirit of the Lord is upon
Me, for He hath anointed Me;
To evangelize the poor He hath
sent Me . . .

And He rolled up the volume
and returned it to the attendant
and sat down.

And the eyes of all in the synagogue were gazing upon Him.

And He began to say unto them,
"Today in your hearing
is this Scripture fulfilled" (Luke iv,16–21).

Lesson from the Epistle of the blessed Paul the Apostle to the Hebrews (v,1–11).

Brethren: The purpose for which any high priest is chosen from among his fellow-men, and made a representative of men in their dealings with God, is to offer gifts and sacrifices in expiation of their sins. He is qualified for this by being able to feel for them when they are ignorant and make mistakes, since, he, too, is all beset with humilations, and, for that reason, must needs present sin-offerings for himself, just as he does for the people. His vocation comes from God, as Aaron's did; nobody can take on himself such a privilege as this.

So it is with Christ. He did not raise Himself to the dignity of the high priesthood; it was God that raised Him to it, when He said: Thou art My Son, I have begotten Thee this day; and so, elsewhere, Thou art a priest for ever, in the line of Melchisedech.

Christ, during His earthly life, offered prayer and entreaty to the God who could save Him from death, not without a piercing cry, not without tears, yet with such

In that passage we see how Christ deliberately chose a definite portion of the Sacred Writing with a view to its suitability to the occasion. And, whereas in the Divine Office the Scripture passages are for the most part read continuously from day to day, in the Mass the Church carefully selects definite passages for every occasion.

Formerly the Roman Mass always had *two* Lessons before the Gospel, but now on Sundays there is never more than one, and since this is invariably from the canonical *Epistles,* the lesson is itself called the Epistle.

piety as won Him a hearing.

Son of God though He was, He learned obedience in the school of suffering, and now, His full achievement reached, He wins eternal salvation for those who render obedience to Him.

A high priest in the line of Melchisedech, so God has called Him. Of Christ as priest we have much to say, and it is hard to make ourselves understood in the saying of it.

R: Thanks be to God.

Gradual

Called *Gradual* because once led by a chanter standing on a *step* (*gradus*) of the pulpit, this alternate singing of a psalm-verse by the soloist and the recurring refrain by the people served to emphasize what had been read.

(Luke iv,18.) The spirit of the Lord is upon Me; He has anointed Me. *V.* And sent Me out to preach the gospel to the poor, to restore the broken-hearted.

Alleluia Anthem

The Alleluia-verse, which originally replaced the psalm-chanting after the *second* Scriptural lesson, is musically the most brilliant part of the entire Mass, and has for its function to attune the minds for the hearing of Christ's own words in the Gospel.

Alleluia, Alleluia. *V.* (Heb. vii,24) Jesus continues for ever, and His priestly office is unchanging. Alleluia.

Preparation for Gospel

The impending proclamation of Christ's message evokes anew a sense of guilt and unworthiness in the human herald, and so he makes

The priest bowing in the middle of the altar prays silently:
Cleanse my heart and my lips, almighty God, who didst cleanse the

bold to pray that his lips might be cleansed as by fire! The prayer dates as of about the year 1100.

lips of the prophet Isaias with a live coal. In Thy gracious mercy deign so to cleanse me that I may be able fitly to proclaim Thy holy gospel: through Christ our Lord. Amen.

(Frankish)

In the foregoing formulary, and this adaptation to himself of the blessing given to the deacon at Solemn Mass, the first-person singular marks medieval origin.

Lord, grant a blessing.
The Lord be in my heart and on my lips, so that I may fitly and worthily proclaim His gospel. Amen.

(Frankish)

Gospel

"And Esdras opened the book before all the people: for he was above all the people: and when he had opened it, all the people stood" (II Esd. viii,5). The little picture from Old Testament times could serve as a partial description of the impressive and rich ceremonial surrounding the reading of the Gospel, the Good Tidings of God spoken by His Son. If to the act of standing as a mark of deepest reverence, were added the carrying of candles and incense, the use of a pulpit (or altar-corner at low Mass), the kissing of the sacred page, the signing it with the Cross, and so forth, the enumeration of rites in honor of the Gospel would be more what we see at Mass. All this serves to show the intimate connection between even the most didactic parts of our service and the latreutic purpose of worship.

P: The Lord be with you.
R: And with you.
P: A passage from the holy Gospel according to Luke.
R: Glory to Thee, Christ.
At this time: Jesus sat down with the twelve apostles, and He said to them, I have longed and longed to share this paschal meal with you before My passion; I tell you, I shall not eat it again, till it finds its fulfillment in the kingdom of God.

And He took a cup, and blessed it, and said: Take this and share it among you; I tell you, I shall not drink of the fruit of the vine again, till the kingdom of God has come.

Then He took bread, and blessed, and broke it, and gave it to them, saying,

This is My Body given for you; do this for a commemoration of Me.

In the Gospel-lesson the Ante-Mass reaches its structural climax: God has spoken by New and Old Testament heralds, here He speaks Incarnate. The sermon is as a commentary on the *Gospel* (O.E., *god spel*, Good Tidings).

And so with the cup, when supper was ended.

This cup, He said, is the New Testament, in My Blood which is to be shed for you.

R: Praise to Thee, Christ.

The priest kisses the book, saying:

P: Through the Gospel words may our sins be wiped away.

(*Jewish*)

Creed

The Creed. In an age when heresies were as common as books were rare, it was essential to have clearly articulated creeds available for everyone. This feeling led a certain archbishop of Antioch, called John the Fuller, to introduce the recitation of an official *Credo* in his Mass early in the fifth century. This custom spread over the East, and penetrated into Europe where so much from the East has found entrance, through the Spanish peninsula. From this new point of radiation, the practice spread until by the ninth century it had covered all of Europe. But, oddly enough, it was as a protection against a new Moslo-Christian error, that Christ was an adopted Son of God, then ravaging the Spanish Church, that the Creed was added to our Mass. It has recently come to light that this was done about 798 by one of Charlemagne's great advisers, St. Paulinus of Aquileia. Paulinus is the author of the Latin formula of our missals. This Creed is often called the

I believe in one God, the almighty Father, maker of heaven and earth, and of all things visible and invisible. And in one Lord Jesus Christ, only-begotten Son of God, born of the Father before all ages; God from God, light from light, true God from true God; begotten, not made, of one essence with the Father; through whom all things were made. He for us men, and for our salvation, came down from heaven (*here he genuflects*) and was incarnate by the Holy Ghost from the virgin Mary; and was made man. He was also crucified for our sake under Pontius Pilate: suffered, and was buried. And the third day He rose again according to the Scriptures. And He ascended into heaven, and is seated at the right hand of the Father. He will come again with glory to judge the living and the dead; and of His reign there shall be no end. I believe too in the Holy Spirit, Lord and life-giver, who proceeds from the Father and the Son; who together with the Father and the

Nicene Creed, and a long passage of it, referring to the consubstantiality of the Son, was solemnly promulgated at the Council of Nicaea, 325. Again, it is referred to as the Niceo-Constantinopolitan Creed, because the final sections on the Holy Spirit are repeated as solemnly defined in the Council of Constantinople of the year 381.

After repeating the salutation, and intoning *Oremus — Let us Pray*, the Ante-Mass abruptly ends. Formerly the Prayers For All Classes were said here.

Son is adored and glorified; who spoke through the prophets. And I believe in one holy, catholic and apostolic Church. I acknowledge one baptism for the remission of sins. And I look forward to the resurrection from the dead, and the life of the world to come. Amen.

(Greek)

The priest turns to the people and says:
P: The Lord be with you.
R: And with you.
P: Let us pray
(Jewish)

End of the Ante-Mass.

Summary. Viewed as a whole, the Ante-Mass is seen to be a slightly modified form of the non-sacrificial worship of Israel, a continuance of the old synagogue rites. By attending these "according to His custom on the Sabbath," Christ Himself was carrying forward usages of a venerable antiquity.

Luke iv,16

When the Ante-Mass and the Mass had come to be looked upon as one service, a few features of the former rite were transferred to the latter. Lastly, with the passing of the organized catechumenate, there disappeared, too, the dismissal of the catechumens, of which a very tactful and polite form closes one of St. Augustine's sermons.

Twelfth-Century Source Material

(*A beautiful and thought-provoking consideration of Mary's role in the Mystical Body is afforded by this sermon-passage of Isaac of Stella, an English Cistercian.*)

The First-born of many brothers, who was the only Son by nature, has by grace taken to Himself many brothers, who are one with Him. . . . Of themselves, by reason of their birth according to the flesh, they are many; but by their new, divine birth they are one with Him. The one and complete and sole Christ is the Head and the body. This One is the only Son of one God in heaven and of one Mother on earth. There are many sons, and there is but one Son.

And, as the Head and members are one Son and many sons, so Mary and the Church are one Mother and two mothers, one Virgin and two virgins. Both have conceived, by the power of the same Holy Spirit, without concupiscence; both have brought forth children to God the Father without sin. The first, without any sin, has given the body its Head; the other, by the remission of all sins, has given the Head its body. Both are Mothers of Christ; but neither has given birth to the whole Christ without the other. Hence in the divinely inspired Scriptures, what is said in general of the virgin mother Church is true of the Virgin Mother Mary in particular; and what is said of the Virgin Mother Mary in particular is to be understood also of the virgin mother Church in general, so that whatever is said of the one may ordinarily be applied equally to the other. — Quoted by permission of Bruce Publishing Company, from Mersch-Kelly, *The Whole Christ.*

Topics for Further Discussion:

With the aid of the missal, list the places where the ideas of the "Great Intercession for All Classes" are now scattered throughout the Mass.

The drama of today descends from the medieval mystery plays, which originated as musical tropes in connection with the Alleluia-verse.

"The Mass is the greatest synthesis of beauty that man has ever achieved." — *Cram.* The history of modern painting, or sculpture, or architecture are chapters in the history of the Mass.

"Before one can preach the Catholic solutions of modern economic problems, he has to indoctrinate his audience with the notion of the mystical body."

Entirely apart from all questions of church support, what is the idea underlying almsgiving as a form of worship?

Readings:

Pope Pius XII, *Christian Worship* (Encyclical Letter, Nov. 20, 1947), translated by Canon G. D. Smith (London: CTS, 1948).

F. Boeser, *The Mass-Liturgy* (Milwaukee: Bruce, 1932); "The Mass of the Catechumens," pp. 19–37.

W. R. Bonniwell, *Interpreting the Sunday Mass* (New York: Kenedy, 1949), Introduction.

F. Cabrol, *The Mass, Its Doctrine, Its History, The Story of the Mass in Pen and Picture* (New York: Kenedy, no date); "The Mass of the Catechumens," pp. 24–26.

W. Drum, "Synagogue," *CE.*

A. Fortescue, *The Mass, A Study of the Roman Liturgy* (New York: Longmans, Green, 1937); "The Influence of Jewish Ritual," pp. 70–75.

M. B. Hellriegel, *The Holy Sacrifice of the Mass* (St. Louis: Pio Decimo, 1944), "The Fore-Mass," pp. 21–40; excellent diagrams.

R. Kelley, "Religious Education," *The Sacramental Way* (New York: Sheed & Ward, 1948), pp. 291–307.

N. Maas, *The Treasure of the Liturgy* (Milwaukee: Bruce, 1932); "The Beginning of the Mass," pp. 37–68.

M. S. MacMahon, *Liturgical Catechism, The Church, The Mass, The Year* (Dublin: Gill and Son, 1926); "The Mass of the Catechumens," pp. 87–98.

C. Marmion, *Christ the Life of the Soul* (St. Louis: Herder, 1923); "The Eucharistic Sacrifice," pp. 257–278.

C. C. Martindale, *The Prayers of the Missal: I, Collects* (New York: Sheed and Ward, 1937); *passim.*

V. Michel, *The Liturgy of the Church* (New York: Macmillan, 1937); "The Liturgical Sacrifice," pp. 149–170.

T. H. Moore, *Beyond the Altar Rail* (New York: Fordham Univ., 1939); "Mass of the Catechumens," pp. 39–50.

P. Parsch–F. C. Eckhoff, *The Liturgy of the Mass* (St. Louis: Herder, 1936); pp. 46–152.

M. Perkins, *Speaking of How to Pray* (New York: Sheed & Ward, 1944); "An Oblation and a Sacrifice to God," pp. 156–166.

J. Putz, *My Mass* (Westminster: Newman, 1948), "Prologue," pp. 22–31.

The Union Prayer Book for Jewish Worship (Cincinnati Central Conf. Amer. Rabbis, 1934), *passim.*

Chapter XIII

OFFERING, A
REDEEMING AND ATONING FUNCTION

You proclaim the death of the Lord
until He come (I Cor. xi,2).

"WE RENDER *thanks* to the Lord our God, and this is the great rite in the Sacrifice of the New Covenant, touching which you will learn, when you are baptized, *what* it is, and where, and when, and *how* it is offered." So wrote St. Augustine to a *Epis.* cxl,48 prospective convert, because in his day the truths of the Eucharist were revealed to neophytes only *after* Baptism. "If we ask a catechumen," said the same Augustine on another occasion. " 'Do you believe in Christ?' he will answer, 'I believe,' and he signs himself the while with the Cross of Christ: he bears the Cross on his forehead and he is not ashamed of the Cross of his Lord. See, he believes in His Name. Let us ask him, 'Do you eat the Flesh of the Son of Man, and do you drink the Blood of the Son of Man?' and he knows not what we are talking about." In the words *Tract. in Ioan.* xi of the first quotation the great bishop touched upon themes that may well engage us now: the thank-offering, the essence of the Sacrifice of the new and eternal Testament, and something of the rite of its offering.

Christian Passover. In God's relations with His chosen people, He once delivered them from captivity and slavery in Egypt under circumstances familiar to us all. The Jews had been told to sacrifice lambs, and to sprinkle the lintels of their houses with some of the blood. That night, as the Israelites, girded and ready for a journey, hurriedly ate of their sacrifices, angels of God's wrath slew the first-born of all the Egyptians, but *"passed over"* the homes sprinkled with blood. This awful visitation of God compelled the reluctant Pharaoh to grant permission for the departure of the Jews under Moses. By divine ordinance, the Jews kept thenceforth the annual remembrance of the Passover as the most sacred token of God's covenant with their race. The Pasch was the pole star around which revolved the whole religious life of Israel. For over two thousand years it was held with its own sacred rites as "the most joyous night of the year," as the ancient *Mishna* phrased it. The paschal lambs were sacrificed to God in thanksgiving for His numberless mercies and provident care. They were eaten in the family circles with an elaborate ritual, wherein the countless benedictions of God were chanted in the sublime poetry of King David. The mercies of God to Israel were told over one by one, and, as each divine favor was recounted, all answered in song: "For His goodness endureth forever!"

Cf. Ps. cxxxv

I Cor. x,11   **Reality Succeeds Figure.** "Now these things befell them in a figure." Not Israel alone, but *all mankind was to be delivered from Satan's bondage,* one worse than Pharaoh's. Therefore Christ, "the Lamb that taketh away the sins of the world," chose the setting of the Jewish thanksgiving supper at which to institute the new Sacrifice of Blood for the sealing of the New Testament. It was thus in an atmosphere of thanksgiving, one still echoing with the hymns of God's endless mercies to mankind, that Christ gave Himself for us. What should not be man's thankfulness in accepting that boon from the hand of the Mediator? "This do ye in remembrance of Me," the command accompanying the great Gift, gave us the Sacrifice of the Mass.

John i,29

I

Summit and Center. "The summit, we may also say the center, of the Christian religion," says Pope Pius XII in his encyclical on *Christian Worship,* which we are to cite at some length, "is the Mystery of the Most Holy Eucharist, instituted by Christ the High Priest and by His command renewed perpetually in the Church through His ministers. . . . Christ our Lord, 'priest forever according to the order of Melchisedech,' 'loved His own that were in the world'; and accordingly 'at the Last Supper, on the night on which He was being betrayed, He willed to leave to His beloved bride the Church a visible sacrifice such as the nature of man requires; one by which the bloody sacrifice that was to be enacted once upon the Cross should be represented and its memory remain until the end of the world, and its salutary power be applied for the remission of the sins that are daily committed by us. . . . He therefore offered His body and Blood to God the Father under the appearances of bread and wine, and under the symbols of the same delivered them to be taken by the Apostles, whom He at that moment was making

Ps. cix,4
John xiii,1

C. of Trent, xxii,1
priests of the New Testament; and to them and their successors in the priesthood He gave command to offer.' "

The Mass and Calvary. "The august Sacrifice of the altar," it is the same papal message we cite, "is therefore no mere simple commemoration of the Passion and Death of Jesus Christ; it is truly and properly the offering of a sacrifice, wherein by an unbloody immolation the High Priest does what He had already done on the Cross, offering Himself to the eternal Father as a most acceptable victim. 'One . . . and the same is the victim, one and the same is He who now offers by the ministry of His priests and who then offered Himself on the Cross; the difference Trent, xxii,2 is only in the manner of offering.' "

The Same Priest. "The priest, then is the same, Christ Jesus, whose sacred person is represented by His minister. The consecration which the St. Thom., S.T. III, Q xxii,a.4 minister received when he was ordained to the priesthood assimilates him to the High Priest and enables him to act by the power of Christ Himself and in His name. And therefore when he exercises his priestly St. Chrys., In Ioann., lxxxvi,4 power he, as it were, 'lends Christ his tongue and gives Him the use of his hand.' "

Victim Offered Differently. "The victim, too, is the same," the pope reminds us, "the divine Redeemer according to His humanity and in His true Body and Blood. But the manner in which Christ is offered is different. On the Cross He offered to God the whole of Himself and His sufferings, and the Victim was immolated by a bloody death voluntarily accepted. But on the altar, by reason of the glorious condition Rom. vi,9 of His humanity, 'death will no longer have dominion over Him,' and therefore the shedding of His Blood is not possible. Nevertheless the divine Wisdom has devised a way in which our Redeemer's Sacrifice is marvelously shown forth by external signs symbolic of death. By the 'transubstantiation' of bread into the Body of Christ and of wine into His Blood both His Body and Blood are rendered really present; but the Eucharistic species under which He is present symbolize the violent separation of His Body and Blood, and so a commemorative showing forth of the death which took place in reality on Calvary is repeated in Christian Worship each Mass, because by distinct representations Christ Jesus is signified and shown forth in the state of victim."

The 'Ends' or Purposes: Praise. The same source states: "The ends of the sacrifice are likewise the same. The first of these is the giving of due glory to the heavenly Father. From the beginning of His life

until His death Jesus Christ was aflame with zeal for the glory of God; and from the Cross the immolation of His Blood went up to heaven breathing out fragrance. And in order that this hymn of praise may continue without ceasing, in the Eucharistic Sacrifice the members are united with their divine Head and with Him and in company with the angels and archangels sing undying praise to God, offering to the almighty Father all honor and glory." *Preface*
Canon

Thanksgiving. "The second end is the giving of due thanks to God. Only the divine Redeemer, because He is the most beloved Son of the eternal Father and fully knows His unbounded love, could offer Him a worthy hymn of thanksgiving. This is what He intended, this is what He willed, when at the Last Supper He 'gave thanks.' Hanging on the *Mark xiv,23* Cross He continued to give thanks; He continues to do so in the august Sacrifice of the altar, which is called by the name of Eucharist, *Preface* or 'thanksgiving'; for this is 'truly worthy and just, right and salutary.' "

Propitiation. "The third end," we read, "is expiation, propitiation, and reconciliation. No other than Christ could make full satisfaction to almighty God for the sins of the human race; and therefore He willed to be immolated on the Cross, being 'the atonement made for our sins, and not only for ours, but for the sins of the whole world.' On our altars *I John ii,2* also He offers Himself daily for our redemption, so that we may be rescued from eternal damnation and numbered in the flock of the elect. And this He does not only for us who are still living on earth, but also 'for all who are at rest in Christ, and who have gone before us with *Canon* the sign of the faith and are asleep in peace.' For whether we live or *St. August.,* die, 'we are not separated from the one Christ.' " *Trin., xiii,19*

Impetration. The encyclical on *Christian Worship* goes on to say: "The fourth end is impetration. Like the prodigal son, man has misspent and wasted all the goods that he had received from his heavenly Father, and is thus reduced to extreme poverty and destitution. But from the Cross Christ 'offered prayer and entreaty . . . not without a piercing cry, not without tears; yet with such piety as won Him a hearing.' *Heb. v,7* And with equal efficacy on our altars He is our advocate with God, asking that we may be filled with every blessing and grace.

We can therefore well understand why the Council of Trent affirms that the saving power of the Cross is applied to us through the Eucharistic Sacrifice to destroy our daily sins." *Trent, xxii,1*

Calvary Sufficient in Merit. "In proclaiming the perfection and superabundance of the Sacrifice of the Cross St. Paul says that Christ 'by a single offering has completed His work for all time, in those whom Heb. x,14 He sanctifies.' The merits of this Sacrifice are utterly boundless; without limits they extend to all men at all times and in all places. And the reason is because the Priest and Victim of it is God Himself made man; because His immolation, like His obedience to the will of His eternal Father, was quite perfect; and because He went to meet death as the Head of the human race. 'Behold the transaction by which we are purchased; Christ hangs on the Cross, such is the price He paid for us. He shed His Blood, with His Blood He bought us; He bought us with the Blood of the spotless Lamb, with the Blood of the only Son of God. St. August., In Psalm., cxlvii,16 The buyer is Christ; the price is His Blood; what He buys is the whole world.' "

Contact With Calvary by Mass. "But this purchase does not take full effect immediately. Having bought the world with this great price which is Himself, Christ has yet to take actual possession of men's souls. And so, in order that the redemption and salvation of individuals in all ages until the end of the world may become effective and be ratified by God, it is necesary for each member of the human race to get vitally in touch with the Sacrifice of the Cross, so that the merits which flow from it may be bestowed upon him. We might say that on Calvary Christ has provided a bath of expiation and salvation, filled with the Christian Worship Blood He has shed for us; but unless men plunge into it and there wash away the stains of their sins, they cannot be cleansed and saved."

Individual Collaboration Required. "Therefore if individual sinners," the context continues, "are to be purified in the Blood of the Lamb, Christians themselves must co-operate. Although Christ, universally speaking, has reconciled the whole human race to the Father by His death, yet He has willed that all men should come and be brought to His Cross, especially by means of the Sacraments and the Mass, and so take possession of the fruits which through the Cross He has won for them. By this active and personal co-operation, the members become ever more and more like their Head, and at the same time the salvation that flows from the Head is applied to the members themselves; and so Gal. ii,19,20 each of us can repeat the words of St. Paul: 'With Christ I hang upon the Cross; and yet I am alive; or rather, not I; it is Christ that lives in Mystical Body, 1943 me.' To quote what we wrote on another occasion in dealing more fully with this subject: Christ Jesus 'dying on the Cross, bestowed upon His

Church the boundless treasure of the Redemption without any co-operation on her part; but in the distribution of that treasure He not only
shares His work of sanctification with His spotless bride, but wills it
to arise in a certain manner out of her labor.' " *Christian Worship*

Pre-eminence of the Mass. The section of the encyclical we have
been quoting concludes: "Among the instruments for distributing to
believers the merits that flow from the Cross of the divine Redeemer,
the august Sacrifice of the Mass is pre-eminent: 'As often as the com-
memoration of this Victim is celebrated, the work of our Redemption is *Missal, 9th S. aft. Pent.*
performed.' But this in no way derogates from the dignity of the Sacrifice
of the Cross; on the contrary it is a clear proof — as the Council of *Sess. xxii,2, can. 4*
Trent asserts — of its greatness and necessity. The daily immolation is
a reminder to us that there is no salvation but in the Cross of our Lord
Jesus Christ; and that the reason why God wills the continuation of this Gal. iv,14
Sacrifice 'from the rising of the sun to its going down' is in order that Mal. i,11
there may be no pause in that hymn of praise and thanksgiving. This is
a debt which men owe to their Creator precisely because they stand in
constant need of His help, and in constant need of the divine Redeemer's
Blood to destroy the sins that call for His just retribution." *Christian Worship*

II

How Laity Should Offer. "It is therefore important," states the
papal encyclical on *Christian Worship*, "for all the faithful to understand that it is their duty and highest privilege to take part in the
Eucharistic Sacrifice; and to take part in it, not passively or negligently
or with distracted mind, but with such active devotion as to be in the
closest union with the High Priest, according to the words of St. Paul:
'Yours is to be the same mind which Christ Jesus showed'; and to offer Phil. ii,5
it together with Him and through Him, and with Him to surrender
themselves."

Lay-'priests,' Lay-victims. "Christ is Priest indeed," the Pontiff
states, "but He is Priest for us, not for Himself. It is in the name of
the whole human race that He offers prayer and acts of religious homage
to His eternal Father. He is likewise victim; but victim for us, since He
substitutes Himself for guilty mankind. Now the Apostle's exhortation,
'Yours is to be the same mind which Christ Jesus showed; requires all
Christians, so far as human power allows, to reproduce in themselves the
sentiments that Christ had when He was offering Himself in Sacrifice:

sentiments of humility, of adoration, praise and thanksgiving to the divine Majesty. It requires them also to become victims, as it were; cultivating a spirit of self-denial according to the precepts of the Gospel, willingly doing works of penance, detesting and expiating their sins. It requires us all, in a word, to die mystically with Christ on the Cross, so that we may say with the same Apostle: 'With Christ I hang upon

Gal. ii,19 the Cross.' "

Priestly Offerers and Lay Offerers. "But the fact that the faithful take part in the Eucharistic Sacrifice does not mean that they also possess the power of the priesthood. The members of your flocks, venerable brethren, must be made to understand this quite clearly. There are some, who, holding a view not far removed from errors that have already been

Trent, xxii,4 condemned, teach that the New Testament knows of no priesthood other than that which is common to all the baptized; that the command which Jesus Christ gave to His Apostles at the Last Supper, to do what He Himself had done, was addressed directly to the whole community of the faithful; and that thence and only later the hierarchical priesthood took its rise. They therefore maintain that the people possess the true priestly power, and that the priest acts only in virtue of a function delegated to him by the community. Consequently they regard the Eucharistic Sacrifice as a true 'concelebration,' and think that it is much better for

Christian priests to assist and 'concelebrate' with the people than to offer the

Worship Sacrifice privately when the people are not present."

Priest, a Mediator; Layman, Not. "It is not necessary to show how plainly these captious errors contradict the truths we asserted above, in speaking of the special position that the priest holds in the Mystical Body of Jesus Christ. One thing we think it advisable to repeat: that the priest acts in the name of the people precisely and only because he represents the person of our Lord Jesus Christ, considered as Head of all the members and offering Himself for them; that the priest, therefore,

St. R. Bell. approaches the altar as Christ's minister, lower than Christ, but higher

Missa, III,6 than the people; that the people, on the other hand, because it in no

Christian way represents the person of the divine Redeemer and is not mediator

Worship between itself and God, can in no way possess the priestly right."

Yet Laity Offer Sacrifice. "All this is certain with the certainty of faith. Yet it must be said that the faithful do also offer the divine victim, though in a different way. The fact is clear enough from the statements of some of our predecessors, and of some Doctors of the

Church. 'Not only do priests offer,' wrote Pope Innocent III, 'but all the *De Sac. Alt.* *Mys.,* III,6
faithful offer too; what is performed in a special way by the ministry
of the priests is done in a general way by the desire of the faithful.'
And from among several assertions of St. Robert Bellarmine on this
subject we may quote the following: 'The Sacrifice is offered principally
in the person of Christ. Therefore this offering that follows the consecration bears witness, as it were, that the whole Church agrees with
the oblation made by Christ and offers together with Him.'" *Missa, i,27*

The Prayers Assert This. "The rites and prayers of the Mass show
no less clearly that the offering of the victim is made by the priest together with the people. After the offertory of the bread and wine the
sacred minister turns to the people and says: 'Pray, brethren, that my
sacrifice and yours may become acceptable in the sight of God the
Father Almighty.' Moreover, the prayers by which the divine victim is *Ordinary*
offered to God are said for the most part in the plural, and they more
than once indicate that the people have a part in this sacrifice as being
offerers of it; for example: '. . . For whom we offer to Thee, or who
offer to Thee . . . ; we beseech Thee, Lord, graciously to receive this
offering of us Thy servants, indeed of the whole of Thy household. *Canon*
. . . We, Thy servants, indeed the whole of Thy holy people, offer to Thy
august Majesty, from the gifts which Thou hast given us a pure victim,
a holy victim, a spotless victim.'" *Canon*

Members All of Christ the Priest. "And there is no wonder that
the faithful are accorded this privilege: by reason of their baptism
Christians are in the Mystical Body and become by a common title
members of Christ the Priest; by the 'character' that is graven upon
their souls they are appointed to the worship of God, and therefore,
according to their condition, they share in the priesthood of Christ *Christian*
Himself." *Worship*

Laymen Ask an Explanation. The document here cited goes on to
say: "In the Catholic Church the human mind, enlightened by faith,
has always sought to reach the deepest possible understanding of divine
truth. It is therefore right that the Christian people should reverently ask
in what sense they also are said in the Canon of the Mass to offer the
Eucharistic Sacrifice: and to meet this reverent desire we give here a
brief and concise explanation."

Remote Reasons. "First, there are remote reasons: the fact that in
a number of cases the faithful assisting at Mass recite their prayers

alternately with those of the priest; the fact that sometimes — in ancient times more frequently — they present bread and wine to the sacred ministers that they may become the Body and Blood of Christ; the fact that they give alms in order that the priest may offer the divine victim for their intention."

Christian Worship

Proximate Reasons, and a Distinction. "But there is also a deeper reason why all the faithful, especially those present at Mass, are said to offer. To avoid any mistake in this very important matter we must clearly define the exact meaning of the word 'offer.' The unbloody immolation by which, after the words of consecration have been pronounced, Christ is rendered present on the altar in the state of victim, is performed by the priest alone, and by the priest in as far as he acts in the name of Christ, not in so far as he represents the faithful. But precisely because the priest places the divine victim on the altar he presents it as an oblation to God the Father for the glory of the Blessed Trinity and for the benefit of the whole Church. Now, understood in this restricted sense, the oblation is in their own way shared by the faithful, and for two reasons: first because they offer the Sacrifice *through* the priest, and secondly because, in a certain sense, they offer it *with* him. And because they have this part in the Sacrifice the people's offering also pertains to liturgical worship."

Christian Worship

People Offering Through the Priest. "That the faithful offer through the priest is clear from the fact that the minister at the altar acts in the name of Christ considered as Head, and as offering in the name of all the members; and this is why it is true to say that the whole Church makes the offering of the victim through Christ."

People Offering With the Priest. "But when the people are said to offer with the priest, this does not mean that all the members of the Church, like the priest himself, perform the visible liturgical rite; for this is done only by the minister appointed for the purpose. No, they are said to offer with him inasmuch as they unite their sentiments of praise, entreaty, expiation, and thanksgiving with the sentiments or intention of the priest, indeed with those of the High Priest himself, in order that in the very oblation of the victim, those sentiments may be presented to God also by the priest's external rite. The external rite of sacrifice must of its very nature be a sign of internal worship; and what is signified by the Sacrifice of the New Law is that supreme homage by which Christ, the principal offerer, and with Him and through Him all

His mystical members, pay due honor and veneration to God. We rejoice to know that this doctrine has been brought into prominence, especially in recent times, through a widespread and more intense study of the liturgy. . . ." *Christian Worship*

Lay Victimhood Also Demanded. "But if the oblation," the Pope says, "whereby the faithful in this Sacrifice offer the divine Victim to the heavenly Father is to produce its full effect, they must do something further: they must also offer themselves as victim. And this immolation is not restricted to the liturgical Sacrifice. The Prince of the Apostles would have us, precisely because we are built upon Christ like living stones, to be 'a holy priesthood, and offer spiritual sacrifices *I Pet. ii,5* acceptable to God through Jesus Christ'; and St. Paul makes no discrimination of time when he exhorts Christians 'to offer up your bodies as a living sacrifice, consecrated to God and worthy of His acceptance: *Rom. xii,1* the worship due from you as rational creatures.' "

At Mass Especially. "But, inevitably, it is when the faithful are taking part in the liturgical action, with such attention and devotion that it may be truly said that their 'faith and devotion are known to Thee,' that their faith will more eagerly work by charity and their *Canon* devotion grow more fervent; it is then especially that they will all consecrate themselves to the glory of God, desiring intensely to make themselves as like as possible to Jesus Christ who suffered so much, as offering themselves as a spiritual victim with and through the High *Christian* Priest Himself." *Worship*

Proof From the Prayers. ". . . The liturgical books similarly admonish those who approach the altar to take part in the sacrifice: 'On this altar let innocence be cultivated, pride sacrificed, anger immolated, all lust and evil desire done to death: let the gift of chastity, not turtle doves, be your offering; and let innocence, not young pigeons, be your *Pontifical,* sacrifice.' As we stand at the altar, then, we must change our hearts: *cons. altar* uproot the sin that is in them, and carefully tend and foster in them everything, that, through Christ, may avail for supernatural life. So, together with the Immaculate Victim, shall we become an oblation pleasing to the eternal Father."

Head and Members Offering Together. ". . . Let this be the aim of the faithful, then," this section of the encyclical concludes, "as they offer the divine victim in the Mass. St. Augustine tells us that on the *Serm., 272* table of the Lord lies 'our mystery,' that is to say, Christ our Lord

Himself: Head and symbol of that compact unity whereby we are the Body of Christ and members of His Body. St. Robert Bellarmine (who writes in the spirit of St. Augustine) says that the sacrifice of the altar signifies the universal sacrifice by which the whole Mystical Body of Christ, that is, the whole city of the redeemed, is offering to God through the High Priest.' This being so, nothing could be more right and just than that all of us, together with our divine Head who suffered for us, should immolate ourselves to the eternal Father. For, in the Sacrament of the altar, as St. Augustine also tells us, 'a sign is given to the Church that in the sacrifice she offers she herself is offered.' "

I Cor. xii,27
Eph. v,30

Missa, II,8

City of God,
x,6

III

ORDINARY OF THE MASS: SECOND PART, OBLATION OF GIFTS

Offertory Anthem

Eloquent of the spectacular setting of the gift-bringing of old, and of the *ceremonial* insignificance it holds today, is the Offertory Anthem. This is the surviving refrain, sung with psalmody, as the people presented their bread and wine.

Christ sits forever at the right hand of God, offering for our sins a sacrifice that is never repeated: by a single offering He has completed His work for all time, in those whom He sanctifies (Heb. x,12–14).

Offering of Bread

It has been said that, while the layman's Offertory was formerly an *act,* now it is a prayer. It would be more accurate to say that it was formerly a *prayer-expressed-in-action,* but now, at most, a *prayer.* The interior act of self-surrender, symbolized in the presentation here of the bread, a moment later, of the wine, is given a suitable verbal accompaniment by the Offertory prayers.

Holy Father, almighty, everlasting God, accept this unblemished sacrificial offering, which I, Thy unworthy servant, make to Thee, my living and true God, for my countless sins, offences, and neglects, and on behalf of all who are present here; likewise for all believing Christians, living and dead. Accept it for their good and mine, so that it may save us and bring us to everlasting life. Amen.

(Frankish)

Mixing of Wine and Water

Of this symbolic act of mixing water and wine the Council of Trent says: "It has been enjoined by the Church on priests to mix water with the wine that is to be offered in the chalice; as well because it is believed that Christ the Lord did this (John xix,34) . . . and, whereas in the Apocalypse of blessed John (Apoc. xvii,15) the

O God, by whom the dignity of human nature was wondrously established and yet more wondrously restored, grant that through the sacramental rite of this water and wine we may have fellowship in the Godhead of Him who deigned to share our manhood, Jesus Christ, Thy Son, our Lord, who is God, living and reigning peoples are called waters, the union of that faithful people with Christ their Head is hereby represented" (*Sess.* xxii).

with Thee in the unity of the Holy Spirit, for ever and ever. Amen.

(*Frankish adaptation of Roman prayer*)

Offering of the Chalice

The end of all sacrificing, of course, is that God deign to accept the gift-offering. *Christ's* gift God is bound to receive, and so we multiply petitions that He accept ours in one and the same act.

We offer Thee, Lord, the chalice of salvation, entreating Thy mercy that our offering may ascend with *a sweet fragrance* (Eph. v,2) in the presence of Thy divine Majesty for our own and the whole world's salvation. Amen.

(*Frankish*)

Offering of Ourselves

"The sacrifice which is offered externally," says St. Thomas, "betokens the internal, spiritual sacrifice, by which the soul surrenders itself to God" (*S.T.* II, II. Q. lxxxv,*a*.2). This *self-oblation* is here voiced in the words of the three youths cast into fire for God's law!

Humbled in spirit and contrite of heart, may we find favor with Thee, Lord; and may our sacrifice be so offered in Thy sight this day that it may please Thee, Lord our God (Dan. iii,39,40).

(*Frankish*)

We think now of what is symbolized by the bread and wine — our own interior dispositions, which so need God's sustaining aid.

Come, Thou Sanctifier, almighty, everlasting God, and bless these sacrificial gifts, prepared for the glory of Thy holy name.

(*Frankish*)

Blessing of Incense

Incense, a natural symbol of prayer, and itself often one of the symbolical gifts in sacrificial worship, is here to be used in a solemn rite expressive of several ideas. But before being offered, the incense is blessed with a prayer that its sweetness delight God.

At the intercession of blessed Michael the *archangel, who stands at the right hand of the altar of incense* (Apoc. viii,3), and of all his elect, may the Lord deign to bless this incense, and to accept its *fragrant sweetness* (Eph. v,2): through Christ our Lord. Amen.

(*Frankish*)

Incensing the Oblations

This incensing of the oblations on the altar is best understood as a signal mark of honor shown to them.

With Thy own blessing, Lord, let this incense rise to Thee, and bring down upon us Thy mercy.

(Frankish)

Incensing the Altar

The first verse of this Scripture passage is the keynote of the elaborate action of incensing, first the crucifix, then the altar, back, table, ends, base. One is thinking mostly of *prayer*, secondarily of incense. It is prayer that pleases God, prayer that is the evening sacrifice, prayer that is the watch set over our unruly inclinations.

Welcome as incense-smoke let my prayer rise before Thee, Lord; when I lift up my hands, be it as acceptable as the evening sacrifice. Lord, set a guard on my mouth, and a barrier to fence in my lips, lest my heart turn to the thoughts of evil, to cover sin with smooth names (Ps. cxl,2–4).

(Frankish)

Returning Censer

The incensing of celebrant, ministers, and laity is again an expression of honor paid to the members because of the Head.

May the Lord kindle within us the fire of His love, and the flame of everlasting charity. Amen.

(Frankish)

Lavabo

When the laity made their gift-offerings in kind and directly into the hands of the celebrant, practical considerations dictated a washing of the hands at this point. Now that the oblations are no longer presented in the ancient manner this washing of the hands has a purely symbolical meaning. The closer the moment of sacrifice approaches the more the priest multiplies his efforts to purify his soul — and to that end washes yet once again his hands.

At a Solemn Mass the celebrant washes all his fingers — not just

With the pure in heart I will wash my hands clean, and take my place among them at Thy altar, Lord, listening there to the sound of Thy praises, telling the story of all Thy wonderful deeds. How well, Lord, I love Thy house in its beauty, the place where Thy own glory dwells! Lord, never count this soul for lost with the wicked, this life among the bloodthirsty hands ever stained with guilt, palms ever itching for a bride! Be it mine to guide my steps clear of wrong; deliver me in Thy mercy. My feet are set on firm ground; where Thy people the tips of the thumbs and fore-fingers as he does at Low Mass. The reason is that he has been handling the thurible and incense boat.

gather, Lord, I will join in blessing Thy name (Ps. xxv,6–12).
Glory be to the Father, and to the Son, and to the Holy Ghost. As it was in the beginning, is now, and ever shall be, world without end. Amen.

(Frankish)

The prayer before us, which is of rather late medieval composition, embodies a quotation from the Canon of the Mass, "in memory of the Passion, Resurrection and Ascension." Almost the whole theology of sacrifice is sketched in this one short formula:

we offer
a tangible gift
to God alone
in memory of Christ's death
in honor of Mary and the saints
with a prayer for its acceptance
unto our salvation
through our Mediator Christ
Jesus.

Bowing slightly, the priest continues:
Holy Trinity, accept the offering we here make to Thee in memory of the passion, resurrection, and ascension of our Lord Jesus Christ; and to the honor of blessed Mary, ever-virgin, of blessed John the Baptist, of the holy apostles Peter and Paul, and of these, and of all the saints. To them let it bring honor, to us salvation; and may they whom we are commemorating on earth deign to plead for us in heaven: through the same Christ our Lord. Amen.

(Frankish)

Orate Fratres

This mutual exhortation to prayer is found in a wide variety of forms in old missals. The encouraging response to it is a still later addition, and is not found, for instance in the Rite of the Dominican Fathers.

P: Pray, brethren, that my sacrifice and yours may prove acceptable in the eyes of God the almighty Father.
R: May the Lord accept the sacrifice at your hands, to the praise and glory of His name, for our welfare also, and that of all His holy Church.
P: Amen.

(Frankish)

Silent Prayer

This Silent Prayer, the oldest Offertory prayer, has for purpose to express our double role of co-priests and co-victims. St. Albert the Great characterizes it as expressing nothing other than the people's oblation of itself in these gifts and through these gifts to God for "incorporation in the unity of the Body of Christ" (*De Off. Miss.* III,2,5).

May *Jesus Christ* our *Mediator* (I Tim. ii,5) commend these offerings to Thy favor, Lord, and present us, together with Himself, as sacrificial gifts for Thy acceptance: He who is God, living and reigning with Thee, in the unity of the Holy Spirit.

(*Roman*)

CANON OF THE MASS: FIRST PART

Dialogue

This dialogue before the Preface is found in identical terms in all the oldest rites. Tradition ascribes it to apostolic times. "You were invited to *lift up your heart* on high," says St. Augustine to neophytes. "That is proper for members of Christ, for our Head is in heaven" (*Serm.* ccxxvii).

P: For ever and ever.
R: Amen.
He then begins the Preface:
P: The Lord be with you.
R: And with you.
P: Lift up your hearts.
R: We lift our hearts to the Lord.
P: Let us give thanks to the Lord our God.
R: That is right and just.

Preface

In our minds "Preface" is associated with the introductory statement at the head of a book, and the connotation is here a danger insofar as the Preface of the Mass may come to be regarded merely as something preliminary to and introducing the Canon itself. The word "Preface," as used in the Mass, was formerly, it would seem, applied to the *entire Canon,* and

P: Right indeed it is and just, proper and for our welfare, that we should always and everywhere give thanks to Thee, holy Lord, almighty Father, eternal God. By Thy ordinance the salvation of mankind was accomplished on the wood of the Cross, so that life might rise again there where death had its beginning, and that he who conquered through a tree should not merely this chanted opening of it. Obviously, then, it is used in an unusual meaning; it is a solemn public address to God (*praefari*). Thus far, in the Roman Mass, there has been very little said or sung that is the exclusive part of the celebrant. But now comes his "grand and solemn prayer" on the improvisation of which the first Christians set such store.

on a tree himself be conquered: through Christ our Lord.

It is through that same Christ our Lord that Thy Majesty is praised by Angels, adored by Dominations, feared by Powers; through Him that the heavens and the celestial Virtues join with the blessed Seraphim in one glad hymn of praise. We pray Thee let our voices blend with theirs, as we humbly praise Thee, singing:

(*Jewish*)

The Hymn of Thanksgiving is here interrupted by the "Holy, holy, holy." This is almost word for word from Sacred Scripture, recalling the visions of Isaias and St. John the Apostle. The last line is the Palm Sunday acclamation slightly modified.

Holy, holy, holy, Lord God of hosts. Thy glory fills all heaven *and earth* (Isa. vi,3). *Hosanna in high heaven! Blessed is He who is coming in the name of the Lord* (Apoc. iv,8). *Hosanna in high heaven!* (Mark xi,9,10.)

(*Jewish*)

CANON OF THE MASS: SECOND PART

Canon means in the Greek a fixed rule, or norm, or standard. The Canon of the Mass is a fixed norm of consecratory prayer, which remains substantially what it was in the time of St. Gregory the Great. "For it is composed" as the Fathers of Trent said with reverence, "out . . . out of the very words of the Lord, the traditions of the Apostles, and the pious institutions also of holy pontiffs" (*Sess.* xxii).

And so, through Jesus Christ, Thy Son, our Lord, we humbly pray and beseech Thee, most gracious Father, to accept and bless these offerings, these oblations, these holy and unblemished sacrificial gifts, which we offer Thee in the first place for Thy holy Catholic Church, praying that Thou wilt be pleased to keep and guide her in peace and unity throughout the world; together with Thy servant our Pope *N.*, and *N.* our bishop, and all who truly believe and practice the Catholic and Apostolic faith.

In the *First Book of Machabees* we read in Jonathan's celebrated letter to the Spartans:

We therefore at all times without ceasing,
both in our festivals
and other days wherein it is fitting,
remember you in the sacrifices that we offer,
and in our observances,
as it is meet and becoming to remember brethren (I Mach. xii,11).

The same propriety dictates that we, in our grateful gift-bringing, think of the whole Church, her visible head, the pope, her local shepherd, the bishop, and all its members everywhere. This prayer, and the several "remembrance prayers" are additions to the original Canon of the Roman Mass.

For the sake of comparison we here give the oldest Mass Canon extant, that of Rome about 225.

Roman Canon of about 225

The deacons bring him [the bishop] the oblation . . . he lays his hands upon it with all the priests and gives thanks saying:

"The Lord be with you."
And all answer:
"And with thy spirit."
"Lift up your hearts."
"We have lifted them up to the Lord."
"Let us give thanks to the Lord."
And he thus continues:

Remember, Lord, Thy servants, *N.* and *N.* (*here the celebrant makes silent mention of those for whom he wishes to pray*), and all here present, whose faith and devotion are known to Thee, and for whom we offer, or who themselves offer up this sacrifice in praise of Thee, on behalf of themselves and all who are theirs, for the redemption of their souls, to gain the hope of safety and well-being, and who pay homage to Thee, their *living, true, eternal God* (I Thes. i,9).

In the unity of holy fellowship we reverence the memory, first of the glorious ever-virgin Mary, Mother of our God and Lord Jesus Christ, and likewise that of Thy blessed apostles and martyrs, Peter and Paul, Andrew, James, John, Thomas, James, Philip, Bartholomew, Matthew, Simon and Thaddeus: of Linus, Cletus, Clement, Sixtus, Cornelius, Cyprian, Lawrence, Chrysogonus, John and Paul, Cosmas and Damian; and of all Thy saints. Grant for the sake of their merits and prayers that in all things we may be guarded and helped by Thy protection: through the same Christ our Lord. Amen.

The bell is rung as he spreads his hands over the gifts:

And so, Lord, we Thy servants, and likewise Thy whole household, make this peace-offering which we entreat Thee to accept. Order our

"We give thanks to Thee, O God, through Thy beloved Son Jesus Christ, whom in these last days Thou hast sent to us [to be] the Redeemer and Saviour and Messenger of Thy will; who is Thy inseparable Word, through whom Thou didst create all things, and who was acceptable to Thee; whom Thou didst send from heaven into the Virgin's womb, and who in her womb was made Man and was manifested [as] Thy Son of the Holy Ghost and born of the Virgin; who fulfilling Thy will, and buying for Thee a holy people, stretched forth His hands, when He suffered, that by His passion He might deliver those who believed in Thee; who when He was delivered over to His passion of His own will, to destroy death, to break the bonds of the devil, to trample upon hell, to enlighten the just, to set a term and to manifest His Resurrection, taking bread, giving thanks to Thee, said:

TAKE YE, THIS IS MY BODY, WHICH SHALL BE BROKEN FOR YOU.

And taking likewise the chalice, saying:

days in Thy peace, and command that we be rescued from eternal damnation and numbered with the flock of Thy elect: through Christ our Lord. Amen.

We pray Thee, God, to make this same offering wholly blessed, to consecrate it and approve it, making it reasonable and acceptable, so that it may become for us the Body and Blood of Thy dearly beloved Son, our Lord Jesus Christ.

He takes the host in his hands and consecrates it:

He, on the day before He suffered death, took bread into His holy and worshipful hands, and lifting up His eyes to Thee, God, His almighty Father in heaven, and giving thanks to Thee, He blessed it, broke it, and gave it to His disciples, saying: *Take, all of you, and eat of this,* for

THIS IS MY BODY.

The bell is rung thrice as he genuflects, shows the Sacred Host to the people, and genuflects again. He consecrates the wine, saying:

In like manner, when He had supped, taking also this *goodly cup* (Ps. xxii,5) into His holy and worshipful hands, and giving thanks to Thee, He blessed it, and gave it to His disciples, saying: *Take, all of you, and drink of this,* for

THIS IS MY BLOOD, WHICH IS SHED FOR YOU;

WHEN YOU DO THIS,

YE MAKE COMMEMORATION OF ME.

"Mindful therefore of His death and resurrection, we offer Thee this Bread and Chalice, giving thanks to Thee, because Thou hast held us worthy to stand before Thee and to minister to Thee. And we beg, that Thou wouldst send Thy Holy Spirit upon the Oblation of the holy Church, and gathering into one all who have received [It] in the fullness of the Holy Ghost unto the confirmation of the faith in truth. That we may praise and glorify Thee through Thy Son Jesus Christ, through whom is to Thee glory and honor, to the Father and the Son with the Holy Spirit, in Thy holy Church both now and forever. Amen" (Hippolytus).

The narrative of the Last Supper puts on the lips of Christ the words of institution and the injunction so to keep His memory. In that one Act our gift is offered to God, becomes the Body and Blood of Christ, proclaims His death on the Cross, and is accepted by the Father as pledge of the new, eternal testament. The essence of the Mass is in the twofold consecration.

It is a commonplace division of the Mass of the Faithful to speak of three principal parts, Offertory, Consecration, and Communion. The division would be misleading if one were to imagine that the

THIS IS THE CHALICE OF MY BLOOD, OF THE NEW AND EVERLASTING COVENANT, A MYSTERY OF FAITH (I Tim. iii,9).

IT SHALL BE SHED FOR YOU AND MANY OTHERS, SO THAT SINS MAY BE FORGIVEN.

He genuflects, saying:

Whenever you shall do these things, you shall do them in memory of Me.

He then shows the chalice to the people, genuflecting as before.

He continues:

And now, Lord, we Thy servants; and with us all Thy holy people, calling to mind the blessed passion of this same Christ, Thy Son, our Lord, likewise His resurrection from the grave, and glorious ascension into heaven, offer up to Thy sovereign Majesty, out of the gifts Thou hast bestowed upon us, a Sacrifice that is pure, holy, and unblemished, the sacred Bread of everlasting life, and *the Cup of eternal salvation* (Ps. cxv,13).

Deign to regard them with a favorable and gracious countenance, and to accept them as Thou wast pleased to accept the offerings of Thy good servant *Abel* (Gen. iv,4), and the sacrifice of our father *Abraham* (Gen. xxii), and that which Thy great priest *Melchisedech* (Gen. xiv,18) sacrificed to Thee, a holy offering, a victim without blemish.

offering part of the Mass was over and finished *before* the Consecration. Actually, the *offering* continues straight through the Canon. By the consecration the gifts offered achieve incomparably higher worth and value, as being Christ's excellent and precious Body and Blood. But the act of sacrificing continues to be that of offering as before; it is the same Act elevated to a much higher plane but continuing in the same direction. The Mass, as Christ's gift, is perfect in all respects, but as ours, the token of our internal disposition, "it may displease God," as St. Robert Bellarmine says. "This therefore is why we ask that God deign graciously to regard this Gift *as it is offered by us*" (*Cont.* II,24).

To that end we beg for part and fellowship with the faithful on earth, below the earth (Purgatory), and in glory, saint and angel, and in one last, supreme gesture we again identify ourselves with the Divine Liturgist fitted to our needs, through Christ, with Christ, and in Christ, as we offer Christ-and-our-selves. It is the climax of *our* part of the Mass. To it the people say "Amen."

This "Amen," as the popular

Bowing low over the altar he says:

Humbly we ask it of Thee, God almighty: bid these things be carried *by the hands of Thy holy angel up to Thy altar on high* (Tob. xii,12), before the face of Thy divine Majesty, so that those of us who by taking part in the Sacrifice of this altar shall have received the sacred Body and Blood of Thy Son, may be filled with every grace and heavenly blessing: through the same Jesus Christ our Lord. Amen.

Remember also, Lord, Thy servants, *N.* and *N.,* who have gone before us with the sign of faith and sleep the sleep of peace. (*Here the celebrant makes silent mention of those dead for whom he wishes to pray*). To them, Lord, and all who rest in Christ, grant, we entreat Thee, a place of cool repose, of light and peace: through the same Christ our Lord. Amen.

(*Frankish insertion of Roman variant*)

Striking his breast, and raising his voice a little, he says:
To us also, Thy sinful servants, who put out trust in Thy countless acts of mercy, deign to grant some share and fellowship with Thy holy apostles and martyrs: with John, Stephen, Matthias, Barnabas, Ignatius, Alexander, Marcellinus, Peter, Felicity, Perpetua, Agatha, Lucy, Agnes, Cecily, Anastasia, and all Thy saints. Into their company we pray Thee to admit

ratification of the Sacrifice, is famous, and has echoed through all the Eucharistic literature. Of it St. Justin says so pointedly: "And when he has ended . . . the thanksgiving, the whole people assent, saying 'Amen.' (lxv), words that Ambrose echoes in turn (*De Mys.*, liv). Listen to St. Jerome's rhetorical question: "Where can the 'Amen' be heard to resound as it resounds in Rome?" (*Ad Gal.* II.) "As the people say 'Amen,'" says Pope Pius XII true to tradition, "let them not forget to offer themselves and their anxieties, their sorrows, their troubles, their miseries and their needs, in union with their divine Head crucified."

us, not weighing our deserts, but freely granting us forgiveness: through Christ our Lord.
It is ever through Him that all these good gifts created by Thee, Lord, are by Thee sanctified, endowed with life, blessed, and bestowed upon us.
He makes the sign of the Cross thrice, saying:
THROUGH HIM, AND WITH HIM, AND IN HIM, Thou, God almighty Father, in the unity of the Holy Spirit, hast all honor and glory.
Replacing the Host and Chalice upon the altar:
P: World without end.
R: Amen.

(*Entire Canon, Roman*)

Summary. "Our prayer is public and social," says St. Cyprian, the glorious martyr-bishop of Carthage (258). "When we pray, we pray not for one, but for the whole people, because we the whole people are one. . . . It is the law of prayer." This law of Christian prayer finds its supreme exemplification in their Sacrifice. This Gift is proffered by the last and the least of the faithful as really as by the New Man and Mediator of the New Testament.   *De Dom. Orat.* 9

Thirteenth-Century Source Material

(Of all the successors to St. Peter, Innocent III is judged to have had the most brilliant pontificate. He was also great as an author, and his book on the Mass, here cited, is the medieval classic in this field.)

There are in this Sacrament three separate elements; namely, the visible form, the real Body, and the spiritual strength: There are the species of bread and wine, the true Flesh and Blood, and the bond of unity and charity. The first is seen by the eye, the second is grasped by the mind, the third is felt by the heart. . . . For indeed the species of bread signifies the dual Body [flesh] of Christ, the real and the mystical. It both signifies and contains Christ's real Flesh. It also typifies, but does not contain, Christ's Mystical Body. As a loaf of bread is made from many grains of wheat, and a cup of wine is crushed from a great number of grapes, so Christ's Church is made up of different classes; in the predestined, the elect, the justified, and the glorified. For

He predestined those whom He called,
and He called them and justified them.

Rom. viii,30,31

And, therefore, the Apostle says:

I Cor. x,12

We many are one bread and one body.

As a type of this, the ark of the Lord was made from setim wood — an incorruptible substance like white thorn. The wine, as fluid and red, suggests blood. In its warmth and fragrance it symbolizes charity. And in quickening the blood and exciting love it rejoices the heart of him who partakes of it. It follows, therefore, that the substance of Christ's Body and Blood is both the Sacrament and the effect, though the bond of union and charity, which is the effect, comes from the Sacrament, and the Sacrament itself is the symbol of this bond. The substance, then, belongs to the bread and wine as it is both contained and signified by them under the visible Species; and the substance is the Sacrament or sign of the bond, signifying and effecting as it does, the oneness of the Church (Bk. IV, ch. 36).

Exod. xxv,10

For He is one and the same, the Son of God who descended from heaven, and the Son of Man who ascended into heaven. To Christ Jesus, as to their Head, are joined all the members of the body — those who through faith in the Eucharist

John iii,13

Eph. iv,3

keep the unity of the Spirit in the bond of peace.

And as one body, one person, the one Christ with His members ascends into heaven. In triumph He represents the glorious Church, and manifesting the oneness of its members with His Person, He cries out to God the Father:

This now is bone of my bone and flesh of my flesh:
They will be two in one flesh.

Gen. ii,24

This is, as the Apostle says:

Eph. v,32

A great mystery in reference to Christ and to the Church.

The Eucharist both effects and symbolizes [prefigures] what the Lord said:

He who eats My Flesh and drinks My Blood   John vi,57
abides in Me and I in Him.

By virtue of our human nature which He assumed, we receive from
Him an indissoluble bond of union, so that He who is ineffably united
with the Father, is marvelously one with us, and through Him (He
mediating between both extremes), we are made one with the Father.
He says:

> Holy Father, keep them in Thy Name,
> whom Thou hast given Me,
> that they may be one as We.
> Not for them only do I ask,
> but for them also
> who shall believe
> through their word in Me,
> so that they may be one in Us,
> and the world may believe
> that Thou has sent Me.

John xvii,20,21,
Douay

Unity asks for union, the Word is one with His Father in nature, man
with the Word is one in person, the members are one with the Head (Bk.
IV, ch. 44).

Topics for Further Discussion:

"Sacrifice is positive, not negative; something given, not given up."

The Offertory Anthem and psalmody were introduced into the Latin Mass by
St. Augustine, which is an additional reason for regretting their decadence.

If sacrifice is basically the service of God by gift-giving, is there a much more
profound idea in the coin collection than any question of contributing to the
support of the church?

Let the group formulate a list of the *social aims* for which alert, intelligent
Catholics offer themselves at Mass.

Two people who have quarreled bitterly, see each other at Mass: think out
a suitable Offertory oblation for either one of them.

Readings:

Pope Pius XII, *Christian Worship* (Encyclical Letter, Nov. 20, 1947): translated
by Canon G. D. Smith (London: CTS, 1948).

F. Boeser, *The Mass-Liturgy* (Milwaukee: Bruce, 1932); "The Mass of the
Faithful," pp. 38–99.

F. Cabrol, *The Mass, Its Doctrine, Its History, The Story of the Mass in Pen
and Picture* (New York: Kenedy, no date); "The Mass of the Faithful,"
pp. 27–36; *passim.*

I. Goma–A. J. Willinger, *The Eucharist and Christian Life* (Paterson: Guild
Press, 1949), "As an Essential Act of Catholic Worship," pp. 95–138.

M. B. Hellriegel, *The Holy Sacrifice of the Mass* (St. Louis: Pio Decimo, 1944), "The Sacrifice-Mass," pp. 4–58.

J. A. Jungmann, *The Eucharistic Prayer* [Canon] (Chicago: Fides, 1956).

J. Kramp, *Live the Mass* (St. Paul: Cat. Guild, 1954), "The Structure of the Liturgical Sacrifice," pp. 88–192.

E. Leen, *The True Vine and Its Branches* (New York: Kenedy, 1938); "The Sacred Sign of Calvary," pp. 48–62; "The Sacred Sign of the Christian Altar," pp. 63–77.

G. Lefebvre, *Catholic Liturgy, Its Fundamental Principles* (St. Louis: Herder, 1937); "The Holy Sacrifice of the Mass," pp. 63–76.

N. Maas, *The Treasure of the Liturgy* (Milwaukee: Bruce, 1932); "The Offertory," etc., pp. 69–99.

M. S. MacMahon, *Liturgical Catechism, The Church, The Mass, The Year* (Dublin: Gill and Son, 1926); "The Mass of the Faithful," pp. 99–138.

V. Michel, *The Liturgy of the Church* (New York: Macmillan, 1937); "The Sacrifice-Oblation," pp. 171–191.

T. H. Moore, *Beyond the Altar Rail* (New York: Fordham Univ., 1939); "Bread and Wine," pp. 51–62; "The Consecration," pp. 63–76.

P. Parsch–F. C. Eckhoff, *The Liturgy of the Mass* (St. Louis: Herder, 1936); pp. 153–256.

M. Perkins, *Speaking of How to Pray* (New York: Sheed & Ward, 1944); "An Oblation and a Sacrifice to God" cont'd, pp. 167–177.

J. de Puniet, *The Mass, Its Origin and History* (London: Burns, Oates and Washbourne, 1931); "The Mass of the Faithful," etc., pp. 110–170.

J. Putz, *My Mass* (Westminster: Newman, 1948), "Act Two: The Consecration," pp. 54–79.

F. J. Sheed, *Theology and Sanity* (New York: Sheed & Ward, 1946), "The Mass," pp. 283–286.

M. de la Taille, *The Mystery of Faith, An Outline* (London: Sheed and Ward, 1930); *passim.*

H. R. Williamson, *The Great Prayer* (New York: Macmillan, 1956).

M. Zundel, *The Splendour of the Liturgy* (New York: Sheed and Ward, 1939); "The Liturgy of the Supper," pp. 125–204.

Chapter XIV

COMMUNING,
A PERSONAL AND A SOCIAL FUNCTION

We many are one bread, one body,
for we all partake of the one Bread . . .
Have not they who eat the Sacrifices
fellowship with the altar? (I Cor. x,17,18.)

PERFECT sacrificial worship has always been accompanied by a
sacrificial banquet. The idea of sacrifice implies this banquet in
which the worshipers partake of the sacrificial gifts, in order to
achieve fellowship with the altar, that is, with God, who accepts the gifts
put upon the altar. The logical and psychological processes of this ritual
are as follows: first, the worshipers make an offering of foodstuffs, as
a social symbol of self-consecration to God; in case a living victim be
offered, it is put to death in token of God's sovereignty. These self-
symbolizing foodstuffs become a savory banquet for the Divinity. Then,
in return, God admits us to this banquet, and thus portrays in symbol the
benefits that flow to man in serving Him. God's foodstuffs in His sacrificial banquet thus betoken these three things:

A. The happiness of future union with God in heaven.

B. The sanctification of self through union with God on earth.

C. The intimate union or unity of the whole divine family, "on earth
as it is in heaven."

These things are called the "fruits" or the "effects" of sacrificial
worship. Since God, moreover, is glorified through the same processes
by which man is sanctified, these things constitute the whole why and
wherefore of such worship.

"Gifts of Unity and Peace." It is essential to draw out in some
detail the intrinsic relation of God's Gift-in-Return, which is Communion,
to our gift-bringing, which is sacrifice. At the Offertory we together
presented God with what St. Thomas called our "gifts of unity and
peace," in the Silent Prayer which he composed for the Mass-formulary of

the Feast of Corpus Christi. The Canon of the Mass speaks of them as the *oblation of our service*. But *for what* are we offering and dedicating ourselves to God in every Mass? Our adoration, thanksgiving, petition, and reparation are rendered to God in token of our *acknowledged dependence* upon Him. We are symbolically and dramatically expressing our complete willingness to accept whatever God's service entails *now*. That inevitably entails putting up with much minor unpleasantness from those about us, involves self-renunciation at home, in the classroom, in office, factory, at the theater, at the dance. This oblation of our service is a big order, in fact, our every relationship is part of it. Of itself it isn't easy, much less, is it pleasant. God therefore wished to make it tolerable (and even easy) by drawing us all together into a *living union* with His Son, who will give us the necessary life-force for the task.

Function of Eucharist. Let us ponder the reasons given by the Fathers of Trent "for the institution of this most Holy Sacrament":

> Wherefore our Saviour, when about to depart out of this world to the Father, instituted this Sacrament, in which He poured forth, as it were, the riches of His Divine love towards man, making a remembrance of His wonderful works;

> and He commended us in the participation thereof to venerate His memory, and to show forth His death until He come to judge the world.

I Cor. xi,24
I Cor. xi,26

> And He would also that this Sacrament should be received as the spiritual food of souls, whereby may be fed and strengthened those that live with His life who said:

Matt. xxvi,26

> He that eateth Me,
> the same shall live by Me;

John vi,58

> And as an antidote whereby we may be freed from daily faults and preserved from mortal sins.

> He would, furthermore, have it to be a pledge of our glory to come and everlasting happiness, and thus be *a symbol of that one body whereof He is the Head, and to which He would fain have us as members united* by the closest bond of faith, hope, and charity.

I Cor. ii,3
Sess. xiii

The last and complete function of the Holy Eucharist is its cementing and unifying one: Communion is to be the real Communion Breakfast,

where we are made one body by partaking of the one Bread. And this, I Cor. x,17
Trent tells us, is in God's purpose the great symbol of the mystical body
of Christ.

Integrated into Sacrifice. "Pope Benedict XIV," says his successor Pius XII, "in order that it might be more evident that by receiving Holy Communion the faithful take part in the Sacrifice,
praised the devotion that prompts the desire of some, not only to communicate when present at Mass, but preferably to receive particles
consecrated at the same Mass — although as he himself explains, the
Sacrifice is shared by the faithful even when they communicate with
hosts previously consecrated. . . . 'Nevertheless the Church has never
forbidden, nor does she now forbid, the priest to satisfy the pious
and just request of such as desire to be admitted to a share of that
same Sacrifice, of which they also — in their own way — are the
offerers. Indeed, she approves and encourages this practice, and
would blame any priest through whose fault or negligence such *Certiores*
sharing of the Sacrifice should be denied to the faithful.' . . . It is *effecti, 3*
very fitting that the faithful, in accordance with the liturgical rule,
should approach Holy Communion after the priest has communicated
at the altar; and, as we have already said, it is praiseworthy that
those who are present should receive particles which have been
consecrated at the same Mass, and so give real fulfillment to the
words: 'that as many of us as have received the Body and Blood of *Canon*
Thy Son by partaking of this altar, may be filled with every blessing *Christian*
and grace.' " *Worship*

The Gift-in-Return. Sacrifice, we recall, is essentially a method of
approach to God; hence, it is not an end in itself, but a means. So the
sacrificial banquet is not an end in itself, much less a separate act of
worship in itself, but a *means of participating* in the fruits and blessings
of the Sacrifice. Even when Holy Communion is carried a long way to
the sick, and at any hour of the day or night, this is merely an extraordinary manner of allowing them to share in the completed Sacrifice.
The very concept of Communion remains incomplete if it does not include
this relation to the Gift that has been offered to God. St. Paul used only
four terms to refer to the Holy Eucharist, "eating the Sacrifice," "sharing in the altar," "partaking of the Table of the Lord," and "eating the
Lord's Supper." As the natural complement of the Sacrifice, this sacri- I Cor. x,xi
ficial banquet is the divinely instituted channel through which God gives

man His Gift-in-Return. Thus, to assist at, and share in the Sacrifice, and then needlessly abstain from communicating (it is *always* possible to communicate spiritually), is like presenting a check for payment at the bank, and then walking away without waiting for the money.

Fuller Sharing in Christ-Life. Every aspect of this exalted subject merits our best attention, but none more than the *corporate meaning of Communion.* In Communion we are sacramentally united with the Person of Christ; but that sacramental union is transitory, even momentary. It is itself designed as a means toward something ulterior, the abiding spiritual fellowship of ourselves in Christ and of Him in us;

> He that eateth My Flesh
> and drinketh My Blood
> abideth in Me
> and I in him.

John vi,56

Food must be converted into living flesh and blood and sinew; it must become alive and part of ourselves. The Son of Man came that we might have life, and He communicates this life by causing us to eat His Flesh and drink His Blood, whereby He shares with men the life He has from the Father. Here one acquires *Christ-life* at its very wellspring and fountain:

John x,10

> As I live by the Father,
> so he that eateth Me,
> the same shall live by Me.

John vi,57

"Africans do well," said St. Augustine, "to call baptism by no other name than 'Salvation,' and the Sacrament of Christ's Body none other than 'Life.'" And this usage he himself more than once follows, as in this sermon on St. John's Gospel:

De Pecc. Mer. 1,24

> Let him who will eat, let him who will drink; let them hunger and thirst; they eat life, they drink life. This "eating" means to be nourished, but one is so nourished that that is not diminished whence you are nourished. The "drinking," what is it but "living"? Eat life, drink life, and you shall have life, and your life shall be whole and entire. Then shall it be, that the life force of each will be the Body and Blood of Christ.

Serm. cxxxi,1

Closer Bond with Fellow Christians. The first consequence of this vital union with Christ, in the order of importance, is this: the selfsame act which thus unites the Christian with Christ, and through Christ with

"IS CHRIST DIVIDED?"
asks Saint Paul.

*"We many are one body
for we all eat one Bread"* says Saint Paul.

God, equally unites him *with all other Christians,* for all are equally by the same token fellow table-guests of God. Fellowship with the physical Body of Christ means fellowship with the Mystical Body of Christ. The very same bond that links the individual with Christ, the Head, links him with the other members of Christ's Mystical Body. Communion is food for the soul of the individual Christian; no less is it the food for the building up of the Mystical Body:

> Because one is the Bread,
> one body are we the many,
> who partake of the one Bread.

I Cor. x,17; variant reading

S.T. III. Q. lxxiii, a.3

Ibid. lxxxii,a.9

"The total effect of this Sacrament," says St. Thomas, "is union with the Mystical Body. . . . The unity of the Mystical Body is the consequence of the real [physical] Body sacramentally received."

The thought of the bread made from numberless grains of wheat, and the wine pressed from countless grapes, *as symbolizing the living unity of Christians,* echoes through the whole of the early Christian literature. We shall limit ourselves here to one citation, the kernel of an Easter sermon by St. Augustine, preached to the "infants" baptized the previous night.

> When you were enrolled as catechumens [says St. Augustine], you were stored in the Christian granaries. Later, when you handed in your names as candidates for Baptism, you began to be ground by the millstones of fasting and exorcisms [in the Lenten exercises of the catechumenate]. Then ye came to the font, and were moistened and made one paste; and then the fire of the Holy Spirit coming upon you [in Confirmation], ye were baked and became the Lord's Bread. See what you have received. *See how this unity has been brought about,* and be of one accord, cherishing one another, holding to one faith, one hope, and love. . . . Thus, too, the wine was once in many grapes, but now is one. . . . Ye now dine at the Lord's Table, and ye there share in His Cup. We are there with you; *together* we eat, *together* we drink, for

Serm. ccxxix   we live *together.*

The highest function of the Christian life on earth is this harmonious activity of the Mystical Body of Christ: its last goal is the brotherhood of the sons of God in the homeland of heaven.

Frequent Communion, For Whom? "God grant that all the faithful," says Pius XII, "may willingly respond to these urgent invitations of the Church; that daily, if possible, they may share the divine

Sacrifice not only by a spiritual Communion, but by receiving the Blessed Sacrament, taking the Body of Jesus Christ, which has been offered for all to the eternal Father. Arouse in the hearts of those under your care, venerable brethren, an eager and almost insatiable hunger for Jesus Christ; as the result of your teaching let the altars be thronged with *children* and *adolescents,* offering themselves, their innocence, and their energetic enthusiasm to the divine Redeemer. Let *married people* come in their crowds, so that from the food they receive at the sacred Table they may derive the power to train their children to be like Jesus Christ and to love Him. Let *workers* be urged to receive the food that will effectively and unfailingly restore their strength and prepare an everlasting reward in heaven for their labors. Invite them all, *men and women, of every class and degree,* and compel them to come in; for this is the Bread of life of which they all stand in need. This is the only Bread the Church of Jesus Christ has at her disposal; a bread to satisfy all the longings of our souls, to unite them closely to Jesus Christ, to form 'one body' and one community of brethren of all those who sit at the same heavenly Table, so that breaking one Bread they may receive the medicine that gives immortality.' " *Luke xiv,23* *I Cor. x,17* *St. Ign. M., Ad Eph. 20* *Christian Worship*

Communion Rites Long Varied. Before reviewing in detail the text or rites of this part of Holy Mass, which might well be called "The Communion Service," it is well to point out a general peculiarity, in which it differs from the Canon, or even the Ante-Mass. The *present rites* were not definitely fixed, or imposed as obligatory, until *comparatively recent* times. It was only at the appearance in 1570 of the reformed edition of the Roman Mass Book requested by the Council of Trent, that this part of the Mass lost the freedom of local variation. Up to that time ceremonial usages, while following the same general lines throughout Latin Christendom, still differed widely in matters of detail. The prayers we now have, therefore, result from a final, selective adoption of elements old and new.

THE ORDINARY OF THE MASS: THIRD PART, SACRIFICIAL BANQUET

This little introductory formula to the Lord's Prayer is found in the writings of St. Jerome (4th cent.) (*Cont. Pelag.* III, 15).

Let us pray. Urged by our Saviour's bidding, and schooled by His divine ordinance, we make bold to say:

Lord's Prayer

We owe it to St. Gregory the Great that the preparation for Communion begins with the *Our Father* (PL. lxxvii,956). In that prayer of divine composition the first petition is for "our daily bread," a request which Origen, Tertullian, Cyprian and all subsequent tradition have applied to the needs of the spirit and only secondarily to those of the flesh. So it is of "the living Bread come down from Heaven" (John vi,51) that we are first concerned.

This whole section of the Mass, in immediate conjunction with the reception of Christ in Holy Communion, turns upon the theme of peace, and the conflict of evil against peace. Here we are asking, through our great and powerful intercessors, to be delivered from that which is opposed to our peace. That means the absence of sin (interior peace), and the absence of external disturbance. The path to peace, of course, is that of fellowship, of loving association with our fellow men. Here we are gathering the 'fruits' of our Offertory sacrifices.

Our Father, who art in heaven, hallowed be Thy name. Thy kingdom come, Thy will be done on earth as it is in heaven. Give us this day our daily bread. And forgive us our trespasses, as we forgive them that trespass against us. And lead us not into temptation: (Matt. vi,9–13; Luke xi,2–4)
R: But deliver us from evil.
P: (*silently*) Amen.
(Jewish)

Deliver us, we pray Thee, Lord, from every evil, past, present, and to come, and at the intercession of the blessed and glorious ever-virgin Mary, Mother of God, of Thy blessed Apostles, Peter and Paul, of Andrew, and of all the saints (*he crosses himself with the paten and kisses it*), be pleased to grant peace in our days, so that with the manifold help of Thy compassion we may be ever free from sin and safe from all disquiet. Through the same Jesus Christ, Thy Son (*breaking the Host*), who is God, living and reigning with Thee in the unity of the Holy Spirit.

P: (concluding aloud) World without end.
R: Amen.

(Roman)

Pax Domini

The breaking of the Bread, preparatory to distributing it, is made to subserve the peace-theme.

P: The peace of the Lord be always with you.
R: And with you.

(Jewish)

The unity of Christ's Sacrifice in time and place, and its single hallowing effect on all participants is, in a measure, expressed by this commingling of the Species.

Breaking the Host, he puts a particle into the Chalice, saying: May this mingling and hallowing of the Body and Blood of our Lord Jesus Christ be for us who receive it a source of eternal life. Amen.

(Frankish)

Agnus Dei

In Oriental Christianity, what we call the Host was often called simply "the Lamb" (cf. Acts viii,32,33). How natural, then, that they should think of the words of John the Baptist at this juncture (Isa. liii,7,8). It was a pope from the Orient who added this to our Mass.

He strikes his breast three times as he says aloud:
Lamb of God, who takest away the sins of the world (John i,29), have mercy on us.
Lamb of God, who takest away the sins of the world, have mercy on us.
Lamb of God, who takest away the sins of the world, give us peace.

(Greek)

Prayers before Communion

This prayer is now taken as referring primarily to Communion. Originally it referred to the general *kiss of peace*. Innocent III explained the people's kiss as a substitute for the reception of Communion! (*De Alt. Mys.* vi,5.)

Lord Jesus Christ, who didst say to Thy apostles: *I leave peace with you; it is My own peace I give you* (John xiv,27): look not upon my sins but upon the Church's faith, and deign to give her peace and unity in accordance with Thy will: Thou who art God, living and reigning for ever and ever. Amen.

(Frankish)

Kiss of Peace

The general kiss of peace, so frequently mentioned in the New Testament, was eloquent testimony that Catholics "did not offer their gift at the altar, until they had first been reconciled with their brethren" (Matt. v,23).

In this prayer and in the next, which are both more personal forms of preparation, we have enumerated most of the effects of the Eucharist. Thus we profess our belief that it:

cleanses from all sin,
unites recipient with Christ,
is a means of salvation,
is protection of body and soul,
frees one from all evil,
acts as shield against Satan,
preserves soul unto life everlasting,
will work damnation if unworthily received.

We might most profitably recall here the burning words of Trent on Communion as our bond of union:

"This holy Synod with true fatherly affection, admonishes, exhorts, begs and beseeches, through the bowels of the mercy of our God, that all and each of those who bear the Christian name, would now at length agree and be of one mind in this sign of unity, in this bond of charity, in this symbol of concord" (*Sess.* xiii).

After kissing the altar the celebrant gives the kiss, saying:
P: Peace be with you! (John xx,19.)
R: And with you.

Lord Jesus Christ, *Son of the living God* (Matt. xvi,18), who, by the Father's will and the co-operation of the Holy Spirit, didst by Thy death bring life to the world, deliver me by this most holy Body and Blood of Thine from all my sins and from every evil. Make me always cling to Thy commandments, and never allow me to be parted from Thee: who with the selfsame God the Father and the Holy Spirit art God, living and reigning for ever and ever. Amen.

(English)

Let not the partaking of Thy Body, Lord Jesus Christ, which I, unworthy as I am, make bold to receive, turn against me into judgment and damnation, but through Thy lovingkindness let it be for me a safeguard of mind and body, and in it let me find healing: Thou who art God, living and reigning with God the Father in the unity of the Holy Spirit, world without end. Amen.

(Spanish)

The Priest's Communion

These words of Psalm 115, here slightly modified, occur again.

With the Host in his hand he says:

Everyone recognizes that this aspiration applies to the recipient the sentiments of the noble Roman of Capharnaum.

Right after communicating, the priest is enjoined by the Missal "to remain for a little while meditating on the most Blessed Sacrament."

Perhaps at no place in the entire Mass does the sacred text more accurately reflect the psychological emotions of our day than these simple, stirring words. Yet they are words of David of three thousand years ago!

This form parallels that which accompanies the priest's reception of the Species of Bread.

I will take the Bread of Heaven, and will *call upon the name of the Lord* (Ps. cxv,13).
(Italian)
Striking his breast thrice, he says:
Lord, I am not worthy that Thou shouldst enter beneath my roof, but *say only the word,* and my soul *shall be healed* (Matt. viii,8).
(Italian)
Receiving the Host, he says:
The Body of our Lord Jesus Christ preserve my soul for everlasting life. Amen.
(Frankish)
Taking the Chalice, he says:
What return shall I make to the Lord for all that He has given me? I will take the chalice of salvation and invoke the name of the Lord (Ps. cxv,12,13). Praised be the Lord! When I invoke His name I am secure from my enemies.
(Italian)
Receiving the Blood of our Saviour, he says:
The Blood of our Lord Jesus Christ preserve my soul for everlasting life. Amen.
(Italian)

The People's Communion

There is a certain amount of repetition in these forms for the Communion of the people. Viewed strictly from the standpoint of unity, they are not really necessary, since the *Confiteor* at the beginning of the Mass could serve for people as well as for priest as preparatory to Communion.

The things contrasted in this short prayer, mouth and mind,

I confess to almighty God, etc.
Behold the Lamb of God, behold Him who takes away the sins of the world (John i,29). *Lord, I am not worthy that Thou shouldst enter beneath my roof, but say only the word, and my soul shall be healed* (Matt. viii,8). (*Thrice*)
(Frankish)

That which our mouths have taken, Lord, may we possess in purity of temporal gift and eternal remedy, remind us again that Catholicism must be *lived* to be effective.

The expressions in the first person singular would indicate that this form is neither very ancient, nor Roman. On investigation it turns out to be a Visigothic or medieval composition. The thought-content is about the same as in the foregoing form.

mind; and may the gift of the moment become for us an ever-lasting remedy.

(Frankish)

May Thy Body, Lord, which I have taken, and Thy Blood which I have drunk, cleave to every fibre of my being. Grant that no stain of sin be left in me, now that I am renewed by this pure and holy Sacrament: who livest and reignest world without end. Amen.

(Spanish)

Communion Anthem

The Communion Anthem is the refrain once sung over and over, between verses of a psalm, at the distribution of Communion. To come singing to Communion, and to recede singing from the celestial Repast may again be as common as it once was.

This is My Body, given up for you; this is the cup of the New Testament in My Blood, says the Lord: *do this whenever you drink it for a commemoration of Me* (I Cor. xi,24–25).

(Roman)

Postcommunion

The Roman form of public thanksgiving after Communion is that collect we call the Postcommunion. Here is where one can best find the Church's basic attitude toward the "fruits" of Communion. Such precision of form is used that only one thought is usually expressed. God is thanked for spiritual nourishment, for soul-health, for a sense of corporate unity. If all have been further incorporated into Christ, then they are "Concorporate" with each other!

P. The Lord be with you.
R: And with you.
P. Let us Pray. We pray Thee, Lord, that the divine victim which we have offered, and of which we have partaken, may endow us with new life and unite us to Thee by enduring bonds of love, so that we may bring forth everlasting fruit: Through our Lord Jesus Christ, Thy Son, who is God, living and reigning with Thee, in the unity of the Holy Spirit, for ever and ever.
R: Amen.

(Roman)

The Mass comes to a rapid ending now. The dismissal echoes a bidding of the Jewish synagogue service.

P: The Lord be with you.
R: And with you.
P: Go, this is the dismissal.
R: Thanks be to God.

(*Jewish*)

This prayer, now reckoned as part of the Mass, was originally written to supply the celebrant's private devotion with suitable thoughts as he left the altar. It can well afford us now a momentary examination on how worthily we have tried to take part in the celebration of the great Mysteries.

Bowing, the celebrant says, silently:

May the tribute of my homage be pleasing to Thee, Holy Trinity. Grant that the Sacrifice which I, unworthy as I am, have offered in the presence of Thy Majesty may be acceptable to Thee. Through Thy mercy may it bring forgiveness to me and to all for whom I have offered it: through Christ our Lord. Amen.

(*Frankish*)

The Blessing

How fruitful if we always recalled how Christ blessed the Apostles as He commissioned them His co-workers!

Blessing the people he says:
Almighty God bless you: the Father, the Son, and the Holy Ghost.
R: Amen.

(*Jewish*)

The Last Gospel

St. John's Summation. The sublime passage at the head of St. John's Gospel has been held in the highest esteem from the very dawn of Christianity. St. Augustine tells us of a Platonist philosopher (*De Civ. Dei*, x,29) who considered it "fit to be written in letters of gold and set up to be read in the highest places." Christians used to read this passage to comfort the sick, to strengthen the dying: in short, there were all sorts of practices

P: The Lord be with you.
R: And with you.
P: The beginning of the holy Gospel according to John:
R: Glory to Thee, Lord.

P: At the beginning of time the Word already was; and God had the Word abiding with Him, and the Word was God. It was through Him that all things came into being, and without Him came nothing that has come to be.

connected with it in the private devotional lives of the people. A local council at Seligenstadt, Germany, in 1022, complained of a superstitious desire of some to hear this Gospel every day (*Mansi*, xix,398). After priests had begun to recite this passage, as part of their thanksgiving as they left the altar, it was not long before popular devotion found a way to insist on its recital at the altar. The movement seems to have spread from Germany. The custom of reciting this Gospel passage at the end of Mass had become quite common, when it was finally sanctioned by the reformed Mass Book of 1570.

We may be very grateful for its introduction. A more beautiful *summary of the whole work of Redemption,* which the Mass itself renews, does not exist than those golden words:

> The Word was God. . . .
> In Him was life,
> and the life was the light of men. . . .
> The light shineth in the darkness,
> and the darkness hath not overcome
> it. . . .
> *To as many as receive Him,*
> *He gave power to become the children of God.* . . .

There is no better sentiment in which to come away from the Table of Sacrifice.

In Him there was life, and that life was the light of men. And the light shines in darkness, a darkness which was not able to master it.

A man appeared, sent from God, whose name was John. He came for a witness, to bear witness to the light, so that through him all men might learn to believe. He was not the Light; he was sent to bear witness to the light.

There is one who enlightens every soul born into the world; He was the true Light. He through whom the world was made, was in the world, and the world treated Him as a stranger. He came to what was His own, and they who were His own gave him no welcome.

But to all those who did welcome Him He empowered to become the children of God, all those who believe in His name; their birth came, not from human stock, nor from nature's will or man's, but from God. (*Here all genuflect.* And the Word was made flesh and came to dwell among us; and we had sight of His glory, glory such as belongs to the Father only-begotten Son, full of grace and truth.

R: Thanks be to God.

(*German*)

Fourteenth-Century Source Material

(One of the Church's most influential women was the unlettered Dominican nun, St. Catherine of Siena [died 1380]: In her dictated DIALOGUE *she speaks as in the person of God the Father.)*

I am their bed and board, and My sweet and loving Word is their food, for they eat the Bread of souls in the Person of this glorious Word, for I give Him to you, that is, His Flesh and Blood, wholly God and wholly man, in the Sacrament of the Altar, by My Goodness, while you are still pilgrims and wayfarers, so that you may not slacken your pace through faintness, or lose the memory of the benefits of the Blood shed for you with so much fire of love. . . . The Holy Spirit serves those souls, for He is the affection of My Charity which ministers to them both gifts and graces. This sweet Servant both fetches and carries to Me their painful but sweetly loving desires, and to them the fruit of the Divine Love, and of their labors, so that they feed on the sweetness of My Charity, so that, as thou seest, I am the Table, and My Son is the Food, and the Holy Spirit proceeding from Me, the Father, and from Him, the Son, is the server . . . (Ch. lxxviii).

By receiving this sacrament, she [the soul] dwells in Me and I in her, as the fish in the sea, and the sea in the fish — thus do I dwell in the soul, and the soul in Me — the sea pacific . . . (Ch. cxii).

I also say to thee, that as the Mystical Body of the Church now abounds in tribulation, so it shall one day all the more abound in sweetness and consolation, and this shall be its sweetness, the reform produced by good and holy pastors . . . (Ch. xii). [The clergy] are placed in the Mystical Body to feed your souls, administering to you the Blood in the Sacraments which you receive from the Church, their task being to extract the thorns of mortal sin, and to plant in you the seed of grace. They are My laborers in the vine of your soul, grafted upon the Vine of the holy Church. . . . I am the Husbandman who planted the true Vine of My only-begotten Son in the earth of your humanity, so that you, being branches joined to the Vine, may bring forth fruit (Ch. xxiii).

Laboring their own vine, they labor their neighbor's for they cannot labor one without the other. . . . Remember then that all rational creatures have their own vine indeed, but it is joined directly to their neighbor's vine, so closely that no one can do good or harm to his neighbor, without doing it to himself, and all of you together make up the universal

Vine, which is the whole congregation of Christians who are united in the Vine of the Mystical Body of holy Church, from which you draw your life. . . . See, then, that I have placed you all as husbandmen, and now again I invite you to labor, because the world is reaching an evil pass. . . . I wish you then to be true husbandmen, and with great zeal to cultivate souls in the Mystical Body of the Holy Church, and this I say because I wish to do mercy to the world (Ch. xxiv).

*   *   *

St. Catherine, acting as a peace envoy, was once set upon by a mob, but they refrained from killing her. "I am right in weeping," she wrote of it, "because I am not worthy that my blood . . . should wall up a stone in the Mystical Body of holy Church."

Topics for Further Discussion:

"The fact that the sacred function . . . has come to an end does not dispense one from making his thanksgiving." — *Pius XII.*

The precept to assist at Mass binds weekly, that to communicate, only yearly: how is such an anomaly to be explained?

"The Eucharist makes men men." — *G. K. Chesterton.*

Two Catholics who "cannot stand" each other, live in the same building and attend the same church. Show how the Eucharist can bridge their antipathy.

A workman out on strike finds himself next to his employer at the Holy Table: Suggest a suitable prayer of thanksgiving for each of them as *addressed to Christ just received into the heart of the other.*

Readings:

Pope Pius XII, *Christian Worship* (Encyclical Letter, Nov. 20, 1947); translated by Canon G. D. Smith (London: CTS, 1948); *passim.*

F. Boeser, *The Mass-Liturgy* (Milwaukee: Bruce, 1932); "The Communion," etc., pp. 100–141.

F. Cabrol, *The Mass, Its Doctrine, Its History, The Story of the Mass in Pen and Picture* (New York: Kenedy, no date); "Mass of the Faithful," pp. 27–36; *passim.*

I. Goma–C. J. Willinger, *The Eucharist and Christian Life* (Paterson: Guild Press, 1949), "As Sacrificial Communion," pp. 141–191.

A. Goodier, *The Inner Life of the Catholic* (New York: Longmans, Green, 1933); "The Sacrifice of the Mass," pp. 76–92.

C. Grimaud–J. F. Newcomb, *"My" Mass* (New York: Benziger, 1928); "Communion during Mass," pp. 211–230.

M. B. Hellriegel, *The Holy Sacrifice of the Mass* (St. Louis: Pio Decimo, 1944), "Communion," pp. 60–66.

J. Kramp, *The Liturgical Sacrifice of the New Law* (St. Louis: Herder, 1926); "The Sacrificial Repast," pp. 159–200.

—— *Live the Mass* (St. Paul: Cat. Guild, 1954), "The Sacrificial Banquet of Holy Communion," pp. 270–301.

E. Leen, *The True Vine and Its Branches* (New York: Kenedy, 1938); "The Principle of Unity in the Mystical Body," pp. 78–91.

G. Lefebvre, *Catholic Liturgy, Its Fundamental Principles* (St. Louis: Herder, 1937); "Holy Communion," pp. 77–92.

N. Maas, *The Treasure of the Liturgy* (Milwaukee: Bruce, 1932); "The Communion," pp. 98–114.

M. S. MacMahon, *Liturgical Catechism, The Church, The Mass, The Year* (Dublin: Gill and Son, 1926); "The Communion," pp. 130–170.

V. Michel, *The Liturgy of the Church* (New York: Macmillan, 1937); "The Sacrifice-Banquet," pp. 192–209.

T. H. Moore, *Beyond the Altar Rail* (New York: Fordham Univ., 1939); "The Sacrament of Oneness," pp. 77–88; "Beyond the Altar Rail," pp. 97–106.

P. Parsch–F. C. Eckhoff, *The Liturgy of the Mass* (St. Louis: Herder, 1936); pp. 257–318.

M. Perkins, *Speaking of How to Pray* (New York: Sheed and Ward, 1944); "For the Building Up of the Body of Christ," pp. 190–205.

J. de Puniet, *The Mass, Its Origin and History* (London: Burns, Oates and Washbourne, 1931); "The *Pater Noster* and the Fracture," etc., pp. 171–195.

J. Putz, *My Mass* (Westminster: Newman, 1949), "Act Three: the Communion," pp. 79–101.

M. Scheeben, *The Mysteries of Christianity* (St. Louis: Herder, 1946), "Mysterious Significance of Our Reception of the Eucharist," pp. 523–535.

F. J. Sheed, *Theology and Sanity* (New York: Sheed & Ward, 1946), "Idyll and Fact," pp. 393–399.

M. Zundel, *The Splendour of the Liturgy* (New York: Sheed and Ward, 1939); "The Liturgy of the Supper," pp. 211–253.

Chapter XV

LAY PARTICIPATION,
A PARISH AND A COSMIC FUNCTION

If thou bless [God] in spirit [alone],
how shall he that filleth the place of the layman
say the AMEN *to thy Eucharist?* (I Cor. xiv,16.)

THOSE who are now young may confidently expect to witness in our country a gradual but most profound change in the normal conduct of public worship, and especially of Mass-worship. Those privileged to travel in Europe may even now observe the same change in a much more advanced stage of realization. While with us this matter is still largely in the preparatory stage, and is far more in evidence in the school than in the church, the situation nonetheless definitely challenges those in training for the tasks of tomorrow. Both the goal of the movement and its peculiar urgency in the age in which we live are indicated in these words of Pope Pius XI: "A need of our times is social, or communal, praying, to be voiced under the guidance of the pastors, in enacting the solemn functions of the liturgy. This will be of the greatest assistance in combating the numberless evils which disturb the minds of the faithful, and weaken the faith in our age." The immediate objective of the new mode of public worship is an *active,* as opposed to the long prevalent *passive participation* on the part of the lay worshipers. The present-day necessity for this communal praying was more completely developed by the sovereign Pontiff in an audience to representatives of capital and labor the world over:

1929

> You are twice and thrice welcome, while from so many nations far and near you bring Us so worthy a representation of the workers of the entire world. You bring Us a representation actuated by that happy concord and union of employees and employers, and directors and workmen, which is necessary for the advantage of every one. . . .
> We have promised to give you something very short and which can put into three words all the eloquence of the *Rerum Novarum* [Leo

XIII's *Encyclical on the Condition of Labor*] and of the *Quadragesimo Anno* [*Encyclical on the Reconstruction of the Social Order on Christian Principles*], for whatever the Catholic program of Catholic direction, individual or social needs.

Here are the three words: prayer, action, sacrifice. . . .

Prayer in the first place. . . . Prayer, individual, domestic, public and social, *particularly social*. . . . That is what you need, you, the workers; you, the financiers: you, who underwrite all industry; you, who labor in justice and charity, in fraternity and in peaceful co-operation; in the practice of all virtues, in the respect of all rights and values, and particularly moral values.   1931

Thus, the harmonious co-operation of Catholics of all classes in applying Christian principles to our social ills is what is envisaged as the result of the new mode of communal worship. And since the whole movement is of today and tomorrow, we propose to build this chapter, also, for the most part, on that epochal letter on *Christian Worship,* given us by Pius XII in 1947, and cited at length in foregoing pages.

Liturgical Movement Appraised. "The end of the last century," says His Holiness, "and the beginning of the present have seen an unprecedented revival of liturgical studies, due in part to the admirable initiative of a number of individuals but especially to the devoted zeal of certain monasteries of the renowned Benedictine Order. The laudable and useful spirit of emulation thus aroused, not only in many parts of Europe but also overseas, has yielded a salutary harvest in the field of sacred study with a wider knowledge and deeper understanding of the liturgical rites of the Eastern and Western Church; and it has also proved beneficial to the spiritual life of many Christians. The venerable ceremonies of the Mass are in consequence better known and valued, the Sacraments more generally and frequently received, the prayers of the liturgy more devoutly appreciated; and the worship of the Eucharist has come to be seen for what it is: the source and center of Christian devotion. Another advantage of the movement has been to call special attention to the doctrine that all the faithful form one closely-knit body of which Christ is the Head, and that it is the duty of the Christian people to take its appointed part in the liturgy. . . . But although we are greatly consoled by the beneficial results of these studies, yet, in view of certain tendencies already apparent, our duty requires

The Oblation

us to give careful attention to this 'revival' and keep the movement free
from exaggeration and error."

Christian Worship

Lay Collaboration. "Let the faithful, then," we read in the same
instruction, "learn to appreciate the dignity to which they have been
raised by the Sacrament of Baptism. They must not be content to
take part in the Eucharistic Sacrifice by the general intention which
all the members of Christ and children of the Church ought to have;
they ought, also, in the spirit of the liturgy, to unite themselves closely
and of set purpose with the High Priest and His minister on earth,
especially at the moment of the consecration of the divine Victim, and
join with him in offering it as the solemn words are pronounced:
'Through Him, and with Him, and in Him, is given to Thee, God the
Father Almighty, in the unity of the Holy Spirit, all honor and glory

Canon

for ever and ever.' And as the people answer 'Amen,' let them not
forget to offer themselves and their anxieties, their sorrows, their troubles,

Christian Worship

their miseries and their needs, in union with their divine Head crucified."

Methods of Collaboration. "We therefore highly commend, says

the Pontiff, "the zeal which, to enable the faithful to take part more easily and more profitably in the Mass, seeks to adapt the Roman Missal to their use, so that they may join in prayer with the priest, using his very words and uttering the sentiments of the Church herself. We also approve the efforts of those who want to make the liturgy a sacred action in which, externally also, all who are present may really take a part. There are *several ways* in which this may be done: The whole congregation, always conformably with the rubrics, *may recite the responses* in an orderly manner; they may *sing chants* corresponding to the various parts of the Mass; or they may *do both*. Or, at High Mass, the people may sing the *responses* and join in the *liturgical chants*." *Christian Worship*

Unifying Purpose. "But these methods of taking part in the Sacrifice," the Pope reminds us, "are to be commended only when they are in exact conformity with the rules of the Church and rubrical instructions. Their chief purpose is to foster the devotion of the faithful and their close union with Christ and His visible minister, and to arouse in them those sentiments and attitudes of mind in which they must become like the High Priest of the New Testament." *Christian Worship*

Natural Limitations. The message continues: "At the same time, although such methods do externally indicate that the Mass being offered by the Mediator between God and men, is to be regarded as the act of the whole Mystical Body, it must be understood that they are by no means necessary to give it its public and communal character. . . . It is to be observed also that it is wrong and irrational, and betrays false assumptions, to exaggerate the importance of these incidental circumstances to the extent of saying that without them the Sacrifice cannot achieve its purpose."

I Tim. ii,5

Christian Worship

Missal-Manual. "You priests," said Pius XII, addressing Rome's Lenten preachers, March 13, 1943, "who at the altar use the Missal every day, the Church's greatest book of devotion, know what treasures of holy thoughts it contains, what sentiments of adoration, praise, and yearning for God it recalls and evokes. You are aware of the force with which it impells one towards things eternal, and what treasures of salutary counsels for the religious life of the individual which it affords." Yet His Holiness went on to deprecate too much insistence on Missal-use, as if such use were obligatory. A Belgian author, who signalized his sound psychology in promoting corporate worship, Émile Mersch, says in this connection: "It even happens that a too literal fidelity to the liturgy as, for example, the effort on the part of one of the faithful to read as quickly as the celebrant all the prayers of the holy Sacrifice, interferes with piety. Too much preoccupation with the letter stifles the spirit: in his endeavor to keep the markers of his missal moving, the individual forgets what is going on, and he no longer thinks of uniting himself with all his heart and with all his soul to God, and to all his brothers in Christ, Who is giving Himself. . . . The faithful should make use of the Missal, not in the manner of the priest who says the prayer for the group, but in the manner of the faithful . . . with a liberty which the official minister does not have." So Pius XII recalls limitations of feasibility.

As Feasibility Permits. "A great number of the faithful," the encyclical states, "are incapable of using the Roman Missal even in a vernacular translation; nor are all equal to a proper understanding of the rites and formulas of the liturgy. People differ so widely in character, temperament, and intelligence that it is impossible for them all to be affected in the same way by the same communal prayers, hymns and sacred actions. Besides, spiritual needs and dispositions are not the same in all, nor do these remain unchanged in the same individual at different times. Are we therefore to say — as we should have to say if such an opinion were true — that all these Christians are unable to take part in the Eucharistic Sacrifice or to enjoy its benefits? Of course they can, and in ways which many find easier: for example by devoutly meditating on the mysteries of Jesus Christ, or by performing other religious exercises and saying other prayers which, though different in form from the liturgical prayers, are by their nature in keeping with them." *Christian Worship*

Liturgical Apostolate, Diocesan Direction. "We therefore exhort you, venerable brethren," urges Pius XII, "in your diocese or within the sphere of your jurisdiction, to see that the way in which the faithful take part in the liturgy conforms to the rules laid down in the Missal and the instructions issued by the Congregation of Rites and in the Code of Canon Law; so that everything shall be conducted with due order and seemliness, and no private individual, even though he be a priest, be allowed to use the church for the purpose of arbitrary experiments. To this end we would desire that besides a Commission for the regulation of sacred music and art, each diocese should also have a Commission for promoting the liturgical apostolate, so that under your watchful care the instructions of the Apostolic See may in all things be observed." *Christian Worship*

Emerging From Silence. One of the 'new' features of this modern liturgical movement is that known as Dialogue Mass, or *Missa Recitata*. The two names suggest low Mass celebrations in which the responses ordinarily said by the servers are now said in common dialogue between priest and people, or in which (in addition to these responses) certain other parts are recited aloud by the congregation with the celebrant. A good deal of recent history in this matter is summed up by a writer in India: "The *missa dialogata* (in which the laity answer the celebrant in unison with the server) was at first treated by the Roman authorities with cautious reserve; for in 1921 it still appeared as a novelty. However, the Bishops were permitted to use their discretion. The practice spread rapidly, and in 1935 Rome declared it 'praiseworthy.' At present it is used all over the world; some Bishops have imposed it on the parishes, religious communities and schools of their dioceses. As a matter of fact, a completely silent liturgy is something abnormal; and certain prayers were originally meant to be said by the laity. But to introduce the *missa dialogata* permission must still be obtained from the bishop" (Putz).

Comformably With the Rubrics. "We also approve the efforts of those," runs a passage already quoted above from this encyclical, "who want to make the liturgy a sacred action in which, externally also, all who are present may really take a part. There are several ways in which this may be done: The whole congregation, always conformably with the rubrics, may recite the responses in an orderly manner." There are two forms of Dialogue Mass in widespread use. In the simpler form some or all of the server's responses are made in common. In the more elaborate form, besides these responses, *Gloria, Credo, Sanctus* and *Agnus Dei* are recited in unison with the celebrant. A third form of Dialogue Mass ('seminary type'), locally endorsed by bishops for special groups, admits the choral recitation also of Introit, Gradual, Offertory Anthem and Communion Anthem. Thus the Dialogue Mass offers scope for much variety in congregational effort.

Songs That Match the Mass. "The whole congregation, always conformably with the rubrics . . . may sing chants corresponding to the various parts of the Mass," says Pius XII in the encyclical. Conformity to the rubrics as to when hymns may be sung in the course of a low Mass is indicated in the regulation, prescriptive at Rome, directive elsewhere, and phrased as follows by Pius X's Vicar for the Diocese of Rome: "During low Masses motets may be sung, and the organ be played, as the rite permits. It is, however, important to observe the rule that *voices and organ shall only be heard during those times when the priest is not reciting aloud,* namely: besides the time of Preparation and Thanksgiving, from the *Offertory* to the *Preface,* from the *Sanctus* to the *Pater,* from the *Agnus Dei* to the *Post-Communion,* the singing being suspended if Holy Communion be given for the recital of the *Confiteor* and the *Ecce, Agnus Dei.*" Conformity is sought also as to *what songs* may be sung during the holy Sacrifice. Here the papal watchword is the common-sense one of relevance, "chants *corresponding to the various parts of the Mass.*" An unrelated song, however good in itself, is highly disruptive of the joint Mass-Action, which is to go forward with the greatest possible union of mind and spirit between Christ and celebrant and congregation. The combination of group-recitation and group-singing at a Dialogue Mass is expressly provided for in a papal passage cited above, "or they may do both."

Feb. 2, 1912

Like Roaring Ocean Waves. At low Mass, by relevant hymns, at High Mass, by chants in the ancient, the polyphonic or the modern modes, there should be *singing congregations.* "We also urge you, venerable brethren, to encourage congregational singing in our churches. Let it be well executed and with due decorum, for it does much to enliven and increase the devotion of the faithful. Let the loud and harmonious song of our people rise to heaven like the roar of the ocean waves, and let them give proof of their melodious voice that they are indeed of one heart and one soul, as befits those who are brethren and children of the same Father." But even though thus adorned with unifying prayer and song, "the Dialogue Mass cannot be substituted for the solemn High Mass; this, even though celebrated with only the sacred ministers present, has a dignity all its own by reason of the solemnity of its rites and the splendor of its ceremonies; although such splendor and solemnity are greatly enhanced if, as the Church earnestly desires, a large and devout congregation assists at it."

Ambrose, Hex, 3,5,23

Acts iv,32 Christian Worship

Christian Worship

Pius X, Pius XI, Pius XII — and Gregory. This large and devout congregation, "thronging our churches and altars, united as living members with their divine Head, . . . with Him and through Him celebrating the august Sacrifice" demands fit music for High Mass also. Nor are we left without direction: "We enjoin the strict observance of the clear and definite rules that have been laid down by this Apostolic See. Gregorian chant, which the Roman Church regards as a thing of her own, having received it as a legacy from ancient times and preserved it throughout the ages under her special guardianship, and which she also exhibits to the faithful as their property and even imposes in certain parts of the liturgy, not only adds to the seemliness and splendor of the celebration of the sacred Mysteries, but also contributes greatly to the faith and devotion of the congregation. In this connection our predecessors Pius X and Pius XI decreed — and we willingly confirm their decrees by our authority — that in seminaries and religious houses careful attention should be paid to Gregorian chant, and that, at least in the chief churches, the ancient *scholae cantorum* should be restored — which has in fact been done with great success in many places."

Nov. 22, 1902

Dec. 20, 1928

Christian Worship

Our Saviour Singing With His Children. A bold and beautiful harmony suffuses the papal directive as we read: "Moreover, 'to enable the faithful to take a more active part in the divine worship, let

Gregorian chant be restored to congregational use, so far as it is the function of the people to sing it. It is truly necessary that the faithful should not assist at the sacred rites as merely detached and silent on-lookers, but should be filled with a sense of the beauty of the liturgy and sing alternately with the priest or the *scholae cantorum* as the rubrics prescribe. If they do this, we shall no longer have the spectacle of a congregation either not joining at all in the Latin or vernacular prayers of the community, or else contributing only a feeble murmur.' If the congregation pays careful attention to the Mass, that nuptial song of His boundless love *which our Saviour sings together with His children* whom He redeemed with His sacred blood, then surely it cannot keep silent, for 'the lover always wants to sing,' and according to the ancient proverb, 'he who sings well prays twice.' In this the Church Militant, people and clergy together, unites her voice with the canticles of the Church Triumphant and the angelic choirs, to sing one magnificent and eternal song of praise to the Blessed Trinity. Do we not say in the Preface: 'With whom, we pray, bid our voices also be joined'?"

Pius XI, Div. Cultus

August., Serm. 336

Christian Worship

Reverent Polyphony and Current Compositions. But strong as is this triple papal endorsement of Gregorian plainsong, the Church has never disowned the religious character of reverent polyphony nor does she exclude the compositions of our own day and age. "But the desire to restore everything indiscriminately to its ancient condition, is neither wise nor praiseworthy. It would be wrong, for example . . . to condemn polyphonic chants, even though they conform to the regulations of the Apostolic See," the same context informs us, and, as for modern music we are reminded: "It cannot be maintained that modern music and singing are to be completely barred from Catholic worship. On the contrary, they are certainly to be admitted to our churches, as long as they are free from a worldly spirit or anything unbefitting the sacred character of the place and the liturgical functions, and as long as they are not inspired by a meaningless striving after extraordinary effects. Under these conditions they can contribute greatly to the splendor of the sacred rites, and help to elevate the minds of the hearers and foster their true devotion."

Christian Worship

Even Art Serves Corporate Function. Everything within the sacred temple subserves the sacred purpose of the Mystical Body worshiping God. "What we have said of music is to be said proportionately of the other fine arts, especially of architecture, sculpture and painting. Modern pictures and statues, whose style is more adapted to the materials in use at the present day, are not to be condemned out of hand. On condition that these modern arts steer a middle course between an excessive realism on the one hand and an exaggerated symbolism on the other, and take into account more the needs of the Christian community than the personal taste and judgment of the artist, they should be allowed full scope if with due reverence and honor they put themselves at the service of our churches and sacred rites. Thus modern art too may lend its voice to the magnificent chorus of praise which great geniuses throughout the ages have sung to the Catholic faith." *Christian Worship*

Union of Priest and People. In such a sacred setting, church and altar are kept in seemly condition, and "even in the absence of great riches or splendor, everything in the church, whether it be vestments or liturgical furniture, is kept clean and tidy, because it is dedicated to the majesty of God. . . . Everything that concerns the external conduct of divine worship has its importance; but the most necessary thing of all is that Christians should live the liturgical life, and nourish and foster the liturgical spirit in themselves. . . . Strive earnestly, also, by methods and means which your prudence judges most effective, to bring about a close union of mind and heart between the clergy and people; that the faithful may take so active a part in the liturgy that it becomes really a sacred action in which both priest — especially the priest in his own parish — and people join in offering to almighty God the worship that is His due." *Christian Worship*

As It Is in Heaven. "Let it be the first object of your zealous apostolate," the Pope says in conclusion, "that all the faithful should attend Mass; and that, in order that they may derive the greatest possible benefit from the Sacrifice, exhort them to take part in it in the legitimate ways that we have above described. The august Sacrifice of the altar is the principal act of divine worship, and must therefore be the source and centre of all Christian devotion. And let your apostolic zeal not be satisfied until you see the members of your flocks approaching Holy Communion in great numbers, for this is the Sacrament of devotion, the sign of unity, the bond of charity. . . . May we so take part in the sacred liturgy during our earthly exile that it may be a preparation and prophetic token of that heavenly liturgy wherein, as we trust, together with her who is the august Mother of *August., In Ioan. XIII*

Apoc. v,13
Christian
Worship
God and our most dear Mother, we shall one day sing: 'Blessing and honor and glory and power, through endless ages, to Him who sits on the throne and to the Lamb!' "

New Life, Old Forms. We read of 85,000 men at Mass in Paris: "Night fell on Paris, slowly, and everything was still steeped in light. In the immense stadium — the Parc du Prince — decorated with banners, 85,000 people were assembled — live wheat rippling on the stands, right up to the very top, and over the staircases and platforms. In the middle of the arena, on a high stage, a young speaker, like the celebrant of a new rite, stood up dressed in white. His voice, amplified by a hundred loud-speakers, filled all the air, and every now and again with a perfect rhythm of a powerful cadence, the immense crowd answered his prayer: for a prayer it was, a gigantic prayer, that was being lifted toward heaven by thousands and thousands of voices, and this imprecation left in one's heart the most powerful impression of unity. Each of us experienced to our very depths the joy of being an ant among these thousands of minute white spots in the night, and of breathing in unison with all.

"At the call of the voice, the workers rose. Each delegation of workers had brought the sign of its labor. And each, in a slow offering, came to place it on the central stage, thus constructing a strange and moving altar, showing with admirable symbolism the Christian identification of prayer and work. The miners from the north brought a lump of coal. Those from the east a piece of iron. The furniture-makers brought their plank of wood. There were others who brought stuffs and flowers. From the four points of the horizon the weavers approached the growing altar and, as they came, formed with four long strips of stretched linen a gigantic white cross on the green grass. Finally a slow procession crossed the length of the arena, bearing on many shoulders a cross ten meters long. They were the invalids and their nurses. For suffering is still richer in worth than effort.

"There followed a moment of inexpressible purity. Slowly, in the darkness that was lit up only by thousands of torches encircling the course, the cross was raised on the altar. It was white, clear, triumphant. Meanwhile, pure voices were raised in the poignant silence appealing for a superhuman blessing from her by whom the Saviour of mankind was born. At that moment no one could doubt that once again in history Christian France had rediscovered her mission, the same mission which was evoked in the nave of Notre Dame by the Cardinal Legate, speaking to all France."[5]

Summary. One of the most notable features of present-day Catholicism is a reform of public worship, in which passive participation is yielding to active participation in the conscious acting as a member of the Mystical Body, by the use of the missal, the Dialogue Mass, the chanted high Mass, and the frequent, even daily, participation in Mass with the integral crown of Communion.

I ~ te,   mis ~ sa est.
De ~ o   gra ~ ti ~ as.

Fifteenth-Century Source Material

(John Burckard, after years of service as papal master of ceremonies, published in 1502 an ORDER OF THE MASS *from which the rubrics now in force were largely drawn: provisions reflecting the Dialogue Mass that have passed into our Missal are italicized.)*

The Psalm, "Iudica . . ."

The celebrant: "Judge, me, O God . . ."

The server and those present say all or only the alternate verses, and *they respond to the other parts* as indicated below.

Confiteor

[After the celebrant has said the Confiteor], *the Supreme Pontiff,* a cardinal, a legate, a patriarch, and archbishop or a bishop, *and the server and those present,* kneeling, say: "Misereatur . . ."

Kyrie

The celebrant, standing at the center of the altar, with hands joined, says in the same tone of voice (that is, a tone loud enough so that all hearing him can *understand* what is said): "Kyrie, eleison . . ." *If the*

[5]By Daniel-Rops, *Colosseum,* Dec., 1937; pp. 218, 219: permission of Sheed and Ward.

server, or those present should not make the response, the celebrant himself says everything.

Receiving the Offerings

If there are any present who wish to make an offering, the celebrant
goes to the corner on the Epistle side. Standing with uncovered head
and with his left side toward the altar, he removes the maniple from his
left forearm, and holding it in his right hand, offers the extremity of it
to be kissed by the offerers, saying to each: "May your sacrifice be pleasing to God Almighty," or, "May you receive a hundredfold, and possess
life everlasting." After receiving the oblations, the celebrant replaces the
maniple on his left forearm, and returns to the center of the altar. . . .

After the Offertory

Then with hands joined before his breast and with downcast eyes, he
turns toward the people from right to left, and facing them says in a
somewhat louder voice: "Orate, fratres . . ." and continues in silence.

The server and the others present, kneeling, with uncovered heads,
answer, saying in a low tone, "Suscipiat Dominus . . ."

But should the server and the others present not answer, the celebrant
himself says the response in a low voice.

Topics for Further Discussion:

"Resolved, that our zeal be exerted, first, to effect a more active participation
of all the faithful in offering this divine Sacrifice; and secondly, to increase
among the faithful frequent and daily assistance at this same august Sacrifice."
— *Resolutions of Sixth National Eucharistic Congress,* Omaha, 1930.

In the light of the principle of active participation, criticize the current expression, "to hear Mass." What would you substitute for it?

The pedagogical principles, as aside from spiritual reasons, for active participation are these:

Activity is a better teacher than passivity.
An eye and an ear, a voice and a posture are together better than an ear.
External activity both releases and increases internal sentiments.
Joint external activity on the part of the group makes their worship a social
communal act, thus fostering unity.

Criticize the expression: "Good voices are the poorest material for plainsong
because they want to be heard individually."

Is Evelyn Underhill (non-Catholic) correct, when she writes (*Worship,* p
98): "If we have to choose between extreme cases it is better to stand up an
sing, 'Thine for ever, God of love,' surrounded by other Christians of all sort
and sizes, from the Mayor and Corporation to the Brownies and Cubs, than t

elude this bracing discipline and murmur the same sentiment in a nice, quiet corner of the church?"

"The recitation of the Rosary, morning prayers, acts of faith, etc., are *good things*. But it is a *better thing* for the people to join their voices with the server and the priest at the altar." — *Cardinal Archbishop Minoretti*, Genoa, 1933.

"Every effort that is made to bring the Catholic people really to participate in the liturgical worship of the Church is a service of inestimable value to the cause of Christ." — *Bishop E. V. O'Hara* (Great Falls, now Kansas City), 1936.

Readings:

Pope Pius XII, *Christian Worship* (Encyclical Letter, Nov. 20, 1947): translated by Canon G. D. Smith (London: CTS, 1948); *passim.*

Catholic Church Music, Legislation of Pius X, Benedict XV, and Pius XI (London: Burns, Oates and Washbourne, 1933); *passim.*

The Chant of the Church (Collegeville: Liturgical Press, 1930); "The Reform of the Church Music," Mrs. Justine B. Ward, pp. 3–22. Pamphlet.

W. Douglas, *Church Music in History and Practice* (New York: Scribner, 1937); "Foundation Principles of Church Music," pp. 3–30.

J. Fitzsimons–P. McGuire, *Restoring All Things* (New York: Sheed and Ward, 1938); G. Lefebvre, "Catholic Action and the Liturgy," pp. 16–50.

D. Hume, *Catholic Church Music* (New York: Dodd, Mead & Co., 1956); "The Voice of the Congregation," 84–93; *passim.*

J. Kearney, *The Meaning of the Mass* (London: Burns, Oates and Washbourne, 1936); "The Mass Is Our Sacrifice," pp. 128–166.

E. Mersch–D. F. Ryan, *Morality and the Mystical Body* (New York: Kenedy, 1939); "Prayers of Christians, Prayers of Members," pp. 114–137.

V. Michel, *The Liturgy of the Church* (New York: Macmillan, 1937); "The Liturgical Chant," pp. 316–340.

J. Putz, *My Mass* (Westminster: Newman, 1948); "Active Participation," pp. 134–143.

A. Robertson, *The Interpretation of Plainchant* (London: Oxford Press, 1937); "General Survey," pp. 1–9; *passim.*

R. R. Terry, *The Music of the Roman Rite* (London: Burns, Oates and Washbourne, 1931). Choirmaster's manual.

E. Vitry, "Eucharistic Dynamism in the Parish," *The Sacramental Way* (New York: Sheed & Ward, 1948), pp. 212–222.

Pocket Manuals:

Monks of St. John's Abbey, *Parish Kyriale* (Collegeville: Liturgical Press, 1935).

Mass of the Angels (Collegeville: Liturgical Press, 1938).

Chapter XVI

PRAYING WITH CHRIST

> *In psalms, hymns, and spiritual canticles*
> *sing . . . to God by His grace* (Col. iii,16).

THE paramount position of sacrifice in worship has been consistently stressed in these pages. Thus far nothing has been said about the worship of corporate prayer. Obviously, since sacrifice is the crowning act of corporate prayer, a public prayer-in-action, as it were, it necessarily rests upon a broad and deep foundation of corporate prayer. In the realm of Christian worship the Divine Sacrifice of the Mass is as a sun, around which daily revolve, like so many planets, the seven Hour Prayers of the day and the three Prayer Watches of the night. Besides these regular satellites in our worship of prayer, there are stars of all magnitudes and orbits, the innumerable and widely varying services held in the churches throughout the year. These services are public, and consequently fairly well known to us, but with the unseen, systematic prayer-world of the Divine Office, as it is called, it is highly desirable to make fuller acquaintance. "The 'Divine Office,'" says Pope Pius XII, "is the prayer of the Mystical Body of Jesus Christ, offered to God in the name of all Christians and for their benefit, since it is recited by priests, by other ministers of the Church, and by religious, who are officially appointed by the Church to that function. . . . The Word of God, when He assumed a human nature, introduced into this land of exile the hymn that in heaven is sung throughout all ages. He unites the whole community of mankind with Himself and associates it with Him in singing this divine canticle of praise."

Christian Worship

Mass in Cycle of Prayer. Besides the religious, men and women, who perform the Office publicly in choir, *all priests,* as everyone knows, *recite the Office* privately every day, just as they are privileged to offer the Sacrifice daily. In this private recitation of the Office it is not easy for the laity to see how the *Mass has daily a definite position* in the prayer cycle, of which it forms the great climax. Where Christians have the opportunity to assist at the Office rendered in public, they notice how the Mass occurs now after this Hour, and now after that, according to the rules as fixed as the phases of the moon.

Evening to Evening. As a rule, our *prayer-day begins at sundown,* when the Office called Vespers, or Evensong, inaugurates the worship of the day. Somewhat later, at nightfall, there is the Office called Compline, short prayers said before retiring to rest. To pray during the quiet of the night is another one of those natural promptings of the religious impulse, and was found widely among the pagan and Jewish religions of the past. It will be recalled that the early Christians held such nocturnal services for prayer and instruction, to which the Sacrifice might or might not be added. These ancient vigils, as they were called, live on in the three Night Watches of our office of *Matins,* which is now followed directly by Mass only once in the year. The midnight Mass of Christmas canonically follows immediately after Matins. On all other days this Office is followed by the joyous service of praise called *Lauds,* "which hail the rising sun as the image of Christ triumphant." When certain Masses of Requiem are celebrated, they follow upon the next Hour, called *Prime.* On all Sundays and feast days of higher rank, technically known as doubles and semidoubles, Mass follows upon the office of *Terce;* while on those of lower rank, known as simples, Mass comes after the hour of *Sext.* On penitential days, as in Lent, it is only after *None* that the Sacrifice is offered. In many ways Mass and Office are interrelated. Here let mention be made of only three: the Office of the day reviews the life of the saint in whose honor Mass is being celebrated; it provides a homily on the Gospel of the Mass; and it re-echoes hour after hour the Collect of the Mass.

These "Hours" Mostly Jewish. Although many details of the origin of the Divine Office are lost in the impenetrable mists of history, there seems no reason for doubting that the framework of the Christian *prayer-day,* as sketched above, is part of our *inheritance* from Israel. That the Night Watches, or Matins, are continuations of the nocturnal vigils connected with the Mass of the Catechumens, itself an adaptation of Synagogue worship, seems quite clear. Evensong and the morning Lauds are mentioned even in the meager records of the first century, and they would be natural continuations of the domestic prayers of the Jews. Even the custom of praying at the third, and sixth, and ninth hours has direct parallels in Israelitic worship. At those hours in the morning and afternoon sacrifices were offered at Jerusalem as trumpets sounded the call to prayer. This, it should be noted, was private prayer, but performed at these times. It was while the Apostles were in prayer at the *third* hour that the Pentecostal Spirit descended upon them; it was while Peter prayed at the *sixth* hour that he received the important vision about admitting Gentiles to the Brotherhood; and as Peter and John entered the Temple precincts to pray at the *ninth* hour they cured the man born lame.

Acts ii,15

Acts x,9

Acts iii,1

Tradition Becomes Christian. The first-century treatise, *The Teaching of the Twelve Apostles,* is silent as to the specific hours of prayer during the day, merely bidding all recite the *Our Father* three times daily. In the next century, Tertullian speaks of the third, sixth, and ninth hours as set times of private prayer. In the early third century, Hippolytus, in the *Apostolic Tradition,* shows how the Romans observed these prayer-pauses throughout the day:

viii,3

> If thou art in thy house, pray at the third hour, and glorify God; and if elsewhere, and that hour be come, pray in thy heart to God; because at that hour they stripped Christ and nailed Him to the Cross. . . . Pray at the sixth hour, for at that hour . . . the day was divided and darkness came; and they shall pray at that hour a strong prayer. . . . And at the ninth hour he shall be long in prayer with glorifying. . . .

Other prayers mentioned by Hippolytus for the faithful were at midnight, on rising in the morning, and at the supper hour. All these were private, except the last named, which was social, and linked with an evening meal in common at the beautiful service known as the Lighting of the Lamps.

Roman Office Popular throughout West. Thus, even from Apostolic times the Christians' daily prayers, whether public or private, were arranged in a rhythmic sequence extending throughout the day and night. Now, it was not long before there were numberless persons of both sexes consecrated by vow to the special service of God, and so this whole realm of prayer was speedily *organized into public, social*

Sext
Terce
None
Prime
Vespers
Lauds
Compline
Three Nocturns of Matins

Day unto day
declareth the message.
Night unto night
revealeth the knowledge.
(Ps. XVIII - 3)

worship. The full complement of the seven Day-Hours, as we have them now, and the three Night Watches, existed in approximately their present modes as early as the fifth century. How this worship of social prayer spread throughout the West with the expanding frontiers of Christendom is the history of the illustrious Benedictine Order, whose founder had written in his *Rule*:

Ps. cxviii,164   The prophet says: "Seven times a day do I praise Thee"; and we observe this sacred number in the seven services of the day; that is, matins, prime, terce, sext, nones, vespers, and completorium; for the hours of the daytime are plainly intended here, since the same prophet provides for the nocturnal vigils,[1] when he says in another place: "At *Ps. cxviii,62*   midnight I will rise and give thanks unto Thee." We should therefore praise the Creator for His righteous judgments at the aforesaid times: matins, prime, terce, sext, nones, vespers, and completorium; and at night we should rise and give thanks unto Him.

"Men of One Book." As soon as one asks *what* prayers were said by the primitive Church, or the early Middle Ages, the answer is everywhere and always "The Psalms: the Psalms and Christian hymns." Psalm means in the Greek a *chant,* and the word was always used to designate the collection of one hundred and fifty prayer-poems of Holy Writ. These had been the substance of both private and public prayer among the Jews, and, as such, were used by Christ and the Apostles from childhood. Naturally they passed into the prayer-life of the Church, and they remain to this day the major portion of the Church's fixed prayer. Since the great break with tradition at the time of the Reformation, the laity of today can hardly be said to know the Psalms. And yet as far as fixed formulas of prayer were concerned, *Christians* for fifteen hundred years *were men of this one book.*

Prayer-Songs Inspired. "The psalms, as everyone knows," says Pius XII, "form the main body of the Divine Office. They embrace the whole day and sanctify it. Speaking of the psalms as distributed in the Divine Office in his day, Cassiodore writes: 'Joyfully in the morning they greet the coming day, they dedicate our *first* hour, hallow the *third,* cheer the *sixth* in the breaking of the bread; at the *ninth* they break our *Explic. in*   fast, they close the end of our day, and, as night comes on, they protect *Psalt.*   our souls from darkness.'

One God, one hope. "They recall to our minds," continues the Pontiff in the same context, "the truths that God revealed to His chosen people, truths terrible sometimes, sometimes full of the greatest consolation. They arouse and foster the hope of the promised Deliverer, which

---

[1]What Benedict called vigils are now called Matins, and what he designated as Matins we now call Lauds.

in ancient times was kept alive by the singing of psalms at home or in the solemnity of the temple; in prophecy they foretell marvelously the glory of Jesus Christ and His supreme and eternal power; His coming upon this earth of our exile and His humiliation; His kingly dignity and His priestly power; His labors for men's good and the shedding of His blood for our redemption. With equal effect they give expression to all the sentiments of our hearts: joy, sorrow, hope, fear, utter confidence in God and love for Him, and our mystical ascent to His dwelling-place."

Christian Worship

Sung in Fields and Vineyards. St. Ambrose said of the Psalms that they are suitable for all, and loved by pious souls in every age. "We find in them," he goes on, "instruction as well as beautiful poetry. We *sing them to enjoy the latter* and we study them to profit by the former." He here touches a note well worth our attention. The Christians sang the Psalms for very enjoyment. Even apart from the public assemblies, in which the Psalms were sung together, these prayer-songs rose spontaneously to the lips. St. Paula, a Roman matron and friend of St. Jerome, related how in her day, "The farmer at his plough used to sing the *alleluia;* the sweating harvester lightened his labor with the singing of the Psalms; the vintager wielding the curved pruning knife chanted some snatch of Davidic poetry." David's measures echoing over hill and dale filled the pagans with wonder, and Eusebius, the historian of the persecutions, relates how this holy enthusiasm of the Christians brought the pagans in shoals to their assemblies. Here the beauty of the Christian rites further won them.

Ep. 46,12

H. E. X,iii

Sung at Common Worship. The part played by these chants in the conversion of Augustine has been told a thousand times. In the period of indecision, prior to his surrender to grace, Augustine could sit unmoved even through sermons of St. Ambrose pleading in such words:

In Christ, then, are all things. Christ is everything to us. If thou hast wounds to be healed, He is thy *physician;* if fever scorcheth thee, He is a *fountain;* wouldst thou punish evil doing, He is *justice;* dost thou need help, He is *strength;* dost thou fear death, He is *life;* dost thou long for Heaven, He is the *way;* dost thou flee from darkness, He is *light;* dost thou hunger, He is *food.*

De Virg. I,6

But when the people rose to chant the Psalms, Augustine's stubborn heart melted quite within him. Looking back upon that time even years afterward, he would write in his *Confessions:*

How I have cried, my God, over the hymns and canticles when the sweet sound of the music of Thy Church thrilled my soul! As the music flowed into my ears, and Thy truth trickled into my heart, the tide of devotion swelled high within me, and the tears ran down, and there was gladness in those tears.

IX,6

Testimony of Newman. The Office, too, was a milestone in the conversion of a modern Augustine, Cardinal Newman. He narrates how profoundly moved he was, while still an Anglican, on making the acquaintance of "that most wonderful and most attractive monument of the devotion of the saints." Elsewhere, and still an Anglican, he wrote:

Apol. II

There is so much excellence and beauty in the services of the Breviary, that, were it skillfully set before the Protestant by Roman controversialists as the book of devotions received in their Communion, it would undoubtedly raise a prejudice in their favor.

Tracts, 75

The Holy Church in Prayer. It would be pleasantly instructive here to open one or other of the four volumes of the breviary and quote this Psalm or that, or read together some of the hymns ("private psalms" they were once called) of Ambrose, or Damasus, or Sedulius, or Fortunatus, or Gregory the Great among the ancients, Thomas Aquinas among the Schoolmen, or Robert Bellarmine among the moderns. But instead, let us turn to the *social aspect of this worship of prayer.* The priest with breviary in hand, the monks and nuns in choir, are the voice of the Church at prayer. Pope Pius XI took occasion to describe it thus:

What a spectacle for Heaven and earth is not the Church in prayer! For centuries without interruption, from midnight to midnight, is repeated on earth the divine psalmody of the inspired canticles; there is no hour of the day that is not hallowed by its special liturgy; there is no stage of life great or small that has not its part in the thanksgiving, praise, supplication, and reparation of the common prayer of the Mystical Body of Christ, which is the Church.

Ency. on Reparation, 1932

In lines, every word of which is charged with historic significance, the same supreme pontiff sketched the incomparable teaching role of this corporate prayer:

These general supplications . . . were at one time made both day and night in the presence of great bodies of the faithful. And it is remarkable how much from earliest times those noble songs . . .

contributed to fostering piety among the people. For especially in the ancient basilicas, where bishop, clergy, and people *joined alternately* in singing the divine praises, liturgical chants were of no little avail, as history records, in *winning a great many of the barbarians* to Christian worship and civilization. In the Christian temples the opponents of Catholicity *learned* more deeply the *dogma of the communion of saints;* wherefore the Emperor Valens, an Arian, before the majesty of the divine mystery as performed by St. Basil, was seized with strange stupor and fainted; and at Milan St. Ambrose was charged by heretics with *charming the multitudes by his liturgical chants;* and Augustine, greatly impressed by these, decided to embrace the faith of Christ. Later on, into the churches, where *all the citizens formed* themselves into *a great choir,* came *artisans, builders, sculptors,* and even *students of letters* who *were embued through the liturgy* with that knowledge of theological matters, which today shines forth so clearly and which we admire in those remarkable monuments of the Middle Ages. *On Promoting the Liturgy, 1928*

Morning and Evening Service. "In ancient times the faithful used to attend the recitation of the Office in greater numbers; but this custom has gradually died out and now, as we have said," the Pope speaks again, "its recitation is the *duty* only of the clergy and religious. The law, therefore, lays no obligation upon the laity in this matter; but it is *greatly to be desired* that they should take part in the recitation or singing of Vespers or Compline[2] on Sundays and feast days in their own parish churches. We therefore urge you and your flocks, venerable brethren, to see that this pious custom does not lapse, or, in cases where it has fallen into disuse, to revive it where possible. And the practice will be attended with greater fruit if the evening hours are sung, not only with proper dignity and decorum, but also in such a manner as, by various means, to arouse the devotion of the faithful. . . .

Let Everyone Do His Best. "Sundays and holydays of obligation," further urges Christ's Vicar, "are to be set aside and consecrated to the things of God: to the worship of God and the heavenly nourishment of the soul. And although the Church commands us only to abstain from servile work and attend Mass, and imposes no command in regard to evening worship, yet she earnestly desires that we should do more than is actually of obligation; indeed more is required by the need which we all have to propitiate God and obtain His benefits. . . . Everybody should go to church, to learn Christian doctrine, to receive the Benedic-

---

[2] *"horarias illas preces. . . quae. . . sub vesperum habeantur."*

tion of the Blessed Sacrament, and so obtain heavenly help against the adversities of this life. Let everyone do his best to learn by heart the formulas that are sung at the evening prayer, and let their meaning become deeply impressed upon their hearts."

*Christian
Worship*

Christ Praying for Us. There is a further consideration in the social aspect of this Christian prayer. The Divine Office is not only the voice of the Church on earth, but of the Church in heaven, *the voice of the Sole-Begotten,* in whom the Father is well pleased, adoring, praising, interceding, and making amends before the Most High for Himself-in-us and for us-in-Himself. Thinking of this endless mediation of Christ, St. Augustine, in commenting on the Eighty-Fifth Psalm, penned one of his most beautiful pages. It deserves quotation at length.

> No greater gift could God possibly bestow upon mankind than the gift of His Word by whom He made all things, constituting Him their Head, and conforming them with Him as members, so that He should be at once Son of God and Son of Man, one God with the Father, one Man with men.

> Thus when we address God in prayer we do not separate His Son from Him; and when the Body of the Son (the Church) prays, it does not separate itself from its Head; and He Himself becomes the *Saviour of His Body,* our Lord Jesus Christ, the Son of God, who prays for us, and prays in us, and is prayed to by us; He prays for us as our Priest; He prays in us as our Head; He is prayed to by us as our God. Let us then recognize our utterances in Him, and His utterance in us. . . .

Eph. v,23

> Let our mind, however, rouse itself, and be awake in its faith, and see that He whom it was contemplating just now *in the form of God,* has also taken *the form of a servant and humbled Himself,* and hanging on the Cross has willed to make His own those words of the Psalmist, *My God, My God, why has Thou forsaken Me?* He is prayed to, therefore, in the form of God; He prays in the form of a servant; there as Creator, here as the created, assuming without change the created nature that He was to change, and making us one man with Himself, Head and Body.

Phil. ii,7,8

Ps. xxi,2

> We pray, then, to Him, through Him, in Him; we speak with Him, and He speaks with us: we speak in Him, and He speaks in us the prayer of this Psalm, which is entitled *A prayer of David,* because our Lord according to the flesh is the son of David, while according to His Godhead He is the Lord of David. . . .

> Let none then, when he hears the words of this Psalm, say, "It is not Christ that speaks," or again, "It is not I that speak." Nay, if he

recognizes himself in the Body of Christ, let him say both *"Christ speaks and I speak."*

Speaking with Christ. This joint speaking to God of Christ and Christians goes on whether we advert to it or not. But it is in keeping with the growing consciousness of the Mystical Body and all it connotes, that the *laity are* nowadays *learning* to speak in the Church's Hour-Prayers with the speaking Christ. The movement, thus far, is not visible in any large way in America, but even now it becomes commoner year by year for the faithful to assist at Vespers and *to make their own* the Hour-Prayers of *Prime* and *Compline.* By way of illustrating a page from this great prayer book of the ages, Compline for Sundays is set out below. The prayer is not very different now from what it was fifteen hundred years ago.

COMPLINE FOR SUNDAYS

Pray, Father, bless us.
Pr. May the Lord Almighty grant us a quiet night and a perfect end.
Ch. Amen.

Short Lesson

Brethren, be ye sober and watch. Your adversary the devil goeth about like a roaring lion, seeking whom he may devour. Whom withstand ye, steadfast in the faith. And do Thou, O Lord, have mercy on us.   I Pet. v,8,9
Ch. Thanks be to God.
Pr. Our help is in the Name of the Lord,
Ch. Who made heaven and earth.
Our Father, *silently.*

After the Our Father, the Priest says the "Confiteor" and the congregation answers:

Ch. May the Almighty God have mercy on you, and forgive you your sins, and bring you to everlasting life.
Pr. Amen.

The congregation then makes the same confession:

Ch. I confess to Almighty God, to blessed Mary ever virgin, to blessed Michael the Archangel, to blessed John the Baptist, to the holy Apostles Peter and Paul, and to all the saints, and to you, father, that I have sinned exceedingly, by thought, word and act, *through my fault, through my fault, through my most grievous fault.* Therefore I beseech the blessed Mary ever virgin, blessed Michael the Archangel, blessed John the Baptist, the holy Apostles Peter and Paul, and all the saints, and you, father, to pray to the Lord our God for me.

The Priest answers:

May Almighty God have mercy on you and forgive you your sins and bring you to everlasting life.
Ch. Amen.
Pr. May the Almighty and Merciful Lord grant you forgiveness, absolution, and remission of your sins.
Ch. Amen.
Pr. Convert us, O Lord of our salvation.
Ch. And turn away Thine anger from us.
Pr. O Lord, make speed to help me.
Ch. O Lord, make haste to succor me.
Glory be to the Father, and to the Son, and to the Holy Ghost.
As it was in the beginning, is now, and ever shall be. World without end.
Amen.
Antiphon: Have mercy.

Psalm IV

When I call on Him, my just God heareth me.
When I was straitened, Thou didst set me at large,
Be gracious to me, and hear my prayer.

Ye children of men, how long will ye be of hardened heart?
Why love ye the futile; and seek after the false?

Know ye that the Lord hath wondrously favored His worshiper.
The Lord doth hear me when I invoke Him.

Be angry [with me, if ye will]; but sin not.
What ye plan in your hearts repent of on your couches.

Offer a due sacrifice, and put your trust in the Lord.

Many are they who say: Who will give us to see good fortune?
Shown forth upon us is the light of Thy face, O Lord.
Thou givest joy to my heart,

Greater than doth the produce of corn and wine and oil, when these
abound.

In peace I will lay me down, and sleep forthwith.
For Thou, O Lord, makest me abide in calm security.

Glory be to the Father.

Psalm XC

He that dwelleth in the shelter of the Most High,
He that abideth in the shadow of Saddai,
Saith to the Lord: My protector art Thou,
My refuge, my God in whom I trust.

For He rescueth thee from the hunter's snare,
And from the word that destroyeth:
With His pinions He shieldeth thee;
Under His wings thou art secure;
His truth guardeth thee like a shield.
Thou shalt not fear the terrors of night,
Nor the arrow that flieth by day
Nor the plague that creepeth abroad in the darkness,
Nor the demon's attack at the noontide.
If thousands fall at thy right hand,
Yet will [the evil] not reach unto thee;
But with thine eyes thou shalt see,
Shalt see the doom meted out to sinners.

For Thou, O Lord, art my refuge.

Thou hast chosen the Most High as thy refuge:
No evil shall come unto thee;
No plague shall draw nigh to thy tent;
For to His angels He hath given thee in trust
To keep thee in all thy ways:
In their hands they shall bear thee up,
Lest thou dash thy foot 'gainst a stone.
On snakes and adders thou shalt tread,
The lion and the dragon thou shalt trample on.

Because he trusted in Me I will help him;
I will guard him, for he knoweth My Name:

He calleth to Me, and I hear him;
In time of need I am with him;
I rescue him and make him great;
With fullness of days I will sate him;
I will make him see My salvation.

Glory be to the Father.

Psalm CXXXIII

Praise ye the name of the Lord,
    All ye servants of the Lord,
    Ye who stand in the House of the Lord,
In the courts of the House of our God!

In the night raise your hands towards the Sanctuary,
    And praise ye the Lord.

"May the Lord bless thee from Sion,
    He who made heaven and earth!"

Glory be to the Father.
    Antiphon: Have mercy on me, O Lord, and grant my prayer.

Hymn

Now that the daylight fades away,
    By all Thy grace and love,
Thee, Maker of the world, we pray
    To watch our bed above.

Let dreams depart and phantoms fly,
    The offspring of the night,
Keep us, like shrines, beneath Thine eye,
    Pure in our foe's despite.

This grace on Thy redeemed confer,
    Father, co-equal Son,
And Holy Ghost, the Comforter,
    Eternal Three in One.
                Amen.[2]

---

[2]Translation by J. H. Newman.

Little Chapter

Thou art in the midst of us, O Lord, and over us Thy Holy Name is called: do not desert us, O Lord, our God.   Jer. xiv,9

Ch. Thanks be to God.

V. Into Thy hands, O Lord, I commend my spirit.

R. Into Thy hands, O Lord, I commend my spirit.

V. Thou hast redeemed us, O Lord, the God of truth.

R. I commend my spirit.

V. Glory be to the Father, and to the Son, and to the Holy Ghost.

R. Into Thy hands, O Lord, I commend my spirit.

Antiphon: Keep us safe.

The Song of Simeon   Luke ii,29–32

Now dost Thou dismiss Thy servant, O Lord, according to Thy word
    in peace:
For mine eyes have seen Thy Salvation,
That Thou hast prepared before the face of all peoples,
To be a Light for the enlightening of the Gentiles, and to the glory of
    Thy people, Israel.
Glory be to the Father.

Antiphon: Keep us safe, O Lord, while we wake, and guard us while we sleep; that our waking be with Christ, and our repose in peace.

Pr. The Lord be with you.

Ch. And with thy spirit.

Let Us Pray

Visit, we beseech Thee, O Lord, this dwelling place, and drive far from it all the deceits of the Enemy: let Thy Holy Angels dwell herein to keep us in peace, and may Thy blessing be ever upon us. Through Jesus Christ our Lord, who with Thee in the unity of the Holy Ghost liveth and reigneth God, world without end.

Ch. Amen.

Pr. The Lord be with you.

Ch. And with thy spirit.

Pr. Let us bless the Lord.

Ch. Thanks be to God.

The Blessing

May the Almighty and Merciful Lord bless and guard us, the Father, the Son, and the Holy Spirit.

Ch. Amen.

At the end of Compline is sung one of the great hymns in honor of our Lady, according to the season of the year. From Trinity Sunday to Advent is sung:

Hail, holy Queen, Mother of mercy, our life, our sweetness and our hope. To thee do we cry, poor banished children of Eve. To thee do we send up our sighs, mourning and weeping in this valley of tears. Turn then, most gracious Advocate, thine eyes of mercy toward us, and after this our exile, show unto us the blessed fruit of thy womb, Jesus. O clement, O loving, O sweet Virgin Mary.

V. Pray for us, O holy Mother of God;

R. That we may be made worthy of the promises of Christ.

Let Us Pray

Almighty, everlasting God, who with the cooperation of the Holy Ghost, didst prepare the body and the soul of the glorious Virgin Mary to become a habitation meet for Thy Son; grant that, as we rejoice in her commemoration, we may, by her loving intercession, be delivered from present evils and from everlasting death. Through the same Christ our Lord. Amen.

Last of all is said:

V. May the divine assistance remain always with us.

R. Amen.

And the *Our Father,* the *Hail Mary,* and the *Creed,* said silently.

Summary. Besides the worship of sacrifice, the Church through certain designated members, performs an unceasing office of prayer, wherein through the divinely inspired poetry of the Psalms and hymns and other sacred writings, she voices the praise, adoration, and reverence of the Divine Majesty. This prayer is distributed over the seven Day-Hours and three Night Watches. Its importance lies in the fact that it is the prayer of the whole Church, the prayer, therefore, of Christ praying with and for His members. An encouraging sign of our times is the growing interest of the laity in the Divine Office, the *Opus Dei.*

Sixteenth-Century Source Material

(The Divine Office, when attacked by the heresiarchs of the sixteenth century, was eloquently defended by St. Robert Bellarmine in his monumental BOOK OF THE CONTROVERSIES. *He says in part.)*

These prayers and praises are called the Divine Office, since in them is contained our duty toward God, to pray to and to praise whom is the office of Christians, and especially of those who are called clerics and monks. Thus God says by Isaias:

My house shall be called the house of prayer for all the nations.   lvi,7

This is to be taken, not primarily of the material structure, that is, the temples and oratories, but especially of the mystical dwelling-place of God, which is ourselves. For herein lies the difference between Christians and all other peoples: the latter, ignorant of original sin and the corruption and weakness of human nature, trust to their own industry and efforts, whereas Christians rely in all things on the divine assistance, have recourse to God in prayer, and implore His aid and mercy, so that the Church cannot be more briefly defined than as the house of prayer. Although the office of praying by way of petition is something passing, and will not last longer than man's [earthly] pilgrimage, the office of praising God will last forever, according to the words of the Psalmist:

Blessed are they that dwell in Thy house, O Lord;
they shall praise Thee forever and ever.   Ps. lxxxiii,5

If one were to ask for a definition of the Divine Office, let this be given: *The Divine Office is a definite method of publicly praising God and entreating Him, mentally and vocally at the same time, instituted by competent ecclesiastical authority.*

First, we say "*a definite method,*" for not any and every praying to God and praising God is the Divine Office, but a certain definite order of psalms, hymns and prayers, which all who are obligated to recite the Divine Office must follow.

Secondly, we say "*publicly,*" because the Divine Office is recited by public and sacred ministers, publicly, in the name of the whole Church, for the common and public weal. That is why, even when it is said by one man and in a private residence, one does not omit such forms as "The

Lord be with you," "Let us pray," "Let us bless the Lord," and the like. These are addressed to the whole Church, and in the name of the same Church he answers himself, "And with thy spirit," "Thanks be to God," and so forth.

Thirdly, we say *"a method of praising and beseeching,"* because the Office of which we speak entails these two obligations, blessing God for benefits received, petitioning Him for things to be received. In this the Office of the Church Militant differs from that of the Church Triumphant, which, when it shall exult in all its members after the Judgment Day, will contain only the praises of God.

In the fourth place, we say "[a method of praising . . .] *God,"* for the whole Office is properly offered to God alone. This is the sacrifice of the lips, of which we read in the Forty-Ninth Psalm:

xlix, 23   The sacrifice of praise shall glorify me.

Nor should it disturb us that one Office is called "of the Saints," another "of the dead," a third "of the season," and so on. The one is called "of the Saints," when it is offered to God in memory of the Saints, and when God is praised in His Saints, just as another is called "of the dead," when we entreat God therein to grant refreshment and rest to the dead. Finally, whether the Office be designated as "of the dead," or in whatever way, the psalms, hymns, Collects, and other parts of the Office are always directed to God.

Fifthly, we say *"mentally and vocally at the same time,"* because the form of the Office, of human institution, necessarily demands an external act. Hence he would not satisfy his obligation who, praying to and praising God mentally only, and not with his voice, did not pronounce all the words completely and distinctly.

Finally, the definition includes *"instituted by competent ecclesiastical authority."* For no one can prescribe a definite norm of prayer, except the one in authority. . . . Pope Gregory VII, in a General Council, prescribed the number of the Psalms and Lessons, as is seen in the canon. . . .— *De Controv.* III: *De Bon. Oper.* X.

Topics for Further Discussion:

Explain the laity's loss of interest in the Psalms and the Office generally.

The additional sense of solidarity in praising God in the very words used on earth by Christ and by so many millions of Christians.

That no history of literature in any Christian country can overlook the treasures of the breviary.

In former times, when few could read or write, people learned the Latin Psalms, and sang them with delight.

In European countries simplified editions of the Breviary have begun to be used widely within late years.

In England a Magnificat Society of laity is organized in groups of eight members, who divide among themselves the several Hours of the Divine Office.

In the United States, within the past few years, social-minded adults, study clubs, student organizations, sodalities, and the like, have linked themselves together into a League of the Divine Office, and corporately recite on occasion some part of the Divine Office.

Readings:

P. Batiffol, *History of the Roman Breviary* (New York: Longmans, Green, 1912); "The Genesis of the Canonical Hours," pp. 1–29.

J. Baudot, *The Breviary, Its History and Contents* (St. Louis: Herder, 1929); *passim.*

F. Cabrol, "Breviary," "Matins," "Lauds," "Vespers," etc., *CE.*

————— *Liturgical Prayer, Its History and Spirit* (New York: Kenedy, 1922); "Forms of Prayer Used in Antiquity," pp. 32–42.

R. Hoornaert, *The Breviary and the Laity* (Collegeville: Liturgical Press, 1936); *passim.*

V. Michel, *The Liturgy of the Church* (New York: Macmillan, 1937); "The Divine Office," pp. 274–293; "The Daily Cycle of Praise," pp. 294–315.

M. Perkins, *At Your Ease in the Catholic Church* (New York: Sheed and Ward, 1938), "On Time With the Church," pp. 133–141.

J. A. Rickaby, *Readings from St. Augustine on the Psalms* (New York: Benziger, 1925); *passim.*

B. Sause, "As One Man: the Divine Office," *The Sacramental Way* (New York: Sheed and Ward, 1948), pp. 175–182.

E. I. Watkin, *The Catholic Centre* (New York: Sheed and Ward, 1939), "Adoration," pp. 227–247.

Text translations:
Full Breviary:
The Roman Breviary, nuns of Stanbrook translation (New York: Kenedy).
Roman Breviary in English (New York: Benziger, 1950).

Condensed Breviary:
The Short Breviary (Collegeville: Liturgical Press, 1941).

Day Hours:
Nuns of Stanbrook, *The Day Hours of the Church, The Liturgy of the Layfolk* (London: Burns, Oates and Washbourne, 1921).
The Hour of Prime (Collegeville: Liturgical Press, 1935).
C. C. Martindale, *Morning Prayers from the Liturgy* (London: CTS).
A. Fortescue, *Vespers for Sundays* (London: CTS).
D. Attwater, *Into Thy Hands,* Compline for entire week (Collegeville: Liturgical Press).
C. C. Martindale, *Compline for Sundays and Festivals* (London: CTS).

Chapter XVII

A CHRISTIAN BECAUSE CHRIST-ED

Unless a man be born anew
of water and of Spirit
he cannot enter into the Kingdom of
Heaven (John iii,5).

IT HAS been the theme of all the preceding chapters of this book
that Christians lead a super-life, living in a Christocentric sphere,
where they share by communication in the life and prerogatives of
Christ. Attention was especially focused on the supreme function of
sacrificial worship, wherein, as participants of the priesthood of Christ,
all Christians have important roles to play. It will now be necessary to
broaden the scope of inquiry, and study the whole *"cultual"* aspect of
Christian life. At least all the more important elements in this divinely
instituted scheme for the fullest and most adequate human existence must
be examined in purpose and function. First and foremost it is essential
to see by what means we were initiated into Christianity, how we were
ingrafted into the Mystical Body of Christ. Belief in Christ's doctrine,
even the most self-sacrificing surrender in living the doctrines of Christianity, do not suffice to make a Christian. We are Christians because
we have been "reborn" in sacramental baptism. The word *christen*
meant literally to make Christian, and this was done by baptism, but
that basic meaning having worn smooth with long usage, modern writers
speak of baptism as the act by which we are Christ-ed.

Purification by Water. "Baptism" etymologically means being *dipped*
or plunged *into water*. As a natural religious rite it means submitting to
a ceremonial washing, or cleansing, at the hands of another. It is thus
an exterior act which of itself expresses a consciousness of guilt, a voluntary surrender of self in order to be purged of the guilt, and bodily
cleansing in token of interior purification. It is seen to be an eminently

fitting sign to express the most conspicuous features of Christian initiation. As such it was deliberately chosen by Christ.

Sacramental Institution. At the opening of His public ministry, Christ went out to where John the Baptist was preaching penance and this natural baptism as a confession of guilt. John was quite clear and insistent in his preaching that *his* baptism could not directly remit sin, but was merely a token of contrition in the faith of the Mightier One to come. By receiving on His own sinless members the *natural baptism* of penance, Christ wished to *consecrate* this cleansing ablution by giving it the *sacramental efficacy* of spiritual regeneration. It will be seen from St. Matthew's account how each of the Three Divine Persons singly and distinctly concur in instituting sacramental baptism.

> Then cometh Jesus
>> from Galilee to the Jordan
>> unto John, to be baptized by him.
>
> And John was for hindering Him, and said,
>> "It is I
>> who need to be baptized by Thee,
>> and comest Thou to me?"
>
> But Jesus answered and said to him,
>> "Let it be so at this time;
>> for so it becometh us to fulfill all justness."
>
> Then he letteth Him come.
>
> And Jesus, having been baptized,
>> came up straightway from the water,
>> and behold,
>> the heavens were opened,
>> and he saw the Spirit of God descend as a dove
>> coming upon Him.
>
> And behold,
>> a voice from the heavens, saying,
>> "This is My beloved Son,
>> in whom I am well pleased."   Matt. iii,13–17

The New Birth. The rite thus solemnly ordained Christ explained by calling it rebirth, a second birth, a birth of water and the Holy Spirit.

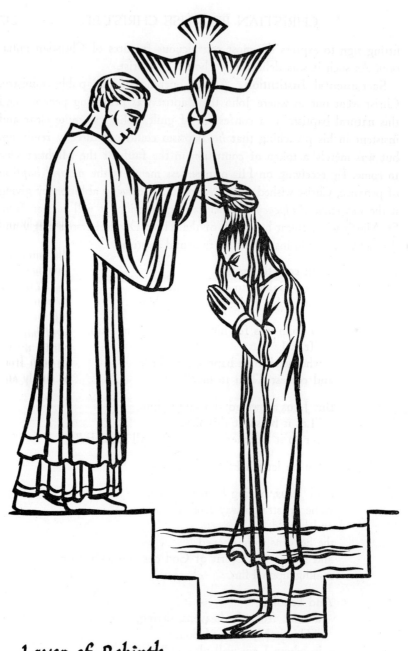

Laver of Rebirth

Unless a man be born anew
of water and of Spirit,
he cannot enter into the Kingdom of Heaven.

That which has come into being from the flesh
is flesh.

That which has come into being from the Spirit
is spirit.

So do not be astonished that I have said to thee, John iii,5–7,
"You must be reborn." tr. by C.C.
Martindale

When Christ sent the twelve Apostles through Galilee, and later the
seventy-two disciples, to preach and heal, St. John narrates how they
baptized. These temporary commissions had their culmination in the John iii,22–26;
final apostolic investiture: iv,1,2

All power in Heaven and earth
hath been given Me.
Go ye, therefore, make disciples of all nations,
baptizing them
in the name of the Father
and of the Son
and of the Holy Spirit:
teaching them to observe all things I have commanded you:
and behold, I am with you all days,
unto the consummation of the world. Matt. xxviii,18–20

On the day of Pentecost, when the throngs ask of Peter, "What are
we to do?" he answers,

Repent ye, and be baptized,
every one of you,
in the name of Jesus Christ
unto the forgiveness of your sins;
and ye shall receive the gift of the Holy Spirit. Acts ii,37,38

From that day onward baptism has been the Christian's initiation, his
supernatural birthday, his entrance into the circle of God's adopted
children, and his incorporation into the Mystical Body of Christ. The
great St. Athanasius sums up all we have said in a few sentences:

It is clear that the descent of the Holy Spirit upon Him at the

Jordan was for our sake, because He bears our body. It was not He derived the advantage of it, but we who through Him have been sanctified. We shared in His anointing in such wise that one could say of us:

I Cor. iii,16

Know you not that you are the temple of God,
and that the Spirit of God dwelleth in you?

When the Saviour, then, purified Himself in the Jordan, it was we in Him and through Him that were purified. And when He received the Spirit it was we who through Him received it.

Cont. Arianos, xlvi

"Rising to New Life." St. Paul's favorite concept of baptism links it with Christ's death and *resurrection from the tomb*. To understand his language, we must recall that the sacrament was normally administered by immersing the candidate into water and then drawing him out of the water. Being *plunged beneath the water* reminded Paul of Christ's going down into the tomb; the rising from the water suggested Christ's glorious victory over death, all the more so since the baptismal waters had all their efficacy from the very fact of Christ's death and resurrection. So the natural man with his sins descended into the water as to a tomb to die to self and to sin, and the sinless Christian arose therefrom to walk in newness of life:

Know ye not,
that as many of us as were baptized unto Christ Jesus,
we were baptized unto his death?
We were buried therefore with Him
through his baptism unto death,
that as Christ was raised from the dead,
through the glory of the Father,
so we also should walk in newness of life.

Rom. vi,3–5

Citizen of Grace-World. "Rebirth" gives a depth of meaning which the Scriptures and the Fathers could never exhaust in numberless explanations. In the words of Christ to Nicodemus, there is a delicate play on words no translation can render; the word ἄνωθεν, rendered "anew," can equally well mean "from above." The new birth from on high implies not only the complete cleansing from all sin, but the entrance into the supernatural life by being implanted into Christ: for all of us,

whether Jews or Greeks,

whether slaves or free,
were baptized into one body. . . .
Now you are [together] the body of Christ,
and severally His members.   I Cor. xii,12,27

And all these members, as those of God's adopted sons, are "sealed against the day of redemption" by the mark of the Holy Spirit. Once Eph. i,14; iv,30 baptized, therefore, always a Christian; the supernatural life here imparted may be killed, but once given this testimonial seal of adoption, there is no process of "unbaptism." This son of God may go astray and be lost, but unto God the son has been born, and son he remains forever.

Oath of Allegiance. Baptism was the first element of Christianity to be called by the Latin word *sacramentum.* This term had meant a solemn, sacred oath, such as the *sacramentum militare,* by which soldiers consecrated themselves and swore fidelity to the military calling. Baptism was called sacrament, or oath, because it involved on the part of the neophyte *an irrevocable undertaking henceforth to serve under the standard of Christ.* How this secondary aspect of baptismal initiation came to designate the whole process becomes clear if we reflect that in Greco-Roman paganism the vilest sins, lying, stealing, impurity, and the like, had been, so to say, deified by being linked with some special god or goddess. The sinful actions had become, as it were, acts of worship to the false divinity in question. Thus the neophyte, who wished to embrace Christianity, had to be taught that baptism entailed forswearing all these depravities, these false gods, and swearing undying allegiance to a God of infinite sanctity.

"Resurrection" on Easter Morning. The Christian teachings had to be slowly unfolded, and assimilated, and to a great extent lived for a fairly long period (three years as a rule), before a catechumen was considered fit for baptism. The baptism itself was *administered in the night preceding Easter Day,* so the neophytes would rise to the new life at the moment Christ rose from the tomb. The Lenten season was given up to a final, intensive training of the Catechumens, and was marked by periodic public scrutinies, or examinations, as the baptismal night drew near. To heighten the psychological impressions of the great act of initiation, the rites of the sacrament itself, at a time when the Mass had hardly passed beyond the simplicity of the Supper Chamber, had taken on a wealth of symbolic richness and elaboration.

Ancient Rites Preserved. The present rites of infant baptism, which are also used in the United States for adults, are a shortened form of an eighth-century ritual: many parts are much older; thus the celebrated questions of renouncing Satan, and his works, and his pomps, were already traditional when Tertullian wrote at the end of the second century. No part of the whole of our worship so truly preserves ancient forms unchanged as this baptismal ritual. In the rites reproduced on page 253 every prayer is word for word from the eighth-century redaction, barring two minor exceptions to be mentioned.

Changes in Ritual. On June 3, 1954, the Holy See granted to the Bishops of the United States a privilege by which the rites of several of the Sacraments may now be administered in the English language in part.

By way of illustrating the new arrangement, and of incorporating the English version thus authorized, at the option of the local bishop, for use in the liturgy, we here reprint the grant in the following manner: what is set in straight type may now be said in English, or in Latin; what is set in *italics* indicates the places where, in administering the Sacraments, *the Latin must be used,* with the English added afterwards at option.

THE RITE OF BAPTISM

The first part of the rite (1–5) reproduces in outline the ceremonies of enrolling a catechumen. It would take place at any time. The candidates were closely questioned as to their motive, status, and occupation. If this last was one connected with pagan worship, or entailing great risks of apostasy, the candidate had to arrange to find a new one. On being accepted by the Church, the candidate was enrolled as a catechumen of the lowest grade, a "hearer" of the Church's teaching.

Text[1]

Reception of the Catechumen. Time, by appointment; place, at door or vestibule of church.

1. *Priest:* What is your name?
Answer: N.
Priest: N, what dost thou ask of the Church of God?
Answer: Faith.
Priest: What does faith offer you?
Answer: Life everlasting.
Priest: If, then, it is life that you wish to enter, keep the commandments. Love the Lord your God with your whole heart, and with your whole soul, and with your whole mind; and love your neighbor as you love yourself.

This and all the exorcisms of the rite are designed to free the baptismal candidate from the power of Satan. If the candidate were an infant, he was subjected to Satan because of original sin; if an adult, still more subject because of evil inclinations, past sins, and the consequent enslavement of the will.

2. **The priest breathes gently upon the face of the child, and says once (to each if there are more than one):**

Depart from him/her, unclean spirit, and give place to the Holy Spirit, the Consoler.

The sign of the cross, at once the symbol of Christ's triumph and the Christian's strength, is solemnly traced upon the candidate that he may become "a temple of God" as one "destined to be born anew."

3. **The priest makes the sign of the cross with his thumb upon the forehead and the breast of the child, saying:**

Receive the sign of the Cross on your ✠ forehead and in your ✠ heart. Have faith in the teachings of God, and live in such a way that from now on you may be enabled to be a temple of God.

---

[1]The translation is from *Collectio Rituum* (Milwaukee: Bruce, 1954).

Let us pray.

O LORD, we implore Thee, in Thy kindness hear our prayers, and guard with unfailing power this Thy chosen N., who has been stamped with the seal of the Lord's cross; so that, holding fast to the first truths he/she has learned of Thy great glory, he/she may, by keeping Thy commandments, attain to the glory of rebirth. Through Christ our Lord. Amen.

The laying on of hands is always one of the Church's most solemn rites. Here it is an act of appropriation: she acknowledges the candidate as her own, places a protecting hand upon him, and commends him meanwhile to God as one now "stamped with the seal of the Lord's cross."

4. The priest lays his hand upon the head of the child (or of each), and afterwards holding the hand extended, he says (in the plural for more than one):

Let us pray.

A LMIGHTY and everlasting God, Father of our Lord Jesus Christ, be pleased to look upon this Thy servant, N., whom in Thy goodness Thou hast called to be instructed in the Faith. Rid him/her of all blindness of heart; break all the nets of Satan in which he/she has been entangled. Open to him/her, Lord, the gate of Thy mercy so that, penetrated by the sign of Thy wisdom [salt], he/she may be rid of the stench of all evil desires and, moved by the pleasing fragrance of Thy teachings, may joyfully serve Thee in Thy Church and daily advance in perfection. Through Christ our Lord. Amen.

5. The priest blesses salt, which, once blessed, may be used at any time thereafter for the same pur-

Salt was for the ancients the universal instrument of purification and preservation. Salt is here blessed, and put upon the tongue of the candidate in order to give expression to the Church's desire that he be preserved from the corruption of sin, and given a relish for heavenly doctrine.

With this giving of blessed salt, a rite which was repeated over and over during the catechumenate, the enrolling of the catechumen was terminated.

pose, in which case the following prayer is omitted.

Blessing of the Salt

O salt, creature of God, I exorcise you in the name of God the Father almighty and in the love of our Lord Jesus Christ and in the strength of the Holy Spirit. I exorcise you by the living God, the true God, the holy God, the God Who brought you into being to safeguard the human race, and commanded you to be consecrated by His servants for the benefit of those who are coming into the Faith, so that by the power of the Holy Trinity you might become a health-giving sacrament to put the enemy to flight. Therefore we beg Thee, O Lord our God, to sanctify by Thy power of sanctification this salt which Thou hast created and to bless it with Thy blessing, so that it may become a perfect medicine for all who receive it and may remain always in every fiber of their being. In the name of our Lord Jesus Christ, Who will come to judge the living and the dead, and the world by fire. Amen.

The priest puts a little of the blessed salt into the mouth of the child, saying (to each):

N., receive the salt of wisdom. May it win for you mercy and forgiveness, and life everlasting. Amen.
Priest: Peace be with you.
Answer: And with your spirit.

After that the priest says (plural for more than one):

Let us pray.

GOD of our fathers, God the Author of all truth, we humbly implore Thee to look with favor on this Thy servant, N., and grant that he/she who is now tasting this salt as his/her first nourishment may not hunger much longer before he/she is given his/her fill of heavenly food, so that he/she may always be ardent of soul, rejoicing in hope, and ever loyal to Thy name. Bring him/her, O Lord, we ask Thee, to the font of the new birth, so that in company with Thy faithful servants, he/she may gain the eternal rewards that Thou hast promised. Through Christ our Lord. Amen.

The rites which follow next (6–7) recall the first great "scrutiny" of the Wednesday after the third Sunday of Lent. The catechumens, now advanced to the rank of "petitioners" for baptism, were being instructed daily and subjected to rigid examinations. Typical elements of the ceremonial part of these scrutinies are here preserved, a repetition of the exorcism, a renewed signing with the cross, and a reiteration of the Church's maternal solicitude as portrayed in the laying on of hands, and an earnest prayer on behalf of the neophytes.

6. Then the priest says:

I exorcise you, unclean spirit, in the name of the Father and of the Son and of the Holy Spirit. Come forth, depart from this servant of God, N., for He commands you, spirit accursed and damned, He Who walked upon the sea and extended His right hand to Peter as he was sinking. Therefore, accursed devil, acknowledge your condemnation and pay homage to the true and living God; pay homage to Jesus Christ, His Son, and to the Holy Spirit, and depart from this servant of God, N., for Jesus Christ, our Lord and God, has called him/her to His holy grace and blessing, and to the font of Baptism.

The priest signs each one and says:

Then never dare, accursed devil, to violate this sign of the holy cross ✛ which we are making upon his/her forehead. Through Christ our Lord. Amen.

7. Continuing, the priest lays his hand upon the head of the child (or of each), and then holding the hand extended, he says (in the plural for more than one):

Let us pray.

O HOLY Lord, almighty Father, eternal God, Source of light and truth, I ask for this Thy servant, N., Thy fatherly love, eternal and most just, so that Thou mayest be pleased to enlighten him/her with the light of Thy understanding. Cleanse and sanctify him/her; grant him/her true knowledge, so that he/she, having been made fit for the grace of Thy Baptism, may retain unwavering hope, true judgment, and sacred teaching. Through Christ our Lord. Amen.

The rites thus far considered are nowadays performed at the door of the church, within the vestibule.

Admittance to the Holy Place and Progress to the Font

The next rites (8–10) enshrine what remains of the most beautiful of the ancient Roman initiation forms. This was the "Great Scrutiny," called also "The Opening of the Ears." This took place on Wednesday of the fourth week of Lent, in the great basilica at St. Paul's tomb.

The final sifting of the cate-

8. The priest places the end of the stole, which hangs from his left shoulder, upon the child (the first, if there are more than one) and leads him into the church, saying:

N., enter the temple of God, so that you may take part with Christ in everlasting life. Amen.

9. After they have entered the church, the priest, leading the way to the font, says aloud, together

chumens had now been made, and the chosen ones were henceforth known as the "elect." After the Gradual of the Mass on this day, four deacons entered in ceremonious fashion, carrying Gospel books, which were deposited on the four corners of the altar. Whereupon a short discourse characterized each gospel in turn, and a deacon chanted its opening passage. Thereupon the *Creed,* which it was forbidden to write, was recited for the catechumens, and then in turn recited *by* the catechumens. Lastly the *Our Father* was recited and explained clause by clause.

The final selection of the catechumens is mirrored in our rites now by the admission at this point to the baptistry. The "giving" and the "giving back" of the *Creed* and *Our Father* are indicated by their recital in common on the way to the baptistry.

The short bidding to enter the church (8) is of medieval composition.

On the morning we call Holy Saturday, took place a ceremonial examination, which, too, is reflected still in our rites. There was first the definitive exorcism of the Evil One (11–13), "that he keep far from this creature of God's making," (soon to be) "a temple of the living God,"

with the sponsors, the Apostles' Creed and the Lord's Prayer.

I BELIEVE in God, the Father almighty, Creator of heaven and earth; and in Jesus Christ, His only Son, our Lord; who was conceived by the Holy Ghost, born of the Virgin Mary, suffered under Pontius Pilate, was crucified, died, and was buried. He descended into hell; the third day He arose again from the dead; He ascended into heaven, and sits at the right hand of God, the Father almighty; thence He shall come to judge the living and the dead.

I believe in the Holy Ghost, the Holy Catholic Church, the communion of saints, the forgiveness of sins, the resurrection of the body, and life everlasting. Amen.

10. OUR Father, who art in heaven, hallowed be Thy name. Thy Kingdom come. Thy will be done on earth, as it is in heaven. Give us this day our daily bread. And forgive us our trespasses, as we forgive them that trespass against us. And lead us not into temptation, but deliver us from evil. Amen.

11.   Final Preparation

Place: at entrance of baptistry
Then before entering the baptistry, with his back to the gate of the baptistry, the priest says:
I exorcise you, every unclean spirit, in the name of God the Father almighty, and in the name of His Son, Jesus Christ, our Lord and

Ancient pagan Romans used saliva as an instrument of diabolic exorcism; ancient Christian Romans remembered how on occasions Christ had used it in His healing, as, for instance, on that occasion in the Decapolis, when they brought Him one deaf and dumb: "He thrust His fingers into the man's ears, and touched his tongue with spittle. And looking up to heaven, He sighed, and saith to him: 'Ephpheta,' that is, 'Be thou opened!' And straightway the man's ears were opened, and the bond of his tongue was loosened" (Mark vii,32–36).

Re-enacting this ceremony in its entirety was liable to give some offense, and hence, as St. Ambrose explains, "For the sake of propriety, the nostrils are touched instead of the tongue."

In 1944 Pope Pius XII made the use of saliva optional on hygienic and similar considerations.

The solemn forswearing of Satan (13) was followed formerly by a solemn swearing of allegiance to Christ. Even though the ceremonial oath has disappeared, this remains the last and most formal step the neophyte can take in entering the service of Christ. The real incorporation is effected by Christ.

Enrolled as a soldier, the neophyte is anointed with oil for the contest with the world, even as athletes used to strengthen their bodies with anointing.

Judge, and in the strength of the Holy Spirit, that you may depart from this creature of God, N., whom our Lord has called to His holy temple in order that he/she may become a temple of the living God and that the Holy Spirit may dwell in him/her. Through Christ our Lord, Who will come to judge the living and the dead and the world by fire. Amen.

12. If circumstances allow, the priest takes saliva and touches the ears and the nostrils of the child (or each) saying (while he touches the ears):

Ephphethá, which means, "Be opened,"

Then touching the nostrils, he says:

so that you may perceive the fragrance of God's sweetness. But you, O devil, depart; for the judgment of God has come.

13. The priest now questions the one to be baptized (or each), as follows:

N., do you renounce satan?
Answer: I do renounce him.
Priest: And all his works?
Answer: I do renounce them.
Priest: And all his display?
Answer: I do renounce it.

14. The priest dips his thumb in the Oil of Catechumens, and anoints the child (each) on the breast and between the shoulders in the form of a cross, saying once (to each):

I anoint you with the oil of salvation, in Christ Jesus our Lord, so that you may have everlasting life. Amen.

The priest wipes his thumb and the anointed places with cotton wadding, or other such thing.

The final act of the neophyte's initiation now begins. The time was as near as possible to the momentous hour wherein Christ "rose again for our justification" (Rom. iv,25); the place was the celebrated baptistry of the Lateran Basilica.

15.   The Baptism

Place: at the fountain.

Standing in the same place, outside the railing or grille, he takes off the violet stole, and puts on a white one. Then he enters the baptistry, as do also the sponsors with the child. The priest, at the font, interrogates again the one to be baptized, the sponsors answering for a little child.

Priest: N., do you believe in God the Father almighty, Creator of heaven and earth?
Answer: I do believe.
Priest: Do you believe in Jesus Christ, His only Son, our Lord, who was born and suffered for us?
Answer: I do believe.
Priest: And do you believe also in the Holy Ghost, the Holy Catholic Church, the communion of saints, the forgiveness of sins, the resurrection of the body, and life everlasting?
Answer: I do believe.

Then the priest says (to each):

N., do you wish to be baptized?
Answer: I do.

Grouped before the bishop, the candidates made a final profession of faith, then one by one they were led down several steps into the saving laver, to be immersed in mystic death to self and to sin, to rise as ingrafted members of the Mystical Body. "It is no longer I that live; it is Christ that liveth in me" (Gal. ii,20); this is not only the ardent cry of a St. Paul; it is the act of faith of every Christian.

16. Then the godfather, or godmother, or both if there are two sponsors, holding the child (touching an adult), the priest takes baptismal water in a small vessel or pitcher, and pours it three times upon the head of the child in the form of a cross, say-

The essential form of baptism is contained in this short formula. This is all that is said by a lay person in administering this sacrament in an emergency.

ing at the same time, only once, distinctly and attentively:

N., I baptize you in the name of the Father (pouring the first time), *and of the Son* (pouring the second time), *and of the Holy Ghost* (pouring the third time).

Royal Unction of the Lord's Adopted

In ancient times the new members of Christ were confirmed immediately after baptism. So, after being clothed with new and snow-white garments, they were led before the bishop that he might impart the plenitude of the Holy Spirit. This anointing with chrism here preserved in our rite is a distant reminder of the former anointing of the confirmation.

17. Then the priest dips his thumb in the holy chrism, and anoints the child (each) on the crown of the head, in the form of a cross, saying:

MAY almighty God, the Father of our Lord Jesus Christ, Who has given you a new birth by means of water and the Holy Spirit and forgiven all your sins, anoint you with the Chrism of salvation in Christ Jesus our Lord, so that you may have everlasting life. Amen.

Priest: Peace be with you.

Answer: And with your spirit.

Bestowal of Symbolic Gifts

In lieu of the new robes formerly given to the baptized as they emerged from the font, the Church now gives a veil by way of preserving this beautiful bit of symbolism. This prayer form is of medieval Gallican origin.

18. Having wiped his thumb and the anointed place, and putting a white garment (or a linen cloth) upon the head of the child, he says (to each):

Receive this white robe and carry it unstained to the judgment seat of our Lord Jesus Christ, so that you may have everlasting life. Amen.

It was with burning torches held aloft that the "newborn from the dead" here marched into the basilica, singing: "I will go unto the altar of God," for their first Holy Mass and Communion in the dawn of Easter morning. To betoken the joy and sweetness of the hour they were at the holy table given to partake of milk and honey.

19. The priest gives to the baptized (or to the sponsor) a lighted candle, saying (to each):

Receive this lighted candle, and keep your Baptism above reproach. Keep the commandments of God, so that when the Lord comes to His marriage feast you may meet Him in the halls of heaven with all His saints, and may live with Him forever. Amen.

The Dismissal in Peace

20. Last of all, he says (plural for more than one):

Go in peace, N., and may the Lord be with you. Amen.

Prayer After Baptism

Almighty and everlasting God, merciful Father, since Thou hast today adopted as Thy child this Thy servant, N., grant, we implore Thee, that, strengthened by the Holy Spirit and nourished by the Bread of Heaven, he/she may grow to full maturity in Christ. And may he/she always keep in mind his/her patron saint, so that by imitating him/her, he/she may attain to the eternal home of the Father. Through Christ our Lord. Amen.

Seventeenth-Century Source Material

(Louis Bourdaloue, S.J. (1632–1704), "the king of preachers and preacher of kings," was one of the greatest lights of the Christian pulpit: he is speaking of our duties toward the Church.)

The Church is a body, I mean a mystical body and a moral one. This body has a Head, who is Jesus Christ, and He has members, and these are the faithful. So the Apostle St. Paul teaches us in various passages, but especially in his *Epistle to the Ephesians,* where he speaks as follows in reference to Jesus Christ:

"He [God] hath subjected all things beneath His feet," and hath given Him for supreme Head to the Church, which is His body, the fulness of Him who is wholly fulfilled in all.

Ps. viii,6

Eph. i,22,23

As if the great Apostle should say: My brethren, we make but one body with Jesus Christ and in Jesus Christ. The assembly of all the faithful, united to Jesus Christ by faith, behold the body of the Church: But the faithful themselves taken separately and considered each one individually, behold the members of the Church. The more the members grow and increase in strength, the more the body deriveth fullness and acquisition of strength: and even the Head Himself receives additional perfection in His quality as Head in the measure in which the body, by the union of its members, strengthens and perfects itself. And this character, our being not only children of the Church, but members of the Church, this is one of the most beautiful titles in which we may glory before God and in respect to God. As members of the Church we belong in a special way to Jesus Christ, since in virtue of the Baptism we have received, and by which we were engrafted into the body of the Church, we have contracted a very close and intimate relationship with Jesus Christ.

Topics for Further Discussion:

The disposition of Providence whereby anyone, even a non-Catholic, can validly baptize.

Since faith and contrition are absolute requisites for adult baptism, the justification of the practice of infant baptism.

The purpose, requisites, and duties of a sponsor at baptism.

The three modes of baptism, by immersion (whole or partial), by infusion (pouring), and by sprinkling.

The use in case of urgent necessity of water mixed with foreign matter, tea, etc.

Readings:

A. d'Alès, *Baptism and Confirmation* (St. Louis: Herder, 1929).
G. Diekmann, "Incorporation Into Christ: Baptism," *The Sacramental Way* (New York: Sheed and Ward, 1948), pp. 88–102.
F. X. Doyle, *The Wonderful Sacraments* (New York: Benziger, 1924); "Baptism," pp. 53–89.
W. H. Fanning, "Baptism," *CE.*

C. Grimaud–J. F. Newcomb, *One Only Christ* (New York: Benziger, 1939); " 'Our' Deification," pp. 99–107.

F. C. Kolbe, *The Four Mysteries of the Faith* (New York: Longmans, Green, 1926); "The Third Mystery as Divine Sonship," pp. 71–77.

C. Lattey, *Six Sacraments, Papers Read at the Summer School of Catholic Studies, Cambridge, 1929* (St. Louis: Herder, 1930); "Baptism," pp. 73–110.

C. Marmion, *Christ the Life of the Soul* (St. Louis: Herder, 1923); "Baptism," pp. 152–168.

J. P. Murphy, "The Sacrament of Baptism," *The Teaching of the Catholic Church* (New York: Macmillan, 1949), II, pp. 767–802.

The New Man in Christ (Liturgical Conference, 1949), *passim*.

M. Perkins, *Speaking of How to Pray* (New York: Sheed & Ward, 1944); "The Mighty Working of His Power," pp. 79–104.

R. Plus, *Baptism and Confirmation* (London: Burns, Oates and Washbourne, 1930).

The Rite for Baptism (Collegeville: Lit. Press, 1957).

W. F. Robison, *The Seven-Fold Gift* (St. Louis: Herder, 1922); "The Gate of Life," pp. 1–30.

M. J. Scheeben, *The Mysteries of Christianity* (St. Louis: Herder, 1946), "The Mystical Nature and Significance of the Sacramental Character," pp. 582–592.

Chapter XVIII

"IN CONFIRMATION THEREOF"

> *Be strengthened powerfully
> through the Spirit
> in the inward man* (Eph.
> iii,16).

ADULT Catholics of our day, and especially college-trained Catholics, are expected by the Holy See to be Christianizing as well as Christian souls. Addressing Catholic collegians of Italy, Pope Pius XI spoke of them as co-apostles, centers radiating beneficent activity even as "radioactive focuses" ceaselessly raying forth Christlike influence. It may strike the modern ear as something of a surprise, not to say anticlimax, to hear the same pontiff say that the zeal and the inexhaustible dynamism needed for such an apostolate is a legacy of the sacrament of confirmation. "If one consider well," writes the Holy Father, "it will be seen that the very sacraments of Baptism and Confirmation impose — among other *obligations* — this Apostolate of Catholic Action. . . . Through *Confirmation* we become soldiers of Christ. A soldier must labor and fight not so much for himself as for others." Nor does it escape the Holy Father that this link with confirmation strikes us as novel. In fact the official Italian *Manual of Catholic Action* elaborates this very idea: *To Cardinal Cerejeira, 1934*

> Confirmation could well be called the Sacrament of Catholic Action. But the dogmatic truths, from which the duty of Apostolate comes forth as a practical corollary, are but little known, little meditated by Christians. In them, too often, the Catholic sense is lacking, and the noble instinct of Apostolate. *Catholic Action must therefore especially study this Sacrament.*[1]

---

[1] L. Civardi, *A Manual of Catholic Action* (New York: Sheed and Ward, 1936), p. 68; quoted with permission.

"The liturgy, well and lovingly understood," continues the papal spokesman in the passage quoted, "gives great help herein." Following such pointed suggestions, alert Catholics the world over are now reappraising the abiding gifts and graces they received in childhood on the day of their confirmation. Is this sacrament making us "radioactive focuses" of the Catholic way of living?

Supernatural Coming of Age. Baptism alone excepted, no one incident of childhood can compare with the reception of confirmation as far as the supernatural life is concerned. No matter how young or how old one may be when he receives this sacrament, it is confirmation that marks the passage from supernatural childhood to *supernatural maturity*. Confirmation is the Catholic's coming of age, attaining his majority, with the strength, the personal *and social* rights and duties of an adult. St. Thomas phrases this with his customary clarity in saying: "The Sacrament of Confirmation confers the fulness of the Holy Spirit in view of the spiritual vigor that befits the adult man. Now man, when adult, begins to communicate his actions to others, whereas at first he lived only to himself." The same idea is set out more fully in another luminous passage of the *Summa*:

S.T. III. Q. lxxii, a.2

> Just as Baptism is a spiritual regeneration unto Christian life, so also is Confirmation a certain spiritual growth bringing man to perfect spiritual age. But it is evident, from a comparison with the life of the body, that the action which is proper to man immediately after birth, is different from the action which is proper to him when he has come to perfect age. And therefore by the sacrament of Confirmation man is given a spiritual power in respect of sacred actions other than those in respect of which he receives power at Baptism. For in Baptism he receives *power to do those things which pertain to his own salvation,* forasmuch as he lives to himself: whereas *in Confirmation he receives power to do those things which pertain to spiritual combat with enemies of the Faith.*

Ibid., a.5

Since we have been confirmed, we are no longer children in the supernatural order, but men. Let us then, with the help of the liturgy, scrutinize this testimonial of our maturity as citizens in the City of God.

Twofold Sign. To begin with the external *sign* of the sacrament, or perhaps one should say "signs," for there are two external features here, the one an anointing with oil, the other a laying on of hands. Both are

Seal of the gift of the Spirit

elemental ritual acts to be met often in natural religions as well as in the revealed religions of Judaism and Christianity.

Anointing. In the Orient the household uses of *oil* were surprisingly varied: in the kitchen it was in constant demand in preparing the foods; in the dining room it was a condiment; in the bath it was the basis of all soaps, unguents, and perfumes (the liberal use of which was a recognized token of joy); in the sickroom it was the instrument of healing; in the reception room it was used to anoint the heads of guests; throughout the whole house it was burned in the lamps. How natural that it should enter conspicuously into the rites of religion, and should have been used in a solemn anointing of kings and prophets and priests! In another connection mention was made of the fact that in Jewish speech one appointed by God for certain special works was by that very fact called "anointed," and that the word *Messiah* is literally rendered "The Anointed One." If *Christians* (the *anointed*) were to become incorporated into Christ (the Anointed), was it not under the circumstances almost inevitable that an anointing with perfumed oil should become an official sign thereof?

This root meaning of "Christian" as "anointed" was sometimes made a matter of taunt against the Church. Thus, about the year 180, we find Theophilus, Bishop of Antioch (where the name originated) defending the name as follows:

> When you laugh at me, calling me a Christian, you do not know what you are saying. First, that which is anointed is sweet and serviceable, and ought not to be laughed at. What ship can be serviceable and seaworthy, unless it be first anointed? Or what tower or house is sightly or serviceable when it has not been anointed? What man, on entering into this life, or when contending in the games, is not anointed with oil? What work can be comely and sightly if it be not anointed and polished? Then even the air and all that is under heaven is, in a kind of way, anointed with light and spirit, and do you not wish to be anointed with the oil of God? We therefore are called Christians on this account, because we are anointed with the oil of God.

Apol. ad Autol.
I,12

Laying On of Hands. Similarly the laying on of hands was a religious rite carrying men's thoughts back through immemorial years, as for instance, to the dying Jacob blessing his sons. Jews would recall how with this solemn act was invested the ministry of the Synagogue. Early Christian neophytes from non-Jewish circles would more readily recall how Christ had laid His hands on the sick in healing, and how this was the usual ceremony of ordination in the *Acts*. This, too, was an appropriate sign to betoken the grant of full and perfect manhood in the supernatural life, and so it is associated with the sacrament of confirmation.

Divine Guest Received. One of the first of the many names by which this sacrament has been known was "Conferring the Holy Ghost." This was a technical term having a definite and circumscribed meaning. "Have you received the Holy Ghost?" conveyed the same idea as our words, "Have you been confirmed?" Now, what is the reality expressed in those words, "conferring the Holy Ghost"? First of all, let us recall momentarily whom we are speaking of as being conferred on us in confirmation. The Holy Ghost is the Third Person of the Triune God, equal from all eternity to the Father and the Son, but distinguished from Father and Son by reason of the proper manner in which He possesses the Divine Nature. God the Father is the first divine Person; God the Son is the second divine Person, begotten eternally of the Father by an act of intellectual generation; God the Holy Ghost is the third divine Person, who proceeds eternally from the Father and the Son as the term of their mutual love. The Holy Spirit, of His very nature, is an outpouring and overflowing of divine life and love and holiness: He is, as it were, God's love personified! Of old God had promised by the prophets that He should pour out His Spirit upon all flesh, and Christ clarified this ancient promise by foretelling His part in its fulfillment:

> I send the promise of My Father upon you;
>   but stay you in the city
> until you be endued with power from on high.   Luke xxiv,49

> I will ask the Father
>   and He shall give you
>   another Advocate,
> that He may abide with you forever.   John xiv,16

On Pentecost the mighty wind and the visible tongues of fire were reserved for those in the upper chamber, but the lifegiving Spirit was for all: "We are all given to drink of the one Spirit." The Advocate and I Cor. xii,13 Helper abides, a permanent Guest, in each of us as in a temple, to be I Cor. iii,16 the glad assurance of our divine sonship, to help us pray, to be to the Rom. viii,16 Father, as a *Pledge,* or Hostage one might almost say in all wonder and Rom. viii,26 reverence. II Cor. i,22

Effects of Sacrament. Two *consequences* of the reception of confirmation are of very special importance: that we thereby share in a higher degree than at baptism in the general priesthood of Christ, and that it gives us a solemn assurance that we *have the strength* to maintain the supernatural life within us, despite all the temptations and storms of life.

Lay Priesthood. It is said in another connection that all Christians share in the priesthood of Christ according to the graduated characters they receive at baptism, at confirmation, and at holy orders. "In a sacramental character," says St. Thomas, *"Christ's faithful have a share in the priesthood of Christ,* in the sense that as Christ has the full power of a spiritual priesthood, so the faithful are likened to Him by sharing a certain spiritual *power* with regard to the sacraments and to things pertaining to divine worship." Baptism is the lowest degree of this participation; it gives the baptized such a share in Christ's priestly functions as minor children have in the actions of a parent. It is a chiefly *passive* sharing. *Confirmation* advances the Christian to the status of an adult with the right and duty of *actively* sharing as co-workers with Christ in His priestly functions, as St. Thomas has it, especially "in those things which pertain to the spiritual combat with the enemies of the Faith." The confirmation *character* is the soul's permanent consecration and deputation for the multiple engagements of social Catholicism. Our duty thus becomes clear, once we realize our abiding capacity, through this character, to be "radioactive" Catholics, bodying forth the Light which is come for the life of the world.

S.T. III. Q. lxiii, a.5

Ibid., Q. lxxii,a.5

Christ-Strong in the Spirit. If the Christian is early called upon to wage battle for his faith and for his salvation, he is in confirmation given the strength to wield the arms of light, and confront danger confidently, knowing that "the Spirit . . . beareth up our weakness." The Christian possesses permanent sacramental powers because "the anointing . . . received from Him abideth." This Christian attitude of humble trust and confidence has nothing of the arrogant error of those who think they are predestined to heaven no matter what they may do. Rather the Christian realizes his own abiding capacity to ruin everything, but knows, too, that as long as he has good will, he will be strengthened, so that

Rom. viii,26

I John ii,27

> temptation will not come upon him
> but such as he can bear;
> and God is faithful
> and will not suffer you to be tempted
> beyond your strength.

I Cor. x,13 Confirmation is the Christian's supernatural life assurance.

Apostolic Practice. The Gospels do not tell us when or how Christ *instituted* this sacrament, but the *Acts* show as clearly as could be desired, the *practice of the apostolic Church*. There was the instance of the evangelization of Samaria by the deacon Philip. He had preached and had begun the initiation of the believers with baptism. Later on the Apostles (the highest grade of the priesthood) came to complete the work by conferring the Holy Ghost. As St. Luke narrates:

> But when they believed
> Philip's preaching of the gospel
>   of the kingdom of God
>   and of the name of Jesus Christ,
> they were baptized, both men and women. . . .

> Now when the Apostles in Jerusalem
> heard that Samaria had accepted the word of God,
>   they sent to them Peter and John,
>   who went down and prayed for them,
>   that they might receive the Holy Spirit;
> for as yet He was fallen upon none of them,
>   but they had *only* been baptized
>   in the name of the Lord Jesus.
> *Then they laid their hands upon them,*
> *and they received the Holy Spirit.*
>   But when Simon saw
>   that the Spirit was given
> through the laying on of the Apostles' hands . . .   Acts viii,12–19

Paul at Ephesus. Some twenty years later, on landing at Ephesus, St. Paul encountered a group of twelve people, who were earnest disciples of Christ. Paul took them for baptized Christians, and asked, as a routine matter:

> "Did ye receive the Holy Spirit when ye believed?"
> But they answered,
> "Nay, we have not even heard
> Whether there be a Holy Spirit."

> And he said: "What baptism, then, did ye receive?"
> They said: "The baptism of John [the Baptist]."

> Then Paul said:
> "John baptized with a baptism of repentance,

telling the people that they were to believe
in Him who was to come after him,
　　that is, in Jesus."

Upon hearing this
they were baptized
in the name of the Lord Jesus;
and when Paul laid his hands on them,
　　the Holy Spirit came upon them,
and they spoke in tongues and prophesied.

Acts xix,2–7

Time of Administration. Since confirmation presupposes and complements *baptism,* the procedure of Paul on this occasion of confirming the neophytes immediately after baptizing them was the normal one in Christian antiquity. Even after infant baptism had become the rule, the Church still kept for a time the custom of confirming infants. This usage is still retained in the Oriental churches, and has not entirely disappeared in the West. There is no doctrinal difficulty involved in the practice, since the conferring of adult *supernatural* standing in no wise depends upon natural age, but the Church came gradually to prefer that this sacrament should be administered *when it is needed;* namely, when the child begins to use his rational faculties (Canon 788), and so must begin to fight for the preservation of the great gift of supernatural life he possesses as a Christian. The Church still regards as ideal that the sacraments be received in the ancient order, baptism, confirmation, Holy Eucharist, but only when this does not entail any delay in admitting the child to eat at the Sacred Table.

Sickroom Administration. Lest children, or others, who are baptized but not confirmed, be cheated by death of their chance to receive this Sacrament of consolation, to their detriment here and eternal loss in heaven, Pope Pius XII, by a decree taking effect January 1, 1947, empowered pastors (and some other priests) to act as *extraordinary ministers* of confirmation. Such priests are thus entrusted with the deathbed configuration of the soul in favor of the faithful within their own territory, when these are truly in danger of death from sickness. None need miss this enlarged sharing in Christ's priesthood. Whether administered by the ordinary minister, or by the extraordinary one, the text of the rite remains the same.

The instructive rite of confirmation follows:

THE RITE OF CONFIRMATION[2]

This introductory versicle admirably expresses the purpose of the sacrament of confirmation. It and the subsequent verses have formed part of the rite since the Middle Ages.

Those who are to be confirmed kneel with hands joined before the minister, who, standing with hands joined, says:

Versicle: May the Holy Spirit descend upon you and may the power of the Most High preserve you from sin.
Response: Amen.
V. Our help is in the name of the Lord.
R. Who made heaven and earth.
V. Lord, hear my prayer.
R. And let my cry come unto Thee.
V. The Lord be with you.
R. And with your spirit.

Then with hands extended above those who are to be confirmed, he says:

Let us pray.

This beautiful prayer, the solemnity of which is heightened by the fourfold "Amen," is the oldest part of the text of this rite. It is contained in a ritual tradition ascribed to Pope Gelasius (492–496). The description of the "sevenfold Spirit" is a citation from the Messianic prophecy of Isaias, of about 800 B.C.:

And the Spirit of the Lord shall rest on Him,
    the Spirit of wisdom and understanding,
    the Spirit of counsel and of fortitude,

*A*LMIGHTY *and eternal God, Who in Thy kindness hast given to this Thy servant a new birth through water and the Holy Spirit, and granted to him/her remission of all his/her sins; send forth from heaven upon him/her Thy sevenfold Spirit, the Holy Paraclete.*
R. Amen.
V. The Spirit of wisdom and understanding.
R. Amen.
V. The Spirit of counsel and fortitude.
R. Amen.

---

[2]The translation is from *Collectio Rituum* (Milwaukee: Bruce, 1954). Confirmation is administered in Latin only.

the Spirit of knowledge and of godliness,

And He shall be filled with the Spirit of the fear of the Lord. (Isa. xi,23.)

It will be noted that this ancient prayer catches up and elaborates the seventh token of the Spirit, according to Isaias, and links it with a solemn sign of the cross. In olden times, when confirmation was administered immediately after baptism, priests or other attendants could help in anointing the sense organs and other parts of the body, but the signing of the forehead with chrism was reserved to the bishop. This is the specific confirmation anointing.

The words here said by the bishop express the final taking possession of the candidate by the power of Christ's cross, and the strengthening that is being imparted. The precise formula was not fixed by Christ, and this one was not adopted as final in the Western Church until the Middle Ages. Older forms abounded in the ritual books. The oldest Roman form we know comes from St. Hippolytus (225): "*I anoint you with holy oil in the Lord the Father Almighty, and Christ Jesus and the Holy Ghost.*" In the ritual of Pope Gelasius (492–496) the form was simply: "*The seal of Christ unto life everlasting,*" which closely resembles that still used in the Oriental churches.

V. *The Spirit of knowledge and piety.*
R. *Amen.*

M ERCIFULLY *fill him/her with the Spirit of Thy fear, and seal him/her with the sign of the cross of Christ, that he/she may obtain everlasting life. Through our Lord Jesus Christ, Thy Son, Who lives and reigns with Thee in the unity of the Holy Spirit, God, forever and ever.*
R. *Amen.*

The minister confirms them as they kneel in order; first the boys and the men, then the girls and the women. In each case, he is told the name to be taken in confirmation and, dipping the tip of his thumb in the holy chrism, he confirms the person as follows:

N., I sign you with the sign of the ✝ Cross and I confirm you with the Chrism of salvation, in the name of the Father, ✝ and of the Son, ✝ and of the Holy ✝ Spirit.
R. *Amen.*

Before beginning to say these words, the minister lays his right hand upon the head of the one to be confirmed, and as he says "of the Cross," he makes the sign of the cross with the holy chrism

The slight blow on the cheek, now usually explained as a reminder that those confirmed must be ready to suffer all things for their Faith, is a ceremonial adaptation of the embrace and kiss originally given adult converts. The rite became a fatherly pat on the cheek when the candidates were normally children. The old salutation remains, "*Peace!*"

These two prayers, and the intervening versicles, eloquently express the idea that the Spirit of God now inhabits the Christian heart as in a temple, but a frail and imperfect temple, one needing al- always to be perfected. As long as the sovereignty of free will remains, it is possible to reject God and the supernatural order. Even in that case, because of the character, as St. Chrysostom says, "We may be recognized as deserters" (In I Cor. ii,1). St. Ambrose dwells upon the more consoling truth: "We are sealed by the Spirit that we may be able to keep within the splendor and likness of Him and His grace . . . *that the Holy Ghost may express in us a picture of His heavenly likeness.*"

Let us listen to a Pentecost sermon by St. Augustine: "The Apostle says, 'One body, one spirit.' Listen, members of that body! The body is made up of many members and one spirit quickens them all. Behold, by the spirit of a man, by which I myself am a man, I hold together all the members; I com-

upon the forehead. Continuing, he makes the sign of the cross over the person at the name of each of the three divine persons.

Then he strikes the confirmed lightly upon the cheek, saying:

Peace be with you.

An attending priest removes the holy chrism from the forehead with cotton batting, which is afterwards burned.

After washing his hands, the minister reads the Antiphon:

CONFIRM, O God, *what Thou hast wrought in us, from Thy holy temple in Jerusalem.*

Glory be to the Father and to the Son and to the Holy Spirit. As it was in the beginning, is now and ever shall be, world without end. Amen.

Then turning to the altar, with hands joined he says:

V. *Show us, O Lord, Thy mercy.*
R. *And grant us Thy salvation.*
V. *O Lord, hear my prayer.*
R. *And let my cry come unto Thee.*
V. *The Lord be with you.*
R. *And with your spirit.*

mand them to move; I direct the eyes to see, the ears to hear, the tongue to speak, the hands to work, the feet to walk. The offices of the members are divided severally, but one spirit holds all in one. . . . What our spirit — that is, our soul — is to our members, that the Holy Ghost is to the members of Christ, to the body of Christ, which is the Church. Therefore the Apostle, when he had spoken of the one body, lest we should suppose it to be a dead body, says, 'There is one body.' I ask: 'Is this body alive?' It is alive. Whence? From the one Spirit. 'There is one Spirit' " (*Sermon* 267).

Two final blessings complete the ceremony. The last of these is justly cherished for its Scriptural language, its depth of feeling, and its venerable antiquity.

Let us pray.

O GOD, *who hast given the Holy Spirit to Thy Apostles, and hast willed that through them and their successors He be given to the rest of the faithful, look with favor upon our humble service, and grant that the Holy Spirit, descending into the heart of this man/woman whose forehead we have anointed with holy Chrism and signed with the sign of the holy cross, may, by dwelling there, make it a temple of His glory. Thou Who with the Father and the Holy Spirit dost live and reign forever and ever.*
R. *Amen.*

Then the minister says:

Behold, so will the man be blessed who fears the Lord.

Turning to those who have been confirmed, and making the sign of the cross over them he blesses them as follows:

M AY *the Lord bless you from Sion, so that you may see the prosperity of Jerusalem all the days of your life and that you may have life everlasting.*
R. *Amen.*

Summary. Confirmation is a sacrament, in which, through anointing and the imposition of hands, the Christian initiation is completed in the conferring of the Holy Ghost; it advances the Christian to adult standing in the Church, and associates him with the highest grade of the priesthood of the laity; it is named from its distinctive characteristic of imparting spiritual strength and confident assurance in God.

Eighteenth-Century Source Material

(Long before 1784, when John Carroll became Vicar-Apostolic and Bishop, the position of American colonists, permanently "deprived of the Sacrament of Confirmation," was most acutely felt.)

Now, coming to the rich and populous provinces of *New England* and *New York* one may find many a Catholic here and there, but they have no opportunity of practicing their religion as no priest visits them, and if we are to judge of the future from the present conditions of the inhabitants, there is not much likelihood that Catholic priests will be permitted to enter these provinces. . . .

Among the old possessions of Great Britain on the continent of America, the only colonies in which priests are permanently located are the provinces of *Maryland* and *Pennsylvania*. In the latter, the Catholic Religion was formerly tolerated by law. In *Maryland*, the laws are opposed to it, as in England; however these laws are rarely put into execution and usually there is a sort of tacit toleration.

It is claimed in *Maryland* there must be around sixteen thousand Catholics, of whom about half approach the sacraments. To take care of these there are twelve missionaries of the Society of Jesus.

The number of Catholics in *Pennsylvania* is between six and seven thousand. They have a public church in Philadelphia, which is the capital of the province. They are ministered to by four priests likewise Jesuits. . . .

There are besides some Catholics in *Virginia*, on the confines of *Maryland*, and in those parts of *New Jersey* which border on *Pennsylvania*. But they have no priests permanently residing among them, their spiritual wants being administered to by missionaries from the two provinces above mentioned. As to *Carolina* and *Georgia*, it is impossible to say whether there are any Catholics there or not. One thing is certain, there are no priests in those provinces.

Florida, a province ceded by Spain in the same Treaty of *Paris,* already mentioned, is almost a wilderness, but the few Catholics who have remained there are allowed the freedom of practicing the Catholic religion in the same manner as the inhabitants of Canada.

Louisiana, or the province of *Mississippi,* which formerly belonged to the French, has for the most part been ceded to the English by the same Treaty, that is, up to the Mississippi River, which gives the province its name. The same freedom of worship has been granted in favor of the Catholic inhabitants, of whom there must be a considerable number. But as to how they are taken care of spiritually the writer has no information whatever. . . .

The great distances of these provinces from his residence [in London] hinders him [the Vicar-Apostolic] from visiting them personally. And therefore he cannot have the information necessary to know abuses and to correct them; *he cannot administer the Sacrament of Confirmation to those faithful who remain totally deprived of this spiritual aid;* he cannot furnish them with priests. . . .

If the Sacred Congregation, moved by these considerations . . . considers it meet to create a Vicar-Apostolic over the other English colonies and islands, it seems that the city of Philadelphia in Pennsylvania would be the place best suited for him to reside in. . . . — *Bishop Richard Challoner,* Vicar-Apostolic of London, to Rome, about 1763. (Quoted from Guilday's *Life and Times of John Carroll* by permission of the Encyclopedia Press.)

Topics for Further Discussion:

That priests by delegation can validly confirm.
Circumstances attending the consecration of the chrism.
Purpose and function of sponsors at confirmation.
The confirmation of infants.
The appropriateness of the Western practice in conferring confirmation at the beginning of adolescence.

Readings:

A. d'Alès, *Baptism and Confirmation* (St. Louis: Herder, 1929).
F. X. Doyle, *The Wonderful Sacraments* (New York: Benziger, 1924); "Confirmation," pp. 90–109.
M. Laros, *Confirmation in the Modern World* (New York: Sheed and Ward, 1938); "The Sacrament of Personality," pp. 17–34; "The Sacrament of Catholic Action," pp. 89–114.
C. Lattey, *Six Sacraments, Papers Read at the Summer School of Catholic*

Studies, Cambridge, 1929 (St. Louis: Herder, 1930); Canon George, "Confirmation," pp. 111–130.

B. Leeming, "The Age for Confirmation," *The Clergy Review,* 41 (1956), 649–663.

——— "The Confirmation of Dying Infants," *The Clergy Review,* 40 (1955), 641–657.

M. Perkins, *Speaking of How to Pray* (New York: Sheed and Ward, 1944); "The Oil of Gladness," pp. 105–116.

R. Plus, *Baptism and Confirmation* (London: Burns, Oates and Washbourne, 1930).

W. F. Robison, *The Seven-Fold Gift* (St. Louis: Herder, 1922); "The Soldier's Signing," pp. 31–63.

T. B. Scannell, "Confirmation," *CE.*

T. W. Smiddy, *A Manual for the Extraordinary Minister of Confirmation* (Milwaukee: Bruce, 1950), *passim.*

G. D. Smith, "The Sacrament of Confirmation," *The Teaching of the Catholic Church* (New York: Macmillan, 1949), II, pp. 803–836.

T. Sparks, "Confirmation, the Completion of the Baptismal Initiation," *The Sacramental Way* (New York: Sheed and Ward, 1948), pp. 103–116.

Chapter XIX

OUR SUPERSUBSTANTIAL BREAD — EMMANUEL

Give us each day our daily bread
(Luke xi,3).

CONSIDERATION of the Holy Eucharist thus far in this book has been limited to the aspect of *Sacrifice*. There is another important realm of Eucharistic truth, that in which this Trust is commonly designated the *Blessed Sacrament*. The Eucharist is both Sacrifice and Sacrament. Like every *sacrifice*, it enables man to approach God by means of a symbolic gift; like the other *sacraments* the Eucharist enables God to approach man, so to speak, by imparting ever new measures of that God-life which we call sanctifying grace. Above all other sacrifices, the Eucharist stands in unapproachable pre-eminence, the fulfillment of what they merely prefigured. And above the other sacraments, the Eucharist enjoys a parallel superiority, for whereas all the sacraments are channels of Christ's grace, this contains and confers Christ, the very fountainhead of grace, Himself. In fact, the multiple relations of the Sacrament of the Eucharist to the other sacraments seemed to the *Catechism of the Council of Trent* to afford the key to the knowledge of the full truth about the limitless riches it contains. That book suggests:

As, however, no language can convey an adequate idea of its utility and fruits, pastors must be content to treat of one or two points, in order to show what an abundance and profusion of all goods are contained in those sacred mysteries.

This they will in some degree accomplish, if, having explained the efficacy and nature of all the Sacraments, they *compare the Eucharist to a fountain, the other Sacraments to rivulets*. For the Holy Eucharist is truly and necessarily to be called the fountain of all graces, containing, as it does, after an admirable manner, the fountain itself of celestial gifts and graces, and the author of all the Sacraments, Christ,

280

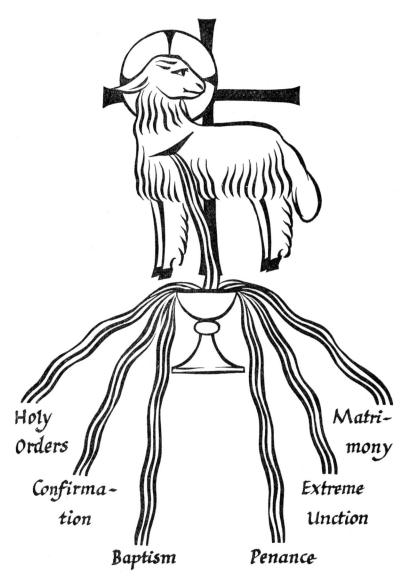

Holy
Orders

Matri-
mony

Confirma-
tion

Extreme
Unction

Baptism

Penance

Compare the Eucharist to a fountain,
the other Sacraments to rivulets.

(Catechism of Trent)

our Lord, from whom, as from its source, is derived whatever of goodness and perfection the other Sacraments possess.

Permanence. In its constitution, so to speak, there is a striking
respect in which the Eucharist differs from the other sacraments — its permanence. In baptism the effects of the sacrament are indeed ineradicably
planted in the soul, but the sacrament itself exists only in the momentary union of the flowing water and the words of administration. So,
too, in confirmation, in penance, and the other sacraments, all are of
momentary duration. The determining words are coupled to the sense
sign and in that instant grace is signified and conferred, and the sacraments as such cease to exist. But it is otherwise with the Holy Eucharist.
Once the species have been consecrated, the Sacrament remains as long
as these remain unchanged. Holy Scripture tells us of the Son of God
emptying Himself of His glory, and humbling Himself to the extent of
assuming our lowly flesh, and enduring death upon the cross. The
Eucharist, as the Fathers have pointed out, entails even a further putting
away of His glory, and a deeper veiling even unto the forms of common
bread and wine. Than this abasement unto bread even divine Love could
go no further. This is the glory of that abiding Presence — Emmanuel.

Transubstantiation. That conversion, by which at the words of consecration, the "substance" of the bread and wine are changed into the
Body and Blood of Christ, while the appearances remain as before, is
called by the Church *transubstantiation*. It is not as though Christ were
hidden within the bread, or permeates the bread — for there is nothing
of bread and wine remaining save the mere sense appearances. Through
this change the actual reality that before was bread or wine is now Christ.
Except for the appearances of bread and wine there is nothing there *but*
Christ, but the living Christ, Christ whole and entire, Body and Blood,
human soul and uncreated Godhead, indissolubly united with the Father
and the Holy Spirit. The former reality is gone, the new Reality is present. This "mystery of faith" is impenetrable to our limited understanding.
The twentieth-century child (or adult) is taught this great truth of the
Eucharist in substantially the same words and phrases as are found in
the oldest catechism we have, that of St. Cyril of Jerusalem, of about 347.
He wrote:

In the figure of the bread is given to thee the Body, and in the figure
of wine the Blood, so that when thou receivest the Body and Blood of

Christ, thou mayest become of one body and blood with Him; for *thus we are become Christ-bearers (Christophoroi)*, when His Body and His Blood are distributed in our members.

What appears to be bread is not bread, although it seems thus to the taste, but is the Body of Christ. . . . At Cana in Galilee He once changed water into wine which is akin to Blood; and shall we not believe Him when He changes wine into Blood? *Cat.* xxii

Two Uses Enjoined. Concerning this Sacrament, by which Christ has committed Himself to our keeping, we have two commands from divine authority, "Do this in memory of Me," and "Take ye and eat." These two uses, *Sacrifice* and *Communion*, coincide fairly well in actual practice, since Communion is designed primarily as a means of imparting to man the return-graces won by the Sacrifice. So inseparably is the Return-Gift connected with the Gift, that without the Communion of at least the priest there is no *integral* Sacrifice. That this truth was once much more commonly appreciated by the vast multitude of the faithful than it is at the present day may, perhaps, be shown by the popular terms with which Communion was referred to. Formerly the common term in the English language for Communion was "Housel," which means etymologically "Oblation," or "Sacrifice." In our own times we speak of the Host and are surprised to learn that for those who first used the term, "Host" (*hostia*) meant sacrificial victim.

Development Brought Other Uses. Christ once compared His Kingdom to a grain of mustard seed, the smallest of seeds when sown, but capable of becoming a tree of stately proportions. And what has been said by way of incidental illustration in the preceding chapters amply illustrates how the offices of Christian worship have undergone a silent but ceaseless development ever since the Pentecostal bath of fire. Just as the great *dogmas* themselves gradually disclosed, and still disclose, their fullest depths and beauties, so the *devotional life* of the Church has become constantly richer by the never-ending blossoming of Catholic piety. In this slow, expansive process, which one cannot observe from day to day, it may even be said that each succeeding age comes into possession of a deeper and fuller Christianity. On looking back one wonders how former ages got along without what we now find so necessary.

A "Thing" and a "Person." In the history of Eucharistic development *an explicitly conscious devotion* to the Real Presence was reserved for the period beginning roughly with the second Christian millennium. No fact is more essential in any historic study touching the Holy Eucharist than this, because this fact gradually brought about such a new reverence for the Holy Eucharist as to effect far-reaching changes in

the *uses* made of it. Of course there was always an implicit realization of, and embryonic devotion to, the Real Presence, but when this passed into the realm of the actual consciousness, the Eucharist, as it were, changed in our estimation of It and attitude toward It from a *thing,* a very holy thing, the holiest of all things, the Body of the Lord, into a *Person.*

Where once people thought it fit and proper to carry the Blessed Sacrament on their persons for safety on embarking on a sea voyage, or to hoist It to the tips of their battle standards, and so plunge into the fray, the newer attitude brought it about that the Eucharist was elevated at Mass, was enthroned upon the altar, was visited, was *prayed to,* in fine, was adored as God. Instead of the Eucharist being wrapped in scarfs and carried on a sea voyage, as formerly, the Eucharistic Lord was now borne in solemn state to bless the vessels by His Presence before sailing.

Still less was the Eucharist now allowed to be kept in little boxes in private dwellings, but instead the families gayly adorned the homes on Corpus Christi Day with whatever of homely finery they possessed, that so their homage might be evidenced as the King was borne through the streets. It can be seen at a glance what a turning point in the history of Christian piety was marked when the full implications of the worship of the Real Presence were realized.

Spread of New Attitude. In the first ages of the Church, whatever *nonsacrificial* uses of the Blessed Eucharist developed (and they were many), these followed by close analogy the two revealed sacrificial ones, Gift and Food. The Eucharist was above all else a *means* to be used in serving God and sanctifying oneself. But it happened that the newer attitude took its rise precisely at a time when, as the *Catechism of the Council of Trent* informs us, people were often accustomed to put off the actual reception of Communion for years at a time. The then existing "Eucharistic void," so to speak, in everyday life caused the new point of view to grow and spread all the more readily. The hunger and thirst, that were not being slaked at the Table of the Lord, were being sated by the very Presence of the Beloved, in visiting and bringing gifts to the Prisoner in the Tabernacle, by attending as a courtier whenever He went through the streets, in uniting with the other villagers to sing His praises and beg His benediction before nightfall, and in other such pious practices. The elevation in the Mass, the tabernacle on the altar, the repository of Holy Thursday, the Corpus Christi processions, the Exposition of Holy Hour, of Forty Hours, our familiar evening Benediction — even the hastiest recollection of what these things mean for us is enough to show what an immeasurable enriching of Christian life has resulted from direct Eucharistic adoration.

Returning to Tradition. But the Church above all else has the trust to be true to her past, to

> guard the good deposit
> through the Holy Spirit
> who dwelleth in us.   II Tim. i,14

Thus it is that, while preserving all the gains of the newer aspect of Eucharistic piety, she is wisely and gradually leading us back once more to the more sacrificial outlook of the more distant past. A modern theologian summed up all we have been saying in the words: "The first ten centuries knew predominantly the *means* aspect of the Blessed Eucharist, the second ten, the *Person* aspect; the day is now dawning when Christians shall simultaneously possess both aspects of this matchless truth."

Personal Values for Super-Life. "The effect of the Sacrament [of the Eucharist]," says St. Thomas, "corresponds to what is done externally in its administration." What is done externally is a social serving of Food. And when directing the modern mind to the older point of view regarding the frequent reception of the Eucharist, Pope Pius X took pains to restate clearly the primary purpose of Communion:

> The desire of Jesus Christ, and of the Church, that *all Christians should daily approach this holy banquet* is based chiefly on this, that Christians united to God through the Sacrament should derive therefrom the *strength* to conquer concupiscence, and should wash away light faults of daily occurrence, and should forestall more serious ones to which human frailty is exposed. The chief thing here is not to safeguard honor and reverence to [our] Lord, [as the Jansenists had taught].

Dec. 20, 1905

This food for the super-life is set before Christians at the conclusion of their social worship of Sacrifice. St. Paul calls the Communion Table "the Supper of the Lord."

I Cor. xi,20

The notable circumstance that the Eucharistic Food, instead of being transmuted into human flesh and blood, as ordinary bodily nourishment, has the singular faculty of itself transmuting men, little by little, into Christs, has been commented upon times without number. Pope Urban IV, who was a contemporary of St. Thomas (thirteenth century), has expressed this thought with classic beauty:

> This Bread is eaten, but not transmuted; it is nowise changed into the consumer, but if it be worthily received, the recipient becomes like to it. This transmutation is brought about by the *streaming in upon us* of the spirit and *life* of Christ. As a result "Christ liveth in us"; our thoughts, our senses and impulses, our will and activity *assume a resemblance* to the hidden Life of the Eucharistic Saviour, and become divine.

Bull, *Transiturus*

St. Thomas describes this primary effect of the reception of the Eucharist under four terms: nutriment, growth, repair, and delight. By this last

S.T. III. Q. lxxix, a.1

he means a certain sense of spiritual exhilaration and a consequent attraction toward God's goodness and sanctity.

Measure of Christ-Life. The good that food does one only commences after eating, when the food begins to be assimilated into living tissue. And the food value of the same diet, taken in the same quantities, remains within narrow limits a constant quantity. But what is the measure of the new Christ-life imparted in Communion? This does *not* remain a constant, but is capable of indefinite expansion and increase, since it corresponds to the *use* that is made of the graces already given. The life value of tomorrow's Communion will depend upon the use being made every hour of today in *living* by the Christ-life given in this morning's Communion.

Today and Tomorrow and the Eucharist. Men and women now everywhere face the threat of a revolution that was characterized by Pope Pius XI as nothing less than relapse into barbarism. "This modern revolution," said this pontiff, "it may be said, has actually broken out, or threatens everywhere, and it exceeds in amplitude and violence anything yet experienced in the preceding persecutions launched against the Church. *Entire peoples find themselves in danger of falling back into a barbarism* worse than that which oppressed the greater part of the world at the coming of the Redeemer." Serenely the Church plans for the future, knowing that she is deathless as long as the world shall run. *On Atheistic Communism, 1937* She will meet the danger by emphasizing the relation of the Eucharist to social solidarity. "To those who read the history of the Church with a discerning eye," explains Archbishop E. A. Mooney (Detroit), "it is clear that each succeeding age has seen insistence instinctively placed on some application of Christian doctrine which meets the special needs of that age. Our own age, with its significant experiments in social solidarity, is witnessing a providential concentration of Christian thought on the doctrine of the Church as the Mystical Body of Christ, and on some of the obvious social implications of that doctrine. . . . It is the one Christ living and working in us. Christ so identifies Himself with the individual members of the Church that our thought of Him would be utterly one-sided and incomplete if it were to consider Him without reference to them. We are members then of one another and of Christ who is our Head. . . . The Holy Eucharist is, to use a phrase which the Fathers of the Church loved, the prime ordinary means of effecting our incorporation with Christ; but St. Paul would have us remember that it is the means of our incorporation with Christ as Head of His Mystical Body, the Church, through which in every age the power of Christ functions in the world, through which the divine work which Christ came to do, is carried on among men."

1935

Summary. The Eucharist is a sacrament (solemnly promised at Capharnaum and instituted at the Last Supper), wherein the Body and Blood of Christ are made present by the power of the words of consecration, under the species or appearances of bread and wine. The Real Presence endures as long as the species remain unconsumed. Besides the divinely appointed uses of the Eucharist in the Christian Sacrifice (as Gift and as Return-Gift), Christian piety has discovered various others, the chief of which is Eucharistic adoration. By its reception as Communion the Holy Eucharist provides the chief channel of God's grace to the individual, and is the chief token of Christian fellowship. As such it is the aspect of Eucharistic doctrine that is particularly emphasized at present.

THE RITE OF HOLY EUCHARIST ADMINISTERED AS VIATICUM[1]

When the priest enters the sickroom he says:

V. Peace be to this house.

R. And to all who live here.

Having put the Blessed Sacrament upon a linen corporal on a table, and genuflecting before It, the priest sprinkles the sick person and the bed with holy water, saying:

Sprinkle me, O Lord, with a hyssop, and I shall be purified; wash me, and I shall be whiter than snow.

Ps. 50: Have mercy on me, O God, because Thou art merciful.

Glory be to the Father, and to the Son, and to the Holy Spirit.

As it was in the beginning, is now, and ever shall be, world without end. Amen.

Sprinkle me, O Lord, with a hyssop, and I shall be purified; wash me, and I shall be whiter than snow.

---

[1]Reproduced from *Collectio Rituum* (Milwaukee: Bruce, 1954). All may be said in English.

V. **Our** help is in the name of the Lord.

R. Who made heaven and earth.

V. O Lord, hear my prayer.

R. And let my cry come unto Thee.

V. The Lord be with you.

R. And with your spirit.

Let us pray.

Hear us, O holy Lord, Father almighty, eternal God, and in Thy kindness send Thy holy angel from heaven to watch over, cherish, protect, be with, and defend all who live in this house. Through Christ our Lord.

R. Amen.

Thereupon he inquires concerning the sick person's need or desire of confessing before receiving Viaticum. With a change of stoles, he hears the confession, gives absolution, and then says:

May the passion of our Lord Jesus Christ, the merits of the Blessed Virgin Mary and of all the saints, and whatever good you have done and evil you have endured be cause for the remission of your sins, the increase of grace, and the reward of everlasting life. Amen.

After this the sick person, or someone in his stead, says the Confiteor:

I confess to Almighty God, to blessed Mary ever Virgin, to blessed Michael the Archangel, to blessed John the Baptist, to the holy Apostles Peter and Paul, to all the Saints, and to you, Father, that I have sinned exceedingly in thought, word, and deed; through my fault, through my fault, through my most grievous fault. Therefore I beseech blessed Mary ever Virgin, blessed Michael the Archangel, blessed John the Baptist, the holy Apostles Peter and Paul, all the Saints, and you, Father, to pray to the Lord our God for me.

The priest says:

May almighty God have mercy on you, forgive you your sins, and bring you to life everlasting. Amen.

May the almighty and merciful Lord grant you pardon, absolution, and remission of your sins.

R. Amen.

Then, having made a genuflection, he holds up the Blessed Sacrament so that the sick person can see It, saying:

Behold the Lamb of God; behold Him who takes away the sins of the world.

He adds in the accustomed manner:

Lord, I am not worthy that Thou shouldst come under my roof; but say only the word, and my soul shall be healed.

Then he gives Holy Communion to the sick person saying:

Receive, my brother/sister, this food for your journey, the Body of our Lord Jesus Christ, that He may guard you from the malicious enemy and lead you into everlasting life. Amen.

If Communion is not given as Viaticum, the priest says, as ordinarily:

May the Body of our Lord Jesus Christ be the guardian of your soul into everlasting life. Amen.

Then the priest washes his fingers in a little water, and wipes them; in due time this water will be thrown into the fire. Then he says:

V. The Lord be with you.
R. And with your spirit.

Let us pray.

O holy Lord, Father almighty, eternal God, trustfully we beg of Thee that the most sacred Body of Thy Son, our Lord Jesus Christ, may be a lasting remedy of both body and soul for our brother/sister who has just received It. Through Him Who lives and reigns with Thee in the unity of the Holy Spirit, God, world without end.
R. Amen.

If any particle of the Sacrament remains, the priest genuflects, rises, and with the Sacrament in the pyx, covered by the burse, makes the sign of the cross over the sick person, saying nothing. Returned to the church, he says the prescribed prayers:

O holy banquet, in which Christ is received, the memory of His Passion is renewed, the soul is filled with grace, and there is given to us a pledge of future glory.
V. Thou hast given them bread from heaven.
R. Containing in itself all delight.
V. The Lord be with you.
R. And with your spirit.

Let us pray.

O God, Who in this wonderful sacrament hast left us a memorial of Thy passion, grant, we implore Thee, that we may so venerate the sacred mysteries of Thy Body and Blood as always to be conscious of the fruit of Thy redemption. Who livest and reignest for ever and ever.

R. Amen.

But if nothing of the Sacrament remains, the priest says in the sick room:

May the blessing of almighty God, Father, ✝ Son, and Holy Spirit, descend upon you and remain forever.

R. Amen.

Nineteenth-Century Source Material

(John Henry Newman, one of the greatest modern champions of Catholicism, writes of Christ and the Eucharist.)

He left His Father's courts, He was manifested, He spake; and His voice went out into all lands. He has taken to Himself His great power and reigned; and, whereas an enemy is the god and tyrant of this world, as Adam made it, so, as far as He occupies it, does He restore it to His Father. Henceforth He is the one principle of life in all His servants, who are but His organs. The Jewish Church looked toward Him; the Christian speaks and acts from Him. What is prior to Him is dark, but all that comes after Him is illuminated. The Church, before His manifestation, offered to Him material elements "which perish with the using"; but now He has sent His Spirit to fill such elements with Himself, and to make them living and availing sacrifices to the Father. Figures have become means of grace, shadows are substances, types are Sacraments in Him. What before were decent ordinances and pious observances, have now not only a meaning but a virtue. Water could but wash the Body in the way of nature; but now it acts toward the cleansing of the soul. "Wine which maketh glad the heart of man," and "bread which strengthens man's heart," nay, the "oil which maketh him a cheerful countenance," henceforth are more than means of animal life, and savor of Him. Hands raised in blessing, the accents of the voice of man, which before could but symbolize the yearnings of human nature, or avail for lower benefits, have now become the "unutterable intercessions" of the

Spirit, and the touch, and the breath of the Incarnate Son. The Church has become His body, her priests His delegates, her people His members.

This is what Christ has done by His coming; but observe, *while* He did all this for His Church, He claimed all He did *as* His own. Henceforth whatever is done is His doing, and it is called what it is. As He is the unseen Source, so must He be acknowledged as the Agent, the present Object of worship and thanksgiving in all that is done; and His instruments are not even so much as instruments, but only the outward lineaments of Him. All is superseded by Him, and transmuted into Him. Before He came there were many masters, but henceforth only One; before He came many Fathers, but He is the One Father of the coming age, as the Prophet styles Him; before He came, all to whom the word of God came were called gods, but He is the One God manifested in the flesh; before He came, there were many angelic appearances with the name of God on them, but now the great Angel of the Covenant is alone to be worshiped; before He came, there were many priests who had infirmity, offering sacrifices year by year continually, but now there is but One High Priest, "who is set on the right hand of the throne of the majesty in the heavens, a minister of the sanctuary, and of the true tabernacle, which the Lord pitched, and not man"; before, there were innumerable sacrifices of bulls and calves which could never perfect the worshipers, now One Immaculate Lamb who taketh away the sin of the world; before, there were judges, kings, and rulers of various ranks, but now there is but One King of kings, and Lord of lords, in His kingdom. . . . There were mediators many, and prophets many, and atonements many. But now all is superseded by One, in whom all offices merge, who has absorbed into Himself all principality, power, might, and dominion, and every name that is named; who has put His holy and fearful Name upon all, who is in and through all things, and without whom nothing is good. He is the sole self-existing principle in the Christian Church, and everything else is but a portion or declaration of Him. Not that now, as then, we may not speak of prophets, and rulers, and priests, and sacrifices, and altars, and saints, and that in a far higher and more spiritual sense than before, but that they are not any of them such of themselves; it is not they, but the grace of God that is in them. There is under the Gospel but One proper Priest, Prophet, and King, Altar Sacrifice, and House of God. Unity is its characteristic sacrament, all grace flows from One Head, and all life circulates in the members of One Body. — Quoted from *A Newman Synthesis,* by permission of Sheed and Ward.

Topics for Further Discussion:

The "matter" of the Eucharist, bread (originally leavened, now unleavened in the Western Church) made from pure wheat flour, and pure grape wine.

The former custom of communicating infants after Baptism with a few drops of the Precious Blood.

Inconveniences attending Communion under both species.

In "offering up" Communion for another, one renders God the same adoration and thanksgiving as in any Communion, and personally receives the sacramental grace (increase of Christ-life), while some of the petitionary and satisfactory values are diverted to the person for whom the Communion is offered.

"The best preparation for receiving our Lord tomorrow is to receive Him today."

The reception of Communion as a divine precept.

That Christ is truly received even by persons in mortal sin.

"Every hour is good for Mass-serving." — *St. John Berchmans.*

Readings:

T. E. Bridgett, *A History of the Holy Eucharist in Great Britain* (London: Burns, Oates and Washbourne, 1908); "The Eucharist in the Life of the People," pp. 217–292.

P. Claudel, *Ways and Crossways* (New York: Sheed and Ward, 1933); "The Physics of the Eucharist," pp. 55–71.

I. Goma–A. J. Willinger, *The Eucharist and the Christian Life* (Paterson: Guild Press, 1949); "The Eucharist . . . as an Object of Catholic Worship," pp. 53–94.

J. C. Hedley, *The Holy Eucharist* (New York: Longmans, Green, 1907); "Apparent Absence of *Cultus* of the Holy Eucharist in the First Thousand Years of the Christian Era," pp. 253–271.

J. Kramp, *Live the Mass* (St. Paul: Cat. Guild, 1954), "The History of Eucharistic Adoration," pp. 302–333.

The Last Rites for the Sick and Dying (Collegeville: Lit. Press, 1957).

E. Leen, *The True Vine and the Branches* (New York: Kenedy, 1938); "The Bread of Life," pp. 92–107.

C. Marmion, *Christ the Life of the Soul* (St. Louis: Herder, 1923); "Panis Vitae," pp. 279–304.

R. Plus, *The Eucharist* (London: Burns, Oates and Washbourne, 1931).

J. Pohle, "Eucharist, the Blessed, as a Sacrament," *CE.*

M. Scheeben–C. Vollert, *The Mysteries of Christianity* (St. Louis: Herder, 1946), "The Incorporation of Christians in Christ Through the Eucharist," pp. 483–497.

Seventh National Eucharistic Congress (Cleveland, 1936); E. A. Smith, Address "Communionism and Communism," pp. 229–233.

G. D. Smith, "The Sacrament of the Eucharist," *The Teachings of the Catholic Church* (New York: Macmillan, 1949), II, pp. 839–879.

H. Thurston, "Benediction," *The Month*, 97, 98 (1901), pp. 587–597, 58–69, 186–193, 264–276; "Our English Benediction Service," 106 (1905), pp. 394–404.

Ninth Eucharistic Congress, Westminster, 1908 (London: Sands, 1909); H. Thurston, "Benediction of the Blessed Sacrament," pp. 452–463.

A. Vonier, *A Key to the Doctrine of the Eucharist* (New York: Benziger, 1925); "Transubstantiation," pp. 176–192.

Chapter XX

THE FATHER OF THE PRODIGAL

If any one have sinned,
we have an Advocate with the Father;
Jesus Christ, the Just
(I John ii,1).

ONE of the reproaches most frequently flung at Christ in His public life was His consorting with sinners. It was a scandal to the religious leaders of the day that He came not to call just Matt. ix men, but sinners, that He conversed with the Samaritan woman, that John iv He dined with Zachaeus, spared the woman taken in adultery, and John viii allowed another woman of ill fame to bathe His sacred feet with her tears. He was, moreover, charged with blasphemy when He claimed to Luke vii remit sin. Matt. ix

"The Friend of Sinners." The attitude then taken toward Christ has been throughout the centuries consistently taken against His Church. What Catholic has not heard the taunt: "Your Church is the friend of the criminal, the lawless, the sinner!" To which the Church serenely responds that the disciple is not above the Master, that her mission is Matt. x,24 precisely to seek out and reclaim what was lost, to bring back to super- Luke xv,4 natural life that which was dead, that she must be ready to forgive those Luke xv,28 who sin against her, not to seven times, but up to seventy times seven. Matt. xviii The Catholic Church is unique among religious bodies now and always, as the whole world knows, in that she provides a regularly constituted ministry of sacramental forgiveness. Something over sixteen hundred years ago, at the very height of the Diocletian persecution, one of the Church's champions made the claim:

> But because all the separated heretical assemblies call themselves
> Christians, and think that theirs is the Catholic Church, you ought to
> know that that is the Catholic Church where there is confession and
> repentance, which soundly cures the sins and wounds to which weak- Lactantius, *De*
> ness of the flesh is heir. *div. Inst.* ix, xxx

Christit is in god

reconciling

the world

unto Himself

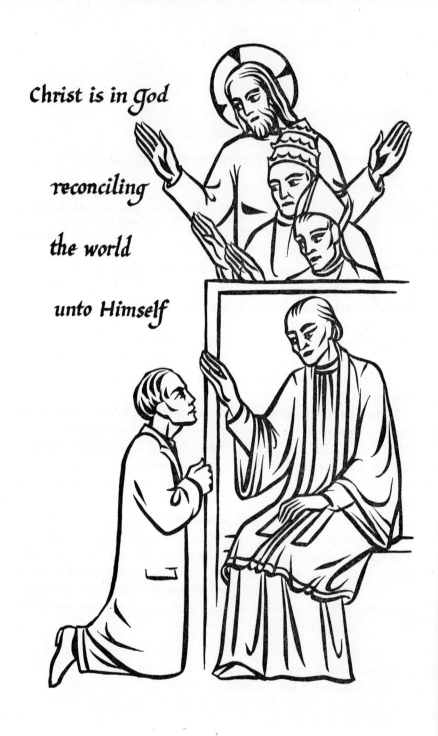

So was Catholicism characterized in the Roman Empire, and so is it characterized in our world of today, as attested by the great modern apologist, Mr. Chesterton:

> When people ask me, or indeed anybody else, "Why did you join the Church of Rome?" the first essential answer, if it is partly an elliptical answer, is, "To get rid of my sins." For there is no other religious system that does *really* profess to get rid of people's sins. . . . The Sacrament of Penance gives a new life, and reconciles man to all living. . . . The gift is given at a price, and is conditioned by a confession. In other words, the name of the price is Truth, which may be called Reality; but it is facing the reality about oneself.[1]

How indeed could the Christian religion be constituted without this saving sacrament? Christ came that through His death we might have supernatural life and strength and effectiveness in actual solidarity with Him.

> If, then, any man be in Christ,
>   he is a new creature:
>   the former things have passed away:
> Behold, all things are made new!
>
> But all things are of God,
>   who hath reconciled us to Himself through Christ
>   and hath given us the ministry of reconciliation:
> God . . . was reconciling the world to Himself in Christ.   II Cor. v,17–19

A Needed Remedy. This atonement with Him is effected by baptism, and lasts *as long as man does not break it by a serious and deliberate violation of God's law.* Such violations, of which St. Paul enumerates as types, impurity, idolatry, drunkenness, serious stealing and cheating, are I Cor. vi,10 *mortal,* are fatal; that is, they kill the supernatural life within, rendering the subject quite incapable of normal supernatural activity. Then what? Are these souls without further refuge? The weakness of our perverted natures, and the blindness to supernatural things, so characteristic of mankind, were known to God, and would be reckoned with in any economy of salvation that *could* be generally workable. In His ministry Christ worked miracles to prove that He personally had power to remit sin, Matt. ix and He more than once promised to Peter and the other Apostles that Mark xvii

---

[1] *Autobiography of G. K. Chesterton* (New York: Sheed and Ward, 1936), pp. 340, 342; quoted with permission.

Matt. xviii   He would confer on them the exercise of a like power in His name.
Then, on the very day on which "He arose from the dead for our justi-
Rom. iv,25   fication," He conferred the great boon of the sacrament of penance on
His Church.

> "Peace be to you.
> As the Father hath sent Me,
> I also send you."

> When He had said this,
> He breathed on them:
> and He saith to them:

> "Receive ye the Holy Ghost.
> Whose sins ye shall forgive,
> they are forgiven them:
John xx,21,22   and whose sins ye shall retain,
> they are retained."

How Used by Apostles. When the religious rebels of the sixteenth
century questioned the traditional interpretation of this passage, as
referring to the institution of the sacrament of penance, the Council of
Trent anathematized them for it. The power here given the Apostles,
Acts v   they *fearlessly exercised.* Peter judged Ananias and Saphira; Paul excom-
I Cor. v;   municated and later pardoned an incestuous Corinthian; he bade
II Cor. ii
I Tim. v   Timothy, "those who sin, rebuke in the sight of all"; James addressed
Christians with the energetic words:

> Make clean your hands,
> ye sinners,
James iv   and hallow your hearts,

while the tenderness of John's disposition moved him to phrase similar
counsels in the terms:

> If we say that we have no sin,
> we deceive ourselves,
> and the truth is not in us.
> If we confess our sins,
> He is faithful and just,
> so as to forgive us our sins,
I John i,8,9   and cleanse us from all iniquity.

If there is one thing clear from the New Testament, it is the infallible Church's conviction of her power to loose and bind the bonds of sin.

Variation in Usage. The Church was *conscious of her sacramental power* of remitting sin (provided the penitent was properly disposed) from Pentecost onwards; yet it is equally true that *her manner of exercising that power* has undergone great changes in the course of time. Our familiar habits of weekly or monthly confession were unknown in antiquity. Rather, as far as the meager records of the time tell the whole story, penance was administered quite differently then. Certain parts of the sacramental ritual or process, which are now strictly private, were then often, if not always, public, and semisocial, in appearance as well as character. Whether the actual confession of sins was private or public, the expression of contrition usually had to be made in public, and the satisfaction, or the "penance" as we call it, was usually public, with the absolution deferred until this satisfaction had been performed before the entire community. The absolution itself was usually administered in public. When we read in *The Teaching of the Twelve Apostles* (of about the year 80): "On the Lord's Day . . . come together, break bread and celebrate the Eucharist, *after confessing your transgressions,* that your Sacrifice may be pure," it is not clear whether this refers to private confession, or to a public confession of guilt couched in more or less general terms, after the manner of our *Confiteor* at the opening of Mass. This latter is, in the light of later custom, more probable.

Before the second century had run its full course, there is clear testimony that *for grievous sins* the organization of public penance was already far developed. (For minor transgressions, sacramental absolution was not needed, but could be had of the bishop on application.) Of the usages connected with the remission of serious sins we can learn much from Tertullian's picture of it. This was written at the very dawn of the third century, and shortly before that ardent spirit was carried away by ultrarigorism against the very system he here describes.

> This act . . . of confessing our sins to the Lord, not indeed as if He were ignorant of them, but because thereby a *satisfaction* is made for them; repentance, too, is born of confession, and by repentance God is appeased. And so confession becomes a disciplinary act of great humiliation and prostration to the penitent; it regulates the *dress,* the *food;* it enjoins sackcloth, and subdues the spirit with anguish; it bids

a man alter his life, and weep over his past sins; it restricts meat and drink to the greatest simplicity possible; it nourishes prayer by *fasting;* it inculcates groans and tears and invocations of the Lord God day and night, and teaches the penitent *to cast himself at the feet of the presbyters,* and to fall on his knees *before the beloved of God,* and to beg of all the *brethren to intercede on his behalf.* . . .

On Penance, c.ix

The body cannot rejoice in the injury of one of its members; all must grieve together and jointly strive for its cure. The Church is in one as well as in the other, and the Church is Christ. When, therefore, you prostrate yourself before the knees of your brethren you are touching Christ, you entreat Christ.

c.x

Early Strictness Mitigated. In the great persecutions of the third century, and the opening years of the fourth, there were many *Christians who fell away* at the hour of trial. Now *apostasy* was one of the mortal sins for which the full rigors of public penance was prescribed by tradition. But the persecutions soon spent themselves, and the "fair-weather Christians" came back in such numbers as to make the *application of the old rules impracticable.* Disputes arose as how the situation was to be handled. The rigorists were for excluding the "lapsed" for good and all, or at least, until the hour of death. The milder spirits, the popes in the van, adopted what seemed to the other party scandalously lax standards, so much so, in fact, that Tertullian and many others preferred to cut themselves off from the Church that stooped to welcome apostates back.

Public Penance in the East. These controversies focused attention on the whole matter of penitential administration, and helped to spread milder ways, but the system as a whole remained on the same basis. When a man had committed one or more of the graver sins, he had to make the fault known to the bishop, or his representative. So much was done, as a rule, in private unless the matter was so notorious that it could not be hidden. The bishop then appointed the culprit to one or other class of penitents, and enjoined a regime of mortification and self-denial which our modern outlook finds almost unbelievably strict. The penitents were (in the East) grouped into "mourners," "kneelers," "hearers," and "by-standers." These terms designated definite degrees of exclusion from participation in common worship. The *mourners* were forbidden even the entrance to the church: stationed outside in sackcloth and squalor they petitioned the prayers of those who entered. *Hearers* could, indeed,

IMPOSING PUBLIC PENANCE
Miniature in an old pontifical. (Reproduced from Thurston's *Lent and Holy Week,* by courtesy of Burns, Oates and Washbourne.)

enter the Church, and remain as long as the catechumens, but they were forbidden to raise their voices in the common prayers. This was allowed the *kneelers,* who, as the second highest class of penitents, knelt in an appointed place and received an imposition of hands before dismissal. *Bystanders* mingled freely with the faithful and were allowed to be present at the Sacrifice, but not to take part in the gift-procession or the Communion. Besides these public exercises of humility and submission, definite fasts, abstinences, almsgiving, prohibitions to bathe, and the like,

EXPELLING THE PENITENTS
Miniature in an old pontifical. (Reproduced from Thurston's *Lent and Holy Week,* by courtesy of Burns, Oates and Washbourne.)

were part of the regime. The general absolution, or reconciliation as it was called, took place on Holy Thursday, so that the entire community could celebrate the Easter solemnities together.

At Rome. The system just described was that of the Orient. A facile writer from Constantinople, Sozomen, having witnessed the Roman penitential discipline about 450, gives this description of it:

> In the churches of Rome the place of those who are in penance is very conspicuous: they stand with downcast eyes and the seeming of mourners. *When the service is concluded,* not being allowed to take part in what is allowed to the initiated alone, with wailing and lamentations they *prostrate themselves* on the ground. The bishop, weeping, comes towards them, and prostrates himself with cries for mercy. Then the bishop first rises and permits those prostrate to rise, and, having said a prayer in fitting fashion over the repentant sinners, dismisses them.
>
> Freely each does penance by fasting, abstention from bathing, abstinence, or whatever is appointed him, and so waits for the time allotted by the bishop. When the appointed day is at hand, he is absolved from his offenses like a debtor that has paid his debt, and he has his place among the people restored to him.

Hist. Eccles. vii,16

In the Lenten weekday Masses we have preserved, in the *Prayer Over the People,* the petition mentioned above as being said with so much ardor at the end of the daily Mass at Rome.

Gradual Transition to Modern Practice. As the Christian centuries unrolled, this *penitential discipline* gradually underwent progressive *mitigation.* At first the rigorous satisfactions demanded began to be commuted to much easier ones; still later, the private features of the rite were enlarged to include what had been heretofore, as a rule, public; lastly, the reconciliation, or *absolution,* was given at the *time of the confession,* on the promise that the satisfaction, "penance" we should say, would be performed as enjoined. The blessed ashes put on our foreheads on the first day of Lent are the one relic surviving of the old regime of public penance. Thus while the acts of both priest and penitent remained substantially the same, the external circumstances attending them came gradually to bear little resemblance to the rigors of an earlier and more robust age. Latterly, the full role of this sacrament of penance in the day-by-day work of character building, the "putting on of Christ," becoming ever clearer, our frequent confession became linked with the daily Sacrifice and Communion in the scheme of the full Christian lives possible in our days.

A Sacramental Judgment. One reason we have dwelt upon these old customs is that they illustrate the nature and character of the several parts of this sacrament better than the more compendious rites of today. "If any one say," declared the Council of Trent, "that the sacramental absolution of the priest is not a *judicial* act . . . let him be anathema [excommunicated]." The acts of the presiding cleric, bishop, or priest as the case may be, under the old regime, assigning a very definite term and measure of penance, overseeing its fulfillment, and then publicly absolving — these were more apt to strike an observer as actions of a judge on the bench than absolution privately and straightway given to all applicants suitably disposed, on their acceptance of a trivial "penance," which seems to bear no comparison to the gravity of the faults committed. But a momentary reflection will show that, as things are at present, all the *judicial* elements are preserved intact. Even now, the priest absolving a penitent judicially acquits him, as it were, of the sins, and this only after he has judged the penitent to be properly disposed. *Sess. xiv, 1551*

Jurisdiction. One of the essentials of this Sacrament seldom understood by the laity is its relation to what is called jurisdiction. Election or appointment confers on a judge in civil life the power of officially interpreting the law, but only in such cases as are referred to him in a court by the State. Holy orders gives the priest once and for all the power of binding and loosing sins, but the priest must be assigned to a tribunal in a given diocese before he can exercise that power. This assigning of a priest to a diocesan tribunal is called a grant of jurisdiction (over sinners); again, such a priest is said to have faculties to absolve sinners applying to his tribunal. This jurisdiction, stemming primarily from Christ's grant to Peter, comes to the priest through the bishop of the diocese. Thus, every confession, far from being a purely personal matter in an obscure corner, represents a cross section of authority exercised by the Church's entire hierarchical structure: Christ–pope–bishop–priest–penitent. In his ringing *Encyclical on the Priesthood*, Pope Pius XI says in this connection:

These words [of absolution] fall, it is true, from the lips of one, who, in his turn, must needs beg the same words of absolution from another priest. This does not debase the merciful gift; but makes it, rather, appear greater: since beyond the weak creature is seen more clearly the hand of God through whose power is wrought this wonder. As an illustrious layman has written, treating with rare competence of spiritual things: ". . . when a priest, groaning in spirit at his own unworthiness and at the loftiness of his office, places his consecrated hands upon our heads; when, humiliated at finding himself the dispenser of the Blood of the Covenant; each time amazed as he pronounces the words that give life; when a sinner has absolved a sinner; we, who rise from our knees before him, feel we have done nothing debasing. . . . We have been at the feet of a man who represented Jesus Christ . . . we have been there to receive the dignity of free men and of sons of God."

The Catholic Priesthood, December, 1935

Self-Accusation. The act from which the whole rite is nowadays popularly denominated, *confession, follows logically from the judicial character* of the power of absolving, as well as from the *medicinal nature* of the sacrament. In regard to this latter, the same Council of Trent aptly quotes a line from St. Jerome: "If the invalid shrink from disclosing his wound to the physician, the latter does not heal that of which he remains ignorant." Regarding the judicial examination to be made by the priest, it is clear that no presiding judge can give a ruling, or verdict, or pardon, until the case has been presented to him. This confession must be, as far as circumstances permit, the full record of the case. There is question here of good will, rather than of absolute, objective integrity of confession. Forgetfulness, ignorance, the affliction of dumbness, the inability then and there to speak the language of the only confessor available, even in emergencies, the lack of time, these render absolute integrity impossible but do not invalidate the confession.

In Eccl. Com. x,11 *Sess.* xiv, 1551

Salutary Sorrow. A more important element, in fact the *most important part* of the whole process, is *sorrow,* or contrition for sin. This means, as everyone knows, detestation and sorrow of heart for sin committed, together with a determination to sin no more. There can be no question of pardon without this. Catholics are often charged with holding that the mere telling of sins in confession is enough to wipe them out, and that afterwards one can return without qualm to the former habits of sin. The most elementary idea of God's justice and sanctity, to say nothing of the constant teaching of the Church, should show how groundless is this charge. If this resolve to sin now no more spring from the love of God and the knowledge that sin outrages His loving kindness, this contrition itself will obtain the pardon of sin, but there remains the obligation of submitting serious sins to the tribunal of penance. Less perfect, but still supernatural, sorrow for sin is sufficient to obtain sacramental forgiveness.

The Function of the "Penance." The role of satisfaction, or the function of the "penance" assigned by the confessor, is in danger of being underestimated in our present usage. Yet it is so important that a penitent cannot be absolved until he has *accepted* the penance enjoined. This is essentially something done as a display of good will, something done personally to expiate the past, and to foreshadow amendment for the future. This satisfaction is to be viewed in its relationship toward God, toward Christ, and toward the fellow members of the Mystical Body. As considered in reference to God, this penance is an acknowledgment that, while the loving mercy of God has condoned the guilt of sin, and its eternal punishment, still His justice demands the restoration of good order by the acceptance of some temporal punishment. As regards Christ, the penance reminds us that the Atonement was primarily a work of satisfaction, and that the members are called upon

> to make up in [their] flesh
> what is lacking of the sufferings of Christ.   Col. i,24

In this connection one should not forget that it is through our Mediator that the modicum of penance here prescribed to us actually has *sacramental efficacy*. The relation of my penance to the entire Mystical Body rests on the principle that the *prayers* and *merits of the Church as a whole* are an important factor in paying this satisfaction to God's justice. St. Pacian, in explaining sacramental absolution of the individual, writes in this strain: "It is obtained by all the faithful." St. Ambrose exhorts the sinner to ask for public penance "so that Christ will intercede for thee, . . . so that the Church pray for thee, so that the entire people weep for thee." There is, in fact, a close cooperation of the entire Christian body in the purification of the sinner, and thus Christ's gift to His Church involves the work of the Mystic Christ as well as that of the Head. In paying our tiny mite of a few Our Fathers and Hail Marys we are in reality drawing a sight draft on the boundless merits of the Mystical Body, Head and members. It is in these terms that the Council of Trent speaks of our "penance":

Rom. v,10
II Cor. iii,5
Rom. viii,17

Phil. iv,13

I Cor. i,31
Cf. Acts xvii,28
Luke iii,8

Sess. xiv, 1551

Whilst we thus, by making satisfaction, suffer for our sins, we are made conformable to Jesus Christ, who satisfied for our sins, from whom all our sufficiency is; having also thereby a most sure pledge that, if we suffer with Him, we shall also be glorified with Him.

But neither is this satisfaction, which we discharge for our sins, so our own as not to be *through Jesus Christ*. For we who can do nothing of ourselves, as of ourselves, can do all things, He cooperating, who strengthens us. Thus, man who has not wherein to glory, but all our glorying is in Christ: in whom we live; in whom we merit, in whom we satisfy; bringing forth fruits worthy of penance, which from Him have their efficacy; by Him are offered to the Father; and through Him are accepted by the Father.

In marked contrast to the severity of by-gone ages, we see and experience the beneficent operation of the great *fund of merit* in the Church, won by Christ, His most blessed Mother, and the saints, upon which we are privileged to draw so easily *by means of indulgences*.

THE RITE OF SACRAMENTAL ABSOLUTION[1]

When the priest wishes to absolve the penitent, after a suitable penance has been imposed and accepted, he says:

May almighty God have mercy on you, forgive you your sins, and bring you to life everlasting. Amen.

This prayer and the next are in reality deprecatory forms of absolution, a wish formally expressed that God will grant the remission of sin. Historians are of the opinion that the original forms of verbal absolution were expressed in this deprecatory manner.

Then with the right hand raised toward the penitent, he says:

May the almighty and merciful Lord grant you pardon, absolution, and remission of your sins. Amen.

The absolution here passes to the direct, indicative mood. The raising of the right hand of the priest is a formal laying on of hands. The oldest absolution ritual we have (about 280) prescribes: "And while the whole people prays over him, *lay hand upon him,* and suffer him henceforth to be in the Church" (*Didascalia,* vii).

MAY our Lord Jesus Christ absolve you; and I by His authority absolve you from every bond of excommunication and interdict, as far as I am able, and you have need. Moreover, I absolve you of your sins, in the name of the Father, and the Son, and of the Holy Spirit. Amen.

This prayer illustrates the multiple relation of the penance, that it is a satisfaction to God, that it has its prime value through the mediation of Christ's death, and through the participation of the merits of the Virgin Mary and the whole Mystical Body.

May the passion of our Lord Jesus Christ, the merits of the Blessed Virgin Mary and of all the saints, and whatever good you have done and evil you have endured be cause for the remission of your sins, the increase of grace, and the reward of everlasting life. Amen.

For any good reason the above prayers may be omitted except

---

[1]Reproduced from *Collectio Rituum* (Milwaukee: Bruce, 1954). When administered as part of the sick-room rites the Prayer, "May the passion of our Lord Jesus Christ," may be said in English.

that beginning "May our Lord
Jesus Christ," etc.

Should any danger of death be
imminent, the priest may say
briefly:

*I absolve thee of all censures and
sins in the name of the Father, and
of the Son, and of the Holy Ghost.
Amen.*

Summary. Penance is a sacrament instituted by Christ to restore
supernatural life and effectiveness to Christians who have committed
mortal sins after baptism. The several acts of the penitent — contrition,
confession, and satisfaction — and those of the priest — absolution and
counsel — are found in the modern as well as in the ancient forms of
administration.

Twentieth-Century Source Material

*(Since St. Francis de Sales [died 1622], perhaps no Catholic has been so in-
fluential in his writings as Columba Marmion, O.S.B. [died 1923]: This extract[1] on penance in Christ is from* CHRIST, THE LIFE OF THE SOUL.)

I Cor. xv,31   "I die daily." Those are St. Paul's words; but if he died daily, it was
that he might the better live the life of Christ.

And in speaking of his sufferings, he wrote those words that appear
so strange and are of such profound depth:

> I . . . make up in my flesh
> what is lacking to the sufferings of Christ,
> on behalf of His [mystical] body,
Col. i,24   > which is the Church.

Is there then something wanting to the sufferings, to the satisfactions of
Christ? Certainly not. Their value is infinite. Christ's sufferings are the
sufferings of the Man-God who substituted Himself for us. Nothing is
wanting to the perfection and plenitude of these sufferings; they were
more than sufficient to redeem us all.

> *He Himself* is a propitiation for our sins . . .
I John ii,2   > also for the *whole* world.

---

[1]Quoted by permission of Herder Co.

Then why does St. Paul speak of "filling up" these sufferings?

St. Augustine gives us the reply. The whole Christ, he says, is formed by the Church united to her Chief, and by the members (which we are), united to the Head (which is Christ). Christ, the Head of this mystical body, has suffered; the great expiation was that of Jesus; the members, if they wish to remain worthy of the Head, must in their turn bring their share of suffering and renunciation:

> The sufferings were indeed filled up, but in the Head: there remained the sufferings of Christ in His body: well, you are His body and members.

In Ps. lxxxvii,3

Contemplate Christ Jesus on His way to Calvary, laden with His cross; He falls under the weight of this burden. If He willed, His divinity would sustain His humanity; but He does not will it. Why? Because, in order to expiate sin, He wills to feel in His innocent flesh the burden of sin. But the Jews fear He will not live to reach the place of crucifixion; they therefore constrain Simon the Cyrenean to help to carry His cross, and Jesus accepts his help.

Simon, in this, represents us all; as members of Christ's mystical body, we must help Jesus to bear His cross. It is a sure sign we belong to Him, if following Him, we deny ourselves and take up our cross:

> If any one will come after Me,
> let him deny himself,
> and take up his cross daily,
> and follow Me.

Luke ix,23

Here is to be found the secret of the voluntary mortifications of faithful souls, privileged souls, holy souls — those mortifications that afflict and macerate the body as well as those that repress even the lawful desires of the mind. Such souls have doubtless expiated their own sins, but love constrains them to expiate for those members of Christ's body who offend their Chief so that the vigor, beauty, and splendor of this mystical body may not be diminished. If we truly love Christ, we shall, following the counsel of a prudent director, generously take our share of these voluntary mortifications which will make us less unworthy members of a crucified Head. Was it not this that St. Paul sought? Did he not write that he had suffered the loss of all things so that he might be admitted to the fellowship of Christ's sufferings and be made conformable to His death?

> That so I may know Him . . .
> what [the] fellowship in His sufferings,
> and become one with Him in His death.

Phil. iii,10

Topics for Further Discussion:

The vast difference in kind between mortal and venial sin.

Matt. iii;
Mark i Confession as a purely natural, psychological need, e.g., of the Jewish crowds moved to repentance by the Baptist.

The medieval ascetical practice of confessing to laymen in the lack of a priest at a moment of grave danger.

The amount of sanctifying grace *restored* by sacramental absolution.

That the pope cannot, outside of the sacrament of penance, remit sin, either his own or others'.

"The confession of faults . . . in some form or other is to be found among all races" (Cf. Karrer, *Religions of Mankind*, p. 90).

Readings:

F. X. Doyle, *The Wonderful Sacraments* (New York: Benziger, 1924); "Penance," pp. 153–177.

L. W. Geddes–H. Thurston, *The Catholic Church and Confession*, Calvert Series (New York: Macmillan, 1928).

E. J. Hanna, "Penance," *CE.*

H. Harrington, "The Sacrament of Penance," *The Teaching of the Catholic Church* (New York: Macmillan, 1949), II, pp. 955–989.

J. C. Heenan, *Priest and Penitent* (New York: Sheed and Ward, 1938); "The Confessor's Point of View," pp. 73–85; *passim.*

J. A. Kane, *The School of Repentance* (Paterson: Guild Press, 1943), "Confession," pp. 61–79.

C. Lattey, *Six Sacraments, Papers Read at the Summer School of Catholic Studies, Cambridge, 1929* (St. Louis: Herder, 1930); F. Cabrol, "Penance," pp. 131–162.

C. Marmion, *Christ the Life of the Soul* (St. Louis: Herder, 1923); "The Sacrament and Virtue of Penance," pp. 187–211.

M. Perkins, *Speaking of How to Pray* (New York: Sheed and Ward, 1944); "According to the Riches of His Grace," pp. 140–155.

R. Plus, *The Ideal of Reparation* (London: Burns, Oates and Washbourne, 1926).

W. F. Robison, *The Seven-Fold Gift* (St. Louis: Herder, 1922); "The Second Hope for Salvation," pp. 64–96.

A. Wilson, *Pardon and Peace* (New York: Sheed and Ward, 1947), *passim.*

Chapter XXI

A MYSTICAL BODY IN MINIATURE

The husband is the head of the wife,
as Christ too is head of the Church . . .
the mystery here is great
(Eph. v,22–32).

THE correct attitude toward Christian marriage is strikingly expressed by a contemporary French writer in the words: "If anyone wants to understand marriage, he must first understand Christ." The superhuman dignity and the inherent sacredness of marriage, as an institution of an all-wise Creator, have always been clear to sane human reason. These convictions, as Pope Leo XIII said, were as if stamped and written on human nature itself. But it was not until Christ had restored the pristine concept of marriage in its purity, and until St. Paul completed the revelation by informing us that marriage is a symbol, or likeness, "a foreshadowing" (Leo XIII), of the Incarnation of Christ and His union with the Church, that the full beauty and effulgence of the divine plan burst upon man. By marriage there is established in each family, as it were, a mystical body in miniature. Let us read this page of the Glad Tidings at the start:

Wives, [be subject] to your husbands
   as to the Lord,
because the husband is the head of the wife,
   as Christ too is Head of the Church,
   Himself being the Saviour of the body.

Well, then, as the Church is subject to Christ,
so also should wives be to their husbands in everything.

Husbands, love your wives,
   as Christ also loved the Church
   and gave Himself up for her sake,

> that He might sanctify her,
> purifying her in the bath of water by means of the word,
> that He might present her to Himself a glorious Church,
> not having spot or wrinkle or any such thing,
> but holy and without blemish.
>
> Even thus ought husbands love their wives
> as their own bodies.
>
> He that loveth his own wife loveth himself.
>
> Surely no man ever hateth his own flesh;
> nay, he doth nourish and cherish it,
> even as Christ the Church;
> because we are members of His body.
>
> For this shall man leave father and mother,
> and shall cleave to his wife,
> and the two shall come to be one flesh.
>
> The mystery here is great —
> I mean in reference to Christ and the Church.

Gen. ii,24

Eph. v,22–32

Like Union of Natures in Christ. In marriage, then, Christian or non-Christian, we have an institution planned and established by God to symbolize and illustrate the union between divinity and humanity effected for our sanctification in the Person of Christ. These are not mere flourishes of rhetoric, but ennobling truths for our enlightenment and happiness. That is why one must say that to comprehend marriage fully, one must know Christ. Let us study this parallel which divine revelation teaches us exists between a family and the Mystical Body.

A Fountain-Head of Life. All *life,* whatsoever it be, comes from God. All created life is owing to that infinite *Act of Love* whereby the *Goodness of God diffuses itself.* There is within the Holy Trinity the intellectual generation of the Son and the eternal procession, *through Love,* of the Holy Spirit: outside, or overflowing beyond the Trinity, there is that temporal outpouring love we call the creation and conservation and provident guidance of the universe. God foreknew that in the fullness of time He should send forth His Sole-Begotten Son wedded to human flesh to restore *supernatural life* to fallen humanity. This unique, indissoluble, and life-giving union of Godhead and manhood we call the Incarnation. From the outset God wished to foreshadow this

Like Christ's Wedding with the Church

ineffable mystery and at the same time He wished to associate man, the lord of the visible world, as closely as possible with Himself in the selfsame Act of Love from which life flows. Therefore He made man male and female, and bade the two become one flesh in a union nothing can dissolve, to cooperate with Himself in propagating life.

Life as Basis for Super-Life. But the union of Godhead and humanity does not end at the Incarnation; in a sense explained in a former chapter it extends itself in the Church to *all Christians* who become *incorporated* therein. Thence exists that mysterious, invisible flow of supernatural life from the Head to the last and the least of the members day after day, year after year, century after century, until the end of time. Similarly in marriage God has appointed that man and woman, as long as the world shall last, shall have His gracious commission to work with Him in diffusing natural life. In the Mystical Body men are endlessly reborn to grace; in marriage men are endlessly born *for* grace.

Man and Woman and God. In the Mystical Body, besides the Person of Christ, and His mystic Bride, the Church, there is Another, God Himself: so in marriage, besides the man and woman, there is the *Third Partner, God.* This is that inherent dignity and sanctity of the very nature of marriage, which has led men everywhere to surround it with sacred, religious rites. That marriage cannot derive from nature alone either its end or its means is forcibly shown by Dr. Karl Adam, a celebrated German professor of theology. "Its principal end," he says, "the generation of children, cannot be attained unless God, the Creator of the spirit, intervene in the paternal function and complete it by the creation of the soul. By that very fact, marriage, even in its natural reality, overflows the confines of this world, and surpasses the forces of this world. From that point of view alone, every marriage is a mystery. Then consider its interior structure. We find there is a sensible, corporeal side, and a moral, spiritual side. Inasmuch as it is placed in the sphere of the senses, marriage is in danger of losing itself by sinking into animality. It must cry for help from above to escape from the preponderance of the corporeal element. On its moral and spiritual side, it is more than a simple alliance of mind and heart; it implies the mutual self-surrender of two persons destined to be welded together in one flesh, a thing which is done in all security only with the Divine good pleasure." The mystery here is great; it is the ever-abiding presence of the Third Partner of the marriage union.

Wedlock Sacramentalized. The foregoing paragraphs viewed marriage as it was first given to man, when God, as Tertullian put it, "after taking the female from the male, recombined in wedlock the two bodies taken from the selfsame substance." But the primal contract of permanent and mutual self-surrender, which constitutes the essence of marriage, demanded of its very nature an exclusive and indissoluble bond. *To His Wife,* iii
If it gave high privileges, it entailed severe and inescapable obligations. The rights of the Third Partner are inalienable, and must be respected whatever be the cost. Therefore, it was decreed that in the New Dispensation God's helps would be proportionately generous. Hence it is that there can now be *no marriage contract* between Christian man and maiden which is *not* at the same time one of *Christ's sacraments,* an efficacious sign of grace which "sanctifies both man and wife." As life in the Council of Trent
Mystical Body is a complete *supernaturalizing* of the character of human existence, so Christian marriage as a sacrament means a complete supernaturalizing of the character of family life.

Permanent Title to Grace. The married state, to which the vast majority of Christians are called, is God's great school of sanctification. Therein all entrants, thanks to the *abiding character* of the sacramental helps for the work at hand, have an *absolute title to all the graces* they shall need for the faithful performance of their duties as long as life shall last. In that truly "epoch-making document," Pope Pius XI's *Encyclical on Christian Marriage,* our Holy Father followed St. Augustine in likening this permanent help to the effects of baptism and holy orders, and said:

> [The faithful at marriage] open up for themselves a treasure of sacramental grace from which they draw supernatural power for the fulfilling of their rights and duties faithfully, holily, perseveringly even unto death. Hence this sacrament *not only increases sanctifying grace,* the permanent principle of the supernatural life, *but also adds* particular gifts, dispositions, *seeds of grace,* by elevating and perfecting the natural powers in such a way that the parties are assisted not only in understanding but in knowing intimately, in adhering to firmly, in willing effectively, and in successfully putting into practice those things which pertain to the marriage state, its aims and duties, *giving them, in fine, right to the actual assistance of grace, whensoever they need it for fulfilling the duties of their state.*   1930

But the same great pontiff bespeaks the need of cooperating with grace, else "the grace of matrimony will remain . . . an unused talent . . . unless the spouses exercise these supernatural powers and cultivate and *develop the seeds of grace they have received.*" St. Thomas speaks in the same strain in a beautiful passage: "And because the *Sacraments effect what they represent,* we must believe that grace is bestowed by this Sacrament upon persons marrying, to enable them to have their part in the union of Christ with His Church; and this aid is very necessary for them, that in their application to fleshly and carnal things, they may not be separated from Christ and the Church."

Cont. Gent. iv,78

Helpmates in Love. One more point of comparison between marriage and the Mystical Body. The Church, as Christ's Bride, is subject to Him, but at the same time, is a queen with her own wide sphere of regal and maternal prerogatives. If the wife in marriage is subject to the husband, this does not in any way infringe her womanly dignity as wife and mother and companion. It means, as Pope Pius XI says: "In this body which is the family, the heart [must not] be separated from the head. . . . For if the man is the head, *the woman is the heart,* and as he occupies the chief place in ruling, *so she may and ought to claim for herself the chief place in love.*" It is of such a Christian marriage that Tertullian gives us the classical picture, in words addressed to his own wife:

Who can tell the happiness of that marriage which is brought about by the Church, confirmed by the Oblation [Mass], sealed with the benediction which the angels proclaim, ratified by the Heavenly Father? Henceforth between the two there is but one flesh and one spirit. They pray together, they prostrate together, they fast at the same time, they instruct each other, exhort and support each other. Together they go to Church, they take their place side by side at the banquet of God, they are united in trial, in persecution, and in joy. They sing Psalms and hymns together, each striving to excel the other in singing the praises of God. To them may Christ send His peace. Whenever two are united there He is also present.

To His Wife, ii, ix

THE MARRIAGE RITE AS WITH THE NUPTIAL MASS[1]

The Sacramental Contract

The parish priest, or other priest appointed to witness and bless the marriage, being properly vested and attended, goes to the altar. Those who are to be married come, with at least two witnesses, and kneel before the officiating priest, who turns to the altar and says:

V. ✝ Our help is in the name of the Lord.

R. Who made heaven and earth.

V. O Lord, hear my prayer.

R. And let my cry come unto Thee.

V. The Lord be with you.

R. And with your spirit.

Let us pray.

O Lord, we implore Thee, let Thy inspiration precede our actions and Thy help further them, so that all our prayers and all our deeds may ever take their beginning from Thee and, so begun, may through Thee reach completion. Through Christ our Lord.

R. Amen.

If there is to be a sermon, it should come next. The following may be used instead:

Instruction Before Marriage

Dear friends in Christ: As you know, you are about to enter into a union which is most sacred and most serious, a union which was established by God Himself. By it, He gave to man a share in the greatest work of creation, the work of the continuation of the human race. And in this way He sanctified human love and enabled man and woman to help each other live as children of God, by sharing a common life under His fatherly care.

Because God Himself is thus its author, marriage is of its very nature a holy institution, requiring of those who enter into it a complete and unreserved giving of self. But Christ our Lord added to the holiness of marriage an even deeper meaning and a higher beauty. He referred to the love of marriage to describe His own love for His Church, that is,

---

[1]The translation is from *Collectio Rituum* (Milwaukee: Bruce, 1954). Whatever is in *italics* must be said in Latin.

for the people of God whom He redeemed by His own blood. And so He gave to Christians a new vision of what married life ought to be, a life of self-sacrificing love like His own. It is for this reason that His Apostle, St. Paul, clearly states that marriage is now and for all time to be considered a great mystery, intimately bound up with the supernatural union of Christ and the Church, which union is also to be its pattern.

This union then is most serious, because it will bind you together for life in a relationship so close and so intimate, that it will profoundly influence your whole future. That future, with its hopes and disappointments, its successes and its failures, its pleasures and its pains, its joys, and its sorrows, is hidden from your eyes. You know that these elements are mingled in every life, and are to be expected in your own. And so, not knowing what is before you, you take each other for better or for worse, for richer or for poorer, in sickness and in health, until death.

Truly, then, these words are most serious. It is a beautiful tribute to your undoubted faith in each other, that, recognizing their full import, you are nevertheless so willing and ready to pronounce them. And because these words involve such solemn obligations, it is most fitting that you rest the security of your wedded life upon the great principle of self-sacrifice. And so you begin your married life by the voluntary and complete surrender of your individual lives in the interest of that deeper and wider life which you are to have in common. Henceforth you belong entirely to each other; you will be one in mind, one in heart, and one in affections. And whatever sacrifices you may hereafter be required to make to preserve this common life, always make them generously. Sacrifice is usually difficult and irksome. Only love can make it easy; and perfect love can make it a joy. We are willing to give in proportion as we love. And when love is perfect, the sacrifice is complete. God so loved the world that He gave His Only begotten Son; and the Son so loved us that He gave Himself for our salvation. "Greater love than this no man hath, that a man lay down his life for his friends."

No greater blessing can come to your married life than pure conjugal love, loyal and true to the end. May, then, this love with which you join your hands and hearts today, never fail, but grow deeper and stronger as the years go on. And if true love and the unselfish spirit of perfect sacrifice guide your every action, you can expect the greatest measure of earthly happiness that may be allotted to man in this vale of tears. The rest is in the hands of God. Nor will God be wanting to your needs; He will pledge you the life-long support of His graces in the Holy Sacrament which you are now going to receive.

Then all stand, and the priest addresses the bridegroom first:
N., will you take N., here present, for your lawful wife according to the rite of our holy Mother, the Church?

The bridegroom answers:
I will.

The priest then asks the bride:
N., will you take N., here present, for your lawful husband according to the rite of our holy Mother, the Church?

The bride answers:
I will.

The consent given, the priest says:
Now join your right hands.

Then, the priest lays the end of the stole on the hands of both and continues:
And say after me:

Groom:
I, N.N., take you, N.N., for my lawful wife, to have and to hold, from this day forward, for better, for worse, for richer, for poorer, in sickness and in health, until death do us part.

Bride:
I, N.N., take you, N.N., for my lawful husband, to have and to hold, from this day forward, for better, for worse, for richer, for poorer, in sickness and in health, until death do us part.

Confirmation of the Marriage Bond

The priest then says:
I join you in matrimony: In the name of the Father ✠ *and of the Son, and of the Holy Ghost.*
R. Amen.

Next:
I call upon all of you here present to be witnesses of this holy union which I have now blessed. "What God has joined together, let not man put asunder" (Matt. 19:6).

After which the priest sprinkles them with holy water.

Blessing of the Wedding Ring, or Rings

Facing the bride and groom, the priest blesses the ring(s) as follows:

V. ✠ Our help is in the name of the Lord.

R. Who made heaven and earth.

V. O Lord, hear my prayer.

R. And let my cry come unto Thee.

V. The Lord be with you.

R. And with your spirit.

For Two Rings

Let us pray.

Bless, ✠ *O Lord, these rings, which we are blessing* ✠ *in Thy name, so that they who wear them, keeping faith with each other in unbroken loyalty, may ever remain at peace with Thee, obedient to Thy will, and may live together always in mutual love. Through Christ our Lord.*
R. Amen.

For One Ring

Let us pray.

Bless, ✠ *O Lord, this ring, which we are blessing* ✠ *in Thy name, so that she who wears it, keeping faith with her husband in unbroken loyalty, may ever remain at peace with Thee, obedient to Thy will, and may live with him always in mutual love. Through Christ our Lord.*
R. Amen.

Then he sprinkles the ring(s) with holy water.

Giving the Ring(s)

Priest:

Now that you have sealed a truly Christian marriage, give this wedding ring/these wedding rings to your bride/to each other, saying after me:

Taking the bride's ring, the groom places it on her finger, saying after the priest:

Groom:

In the name of the Father, and of the Son, and of the Holy Spirit. Take and wear this ring as a pledge of my fidelity.

The bride does the same with the groom's ring, in a double ring ceremony.

The blessing follows:

Blessing

Psalm 127

Happy are you who fear the Lord, who walk in his ways!

For you shall eat the fruit of your handiwork; happy shall you be, and favored.

Your wife shall be like a fruitful vine in the recesses of your home; Your children like olive plants around your table.

Behold, thus is the man blessed who fears the Lord.

The Lord bless you from Sion: May you see the prosperity of Jerusalem all the days of your life;

May you see your children's children. Peace be upon Israel!

Glory be to the Father, and to the Son, and to the Holy Spirit.

As it was in the beginning, is now, and ever shall be, world without end. Amen.

V. Lord, have mercy.

R. Christ, have mercy. Lord, have mercy.

V. Our Father, etc., **in secret**

V. And lead us not into temptation.

R. But deliver us from evil.

V. Grant salvation to Thy servants.

R. For their hope, O my God, is in Thee.

V. Send them aid, O Lord, from Thy holy place.

R. And watch over them from Sion.

V. O Lord, hear my prayer.

R. And let my cry come unto Thee.

V. The Lord be with you.

R. And with your spirit.

Continuing, the priest says:

Let us pray.

Almighty and everlasting God, Who by Thy power didst create Adam and Eve, our first parents, and join them in a holy union, sanctify the hearts and the bodies of these Thy servants, and bless ✝ them; and make them one in the union and love of true affection. Through Christ our Lord.

R. Amen.

With hands raised and extended in blessing over the Spouses, the priest reads the following prayers:

May almighty God bless you by the Word of His mouth, and unite your hearts in the enduring bond of pure love.

R. Amen.

If the Spouses are elderly, this next prayer may be omitted:

May you be blessed in your children, and may the love that you lavish on them be returned a hundredfold.

R. Amen.

May the peace of Christ dwell always in your hearts and in your home; may you have true friends to stand by you, both in joy and in sorrow. May you be ready with help and consolation for all those who come to you in need; and may the blessings promised to the compassionate descend in abundance on your house.

R. Amen.

May you be blessed in your work and enjoy its fruits. May cares never cause you distress, nor the desire for earthly possessions lead you astray; but may your hearts' concern be always for the treasures laid up for you in the life of heaven.

R. Amen.

May the Lord grant you fullness of years, so that you may reap the harvest of a good life, and, after you have served Him with loyalty in His kingdom on earth, may He take you up into His eternal dominions in heaven.

Joining his hands, the priest continues:

Through our Lord Jesus Christ His Son, Who lives and reigns with Him in the unity of the Holy Spirit, God, world without end.

R. Amen.

If Mass does not follow immediately, the priest dismisses the Spouses, saying:

Go in peace, and may the Lord be with you always.

R. Amen.

After this the priest says the Nuptial Mass, observing everything prescribed therein, or as indicated below.

If there is to be no Nuptial blessing, after the Psalm and Versicles, as given on pp. 321–322 above, the priest says the following prayer:

Let us pray.

O Lord, we implore Thee extend to Thy faithful servants the right hand of Thy divine assistance, so that they may seek Thee with their whole hearts and receive from Thee whatever they ask for that is right. Through Christ our Lord.

R. Amen.

The Nuptial Blessing Given Within the Mass

After the "Pater Noster," and before the "Libera nos, quaesumus, Domine," the bride and groom kneel at the foot of the altar and the priest says these prayers in Latin, from the Epistle side:

Let us pray.

Listen with favor, O Lord, to our prayers; and in Thy goodness maintain the ways which Thou hast established for the continuation of the human race, so that the union which has been founded by Thy authority may be preserved by Thy aid. Through our Lord Jesus Christ, Thy Son, Who lives and reigns with Thee in the unity of the Holy Spirit, God, world without end.

R. Amen.

Let us pray.

O God, Who by Thy mighty power hast made all things where before there was nothing; Who, having put in order the beginnings of the universe, didst form for man, made to Thy image, an inseparable helpmate, woman, so that Thou didst give woman's body its origin from man's flesh and teach that it is never right to separate her from the one being whence it has pleased Thee to take her:

O God, Who hast consecrated the union of marriage making it a sign so profound as to prefigure in the marriage covenant the mystery of Christ and the Church:

O God, Who dost join woman to man, and give to that society, the first to be established, the blessing which alone was not taken away in punishment for original sin nor in the doom of the Flood:

Look with kindness on this Thy servant who is now to be joined to her husband in the companionship of marriage and who seeks to be made secure by Thy protection.

May this yoke that she is taking on herself be one of love and peace. May she be faithful and chaste, marrying in Christ, and may she always imitate the holy women. May she be the beloved of her husband, as was Rachel; wise, as was Rebecca; long-lived and loyal, as was Sarah.

May the author of sin have no mastery over her because of her acts. May she hold firm to the Faith and the commandments. Faithful to one embrace, may she flee from unlawful companionship. By firm discipline may she fortify herself against her weakness. May she be grave in her modesty, honorable in her chastity, learned in the teachings of heaven.

May she be rich in children, prove worthy and blameless, and may she attain in the end to the peace of the blessed, the Kingdom of heaven.

May she and her husband together see their children's children to the third and fourth generation and enjoy the long life they desire. Through our Lord Jesus Christ Thy Son, Who lives and reigns with Thee in the unity of the Holy Spirit, God, for ever and ever.

R. Amen.

After the "Benedicamus Domino" (or "Ite Missa est") and before he blesses the people, the priest turns to the bride and groom and says:

May the God of Abraham, the God of Isaac, the God of Jacob be with you, and may He fulfill in you His blessing; so that you may see your children's children to the third and fourth generation and afterward possess everlasting and boundless life. Through the help of our Lord Jesus Christ, Who with the Father and the Holy Spirit lives and reigns, God, for ever and ever.

R. Amen.

Twentieth-Century Source Material

(An indefatigable apologist of our day, Father Martindale, in his booklet, WEDLOCK.)

Nothing Christian is understood save within the all-covering doctrine of our incorporation into Christ, so that Marriage itself, within Christianity, must not on any account be thought of in the very least merely as the most faithful of non-Christian monogamists think of it, but as one of many means whereby Christ fills us with His life, and draws us deeper into His own. . . .

Let us recall again what Marriage, by the law of nature, that is, God's will working itself out in creation and in man in particular, is meant to be. It is a free contract made between two human wills, the wills of a man and a woman promising to live together, and with no one else, and till one or the other dies. The object of this contract is primarily the procreation of children and the furtherance of the race: the inspiration of the contract should be mutual love and trust. . . .

But now Catholic doctrine teaches that our Lord not only preserves all this — so that the very substance of Christian marriage is a free permanent contract between two, but raises this so that it becomes a Sacrament. Christ does not give Grace merely on the occasion of this contract being made, or because it is made, but through and by means of it. Hence it is strictly true to say that the two Christians who make the contract, by that very fact administer each other the Marriage Sacrament. They are its ministers, not the priest. The Church, in the person of her priest, stands by and blesses, and is glad in the Sacrament that she witnesses; but her priest is not its Minister. The bride and bridegroom are that. So that *the very first and infinitely best wedding gift that they make to one another is Grace* — grace in the divinest sense, such as is freely given by means of every Sacrament and by Christ Himself, and grace directed precisely toward making the married life well and truly livable to the end. . . .

For Sacraments *do* what they *symbolize*. Here you have two human persons becoming "unto one flesh. . . ." Christ catches up each one of us who wills, and so unites him with Himself that they make "one Spirit," one mystical wedded Person. Numerically we are not one and the same with Christ, any more than bride and bridegroom cease to be two human individuals. But we do become mystically wedded to Him, and each soul has the right to see itself, if it wills, as the Bride of Christ. Hence Christian Marriage, in which two become "unto one flesh," is the most perfect human symbol of that wedlock between each living Christian soul "in grace" and its Redeemer, and this, in its turn, is the intended reproduction, on that level, of the Incarnation. — Quoted by permission of Sheed and Ward.

Topics for Further Discussion:

"The basis of a happy wedlock and the ruin of an unhappy one is prepared and set in the souls of boys and girls during the period of childhood and adolescence." — *Pius XI.*

The right of the Church to establish and define nullifying impediments to the marriage of Christians.

The purpose of banns.

Famous attempts to force the Church to grant divorces: Philip II of France and Pope Innocent III; Henry VIII of England and Pope Paul III; Napoleon I and Pope Pius VII.

Eugenics is scientifically unsound; enforced sterilization, morally wrong.

Readings:

This Is Marriage (simplified form of Pius XI's *Casti Connubii*) (Loveland: Grailville, 1946).

F. X. Doyle, *The Wonderful Sacraments* (New York: Benziger, 1924); "Marriage," pp. 215–247.

Family Life in Christ (Liturgical Conference, 1947); *passim.*

G. H. Joyce, *Christian Marriage, A Doctrinal and Historical Study, Heythrop Theological Series* (New York: Sheed and Ward, 1933).

C. Lattey, *Six Sacraments, Papers Read at the Summer School of Catholic Studies, Cambridge, 1929* (St. Louis: Herder, 1930); G. H. Joyce, "Matrimony, Dogmatic Theology," pp. 225–241; E. J. Mahoney, "Matrimony, Moral Theology," pp. 242–257.

A. Lehmkuhl, "Marriage, Sacrament of," *CE.*

E. J. Mahoney, "Christian Marriage," *The Teaching of the Catholic Church* (New York: Macmillan, 1949), II, pp. 1062–1100.

T. Mueller, "Marriage in Christ," *The Sacramental Way* (New York: Sheed and Ward, 1948), pp. 117–130.

Pope Leo XIII, *Great Encyclical Letters of Pope Leo XIII* (New York: Benziger, 1903); "Christian Marriage" (*Arcanum divinae*), p. 58.

M. Perkins, *Speaking of How to Pray* (New York: Sheed and Ward, 1944); "The Sacrament of Matrimony," pp. 129–139.

Pope Pius XI, *Encyclical on Christian Marriage* (New York: America Press, 1931).

The Rite for Marriage (Collegeville: Lit. Press, 1957).

W. F. Robison, *The Seven-Fold Gift* (St. Louis: Herder, 1922); "The Consecration of Love," pp. 194–225.

M. J. Scheeben–C. Vollert, *The Mysteries of Christianity* (St. Louis: Herder, 1946), "Christian Matrimony," pp. 593–610.

M. Schlüter–Hermkes–E. R. Smothers, *The Family* (New York: America Press, 1938; pamphlet), *passim.*

H. Thurston, "Marriage, Ritual of," *CE.*

R. Tunick–M. Burbach, *Our Family Book of Life* (Kansas City: Designs, 1949); *passim.*

S. Undset, *Stages on the Road* (New York: Knopf, 1934); "Reply to a Parish Priest."

A. Vermeersch, *What Is Marriage?* (New York: America Press, 1931.)

Chapter XXII

OTHER CHRISTS

As ministers of Christ,
and stewards of the mysteries of God,
so let men account us
(I Cor. iv,1).

A S THE sacrament of matrimony through natural parenthood provides for the natural life of Christians, that of holy orders secures the diffusion of the supernatural life of the Mystical Body. Both sacraments have a markedly social character. Neither is necessary for the salvation of any individual; each in its own way is indispensable for the life of the Church as a body. Marriage cooperates with God in a *creative* act, and is therefore intrinsically holy: the priesthood enables man to cooperate with Christ in the *redemptive* and *sanctifying* process from birth until death, and hence is of incomparable holiness and dignity. The whole of the Christian religion is priestly through and through, since it is merely an extension of, and sharing in, the essentially priestly character of the Mediator. Those baptized and those confirmed, as we have seen, share in the lower degrees of the extension to man of the priestly character and powers of Christ, but the baptized and the confirmed revere the immeasurably higher rank and powers of those in holy orders. The laity share in the *internal* priesthood of Christ, to adopt the language of the *Catechism of the Council of Trent,* whereas the recipients of holy orders share also in the *external* priesthood. To quote:

Regarding the internal priesthood, all the faithful are said to be priests, once they have been washed in the saving waters of Baptism. Especially is this name given to the just who have the Spirit of God, and who, by the help of divine grace, have been made living members of the great High-Priest, Jesus Christ; for, enlightened by faith which is inflamed by charity, they offer up spiritual sacrifices to God on the altar of their hearts. . . .

327

The external priesthood, on the contrary, does not pertain to the faithful at large, but only to certain men who have been ordained and consecrated to God by the lawful imposition of hands and by the solemn ceremonies of holy Church, and who are thereby devoted to a particular sacred ministry.

II, c. vii, Q. xxii

Dignity of Priesthood. Such persons are called by Holy Writ "ministers" (that is "servants"), "stewards of the mysteries of God," "*ambassadors* on Christ's behalf," "yea, God's *fellow workers*," whose duty it is to live the Christian life that they "may present every man perfect in Christ Jesus." They are thus called to the august duty of acting as Christ's agents and representatives. Their work is threefold: they carry on Christ's high function of teaching, and Christ's governing function in the Church, but both of these for the sake of their third duty, that of *sanctifying* the members of the Mystical Body. No one can govern well beyond the measure of his own self-government. No one can effectively teach moral lessons beyond the measure in which he lives them. And although the sanctifying effects of the sacraments are not nullified by the sins or sinfulness of their minister, still, taking things in the large, one may say that none but a holy priest will be able "to present every man perfect in Christ Jesus." While there will be occasional lapses in even the highest positions (there is frailty wherever there is flesh and blood), still the *office* of the priesthood is one of the highest holiness, and the priesthood is the Catholic's pride and joy. No one has expressed the Catholic's attitude toward priests better than St. Francis of Assisi, who out of humility declined to be numbered among them. In his *Testament* he writes:

Col. i,28

The Lord gave, and still gives me, such faith in priests who live according to the form of the holy Roman Church, *because of their clerical character,* that if they should persecute me, I would still have recourse to them. And if I were as wise as Solomon and should find a poor priest in this world, I would not preach against his will in his church. And I wish to fear, love, and honor all priests as my lords. I am unwilling to think of sins in them, because I discern in them the Son of God, and they are my lords. And on this account I wish to perceive in this world nothing of the most high Son of God except His most holy Body and His most holy Blood which they receive in the sacraments, and they alone administer to others.

c.III

The ideal of the priesthood is enshrined in the expression *Alter*

See whose ministry is confided to you.
(Pontifical)

Christus, "another Christ," and despite all shortcomings the distinction of priests before the world is that they do possess what Pope Pius X called "that priceless blessing, a *sense of Christ.*" St. Thomas, who postulated no ordinary holiness, but excelling virtue in the cleric, was merely recording Catholic tradition when he wrote that "each minister of the Church is, in some respect, a copy of Christ," and Pope Pius XI interprets this saying as follows: "The priest, as is said with good reason, is indeed 'another Christ'; for, in some way, he is himself a continuation of Christ."

S.T. III. *Supp.*
*Q. xl,a.*4

Encyclical, *On
the Priesthood*

What hath the Lord not placed in my hand [mused St. Charles Borromeo, Archbishop of Milan], when He hath placed there His Only-Begotten, co-equal and co-eternal Son? In my hand He hath placed all His treasures, His sacraments and graces: he hath placed there souls, His dearest possessions . . . : in my hand He hath placed Heaven, which I can open and shut to others.

So it is that priests "watch over our souls, as men who have to render an account."

Heb. xiii,17

Institution of Sacrament. When and under what circumstances was this sacrament instituted? This is an instructive question. "If anyone say that by the words: *'Do this in commemoration of Me,'* Christ did not constitute *and ordain* the Apostles priests, so that they and other priests might offer His Body and Blood, let him be anathema"; the Council of Trent thus answers our question in clearly formulating the age-old belief of Catholics. In other words, as has often been pointed out, by the very fact of establishing the Christian Sacrifice, and commanding its offering, Christ constituted and ordained the Apostles priests. The Apostles were ordained in a sort of super-sacramental manner: the Sacrifice itself brought the priesthood with it. This circumstance is illuminating, as showing the intimate relationship between the priest and his chief function, to offer sacrifice:

Sess. xxii, 1562

Every high priest,
taken from among men,
is ordained . . .
Heb. v,1   *that he may offer up both gifts and sacrifices.*

Ordination by Imposition of Hands. Christ could (and did) ordain the Apostles priests in this special manner, but for all that He fixed that the mode of initiation for other priests should be the ancient, solemn *rite of laying on of hands*. From Pentecostal days onward this sacrament in its several degrees of diaconate, priesthood, and episcopacy, has been conferred with prayer and a solemn imposition of hands. In the course of time the ordination ritual in the West became enriched with a vast and manifold symbolic ceremonial, during which the vestments and insignia of office are solemnly presented to the candidate. This ceremonial is reverently preserved, but the real essence of the rite remains in the laying on of hands, as the Holy See recently recalled (Nov. 30, 1947).

There is something very special about this ordination imposition of hands. It is not merely an *ordination* rite, that is, the imparting of sacramental powers, but it connotes an election, a calling, a choice on the part of God. *"Clergy"* is a Greek word meaning choice, allotment, portion; the clergy in a special manner are the Lord's choice and portion:

> Ye have not chosen Me,
> but I have chosen you.

In turn God becomes the chosen lot and portion of the clergy themselves: as one is being enrolled in the clerical state, he repeats with joy in the words of King David:

John xv,16

> The Lord is the portion of my cup,
> and mine inheritance.
> Thou art He
> who restorest mine inheritance to me.

Ps. xv,5

Function Seen in Primitive Names. Concerning this same matter of names, one may learn other worth-while lessons by scrutinizing those connected with this sacrament. There is first that of the sacrament itself, *holy order* or *holy orders,* to designate collectively the several ranks or grades of the Christian ministry. The *"deacons"* are so called from a Greek word meaning "servants": the first capacity in which we find deacons in the New Testament is that of serving the common table of the Christian community of Jerusalem. Besides administering all that pertained to the temporal needs of the Christians, they assisted the Apostles in various functions, even that of preaching. It was for his success in preaching that St. Stephen, the protomartyr, won his crown. *"Priests"* or *"presbyters,"* again, are words from the Greek meaning "elders." Even now in ordaining young Levites for the altar, the bishop prays: "May they prove themselves *elders* by the gravity of their conduct and the strictness of their lives; that meditating on Thy law day and night, they may believe what they read, teach what they believe, and practice what they preach." Our word *"bishop"* is a rendering of a Greek word meaning "overseer," or watcher, or superintendent. The Fathers in their homilies often dwell on the truth expressed in that word, that they are set up by God to "watch over" the Christian flock.

Minor Orders. In the chapel of the seminary of the Archdiocese of Chicago the sanctuary is raised four steps above the nave. These four steps are marked respectively with the Latin equivalents of *"Door-keeper,"* *"Exorcist,"* *"Reader,"* and *"Acolyte,"* names which designate the so-called minor orders of the Western Church. As the administrative functions of the early deacons increased, these duties were distributed among inferior assistants, so that gradually there grew up this definite sequence of minor orders. Later on, owing to changes in the manner of administering Church charities, and Church rites, these lower orders fell into desuetude, and for the most part the orders themselves disappeared at Rome. Meanwhile, however, they had been introduced into Gaul, and it was from thence that they returned later on to Rome and were adopted there once more. They remain as ceremonial stages in the promotion of clerics. In the East there is only one minor order, that of Reader, who still enjoys his ancient and important function of chanting the Lessons, other than the Gospel ones, at holy Mass.

Major Orders. Again, the same seminary chapel at Mundelein illustrates the *major orders* in that the altar is set three steps above the sanctuary, and this time the gradations bear the equivalents of *"Subdeacon,"* *"Deacon,"* and *"Priest."* Whether the subdiaconate is really a grade of the sacrament, or merely the last step in the approach to it, is a question on which theologians are not agreed. There is no room for doubt, however, that the diaconate is a divinely instituted grade of the ministry and that its reception is a true sacrament, imprinting a seal or character on the soul. As ecclesiastical life is now organized, deacons are seminarists and have no administrative duties, but by Canon Law their proper functions still include the administration of Holy Communion and baptism (both by delegation).

Priest and Bishop. The *priesthood* is of two grades, that of simple priests and that of bishops. The chief and most important function of the priest is to offer the Sacrifice, and in this matter, as St. Thomas says, "the Pope's power is no greater than that of a simple priest." But priest and bishop possess this power in different ways: the priest has it and can use it himself, the bishop, besides using it, can *impart* it to others. Therein lies the chief difference between these two grades of the priesthood. Thereby Christ provides not alone for the celebration of the Sacrifice but for the perpetuation of those heralds and ambassadors He singled out to be with Him, and work with Him, and to carry His message to the uttermost parts of the earth. Acts i,8

Distinction as Related to Eucharist. St. Thomas, the prince of theologians, has an interesting passage in the *Summa* wherein he derives the distinction of all the grades of holy orders from their separate relationships to the Holy Eucharist. The *episcopacy,* treated elsewhere, is alone not included in this engaging little essay:

> The distinction of Orders is derived from their relation to the Eucharist. For the power of Order is directed either to the consecration of the Eucharist itself, or to some ministry in connection with this sacrament of the Eucharist. If in the former way, then it is the order of *priests.* . . . The cooperation of the ministers is directed either to the sacrament itself, or to the recipients. If the former this happens in three ways. For in the first place there is the ministry whereby the minister cooperates with the priest in the sacrament itself, *by dispensing,* but not by consecrating . . . and this belongs to the *deacon.* . . . Secondly, there is the ministry directed to the disposal of the sacramental matter in the sacred vessels of the sacrament; and this belongs to *subdeacons.* . . . Thirdly, there is the ministry directed to the proffering of the sacramental matter, and this belongs to the *acolyte.* . . . The ministry directed to the *preparation of the recipients* can be exercised only over the unclean, since those who are clean are already apt for receiving the sacraments. Now the unclean are of three kinds, according to Dionysius. For some are absolute unbelievers and unwilling to believe; and these must be altogether debarred from beholding divine things and from the assembly of the faithful; this belongs to the *doorkeepers.* Some, however, are willing to believe, but are not as yet instructed, namely catechumens, and to the instruction of such persons the Order of *readers* is directed. . . . But some are believers and instructed, yet lie under an impediment through the power of the devil, namely, those who are possessed; and to this ministry the Order of *exorcists* is directed.

S.T. III. *Supp.*
Q. xxxvii,*a.*2

Ordination Rites. The length of the rites of ordination makes it impossible to reproduce them here. But even if space requirements did not preclude this, it would no doubt be more profitable to single out for comment some of the more characteristic features of the ritual of episcopal consecration and priestly ordination. Originally these similar promotions had an almost identical rite, a prayer said while imposing hands on the candidate. Throughout the centuries, both rites have grown in complexity, but along remarkably parallel lines. The greatest difference now is that three bishops are required to consecrate a new bishop, while only one is needed to ordain a priest. The most imposing ceremonies are here enumerated in opposite columns. With these lists before one, reference will be facilitated.

Priestly Ordination	Episcopal Consecration
1. Presentation of candidate.	1. Presentation of candidate: reading of papal mandate, examination, profession of faith.
2. Litany of Saints.	2. Litany of Saints.
3. Laying on of hands.	3. Laying on of hands.
4. Investiture with stole and folded chasuble.	4. Investiture with Gospels.
5. Anointing of hands.	5. Anointing of head and hands.
6. Presentation with bread and wine.	6. Investiture with staff and ring.
7. Offertory gift: one lighted candle.	7. Offertory gifts: two lighted candles, two loaves of bread, two barrels of wine.
8. Concelebration of Mass.	8. Concelebration of Mass.
9. New priest given nonconsecrated wine after Communion.	9. Communion under both Species.
10. Investiture with full chasuble.	10. Investiture with miter and gloves.
11. Oath of homage and obedience.	11. Enthronization.

The People's "Veto." Ordination was always a function to which as much *publicity* was given as possible. Some sort of public examination of the candidates and the willingness of the people to accept them as their spiritual leaders is one of the conditions attaching to ordination rites. The examination of the bishop-elect now includes, besides his solemn presentation, the reading of the papal mandate, a formal catechizing, and a public profession of faith. At the ordination of priests the candidates are solemnly presented, and their worthiness then attested by the archdeacon. Then, as a relic of times long past, the bishop bids the people "to freely disclose whatever be known of their conduct and morals." The bidding then goes on:

> Let your assent to their ordination be given because of their merit, rather than through any partiality to them. If anyone, therefore, has anything against them, let him come forward and declare it in God's name and for God's sake; but let him be mindful of his own condition.

Penitential Preparation. It was only *after fasting and prayer* that the early Christians at Antioch "imposed hands on Saul [Paul] and Barnabas"; following this example ordinations have traditionally been Acts xiii,2 conferred only after fasting and strict penitential exercises. From the end of the fifth century, in the Latin churches, the ordination of priests was restricted to the Saturdays of the Ember weeks: for the consecration of bishops a Sunday was chosen (because the Holy Ghost came down upon the Apostles on a Sunday), but even in this case a certain penitential mien marks the beginning of the rites. In the impressive Litany of the Saints intercessions are sent up to all the members of the Mystical Body in glory on behalf of the ordination candidates.

"A Priest Forever." The *imposing of hands* is the august sacramental rite. Of the effects of the imparting of "the Holy and Quickening Spirit," St. Gregory of Nyssa, a brother of St. Basil, wrote in the fourth century:

> The same power of the Word renders the priest venerable and honorable, singled out, by this consecration bestowed on him, from his fellowship with the generality of man. While but yesterday he was one of the multitude, one of the people, he is suddenly rendered a guide, a president, a teacher of righteousness, an instructor in hidden *Orat. in Bap.* mysteries. *Christi*

When the imposing of hands is finished, the sacramental character has been imposed.

Anointing with oil as an ordination rite probably originated with the

Visigoths of Spain, who, about the same time that they revived the Old Testament rites of anointing their kings, also began to anoint the hands of priests at ordination. Later the Franks brought in the anointing of the bishop's hands and then of the bishop's head.

Investiture with Insignia. The many ceremonial investitures which now characterize the ordination ritual are also probably due to an impulse first given by the Visigoths. At any rate the conferring of the stole as an emblem of the priestly office is first found among them. This led to manifold imitation. At this point in the present rites a new priest is clothed with stole and folded chasuble while a new bishop is solemnly given a pastoral staff and ring.

Interesting relics of the one-time *gift-procession* survive in the ordination Mass. But, whereas the priest presents merely a lighted candle, the new bishop offers two such candles, and two loaves of bread, and two small barrels of wine. At the solemn rites of canonization, at a papal Mass, in addition to the gifts just enumerated, the Pope's offering also includes two live doves.

Concelebration. By concelebration of the ordination Mass is meant the simultaneous consecration of the *same* sacrificial elements by the officiating bishop and the ordination candidates. This is another very ancient feature here preserved. At both episcopal consecration and priestly ordination the Mass is concelebrated. The new bishop celebrates partly on a side altar and partly at the main altar with the consecrating prelate. The new priest concelebrates as he kneels before the altar at which the bishop offers the Sacrifice. While we often speak of a new priest's first Mass as being a day or so after ordination, strictly speaking his first Mass is in immediate conjunction with the ordination itself. This is one of the most impressive elements of the ordination rites.

Formerly, as we know, all normally communicated under both sacramental Species. When this was in process of disappearing, the laity often communicated under the Species of Bread and were then given a sip of *nonconsecrated wine*. Both these stages of ceremonial development are mirrored in the ordination ceremonies, for the new bishop communicates under both Species, while the new priest, after communicating under the one Species of Bread, partakes of a chalice of nonconsecrated wine.

At the end of the Mass there is a final investiture. The new priest is robed in the full chasuble, and then pays filial homage to the bishop.

This last little rite preserves for us the *feudal swearing of fealty* to the suzerain. The bishop this time receives his miter and gloves, and is then solemnly enthroned on his episcopal chair.

Summary. Holy orders is a sacrament of three degrees which elevates a layman to the highest communicated grade of the priesthood of Christ, thereby empowering the recipient to administer the sacraments and whatever pertains to the government of the Church according to the degree in which one has received the sacrament. Like baptism and confirmation it imparts an abiding character. It is administered by a bishop with prayer and imposition of hands on a baptized Christian of the male sex.

Twentieth-Century Source Material

(Pope Pius XI, on the priest's relations to the Mystical Body, in the Encyclical Letter, THE CATHOLIC PRIESTHOOD, *1935.)*

Besides this power over the real [here used in the sense of "Sacramental"] Body of Christ, the priest has received other powers, august and sublime, over His Mystical Body. There is no need, My Venerable Brethren, to enlarge upon the beautiful doctrine of the Mystical Body of Christ, a doctrine so dear to St. Paul; this beautiful doctrine that shows us the Person of the Word-made-Flesh in union with all His brethren. For from Him to them comes a supernatural influence, so that they, with Him as Head, form a single Body of which they are the members. Now a priest is appointed

> dispenser of the mysteries of God I Cor. iv,1

for the benefit of the members of the Mystical Body of Christ; since he is the ordinary minister of nearly all the Sacraments — those channels through which the grace of the Saviour flows for the good of humanity. The Christian, at almost every important stage of his mortal career, finds at his side the priest with power received from God, in the act of communicating or increasing that grace which is the supernatural life of his soul.

Scarcely is he born before the priest, baptizing him, brings him by a new birth to a more noble and precious life, and makes him a son of God and of the Church of Jesus Christ. To strengthen him to fight bravely in spiritual combats, a priest invested with special dignity makes him a soldier of Christ by holy chrism. Then, as soon as he is able to recognize and value the Bread of Angels, the priest gives It to him, the living and life-giving Food come down from Heaven. If he fall, the priest raises him up again in the name of God, and reconciles him to God with the Sacrament of Penance. Again, if he is called by God to found a family and to collaborate with Him in the transmission of human life throughout the world, thus increasing the number of the faithful on earth and, thereafter, the ranks of the elect in Heaven, the priest is there to bless his espousals and unblemished love; and when, finally, arrived at the portals of eternity, the Christian feels the need of strength and courage before presenting himself at the tribunal of the Divine Judge, the priest with the holy oils anoints the failing members of the sick or dying Christian, and reconsecrates and comforts him.

Thus the priest accompanies the Christian throughout the pilgrimage of this life to the gates of Heaven. He accompanies the body to its resting place in the grave with rites and prayers of immortal hope. And even beyond the threshold of eternity he follows the soul to aid it with Christian suffrages, if need there be of further purification and alleviation. Thus, from the cradle to the grave the priest is ever beside the faithful, a guide, a solace, a minister of salvation and dispenser of grace and blessing.

Topics for Further Discussion:

The appropriateness of celibacy for the clerical state.

The exclusion of woman from sacramental ministry.

"No loyalty to the Church where disloyalty to the clergy."

The papal condemnation of Anglican Orders. (Cf. "Anglican Orders," CE.)

The relationship of the priest and bishop to the physical Body and the Mystical Body of Christ.

"Not every priest is a saint, but every saint is a priest." In what sense is this true?

Readings:

Pius XI, *Encyclical on the Catholic Priesthood* (New York: *The Catholic Mind,* xxxiv, 1936); pp. 41–79.

H. Ahaus, "Orders, Holy," CE.

J. Bligh, S.J., *Ordination to the Priesthood* (New York: Sheed and Ward, 1956), "The Decree for the Armenians," pp. 47–55.

O. Cohausz, *The Priest and Saint Paul* (New York: Benziger, 1927); *passim.*

C. Cronin, "The Sacrament of Order," *The Teaching of the Catholic Church* (New York: Macmillan, 1949), II, pp. 1022–1061.

F. X. Doyle, *The Wonderful Sacraments* (New York: Benziger, 1924); "Holy Orders," pp. 195–215.

P. A. Kelly, *The Romance of a Priest* (New York: Kenedy, 1927); *passim.*

F. C. Kolbe, *The Four Mysteries of the Faith* (New York: Longmans, Green, 1926); "The Sacraments of Growth," pp. 146–155.

C. Lattey, *Six Sacraments, Papers Read at the Summer School of Catholic Studies, Cambridge, 1929* (St. Louis: Herder, 1930); B. Grimley, "Holy Orders," pp. 163–224.

H. E. Manning, *The Eternal Priesthood* (London: Burns, Oates and Washbourne, 1924); *passim*.

W. F. Robison, *The Seven-Fold Gift* (St. Louis: Herder, 1922); "The Source of Sacred Power," pp. 162–193.

W. Schamoni–O. Eisner, *Married Men as Ordained Deacons* (London: Burns, Oates and Washbourne, 1956); *p sim*.

M. J. Scheeben–C. Vollert, *The Mysteries of Christianity* (St. Louis: Herder, 1946), "The Inner Structure of the Individual Sacraments and Their Relation to One Another," pp. 572–582.

A. G. Schmidt, *The Ceremonies of Ordination to the Priesthood* (Chicago: Loyola Press, 1917). Full English translation of ordination rite.

Chapter XXIII

THE HAND OF THE HEALER

He bound up his wounds,
pouring thereon oil
(Luke x,34).

FROM the very dawn of reason we are taught to pray daily, and many times daily, for special helps "at the hour of our death." For even apart from the fear and natural shrinking at the prospect of departing from life, there is the supernatural aspect of that situation, the all-importance of which cannot be overestimated. For weal or woe, eternity is decided by the dispositions of the will at the hour of death, and Christians have always felt that the archenemy of Christ attacks with "artillery, foot and horse" in what is called the final agony, that is, the supreme struggle for victory. This belief is so described by the Council of Trent:

> Although our enemy seeks and seizes throughout our lives occasions to destroy our souls, still there is no time at which he more strenuously puts forth all the efforts of his cunning to ruin us utterly, and, if he can, shake our confidence in the divine mercy, than when he sees that end of life is imminent.

Now, the loving kindness of God, which, as well as His Wisdom,

reacheth from end to end mightily,
and disposeth all things sweetly,

Wisd. viii,1

has provided special sacramental help for all the other normal and abnormal crises in the Christian life. It was not to be expected that the hour of death, so uniquely critical above every other hour of existence, should be left without its proper sacramental aid. Nor was it. The *crisis of serious illness,* and the collapse of the approach of death, are *provided with a sacrament* wonderfully suited to its proper function; namely, to heal the last wounds of sin, and impart strength and courage at the end.

The customary lucidity of St. Thomas shows to excellent advantage when he treats of the nature and purpose of this sacrament:

> By dispensation of divine justice, the sickness of the soul, which is sin, sometimes passes to the body. Such bodily sickness is sometimes conducive to the health of the soul, where it is borne humbly and patiently and as a penance whereby one may make satisfaction for sin. Sometimes, again, sickness injures spiritual well-being by hindering the exercise of virtues. It was fitting, therefore, to have a spiritual remedy, applicable to sin precisely in this connection of bodily sickness being a consequence of sin. By its spiritual remedy bodily sickness is sometimes cured, when it is expedient for salvation.
>
> *Cont. Gent.* V, iv,73

The Oil of Healing. The therapeutic use of oil is as old as the world, and remains fairly common even nowadays in the form of salves and ungents, and the like. In the domestic life of the Orient this use of oil was a very conspicuous one, and is reflected many times in Holy Writ. When Isaias in a vision foresaw the Redeemer's sufferings, he said:

> From the sole of the foot unto the top of the head,
>   there is no soundness therein:
> wounds and bruises and swelling sores:
>   they are not bound up, nor dressed,
>   nor fomented with oil.
>
> *Isa.* i,6

Of the story of the Good Samaritan, as told by Christ, we recall how he "bound up his wounds, pouring thereon oil." Again, one remembers, *Luke* x,34 that when Christ sent the Twelve to preach the advent of the Kingdom of God, in the second year of the public ministry, the account of their labors is summed up as follows:

> And they went forth and preached repentance,
>   and cast out many devils,
> and anointed many sick with oil, and healed them.
>
> *Mark* vi,12–13

Homely Healing Becomes Sacrament. In Christ's day and long afterwards, anointing with oil in time of sickness was a commonplace household remedy. Nothing could be more appropriate to become the external *sign* of the special sacramental graces with which Christ wished to strengthen the soul in time of sickness than this same, everyday anoint-

god, Physician of souls and bodies,
heal thy servant.

ing. Let it not be thought that, because the anointing of the sick was elevated to the dignity of a sacrament, the ordinary, household, non-sacramental anointing was discontinued. Far from it; it continued to play a prominent part in the lives of Christians. But to return to the consideration of the sacrament known as the last anointing.

Compared with Confirmation. The young child at the dawn of its rational life is anointed in token of strengthening in confirmation: before the last battle the aged warrior is anointed in token of strengthening in extreme unction. In the identical action what different outlooks! The former is the joyous application of the oil of the athlete; the latter, the soothing, softening, penetrating oil of the physician.

Institution Promulgated. The time and place of the *institution* of this sacrament have not been revealed to us; but for the rest, St. James, the brother (a Semitic equivalent for "cousin") of Christ, gives us ample details of its *nature, rite,* and *effects* in the passage:

Is any one among you sick?	(*Subject*)
Let him call in the priests of the Church,	(*Minister*)
and let them pray over him,	(*Rite*)
anointing him with oil in the name of the Lord.	(*Rite*)
And the prayer of faith shall save the sick man,	(*Effect*)
and the Lord shall raise him up	(*Effect*)
And if he have committed sins	(*Conditional effect*)
he shall be forgiven.	Jas. v,14–15

Reserved to Seriously Sick. The first circumstance that stands out emphatically in this passage is that this is *a sacrament for the sick.* The original Greek of James makes it clear that a serious, or dangerous, sickness is meant. Therefore the Church has always understood that she is not at liberty to give this sacrament to one, even in imminent danger of death, but as yet in sound health, as soldiers going into battle, or a criminal about to be executed. On the other hand, the Church urges it upon one sick with a serious illness, although in no apparent danger of a speedy death, as in the case of a consumptive patient, who may well live for months, or eventually recover. The sacrament is intended to give special helps in the crisis of a serious sickness, whether the latter prove fatal or not. The sacrament may be received as often as the sick person falls into a fresh danger of death, even in the course of the same illness, when after rallying from danger, he suffers a relapse.

Former Variety in Rites. Some have thought that, since St. James speaks of *priests in the plural number,* the sacrament must be administered by several of them together; and, indeed, in both East and West, the Last Anointing was often so administered. But the Church has taken care to prevent the notion from gaining ground that it *must* be administered in this multiple fashion. Such a view, in fact, would really put the sacrament out of reach of most people. The Church interprets St. James' expression as referring to priests as a body or group, much as we speak of the clergy.

The *rite* of this sacrament was probably determined by Christ *only in the general terms* recorded by the Apostle, that there should be an anointing accompanied by prayer. Now these two elements could be combined in a limitless variety of ways. Neither did the Church see fit until almost modern times to prescribe detailed forms. Thus there is no sacramental ritual with a more diversified and interesting history than extreme unction. Something of the former ritual diversity will be indicated below in our survey of the present rites.

Twofold Effects. Let us pass to the important question of the proper effects of the last anointing. A glance at St. James' text shows that he indicates, as following upon the anointing, two effects, or classes of effects, the former unconditionally, the latter conditionally: "the Lord shall raise him up" and "*if* he have committed sin, he shall be forgiven." Let us take up these effects, or classes of effects (for each has a twofold nature), in the order in which the Apostle gives them.

How Soul Is Strengthened. The *"raising up"* here promised means, if the Greek words are closely scrutinized, "*an awakening,* a resuscitation, a stirring up, bringing to life from torpor or dullness." Who does not know that sickness, grave sickness, by lowering the vitality, induces "lethargy, exhaustion, inability to concentrate, stupor, even illusions, and hence extreme difficulty in prayer when prayer is the great necessity"? Under such circumstances it is much harder to make the most fruitful use of ordinary means of grace, and in particular, the ordinary means of setting one's conscience in order, the sacrament of penance. Last anointing was called by the Fathers and Schoolmen, and the Council of Trent sanctions and perpetuates the name, "the complement of penance." It must then *complete,* as it were, the sick man's reception of penance, fill up what perchance was lacking to it, and even go further than the latter could go under the circumstances by way of putting the soul in final readiness to meet God face to face. This the sacrament does by supernaturally stirring up, waking up, invigorating, and strengthening the soul for the needs of the hour. From this it becomes clear why this sacrament cannot be given to those who are not sick. The ordinary means suffice for them. It also becomes clear why it cannot be administered to another class, those, namely, who are too young to have committed any sin. Infants before arriving at the use of reason cannot hinder by sin the flow of Christ-life within them, and so neither ordinary nor extra-ordinary means are needed to preserve their measure of divine life intact.

Bodily Healing at Times. The healing effects of the sacrament *need not be limited* to soul-healing. The Church teaches that, *"sometimes, when it is expedient for the salvation of the soul"* (Trent), God uses this sacrament to restore the sick to health. Without invoking or exclud-ing miraculous effects, this is readiest understood as follows: the renewed vigor of soul, the calmness and self-possession, "that immunity from disorder," which St. Thomas called the principal effect of the sacrament, combines so forcibly with the bodily strength in resisting disease, that restoration to health is facilitated. S.T. III Supp.
Q. xxxii,a.2

Remission of Grave Sin. The remission of sin, *if* there be such in the soul of the recipient, is also mentioned by St. James as an effect of this sacrament. How and in what degree does the last anointing remit sin? As far as *mortal* sins are concerned, which after all are the only ones that slay the Christ-life, extreme unction is *not* a substitute for the reception of penance. If the sick person is physically able to show repent-ance in some manner, whether this be complete self-accusation or not, he is absolved before being anointed. Therefore the normal condition of the soul at the reception of last anointing is that of freedom from mortal sin. If, however, a sick person, in the state of mortal sin, be no longer capable of any form of confession, as, for instance, in a comatose state, and have previously conceived at least imperfect contrition for his sins, last anointing makes up for the impossibility of penance, and directly remits mortal sins. Here one sees the ingenuous limits to which divine love can go in providing channels of grace for wayward and willful man.

Remnants of Sin Removed. Venial *sins,* and the *temporal punish-ment* due to remitted sins, mortal and venial, these are remitted accord-ing to the measure of the recipient's contrition. The scope of the remission is limited only by the disposition of the recipient, not by the generosity of the Giver. The Church's traditional teaching in this matter is that, given the proper dispositions on the part of the recipient, that is, a sincere detestation of *all* sin, this sacrament *prepares the soul for immediate entrance into the glory of heaven.* "This sacrament is the last remedy that the Church can give, since it is an immediate preparation S.T. III, 2. 29,
a1; 2. 65, a7 for glory," says the Angelic Doctor, and similarly in another context: "This sacrament . . . leaves nothing in him . . . to hinder his reception into glory." These same views are taught by SS. Albert the Great and Bonaventure, Duns Scotus, Durandus, and many others. But since, as in the familiar case of a plenary indulgence, the recipient may fulfill the conditions to a greater or less degree, and thus receive greater or less remission of punishment, so, too, in the last anointing, the patient is not offered a magical means of escape from purgatory, or from the consequences of a misspent life.

Cont. Gent. iv,73

Extreme unction does give, to sum up, sacramental grace, fresh vigor, assurance of help to the end, and confidence in a merciful welcome at the portals of God's Country.

Names of Sacrament. Before perusing the present rites of the sacrament, let us recall that the common names for it now are *survivals* from a large field. In the West this sacrament was variously denominated "Holy Oil," "Holy Oil of the Sick," "Anointing with Holy Oil," "Chrism," "The Office of Anointing," "Imposition of Hands upon the Sick," "The Sacrament of the Departing," and the like. *"Extreme unction"* is recorded as early as the ninth century, but became common only some five hundred years later. In the Orient this sacrament was sometimes called *Heptapapdum* (*Office of the Seven Priests*), or more commonly, as at present, *Euchelaion* (Prayer-Unction).

THE RITE OF LAST ANOINTING[1]

The rite is here set out according to the norms of the Roman Ritual, although as a general rule in this country extreme unction is administered immediately after the patient has confessed and received Communion in the form of Viaticum, that is, provision for the journey. In that case the priest omits the prayers 1-2, and begins at number 3.

A wealth of picturesque ceremonial usage formerly attached to the administration of extreme unction. Its functional relation to penance was brought out by associating it immediately with that sacrament, instead, as in our present rites, of having it follow the reception of Viaticum. The sacrament was often, especially in monastic institutions, administered by three, or five, or seven priests, who approached the sick chamber in procession. Their entry, and the hallowing of the sickroom, has left little trace in our present rites, but the ancient prayers surviving (3-6) are considerable. Among the features that have now disappeared from this part of the rite

A. Entry and Blessing of Room

On arriving at the place where the sick person lies, the priest enters the room and says:

1. Peace be to this house.
Response. And to all who live here.

2. **Then after placing the oil on a table, being vested in a surplice and violet stole, the priest sprinkles the sick person, the room, and the bystanders with holy water, saying: Asperges, as given below:**

Antiphon: Sprinkle me, O Lord, with a hyssop, and I shall be purified; wash me, and I shall be whiter than snow.

3. *V.* Our help is in the name of the Lord.
R. Who made heaven and earth.
V. The Lord be with you.
R. And with thy spirit.

---

[1] The translation is from *Collectio Rituum* (Milwaukee: Bruce, 1954). Everything in *italics* must be said in Latin.

are: the incensing of the bed chamber, the sprinkling of the room with ashes in token of penance, laying the sick person on a penitential hair-cloth, and the like. These are clearly reminiscent of the rites of reconciliation after public penance.

These prayers (4-6) are very old forms, coming down from the ninth century at the latest. They seem to be of Gallican origin. In tenor and content they are properly prayers for the entry of the clerics come to administer the sacrament.

Let us pray.

4. O LORD Jesus Christ, as we, Thy lowly servants, enter this house, may our coming bring with it everlasting happiness, divine riches, unclouded joy, fruitful charity, enduring health. Let no demons have access here; let the angels of peace be present and all hateful dissension take leave of this house. O Lord, show forth in us the greatness of Thy holy name, and bless ✝ our way of life; bless the entering of Thy lowly servants into this house, Thou Who art holy and loving, Thou Who livest with the Father and the Holy Spirit for ever and ever.
    R. Amen.

5. LET us pray and beg our Lord Jesus Christ to bless ✝ with His own blessing this house and all who live in it. May he give them a good angel for their protector, and cause them to serve Him by considering the wonders of His law. May He turn away from them all the powers of the Enemy, rescue them from all dread and bewilderment, and keep them in this dwelling safe and sound. He Who is God, living and reigning with the Father and

the Holy Spirit for ever and ever.
R. Amen.

Let us pray.

6. HEAR us, O holy Lord,
Father almighty, eternal
God, and send Thy holy angel
from heaven to watch over, cherish,
protect, be with, and defend all
who live in this house. Through
Christ our Lord.   *R.* Amen.

The foregoing prayers may be
omitted in whole or in part, if
urgency demand.

If the sick person wishes to go
to confession, the priest hears him
and absolves him.

Then the Confiteor ("I confess") having been said in Latin
or the vernacular, the priest gives
the general absolution.

In the recitation of the *Confiteor*
at this point is preserved a relic of
the rites of penance, which sacrament was formerly, as was said,
administered at this point. The injunction to the bystanders to recite
the seven Penitential Psalms and
the Litany of the Saints during the
unction reflect conditions when the
actual anointing was much more
elaborate than at present.

I CONFESS to Almighty God,
to blessed Mary ever Virgin, to
blessed Michael the Archangel, to
blessed John the Baptist, to the
holy Apostles Peter and Paul, to
all the saints, and to you, Father,
that I have sinned exceedingly in
thought, word and deed; through
my fault, through my fault,
through my most grievous fault.
Therefore I beseech blessed Mary
ever Virgin, blessed Michael the
Archangel, blessed John the Baptist, the holy Apostles Peter and
Paul, all the saints, and you, Father, to pray to the Lord our God
for me.

MAY almighty God have
mercy on you, forgive you
your sins, and bring you to life
everlasting. Amen.

MAY the almighty and merciful Lord grant you pardon, absolution, and remission of your sins. Amen.

Then before beginning to anoint the sick person, the priest admonishes the bystanders to pray for him.

If time and circumstances allow, the following passage may be read:

Beloved brothers, let us listen to the words of the holy Gospel according to St. Matthew (8:5–10, 13):

At that time, as Jesus came to Capharnaum, there came to Him a centurion who entreated Him, saying: "Lord, my servant is lying sick in the house, paralyzed, and is grievously afflicted." Jesus said to him, "I will come and cure him." But in answer the centurion said, "Lord, I am not worthy that Thou shouldst come under my roof; but only say the word, and my servant shall be healed. For I too am a man subject to authority, and have soldiers subject to me; and I say to one, 'Go,' and he goes; and to another, 'Come,' and he comes; and to my servant, 'Do this,' and he does it." And when Jesus heard this He marvelled, and said to those who were following Him, "Amen, I say to you, I have not found so great faith in Israel." Then Jesus said to the centurion: "Go thy way; as thou hast believed, so be it done to thee." And the servant was healed in that hour.

The priest goes on and those present respond:

Let us kneel down and pray.

V. Lord, have mercy.

R. Christ, have mercy. Lord, have mercy.

V. Lord, that Thou wouldst visit and strengthen this sick man/woman.

R. We beseech Thee, hear us.

V. That Thou wouldst give him/her life and health.

R. We beseech Thee, hear us.

V. That Thou wouldst grant him/her the grace of the Holy Spirit.

R. We beseech Thee, hear us.

V. Lamb of God, Who takest away the sins of the world.

R. Spare us, O Lord.

V. Lamb of God, Who takest away the sins of the world.

R. Graciously hear us, O Lord.

V. Lamb of God, Who takest away the sins of the world.

R. Have mercy on us.

Extending his right hand over the sick person, he says:

In the name of the Father, and of the Son, and of the Holy Spirit. May any power that the devil has over you be utterly destroyed, as I place my hands on you and call upon the help of the glorious and holy Mother of God, the Virgin Mary, and of her illustrious Spouse, St. Joseph, and of all the holy angels, archangels, patriarchs, prophets, apostles, martyrs, confessors, virgins, and all the saints. Amen.

Having moistened his thumb with the Holy Oil, he anoints in turn the eyes, the ears, the nostrils, the mouth, the hands, and the feet — each and all with the sign of the Cross — saying for each unction as follows:

For the Eyes

By this holy anointing and His most loving mercy may the Lord forgive you whatever wrong you have done by the use of your sight. Amen.

For the Ears

By this holy anointing and His most loving mercy may the Lord forgive you whatever wrong you have done by the use of your hearing. Amen.

For the Nostrils

By this holy anointing and His most loving mercy may the Lord forgive you whatever wrong you have done by the use of your sense of smell. Amen.

For the Mouth (Closed)

By this holy anointing and His most loving mercy may the Lord forgive you whatever wrong you have done by the use of your sense of taste and power of speech. Amen.

For the Hands

By this holy anointing and His most loving mercy may the Lord forgive you whatever wrong you have done by the use of your sense of touch. Amen.

For the Feet

By this holy anointing and His most loving mercy may the Lord forgive you whatever wrong you have done by the use of your power to walk. Amen.

In case of necessity a single anointing is sufficient, as, on the forehead:

By this holy anointing may the Lord forgive you whatever wrong you have done. Amen.

The anointing finished, the priest rubs his thumb with a bit of bread, and washes and wipes his hands. This ablution water and the bread are later to be thrown into the fire. The priest says:

V. Lord, have mercy.

R. Christ, have mercy.

Lord, have mercy.

V. Our Father, etc., **in secret**

V. And lead us not into temptation.

R. But deliver us from evil.

V. Grant salvation to Thy servant.

R. For his/her hope, O my God, is in Thee.

V. Send him/her aid, O Lord, from Thy holy place.

R. And watch over him/her from Sion.

V. Be a tower of strength for him/her, O Lord.

R. Against the attack of the enemy.

V. Let the enemy have no power against him/her.

R. And let not the son of evil come near to harm him/her.

V. O Lord, hear my prayer.

R. And let my cry come unto Thee.

V. The Lord be with you.

R. And with your spirit.

Let us pray.

O LORD God, Who didst say through James, Thy apostle: "Is any-one sick among you? Let him bring in the priests of the Church, and let them pray over him, anointing him with oil in the name of the Lord. And the prayer of faith will save the sick man, and the Lord will raise him up, and if he be in sins, they shall be forgiven him," cure, O Redeemer, we implore Thee, by the grace of the Holy Spirit the illness of this sick man/woman and heal his/her wounds; forgive his/her sins, and drive away from him/her all pains of mind and body. In Thy mercy, give him/her his/her health, inward and outward, so that he/she may once more be able to take up his/her work, restored by the gift of

Thy mercy. Thou Who livest and reignest with the Father and the Holy Spirit, God, for ever and ever.
R. *Amen.*

Let us pray.

W E IMPLORE *Thee, O Lord, look with kindness on Thy servant, N., who is growing weak as his/her body fails. Cherish and revive the soul which Thou didst create, so that, purified and made whole by his/her sufferings, he/she may find himself/herself restored by Thy healing. Through Christ our Lord.*
R. *Amen.*

Let us pray.

O HOLY *Lord, Father almighty, eternal God, Who, by pouring the grace of Thy blessing into the bodies of the sick, dost watch with all-embracing care over Thy creatures, be present in Thy kindness as we call upon Thy holy name. Free Thy servant from sickness, restore to him/her his/her health, raise him/her up by Thy right hand, strengthen him/her by Thy power, protect him/her by Thy might, and give him/her back to Thy holy Church, with all that is needed for his/her welfare. Through Christ our Lord.*
R. *Amen.*

Twentieth-Century Source Material

(Gloomy rigorism associated with Purgatory is an excrescence on the ancient traditions, to which modern authors are redirecting our attention, as Professor Bartmann in his book, PURGATORY, A BOOK OF CHRISTIAN COMFORT.)

In Purgatory the virtue of faith remains active and operative, just as it was on earth, and by it the soul knows many things that contribute immensely to its happiness. Faith embraces and includes the whole mystery of our Redemption. . . . Why should not then the Souls in Purgatory experience something of this joy, even more abundantly than God's children on earth? All the more as Christ is the glorious mystical Head of the Souls in Purgatory, as of all those whom faith and charity unite to Him? So we say: these souls are even more intimately connected with the Head of the Church, Christ, than when they were on earth, for no temptation, no doubt, can shake their immovable faith; it cannot be affected by the jeers of freethinkers or the scorn of atheists; on the contrary, the torch of faith burns brightly, clearly, and steadily within the souls that people this mysterious land. The blessed bond of a common faith unites them in a blissful union to Christ and all the other spirits. The best thing about the faith is that, according to St. Paul,

Eph. iii,16   by it Christ dwells in our hearts . . .

To the essential joys of Purgatory and such as are common to all spirits, particular or personal ones may be added. "Every day is a holy day for a soul that tries to bring its will into perfect harmony with God's will." If that is so, then every day in Purgatory is a holy day, for apart from those in heaven, there are no souls more closely united to God's will than those in Purgatory. To these uninterrupted holy days may be added the great anniversaries of our redemption which the Church observes on earth. Since we are all members of one and the same body, whether we be on earth, in Purgatory, or in heaven, we share in all the joys of the whole mystical body of Christ. So we may surely suppose that the splendour of the great festivals which we celebrate here on earth spreads its radiance even as far as Purgatory. It is against our principles to indulge the imagination — the dogma of Purgatory is far too serious and important for that; but the idea that the whole invisible world, insofar as it is peopled by the children of the kingdom of heaven, joins in the celebration of the festivals which the Church of this world observes in honor of Christ, its Head and its Saviour, rests on such solid ground that it cannot simply be brushed aside. Now all our festivals are festivals of grace, and where grace illumines a soul, joy also bursts forth, irrespectively of the point that it may have reached on the road to salvation. . . . And the theme of its song of victory is suggested by St. Paul

II Tim. i,12 when he says: "I know in whom I have believed." Every fresh arrival in Purgatory enters with these feelings of joy and gratitude. Notwithstanding the delay he had to bear with, he knows that in essence and substance his redemption is complete and perfect. . . . There the soul no longer cherishes many hopes: it retains but one, all the others having forsaken it at its entrance into the next world:

> Looking for the blessed hope
> and the manifestation of the glory

Tit. ii,13   of our great God and Saviour Jesus Christ.

— Quoted by permission of Burns, Oates & Washbourne.

Topics for Further Discussion:

A frequent difference of time ranging from a half hour to two hours or so, between the moment of apparent death and actual death, and the consequent duty with respect to last anointing

Neglect to inform a sick person of the gravity of the illness, an omission with probably eternal consequences.

Last anointing *before* a major surgical operation.

Circumstances under which extreme unction is the only means of salvation.

The frustration of extreme unction by impenitence.

Readings:

J. P. Arendzen, "Extreme Unction," *The Teaching of the Catholic Church* (New York: Macmillan, 1949), II, pp. 990–1021.

B. Bartmann, *Purgatory, A Book of Christian Comfort* (London: Burns, Oates and Washbourne, 1936); "Is It Possible to Avoid Purgatory," pp. 204–227.

F. X. Doyle, *The Wonderful Sacraments* (New York: Benziger, 1924); "Extreme Unction," pp. 178–194.

J. B. Ferreres, *Death Real and Apparent* (St. Louis: Herder, 1906); *passim.*

M. A. Jugie, *Purgatory* (Westminster: Newman, 1949), "Means of Avoiding Purgatory: Sacramental," pp. 116–140.

A. J. Kilker, *Extreme Unction* (St. Louis: Herder, 1927).

The Last Rites for the Sick and Dying (Collegeville: Lit. Press, 1957).

C. Lattey, *Six Sacraments, Papers Read at the Summer School of Catholic Studies, Cambridge, 1929* (St. Louis: Herder, 1930); L. W. Geddes, "Extreme Unction," pp. 258–282.

———, *Man and Eternity, Papers Read at Summer School of Catholic Studies, Cambridge, 1936* (London: Burns, Oates and Washbourne, 1937); W. J. O'Donovan, "Death from a Medical Point of View," pp. 72–88.

M. Perkins, *Speaking of How to Pray* (New York: Sheed & Ward, 1944); "Anointing for Glory," pp. 117–123.

W. F. Robison, *The Seven-Fold Gift* (St. Louis: Herder, 1922); "Health or Help," pp. 131–161.

R. H. J. Steuart, *The Inward Vision* (New York: Longmans, Green, 1932); "Dies Irae," pp. 139–147.

P. J. Toner, "Extreme Unction," *CE.*

Chapter XXIV

FROM LIFE TO LARGER LIFE

Touching them that sleep . . .
Grieve not even as the rest
who have no hope (I Thess. iv,13).

THE acid test of man's attitude toward life is his attitude toward death. This silent leveler is often called "God's most eloquent messenger"; undoubtedly death speaks a language all understand. His ceaseless visitations bring it about that, whereas the adolescent and the young number kin and friends mostly among the living, the mature and the aging count *theirs* among the dead. Death takes no holiday. Ever and again we are called to assist at the last, sad rites for some departed friend, so that it gradually becomes borne in upon us that still sharper partings will cut off those nearest and dearest to us on earth. For each individual one of life's chief tasks is to learn to die. Sorrow and grief at bereavement are as natural to man as the bonds of love they sever. Just as natural, too, is the desire to show reverential honor to the departed by investing interment with special religious rites. From immemorial years these two reactions in the presence of death have been reckoned as universal human promptings. They attend the biers of civilized and savage, of Hebrew and Hindu, of the Christless and the Christian. But Christianity hallows and tempers both the sorrow of separation and the dutiful piety of obsequies, for we are not like those "who have no hope."

Pagan's Views on Death. It was a mark of the *degeneration of the ancient pagan religions* that the primitive and reverent customs of burial had gradually given way, by the time Christianity appeared, to the desecration of the funeral *pyre*. But it is really not surprising, in the light of the pagan's utter hopelessness before death, as proclaimed by numberless sepulchral inscriptions along the great highways, that the inhuman and degrading practice of cremation had been adopted quite generally. For what was death in the eyes, let us say, of a Roman of the time of Augustus? With one voice his poets called it *night:* Virgil and Horace, Ovid and Catullus find no fitter phrase for it than "everlasting night," "perpetual night," "black night." His philosophers echoed, it is true, mankind's traditional yearnings for immortality, but in such hollow tones that many, high and low alike, substituted for a belief in the life beyond "a search for the great Perhaps." Romans of every rank set upon their tombs such memorials as these:

INTO NOTHING FROM NOTHING HOW QUICKLY WE GO

or the following:

ONCE WE WERE NOT, NOW WE ARE AS WE WERE

or that reckless sentiment so freely used as to be understood when only the initials of the words were engraved:

I WAS NOT, I WAS, I AM NOT, I CARE NOT

Curses and Blasphemy. Often these pithy messages from the grave express merely bewilderment as in this puzzling admission:

I LIVED AS I LIKED, BUT WHY I DIED, I KNOW NOT

But frequently the bitterness of death becomes a curse against fate, or against God. "Curse the harshness of my lot" begs a boy of ten from his narrow tomb, a tone which is intensified in the passionate blasphemy of a young woman:

I LIFT MY HANDS AGAINST GOD, WHO TOOK ME AWAY, THOUGH I HAD
DONE NO HARM, AT THE AGE OF TWENTY

Christian "Cities of the Dead." It is a good instance of the contrasts always afforded by Christianity to the spirit of the world that only a few steps could separate such pagan tombs along the roadside from the entrances to *Christian burial chambers* where all was vastly different. Here, amid lively, light-hearted, frescoed scenes of garden and grove, the elaborate vaulted rooms and galleries breathe peace in the presence of sorrow, life in the presence of death, and a simple, joyous love following the departed ones now "called from darkness into God's wondrous light." The Christian calls his *necropolis* a "cemetery," which means a I Pet. ii,10 sleeping-place, a new word, coined, it seems, by him, and one that

Interior of a Pagan Columbarium or "Dovecote"

After cremation of the bodies, the ashes were deposited in the small wall niches, which were sealed with tile or marble, and the spot then marked for identification. (Based on illustration in Lanciani's *Pagan and Christian Rome*, courtesy Houghton Mifflin Co.)

puzzled the pagans. Thus, the last edicts of persecution speak of "Christians worshiping in those spots called 'sleeping-places.'" Euseb. *H. E.* vii,13

At First Protected by Law. Although, as the edict just quoted would indicate, the Christian burial places were, in the last persecutions, outlawed and violated, before that they had been *protected and shielded by law* for generations. Even the mangled bodies of the martyrs put to death as outlaws could be reverently caught up, and clothed in fine raiment, and openly carried with flowers and lights and incense and singing to the Christian burial places, whether these were in the open fields, or in the private subterranean vaults of the wealthy members of the community. Thus the burial of St. Cyprian was a spectacle to the entire city of Carthage. Whether in the fields, then, or in the catacombs, as the case might be, the bodies once incorporated into the Mystical Body were reverently laid to rest. The inscriptions on these tombs were such simple, touching messages as these:

IN PEACE

LIVE IN GOD

GOD REFRESH THY SOUL

PEACE BE YOURS IN GOD

MARCIAN SLEEPS IN PEACE

FARE THEE WELL IN CHRIST

PEACE FROM THE BRETHREN

FAREWELL TO THEE IN CHRIST

FAREWELL MY BELOVED IN PEACE

HAPPY FLORENTIUS LITTLE LAMB OF GOD

VICTOR DWELLS IN PEACE AND IN CHRIST

Christians' Views on Death. Here we are in the presence of a radically different attitude toward death, the *Christian attitude,* that of those who *know in whom they have believed,* and who cherish firm hope II Tim. i,12 of life eternal with God. The very air of the Christian sleeping-place is sanctified, because charged with this expectation of a larger, truer life in the unveiled vision of God's Majesty.

Pagan Rites Christianized. Tertullian, who wrote at the end of the second century, tells us of the custom of meeting annually at the graves of the dead to celebrate the Christian Sacrifice. This was a Christianizing of an older, pagan banqueting practice, as was mentioned on page

103. In like manner, *nearly all the other common usages* attending Christian burial today are *adaptations* from the pagan customs of early Christian times. In Tertullian's day it was still reckoned an undesirable relic of paganism that flowers, and wreaths in particular, were strewn upon coffin and grave, but by St. Jerome's time this beautiful custom was accepted without question. Jerome writes to his friend Pammachius: "Husbands spread violets, roses, lilies and purple blossoms on the graves

Epis. 26 ad Pam. of their wives, and so assuage the sorrow of their hearts in these offices."

The great historian of the early persecutions, Eusebius, speaks of the zealous care with which the bodies were *cleansed,* and anointed with sweet-smelling spices, and *wrapped* in white linen cloths. All of which reminds one forcibly of the Gospel story of the burial of Christ. Of St. Cecilia and other famous martyrs it is known they were interred in regal cloth-of-gold. St. Cyprian, in the middle of the third century, gently scolded his flock that at funerals they wore *"black garments of*

De Mort. xx *mourning,* whereas the departed have already put on the shining raiment" of glory. But the wearing of black persisted, and later on even conquered the Church, since it is now found in the sacred vestments and the hangings of altar and bier. St. Jerome contrasts the howling of the heathen funeral procession with the comforting *psalms* as sung by the Christians. The funeral *processions,* held as a rule in the evening, reminded St. John Chrysostom, of Constantinople, of an escort of honor, because of the torches carried, the waving of palm branches, the smoking censer, and oft-echoing cries of *Alleluia.*

Consolation amid Sorrow. Some of the most precious pages of St. Augustine's great letter to God, his *Confessions,* narrate the circumstances of the passing of his saintly mother, Monica. She had said as the end drew near: "Lay this body anywhere; let not the care for that in any way disquiet you. This only I request that you should remember me at the Lord's altar, wherever you be."[1] Augustine relates at what great cost he was able to refrain from weeping then, and "when the sacrificial price of our redemption was being offered for her," and again during the prayers at the grave. Of his tears shed later in private the memory came back to him more than ten years after as he wrote the *Confessions,* and he says of them quite unashamed: "And now let who will judge me as

---

[1] At this time Augustine had no thought of becoming a priest; the expression refers to the custom of a public remembrance of the dead made during Mass.

he will, and if he find sin therein that I wept for my mother and for such a mother, let him not deride me, but rather if he be of large charity, let him weep himself for my sins and ask pardon of Christ for me."

Conf. ix,12

St. Monica died at Ostia near Rome in the summer of 387. From a far-distant quarter, Syria, in the Christian Orient, we have of about that same date summary directions concerning Christian burial:

> In the funerals of your dead [we read in a work called the *Constitutions of the Apostles*] lead them forth with psalms, if they were faithful in the Lord. . . . Offer the acceptable Eucharist, the anti-type of the royal Body of Christ in your churches [for them], and in your cemeteries. . . . Assemble in the cemeteries, reading the Sacred Scriptures and singing psalms for the martyrs . . . and for all the saints [i.e., all departed Christians] . . . and for your brethren.

Con. Apos. vi,32

Larger Life Beyond. Enough has been said to make it clear that our customary offices toward the dead come down to us from remotest times, and sanctified by the sorrows and resignation of all the Christian centuries. It should also be doubly clear that in these rites the Church seeks to give eloquent, if tempered, expression to the genuine human sorrow of the occasion, together with an expression of her *unshakable faith in the fuller life* beyond the grave. If she says in one breath, "Weep for the dead," she adds in the next, "Weep *but little* for the dead, for he is at rest." Excessive sorrow, warns St. Cyprian, is like denying the faith, and gives the Gentiles a chance to say "that we mourn for those who, we say, are alive with God, as if they were extinct and lost." The faith we profess is couched in those matchless phrases spoken near the grave of Lazarus:

Eccles. xxii,10
Eccles. xxii,11
De Mort. xx

> I am the Resurrection and the Life;
> he that believeth in Me, even if he die, shall live,
> and whosoever liveth and believeth in Me,
> he shall never die.

John xi,25

So well had St. Paul plumbed the meaning of these words that he could fearlessly say:

> Christ shall be glorified in this body of mine,
> whether by its life or by its death.
> For with me to live is Christ, *and to die is gain.*

Phil. i,20–21

The Papal Crypt
in the Catacomb of Callistus

The last line of the quotation was graven on his tomb at **Rome.**
Resurrection of the Body through Christ. St. Paul's converts at
Corinth engaged in his absence in endless disputes about the resurrection
from the dead, that of Christ, and their own. His mode of answering
their questions links our own resurrection to Christ's in such a way that
there is, after all, only *one* resurrection from the dead. It is wholly in
virtue of the Christian's solidarity with Christ that he is to rise again:

> But, in truth, Christ *is* risen from the dead,
>   the first fruits of them that sleep.
> For since by a man [came] death,
> by a man also [cometh] resurrection from the dead.
>   For as in Adam all die,
> so in Christ shall all be made to live.
>   But each in his own order:
>   Christ the first fruits,
>   then they that are Christ's [shall rise] at His coming.   I Cor. xv,20–24

This calm assurance Paul never tired of repeating. Let two other short
citations complete our investigation of his thought in this matter. To
the same Corinthians he wrote at a later date:

> For we know that He who raised up the Lord Jesus
>   will raise us up also with Jesus
> and place us along with [the just].   II Cor. iv,14

Speaking to the Romans, Paul attributes the resurrection to the indwelling
of the Holy Spirit:

> If the Spirit of Him who raised Jesus from the dead
>   dwelleth within you,
> then He who raised up Jesus from the dead
> will also bring to life your mortal bodies
> through His Spirit who dwelleth within you.   Rom. viii,11

In short the resurrection of the Head has merited that of the members,
and is the pattern thereof.

Since the abundant consolations the Church's Burial Ritual can
afford will one day *be needed to comfort us* in bereavement, it well repays
one to peruse these rites betimes. Below are set out extracts typical of
the entire service.

EXTRACTS FROM THE RITES OF CHRISTIAN BURIAL[1]

A. Procession to the Altar

The priest, in the house of the deceased, or, in this country, more commonly at the door of the church, sprinkles the corpse with holy water and recites Psalm 129:

Antiphon: If Thou, O Lord, dost mark iniquities

Out of the depths I cry to Thee, O Lord; * Lord, hear my voice!
Let Thine ears be attentive * to my voice in supplication.
If Thou, O Lord, dost mark iniquities, * Lord, who can stand?
But with Thee is forgiveness, * that Thou mayest be revered.
I trust in the Lord; * my soul trusts in his word.
My soul waits for the Lord * more than sentinels wait for the dawn.
More than sentinels wait for the dawn, * let Israel wait for the Lord,
For with the Lord is kindness * and with him is plenteous redemption;
And he will redeem Israel * from all their iniquities.
Eternal rest * grant unto him/her/them, O Lord;
And let perpetual light * shine upon him/her/them.

Antiphon: If Thou, O Lord, dost mark iniquities, O Lord, who can stand?

V. The Lord be with you.

R. And with your spirit.

Let us pray.

O Lord, we commend to Thee the soul of Thy servant, N., that, having departed from this world, he/she may live with Thee. And by the grace of Thy merciful love, wash away the sins that in human frailty he/she has committed in the conduct of his/her life. Through Christ our Lord.

R. Amen.

The corpse is brought to the altar, the symbol of the Heavenly City, where God and His Christ, surrounded by saints and angels, await the coming of the just. To this high assemblage the Church now addresses her petition:

Come to his/her aid, * O saints of God; hasten to meet him/her, angels of the Lord: * Taking up his/her soul, * Presenting it in the sight of the Most High.

---

[1]Translation is from *Collectio Rituum* (Milwaukee: Bruce, 1954). Prayers may be said in English if function is with a low Mass.

V. May you be received by Christ, Who has called you: and may the angels bring you into the bosom of Abraham.

R. Taking up his/her soul, * Presenting it in the sight of the Most High.

V. Eternal rest grant unto him/her, O Lord: and may perpetual light shine upon him/her.

R. Presenting his/her soul in the sight of the Most High.

If the Office of the Dead is to be said, it follows here.

B. Mass for the Dead

Many minor peculiarities characterize a Mass for the Dead, or Mass of Requiem, as it is called. In general these are all indications of an extreme antiquity. These Mass-formularies were among the very first to develop, and spread rapidly. Once they had become well known, popular attachment resisted further change.
Among the proper parts of the funeral Mass are:

Collect

O God, whose *property it is always to have mercy and to spare,* we humbly present our prayers to Thee in behalf of the soul of Thy servant N, which Thou hast this day called out of the world: beseeching Thee not to deliver it into the hands of the enemy, nor to forget it forever, but command it to be received by the holy angels, and to be carried into Paradise; that, as it hoped and believed in Thee, it may not undergo the pains of hell, but may obtain everlasting joys. Through Jesus Christ, Thy Son, our Lord, etc.

Epistle

We would not have you ignorant,
brethren,
touching them that sleep,
that you grieve not,
even as the rest *who have not hope.*
For, as we believe that Jesus died and rose again,
God will likewise bring with Jesus
those who have fallen asleep through Him.
For this we tell you as the Lord's word,
that we who live,
who survive unto the Lord's coming,
shall not precede them that are fallen asleep.

For the Lord Himself at a signal —
the voice of an archangel and the trumpet of God —
shall come down from heaven;
and the dead in Christ shall rise first.
Thereupon we the living, who remain,
shall together with them
be caught up in the clouds
to meet the Lord in the air,
and thus *we shall be ever with the Lord.*

I Thess. iv,12–17   Comfort ye one another, therefore, with these words.

Gospel

At that time: Martha said to Jesus,
"Lord, hadst Thou been here,
my brother had not died;
and even now I know
that whatsoever Thou shalt ask of God,
God will give Thee."

Jesus saith to her,
"Thy brother shall rise again."

Martha saith to Him,
"I know that he shall rise again at the resurrection,
on the last day."

Jesus said to her,
"I am the Resurrection and the Life;
he that believeth in Me, even if he die, shall live,
and whosoever liveth and believeth in Me,
he shall never die.
Believest thou this?"

She saith to Him,
"Yea, Lord, I have believed
that Thou art the Christ, the Son of God,
John xi,21–27   that cometh into the world."

At the Offering

Have mercy, O Lord, we beseech Thee, on the soul of Thy servant, N, *for which we offer this Victim of praise,* humbly beseeching Thy Majesty that by this service of loving atonement he (she) may deserve to attain everlasting rest. Through Jesus Christ, etc.

After the Communion

Grant, we beseech Thee, Almighty God, that the soul of Thy servant, which today hath departed this world, *being purified and freed from sins by this Sacrifice,* may obtain both forgiveness and eternal rest. Through Jesus Christ, etc.

C. The Final Absolution

At the end of the Mass, the priest lays aside the maniple and chasuble, and puts on a black cope. Then standing at the foot of the corpse, he once more solemnly intercedes for the complete freeing of the soul from all penalties due to sin.

O Lord, do not bring Thy servant to trial, for no man becomes holy in Thy sight unless Thou dost grant him forgiveness of all his sins. We implore Thee, therefore, do not let the verdict of Thy judgment go against him/her, whom the loyal prayer of Christian faith is commending to Thy mercy, but rather, by the help of Thy grace, may he/she escape the sentence which he/she deserves, for during his/her earthly life, he/she was signed with the seal of the Holy Trinity; Who livest and reignest for ever and ever. R. Amen.

D. Order of Burial

It is especially in the concluding section of these rites that the reverence for the dignity of a Christian's body is given expression. To this end the body is not interred until its last resting place has been blessed. Blessing the grave the priest says:

*Deliver me, O Lord, from everlasting death on that day of terror: * When the heavens and the earth will be shaken. As Thou dost come to judge the world by fire.*

V. I am in fear and trembling at the judgment and the wrath that is to come.

**When the heavens and the earth will be shaken.*

V. That day will be a day of wrath, of misery, and of ruin: a day of grandeur and great horror:

†*As Thou dost come to judge the world by fire.*

V. Eternal rest grant unto them, O Lord, and let perpetual light shine upon them.

Deliver me, O Lord.

V. Lord, have mercy.

R. Christ, have mercy.   *Lord, have mercy.*

V. Our Father.

V. And lead us not into temptation.

R. But deliver us from evil.

V. From the gate of hell.

R. Rescue his/her/their soul/s, O Lord.

V. May he/she/they rest in peace.

R. Amen.

V. O Lord, hear my prayer.

R. And let my cry come unto Thee.

V. The Lord be with you.

R. And with your spirit.

O God, Who alone art ever merciful and sparing of punishment, humbly we pray Thee in behalf of the soul of Thy servant, N., whom Thou hast commanded to go forth today from this world. Do not hand him/her over to the power of the Enemy and do not forget him/her forever; but command that this soul be taken up by the holy angels and brought home to paradise, so that, since he/she hoped and believed in Thee, he/she may not undergo the punishments of hell, but rather possess everlasting joys. Through Christ our Lord. R. Amen.

Christ's promise of resurrection through Himself is then sung as an antiphon before and after the joyous hymn "Benedictus" [cf. Luke i,68–79], Zachary's song of thanksgiving at the approach of man's redemption. These sentiments of supernatural happiness should fill the Christian mind as it turns away from the grave. God's mercies are hymned that the fruits of redemption have been applied in last and fullest measure to the soul now entering upon the life of glory.

Summary. The universal sanctifying power of Christianity hallows and assuages man's natural sorrow in bereavement. While tenderly allowing the expression of genuine grief, the Church gently turns her funerary rites into a magnificent profession of faith in the Christian's destiny of sharing the God-life forever, and the further promise of the resurrection of the body through the merits of and after the pattern of Christ's own resurrection.

If it be
 in [view of] this life alone
 that we have set our hopes in Christ,
we are more to be pitied
 than all [other] men.   I Cor. xv,19

Twentieth-Century Source Material

(In Gertrude von Le Fort's HYMNS TO THE CHURCH, *done into English by Mrs. Winthrop Chandler, the Mystical Body finds exquisite treatment: the volume closes with the lines here cited):*

The Last Things: IV

But when once the Great End of all mysteries shall begin,

When the Hidden One shall blaze forth in terrible storms of unfettered love,

When His home-call shall rend the welkin like a tempest and the wasted desire of His creation shall shout for joy,

When the bodies of the stars burst into flame and out of their ashes light shall rise delivered,

When the heavy dykes of matter break and open all the sluices of the invisible,

When decades of centuries sweep back like eagles, and embattled aeons come home to eternity,

When the vessels of speech shall be shattered, and torrents of the never-uttered shall burst forth,

When the loneliest souls are washed up into the light, and see there what they never knew about themselves;

Then will the Revealed One raise my head, and before His sight all my veils will rise in flames,

And I shall lie there like a naked mirror in the presence of all worlds.

And the stars shall find in me their praises, and the ages will find in me their eternity, and the souls will find in me their divinity.

And God will recognize in me His love.

And henceforth my head shall wear no other veil than the dazzling light of Him who is my Judge.

And the world will be lost in this veil of light.

And the veil shall be called mercy, and mercy shall be called infinite.

And the infinite shall be called blessedness. Amen.

— Quoted by permission of Sheed and Ward.

Topics for Further Discussion:

The Church's refusal of funeral services to such as order their bodies cremated (Canon 1240).

The attendance of Catholics at non-Catholic funeral services.

The Protestant rejection of prayers for the departed.

The sending of "Mass cards" instead of elaborate floral pieces.

The custom of having anniversary Masses celebrated for departed relatives, etc.

The series of thirty so-called Gregorian Masses.

The medieval fancy of a cessation of purgatorial suffering on Sunday.

"Heaven is *not* heaven, is not a place of happiness, *except* to the holy." — *Newman.*

The word *purgatory* does not occur in the liturgy.

"Life is so short it seems God's greatest joke on man." — *St. Catherine of Siena.*

Texts of the Funeral Rites:

Mass for the Dead and the Burial Service (London: CTS).

Mass on the Day of Burial (St. Paul: The Leaflet Missal, 1931).

Masses for the Dead (Milwaukee: Bruce, 1932).

The Funeral Mass and Burial Service for Adults (Collegeville: Liturgical Press, 1929).

Readings:

J. P. Arendzen, "Heaven, or The Church Triumphant," *The Teaching of the Catholic Church* (New York: Macmillan, 1949), II, pp. 1248–1282.

B. Bartmann, *Purgatory, A Book of Christian Comfort* (London: Burns, Oates and Washbourne, 1936); "The Psychology of the Hereafter," pp. 47–52; "Purgatory in the Church of the Fathers," pp. 88–107; *passim.*

F. Cabrol, *Liturgical Prayer, Its History and Spirit* (New York: Kenedy, 1922); "Death," pp. 296–307.

The Funeral Mass and Burial Service (Collegeville: Lit. Press, 1957).

C. Grimaud–J. F. Newcomb, *One Only Christ* (New York: Benziger, 1939); " 'Our' Death in Christ," pp. 209–219; " 'Our' Resurrection," pp. 220–233; *passim.*

L. Hertling–E. Kirschbaum–J. Costelloe, *The Roman Catacombs and Their Martyrs* (Milwaukee: Bruce, 1956), "The People of God," pp. 143–160.

C. Lattey, ed., *Man and Eternity, Papers Read at the Summer School of Catholic Studies, Cambridge, 1936* (London: Burns, Oates and Washbourne, 1937); F. Moncrieff, "Purgatory and Indulgences," pp. 161–200.

C. Marmion, *Christ, the Life of the Soul* (St. Louis: Herder, 1923); "Coheredes Christi," pp. 388–402.

J. McCann, "The Resurrection of the Body," *The Teaching of the Catholic Church* (New York: Macmillan, 1949), II, pp. 1211–1247.

J. B. McLaughlin, "Purgatory, or The Church Suffering," *The Teaching of the Catholic Church* (New York: Macmillan, 1949), II, pp. 1141–1175.

F. J. Sheed, *A Map of Life* (New York: Sheed and Ward, 1933); "Heaven," pp. 140–144.

H. Thurston, "Burial, Christian," *CE.*

A. Vonier, "Death and Judgment," *The Teaching of the Catholic Church* (New York: Macmillan, 1949), II, pp. 1101–1140.

Chapter XXV

EMANCIPATING AND ENLISTING CREATION

Creation itself shall be freed
from its slavery to corruption . . .
unto the freedom . . .
of the children of God (Rom. viii,21).

WHEN will America have a Catholic culture? Or, when, at least, will American Catholics produce a complete and consistent Catholic culture for themselves in America? It is not a flippant play on assonances to reply that this will be when we allow the aura of our cult to permeate out to the utmost periphery of our living, or when we allow our Catholicism to be catholic in the sense of all-embracing. "Christianity, as no other religion," says Father Karrer, "evokes life in its entire extent and fulness, accepting it to bless it. It regards nothing that exists as contemptible or insignificant. *The entire creation is God's.* But for that very reason the universe is not the sumtotal of being; 'all things are not the All,' — the belief that they are must ultimately lead to despair or stoical resignation. 'God has entered nature to deify nature.' "[1]

Graduated Dependence. All created things have been created for God, but all are not for God in the same way. The several orders of creation have subordinated relationships toward the First Cause. Irrational creatures subserve man, man subserves Christ, Christ subserves God. "All things are yours," says St. Paul, "and ye are Christ's, and Christ is God's." The close relationship between Christ and irrational nature is emphatically repeated in several passages of the same Apostle, nowhere with greater beauty than in *Colossians:*   I Cor. iii,22

> Now He [Christ] is the Image of the unseen God,
> first-born before every creature.

---

[1] O. Karrer, *The Religions of Mankind* (New York: Sheed and Ward, 1936), p. 214.

For *in Him* were created all things in heaven and on earth,
   things seen and things unseen,
whether thrones or dominations or principalities or powers —
   all creation is through Him and unto Him.
   And Himself is prior to all,
   and in Him all things hold together.
   He again is the Head of the body, the Church:
it is He who is the beginning, the first-born from the dead,
   so that among all He Himself may stand first.
   For in Him it hath pleased [the Father]
      that all fullness should dwell,
Col. i,15–20   and through Him to reconcile all things to Himself.

Creation at Large Enslaved. Now, one of the minor tragedies consequent upon the primal fall of man was that it *upset and unbalanced* this divinely planned subordination and movement of *irrational nature* toward its End and Author. Since the unseeing and unreasoning homage of the lower orders is rendered God *by assisting man* in paying his meed of homage, when man refused to serve the Creator, lower nature also, as St. Paul puts it, was thereby made subject to vanity, enslaved, like man, beneath the yoke of sin. Man indeed was redeemed from *his* subjection to vanity by Christ's death, but the full emancipation of nature at large from *its* servitude will come only at the end of time:

Yea, creation with eager straining
awaiteth the manifestation of the children of God.
   For creation was made subject to vanity —
not of its own will, but by reason of him who subjected it —
   yet with hope that creation itself shall be freed
      from its slavery to corruption
unto the freedom of the glory of the children of God.
For we know that all creation doth groan and travail together
Rom. viii,19–22   unto this hour.

Progressive Emancipation. How is nature, thus groaning in enslavement, to use the Apostle's strong language, to be set free? The full and *complete manumission* will come only at "the manifestation of the children of God," that is, at the end of time. But a partial and *progressive liberation* of these enslaved creatures has been going forward in the Church ever since Christ walked the earth in His mortality. It is this idea, with its consequent important bearings on the full Christian life, that is sketched in this chapter. Another sidelight of the Christian's dignity is afforded by examining how the Church liberates and employs the innate, upward tendency of nature toward the spiritual and moral realm, toward inclusion among those things which are brought under the sole scepter of Christ.

Channels of Christ-Life. To start with, one sees how Christ Himself *liberated* and *enlisted certain elemental creatures* by making them channels of His sacramental graces. The water, which now has power to cleanse from original and personal sin, is surely freed from its primal subjection to vanity, and given patents of high nobility among all lower creatures. All water is now in a sense holy water. Likewise the oil, through the sacramental instrumentality of which unfailing strength and assurance are communicated in turn to the adolescent and the dying Christian, is sacred, set apart, and once more fulfills its real destiny of serving God in serving man. The simplest, commonest foodstuffs, bread and wine, are lifted to an unimaginable plane of nobility, when in obeying the transubstantiating Hand of God, their accidents permit us to have a visible Sacrifice and a visible Real Presence. Simple human actions, too, can thus be quickened to the divine touch, and carry the life of God to man. The mutual marriage contract of a man and woman, the ceremonial imposition of hands, and the acts of confession and contrition, all of these are ennobled and enlisted in Christ's "homely" processes of sanctification.

Making Nature Sacramental. Outside the scope of the seven sacraments, which are the work of Christ Himself, the *Church* has been inspired *to emancipate* a vast and indeterminate number of creatures, *sacramentals* as she calls them, and enlist them in her service of God. Thus, in the single act of erecting a building for her worship, the Church has shown countless ways of hallowing and dedicating to *her* use, and thus directly to Christ's use, myriad objects of irrational nature. The stone and brick of the towering structure, the arches, the vaultings, the columns and capitals — are all ennobled by being built into a house of God. The gleaming marbles of the sacrificial altar, or of the Communion table, or of the statuary, the glowing colors of the glasswork, the wrought iron and brass, the tapestries and veils and linens and vestments, the carved crucifix, the jeweled chalices and monstrance — do not all these unthinking objects here subserve their highest possible function by being given a voice in the sweeping oratorio of praise, which a church building is? The poetry of majestic ritual and the strains of noble chant, the fragrance of flowers, the gleaming tapers, the silver-tongued bells, the fuming thurible, the tossing of banners, the palm branches of triumph, the ashes of penance, the black shroud of the cata-falque — all these natural objects the Church has known how to eman-cipate and recruit as aids to sanctity, as subsidiary channels of Christ-life, as strands of "the cords of Adam."

Osee xi,4

But a devout Christian, after all, passes but a small part of the sum total of his life within a church. The long hours of the day are spent in office or factory or market or clinic or court; the precious joys of family life are limited for the most part to the sphere of the home. The scenes of one's occupation and the focal point of the home, both these are of incalculable importance in determining man's life, and therefore in deter-mining the quality of the *Christian life*. Consequently the Church is solicitous that her members should leave nothing undone that might well be done toward emancipating and enlisting as sacramentals the thousand and one natural objects that surround one at home or at work. The munificent hand of the Church is willing and anxious to bless and elevate *all* that pertains to the surroundings of the Christian. Conversely, an enlightened and appreciative use of this power of the Church is a token of the genuine Christian spirit.

Homage and Not Superstition. Before considering in any detail the wealth or variety of the sacramentals, with which Mother Church would surround the Christian life from morning until night, it is well to understand their real value, and to vindicate them clearly from the realm of superstition. Wherein differs the act of a Catholic in putting a blessed medal of St. Christopher on his automobile, let us say, and the act of a savage bushman tying a crooked horn to the axle of his rude cart? The latter, we say, is superstition, while the former is not. But why not? The external action performed may be quite similar in either case. In the case of the crooked horn as a talisman against mishap to the cart, we have a deliberate attempt *to supplement the efficaciousness of prayer* by a means in itself insufficient, but conceived as endowed with religious power. That is superstition. But the medal, by reason of its being blessed by the Church, derives an efficacy from the Church's intercessory powers with God. By the Church's act the medal is embodied into the grace-system, in a real, if subsidiary, way; the medal becomes a radiating-point of God's special relationships with man in His Son. The medal is in God's sight a sign of redemption, invoking in the only Name under Heaven whereby man must be saved a special blessing, which is Acts iv,12 another way to say a special Providence of God. Then, too, the medal is a sign for ourselves, and a reminder of the pious sentiments with which we commended the automobile and its use to God, through the mediation in this case of St. Christopher (Christ-bearer), in the knowledge that God's graces and blessings *are attracted by the continuance of such sentiments.* Sacramentals great or small thus differ from sacraments in this, that the efficacy of the sacramentals depends more upon the sentiments of those using them, than in the case of the sacraments. Again, if one is typing on a machine, say, that has been blessed, he is just as likely to misspell words or strike the keys in the wrong order as if sitting at a machine not so blessed. (The example is chosen quite at random, but the Ritual does provide a blessing for typewriters.) But the knowledge that the machine in the first case has been blessed and dedicated to God will awake in the user, *if he knows and adverts to the fact,* a certain sense of reverence as in dealing with something sacred, and of God's assisting presence, or man's destiny. However fleeting or instantaneous, or even inchoative, these acts may be, they are seeds of faith and hope and love, and so assist man in referring his work to God even though deficient in orthography. By multiplying around us these minor agencies of grace, man is assisted in carrying out the Apostle's injunction:

> Whether you eat or drink or do aught [besides],
> do all for the glory of God.   I Cor. x,31

This right attitude is well expressed in the General Blessing, included in the new "English-Latin Ritual" approved (June 3, 1954) for use in the United States:

Let us pray.

O God, by Whose word all things are made holy, pour down Thy blessing ✠ on this ———/these ——— which Thou hast created, and grant that whoever, giving thanks to Thee, uses it/them in accordance with Thy law and Thy will, may, by calling upon Thy holy name, receive through Thy aid health of body and protection of soul. Through Christ our Lord.   *R.* Amen.

The object(s) is (are) sprinkled with holy water.

Hallowing the Home. In what manifold ways may not the blessings of the Church bring a sanctifying influence into the intimacies of life? Suppose one begins by grouping some of the forms of benediction that concern individuals and family life. First of all the *home* or *apartment* is the object of several blessings. The dwelling is sprinkled with lustral water, as God is besought "to send an angel from heaven to guard, cherish, shield, and defend all who live in this home." Another form for the blessing of the home implores of God that through His blessing it may become "a home of health, chastity, self-conquest, virtue . . . goodness . . . and thankfulness to God the Father, Son, and Holy Ghost." In some Catholic countries, as in Italy, for instance, the custom obtains of having all the homes blessed yearly on Easter Eve. There is another type of quasi-blessing of the Christian home (and *this* is more common among us), the presence in the home of sacred images, crucifixes, statuettes, and religious pictures from the inexhaustible treasury of Christian art.

Mother and Children. The home, of course, exists only for those who dwell in it, and the Church's solicitude in first instance concerns these living members of Christ. The pregnancy of a mother is blessed with beautiful prayers that recall how the Body of Christ was formed through the overshadowing of the Holy Spirit. We are familiar with the blessing of a mother after delivery, a blessing we call in an old phrase "the churching of women." This blessing is desired by every Christian mother, because it brings her into touch with Mary's Purification. The newborn infant's blessing embodies a beautiful prayer addressed to Christ, "the Son of the living God, born before all ages, but who wished to be born an infant in the fullness of time." In a similar strain, "the merciful Lord and consoler of the faithful" is reminded in a blessing for the sick how He once visited and cheered and cured the mother-in-law of Simon Peter. Part of this exquisite formulary is:

> May the Lord Jesus Christ be with thee, to defend thee; within thee, to preserve thee; before thee, to guide thee; behind thee, to protect thee; and above thee, to bless thee.

Eloquent samples of the Church's solicitude for children abound in the Roman Ritual. This one is the final portion of the "Blessing for an Ailing Child" in the new American Ritual:

Blessing of a Sick Child

The priest holds his hands extended:

Let us pray.

O God, by Whose help all things grow to maturity and, once grown, are kept strong, stretch out Thy hand over this, Thy young servant, N., in his/her sickness, that he/she, having regained his/her health and strength, may grow up to full manhood/womanhood, and unfailingly offer Thee a loyal and pleasing service all the days of his/her life. Through Christ our Lord.

R. Amen.

The prayer finished, the priest lays his right hand on the child's head, and says:

V. They shall lay their hands upon the sick.

R. And they shall be healed.

May Jesus, the Son of Mary, Saviour of the world, through the merits and intercession of His holy Apostles, Peter and Paul, and of all the saints, be merciful and kind to you. R. Amen.

He blesses the child, saying:

May the blessing of almighty God, Father, Son, ✠ and Holy Spirit, descend upon you and remain forever. R. Amen.

He sprinkles the sick child with holy water.

When children, or young people in general, are sick, they have to stay home from school, but (sickness apart) how much of their time is not passed in school or college surroundings! Naturally the Church is most anxious that the young child be growing into his or her full stature as a Christian. This comes out in her blessing for schools:

Blessing of a School

Let the priest on entering sprinkle the rooms with holy water saying:

V. Peace to this house.

R. And to all who live here.

V. Our help is in the name of the Lord.

R. Who made heaven and earth.

V. The Lord be with you.

R. And with your spirit.

Let us pray.

O Lord Jesus Christ, Who didst command Thy Apostles to pray

that peace might come to whatever house they entered, sanctify ✝, we implore Thee, by our ministry this house meant for the education of youth. Pour into it the richness of Thy blessing ✝ and of Thy peace. May salvation come to those who live here as it came to the house of Zaccheus when Thou didst enter it. Command Thy angels to guard it and to drive away from it all the power of the enemy. Fill the teachers with the spirit of knowledge, wisdom, and fear of Thee. Strengthen the students with heavenly grace, so that they may grasp with their minds, treasure in their hearts, and carry out in their deeds all the teachings that lead to salvation. And may all here please Thee by practicing every virtue, so that they may one day be welcomed into Thy eternal home in heaven. Through Thee, Jesus Christ, Saviour of the world, Who lives and reigns, God, for ever and ever.

R. Amen.

Common Household Objects. Solicitude for the sick suggests benedictions for the wine of the sickroom, as well as for bandages and medicines and foodstuffs. Mention of these may serve to introduce us to blessings for household objects. At the blessing of the fire, or fireplace, whether this be the old-fashioned hearthstone, or the modern range, the thought of God as "the Light unfailing" is emphasized. Many of the major household objects are or may be recipients of special blessings. Suppose we single out the radio by reason of its paramount possibilities in advancing or hindering "the growth in Christ." The Church would by all means have so important an instrumentality ennobled and enlisted on the side of Christ. She says in blessing it:

O God, who walkest on the wings of the wind, and who alone dost wonderful works; grant, that as by the power implanted in this metal Thou dost bring quicker than the lightning-flash absent things hither, and dost speed things present hence away; so we, taught by new inventions, and supported by Thy grace, may be able more easily and quickly to come to Thee. Through Christ our Lord. Amen.[2]

Blessing of Automobile. Closely resembling the radio, in its capacity for affecting the Christian life, is the automobile. The blessing for this is well suited to impress upon those who have it employed those sentiments spoken of above, which insure God's benediction and special protection. No day passes but that the press abounds in accounts of auto-

---

[2] This form, originally framed for telegraph instruments, is used also for radios.

mobile fatalities, and everyone knows that the use of an automobile, so helpful in every way, is nevertheless attended by constant and serious dangers. In her blessing for an automobile the Church recalls with a certain solemnity how the immeasurable treasure of faith in Christ came Acts viii,27 to the Ethiopian man as he was riding in his chariot, and goes on to beg of God that His guiding Hand and His grace may attend this car through all paths and turnings of life.

Blessing of an Automobile or any Kind of Vehicle

V. Our help is in the name of the Lord.
R. Who made heaven and earth.
V. The Lord be with you.
R. And with your spirit.

Let us pray.

O Lord God, listen favorably to our prayers, and with Thy right hand bless ✠ this car/truck/wagon, etc. Send Thy holy angels to deliver and guard from every danger it and all who will ride in it. And as Thou didst grant faith and grace by Thy deacon, Philip, to the man from Ethiopia sitting in his chariot and reading Holy Scripture, so also show the way of salvation to Thy servants, so that, helped by Thy grace and always intent on doing good works, they may, after all the trials of their pilgrimage and life on earth, attain to everlasting joys. Through Christ our Lord.
R. Amen.

Let it be sprinkled with holy water.

The Airplane. All remember how a small and frail monoplane carried an intrepid American youth in solitary flight across the broad Atlantic. Where Colonel Lindbergh succeeded, many others have failed before and since, at the cost of their lives. But despite these disasters, flying itself goes steadily forward, until the full measure of man's mastery over the air will have been gained. Therefore the Church has prepared a blessing for airships, the first prayer of which is rendered.

O God, who dost all things for Thyself, and hast ordained all the elements of this world for the service of mankind; bless, we beseech Thee, this airship; so that, every evil and danger being far removed, it may promote a wider spreading of the praise and glory of Thy Name, and a more prompt dispatching of human affairs, and that it may foster in the souls of all using it heavenly desires. Through Christ our Lord. Amen.

A second prayer here begs God's blessings on all flyers who commit themselves to Mary's protection, and a third begs for them an angel companion from God on all such journeys.

Blessings for the City. The benedictions just mentioned bring one beyond the home, and out into the world of business. Here, too, the Church would have the sanctification of her presence become ever more prominent. She provides blessings for mills and factories, shops and ships as well as for all manner of agencies more directly social or communal, such as dynamos, telegraph lines, fire-fighting apparatus, ambulances, railway lines and equipment. Printing presses, libraries, archives, schools — all can be enlisted into the corps of the sacramentals, by specially appointed forms of benediction. Just as a city dweller is never far from a church, he need seldom find himself in a place where the hallowing touch of the Church's blessing has not been felt or may not reach.

And for the Country. The vast numbers of Christians engaged in occupations rural or pastoral are not left unprovided for in the Church's armory of blessings. The farm lands themselves are the object of frequent dedications to God; the seed, the sown fields, the ripening crops, the first fruits, the harvest, all are commended to the dominion of Him who alone giveth the increase. The swarming bees, the poultry, the herds and flocks — these, too, may be dedicated to God by prepared and appropriate formulae. Draft animals, man's invaluable servants, are a matter of special concern. Their stable may be placed under heaven's special protection with a prayer that commemorates how "the ox knew its Master and the ass the manger of its Lord" that winter night when there was no room in the inn. Does the farm possess a well, or a pond? In either case, this must have a benediction. Is a bridge building? It will be sprinkled with holy water, while God is asked to depute His angels to protect and defend it, and all who pass over it.

"The Middle Ages Were Ignorant." Of course, a skeptic could point out that much of the value set upon the Church's multiple blessings in ages gone by was due to popular ignorance of the physical sciences. There is truth in the fact that having the modern home protected by a lightning rod is felt to afford that assurance of safety formerly attached to a form of benediction. But when the fullest measure of man's mastery over nature is in every "scientific" way employed, the truest science still proclaims that we are insignificant creatures before the All Mighty. We do well, by the Church's special blessings, and by a thousand informal acts of dedication of our own, to increase and intensify the influence of Christ on the environment, physical and social, in which we live.

Summary. Thus, in whatever place or calling the individual Christian may live, the solicitude of the Church, whose wisdom is not from hence, unwearyingly furnishes him with many minor instrumentalities of sanctification. She seeks thereby to liberate and enlist and bring under the headship of Christ a creation that groans to be freed from its slavery

Rom. viii,20   to corruption. In particular, the Christian should thus envisage all the primary objects of his work and pleasure, his home, office, factory, and instruments of trade. The *rationale* of this attitude is expressed by St. Paul thus:

> Everything God hath created is good,
> and nothing is to be rejected,
> so it be received with thanksgiving,

I Tim. iv,4   for it is sanctified by the word of God and by prayer.

Twentieth-Century Source Material

(Few heralds of religion in our day bear comparison with Father Karl Adam of Tübingen; the passage cited is from his great book, THE SPIRIT OF CATHOLICISM.*)*

And in order that the rhythm of social life may be made harmonious by religious and sacramental concords, the Church approves innumerable confraternities and sodalities, confraternity altars and banners and feasts, in which religious effort aims at a specially intimate and lofty community expression. And to that extent it may be rightly said that Catholicism is the "religion of exalted moments." From out of the infinite abundance of its wealth it is constantly, as the hours pass, bringing new gems and new treasures to light, and these give a constantly new stimulus to the faithful and enrich them and do not suffer their interest to flag. So Niebergall describes the Church as a "mistress of joy to her children." The life and activity of the Church are irradiated with innocent joy, serene brightness, devout gladness. "Gothic architecture," said the Protestant Dean Lechler, "is at home only where the Mass bell rings." And he justly adds: "Without the worship of Catholicism neither

Raphael, nor Fra Angelico, neither Hubert Van Eyck, nor the younger Holbein, nor yet Lorenzo Ghiberti, Veit Stoss and Peter Vischer, would have produced the marvellous achievements of their art and endowed the churches of God on earth with a wealth of sacred beauty which will remain a treasure for all time." I am not sure that this intimate connection of Christian art with the Holy Eucharist, of the cathedral with the Tabernacle, is generally recognized. Catholic churches, whether of ancient or modern times, with all their wealth of beauty, are eucharistitc creations. They have sprung from a living faith in the sacramental Presence of our Lord. And where this faith has departed they lose their deepest meaning and are left without the idea which created and inspired them. They are beautiful but dead, bodies without a soul.

Much more might be said to show how the Church, in her sacramental work for souls, embraces also the inanimate creation, consecrating the altar stone, consecrating also the church's bells. We might speak of her Rogation Days whereon she blesses the produce of the fields, and tell how on Corpus Christi Day she carries the Blessed Sacrament out into the spring-time. The whole of nature, the flowers of the field, the wax of the bee, the ears of corn, salt and incense, gold, precious stones and simple linen — there is nothing which she does not bring into the service of the sacred Mystery, and bid them speak of It with their thousand tongues. Under her hands all nature becomes a "Lift up your hearts" (*Sursum Corda*) and a "Bless ye the Lord" (*Benedicite Domino*). "Everywhere," says Niebergall, "she makes men see the Holy and she fills the whole environment of her adherents with its charm and radiance." And where the Church herself is not active, there her children are at work. With hands that are rude and humble, but with eyes shining with the light of faith, they erect their sacred images and crucifixes in fields and by mountain paths, and carry the light and consecration of the divine up to the soaring peak and down to the foaming torrent. Amid a Catholic folk and in a Catholic land — there statues of our Lady stand by the roadside, there the Angelus bell is heard, there men still greet one another with the words, "Praised be Jesus Christ."

*   *   *

We have endeavored to estimate in a few brief sentences the Church's sacramental and mystical action in the formation of the *homo sanctus,* the saint. We have seen that she is able both comprehensively, and profoundly, with realistic force and with psychological insight, to bring God's grace down to men, and amid the dust and turmoil of everyday life to make the All Holy visible amidst innumerable candles. . . .

— By permission of Macmillan Company.

Topics for Further Discussion:

"Neither is there any other nation . . . that hath gods so nigh them." Deut. iv,7.

"Christians do not hold that the divine Presence must of necessity follow mystic elements and forms of words . . . but that [it] accompanies a calm and Godlike disposition." — *Synesius, a fifth-century bishop.*

Your description of the ideal Christian atmosphere in a factory or store; in a newspaper or magazine office.

That Christian symbolism affords a richer, and truer, conception of the world.

"The liturgy is creation, redeemed and at prayer, because it is the Church at prayer." — *Guardini.*

Readings:

F. Berger, *Cooking For Christ* (Des Moines: Nat. Cath. Rural Life, 1949); "The Liturgical Year in the Kitchen," *passim.*

F. Cabrol, *Liturgical Prayer, Its History and Spirit* (Westminster: Newman, 1950); "Sanctification of Places and Things," pp. 203–244.

Collectio Rituum, Latin-English Ritual for United States (Milwaukee: Bruce, 1954).

A. Fortescue, "Ritual *(Rituale Romanum),*" *CE.*

A. Gasquet, *Sacramentals and Some Catholic Practices* (St. Paul: Lohmann, 1924); "The Sign of the Cross," pp. 24–30; "Blessings and Consecrations," pp. 39–43; "Images," pp. 44–52, etc.

R. Guardini, *Sacred Signs* (New York: Benziger, 1931); Introduction, pp. ix-xiv; "The Sign of the Cross," pp. 3–4; "Holy Water," pp. 35–38; "Blessing," pp. 69–72; "Sacred Space," pp. 73–76; "Sacred Hours," pp. 81–90, etc.

────── *The Church and the Catholic* (New York: Sheed and Ward, 1935); "The Awakening of the Church in the Soul," pp. 28–31.

O. Karrer, *The Religions of Mankind* (New York: Sheed and Ward, 1936); "Christianity Is the Religion of Wholeness," pp. 211–221.

G. Lefebvre, *Catholic Liturgy, Its Fundamental Principles* (St. Louis: Herder, 1937); "The Sacramentals," pp. 105–117.

N. Maas, *The Treasure of the Liturgy* (Milwaukee: Bruce, 1932); "The Sacramentals," pp. 115–210.

V. Michel, *The Liturgy of the Church* (New York: Macmillan, 1937); "The Sacramentals," pp. 253–273.

Rituale Romanum, Table of Contents.

Rogation Day Booklet For Parish Observance (Des Moines: CRLB, 1955).

J. P. Schlarman, *With the Blessing of the Church* (Des Moines: Nat. Cath. Rural Life, 1946); 32 blessings of Ritual translated.

P. T. Weller, *Roman Ritual,* Blessings (Milwaukee: Bruce, 1946); *passim.*

Chapter XXVI

CHRISTOCRACY THROUGH CORPORATE WORSHIP

A glorious Church . . .
holy and without blemish
(Eph. v,27).

GOD does not exist for man, but man exists for God. In a sense nonetheless true, if not so palpably obvious, Christ does not exist for Christians, but Christians exist for Christ. Thus far in this course prominence has been given to the ideas of the supernatural life through incorporation into Christ, and the offices of corporate worship and the sacraments as so many channels of fuller participation in this super-life. The Christian life thus viewed is found to be one of incomparable dignity and nobility by reason of this most intimate association with, and participation in, the life of the God-Man. But our primary concern thus far has been with the question: What is the Church's function in *my* regard? What does the Church do for *me*? Bluntly stating the question in this egocentric way shows how one-sided our view of the Christian life has been, and the singular importance of the proper corrective at this point needs no further exposition.

It behooves us to ask fairly, what are the fruits of the Christian life? If the Christian life is livable, it should produce fruits of personal sanctification through the operation of the immanent, supernatural principle of grace, and fruits of social sanctification, through the measure of the Christian's beneficent influence on those around him. Though growth in grace is not directly measurable, its consequences are so clear there is no mistaking them: "By their fruits ye shall know them." Matt. vii,16

Finding One's Place. Instead of asking, then, what the Church does for me, the question ought to be approached from the other side, and phrased in some such way as this: "Now that I am incorporated into the Church, the Mystical Body of Christ, and live by its super-life, *what is my function in the Church,* what is *my* contribution to the well-being and

385

activity of the Church?" I, even I, am an integral part of the mystic Christ, and as such I have my own proper functions to perform. I must see to it, in the first instance, that I be a sound, a serviceable, smooth-functioning, cooperative unit, that the whole Body be not hindered and lamed on my account.

If one member suffereth,
all the members suffer therewith;

I Cor. xii,26

to the measure in which I fall short, in that measure will the glory of Christ be forever incomplete in me. Christ, who appointed some as Apostles, some as evangelists, some as shepherds and teachers, has ingrafted me into this vast, living Vine of Christ-life, that I may contribute my special fruitfulness to the whole. Definite tasks are envisaged for me in the great work to be done before

we all attain to the unity of the faith
and of the full knowledge of the Son of God,
to the perfect man,
to the full measure of the stature of Christ.

Eph. iv,13

The Work to Be Done. To make Christianity as a whole, humanity as a whole, a faultless reproduction of Himself, is Christ's great task, one to be fully achieved only at the end of time. But, meanwhile, as the myriad gems of the mosaic, each Christian must be separately formed and fashioned and fitted into *his* place in the whole. The Master-Worker is ever at His work, and each one of us, while being ourselves further fashioned in His hand, is at the same time a tool for the fashioning of others.

For we are His handiwork,
created in Christ Jesus for good works,
which God hath prepared beforehand
that therein we may walk.

Eph. ii,10

This fact of cooperating with the Master-Worker gives the Christian life, in unparalleled grandeur, its richness, its joyous creativeness, the gripping enthusiasm of an artist at work shaping Christ in himself and others. Life is given a new and matchless purpose by adoption into the Mystical Body,

that they who live
may no longer live to themselves,
but to Him who died for them
and was raised from the dead.   II Cor. v,14

Solidarity in God vs. Godless Solidarity. Let us consider the up-to-dateness of this Catholic Action on the foundation of the Mystical Body. "A Catholicism with a traditional sociology," observes Gurian in a recent work, "is of little use in a world as it is today." And even before the beginning of this century the centrifugal forces of "post-Christian" civilization had clearly indicated the catastrophe toward which they were bearing us. Reaction, even violent reaction, was inevitable, if civilization was to endure. The Fathers of the Vatican Council (1870) were deliberating, under the guidance of the Spirit of Love, on the doctrine of the Mystical Body as the divine magnet to repolarize, reintegrate, consolidate modern living: "In order that it should be held before the faithful and deeply rooted in their minds, this most excellent concept of the Church . . . *can never be sufficiently emphasized.*" But the sudden outbreak of *Mansi,* 51, 539 war dispersed the Council before that consultation was completed. Meanwhile gospellers of materialist and godless communism saw in hatred and class war the means with which to arrest the march of events and win through to a solidarity, dehumanized and de-souled, it is true, but a solidarity. The two programs are diametrically opposed: the clash of conflict will ring throughout the world.

"The Old Order Changeth." From that time forward the Church has ever more insistently spoken the social language of the Mystical Body. Pius X framed the Church's whole program in the words of an almost untranslatable passage from *Ephesians,* about the integration of all men under Christ's headship,

a dispensation to be realized in the fullness of time,
to bring all things [as] to a head in Christ.   Eph. i,10

Pius XI, throughout his long pontificate, emphatically reiterated the same evangel. "The hypostatic union of Christ," he once phrased it, " . . . brings back and puts before us the image of that unity by which our Redeemer wishes His Mystical Body, the Church, to be distinguished. . . . *The personal unity of Christ exists as the divine examplar with which He wishes the structure of society to conform.*" In the greatest of *Light of Truth,* 1931 his messages, *On the Reconstruction of the Social Order on Christian Principles,* the pontiff twice appeals to the doctrine of the Mystical Body. In the first of these passages he affirms of the social order, as reformed by functional groups from just natural principles, that it will *bear comparison* with the divinely revealed society of the Mystical Body; that it will be, namely, a quasi-mystical body built on the natural plane. Farther on, in treating of the realization of this new order of things, he says that the *intimate conviction* of membership in the Mystical Body of Christ is a prerequisite to the upbuilding of the new social order:

> Then only will it be possible to unite all in a harmonious striving for the common good, when all sections of society have the intimate conviction that they are members of a single family and children of the same heavenly Father, and further, that they are one body in Christ and members each of the other.

Rom. xii,5, Douay

We are fitted to help build a new social order only when we are thoroughly Mystical Body-minded.

"Communication of Christ-Life." The layman is called upon, even obliged, to work on this vast undertaking, by the very fact of his own membership in the Mystical Body. "The very sacraments of Baptism and Confirmation *impose* . . . this apostolate of Catholic Action . . . since through [them] we become members of the Church, or of the Mystical Body of Christ, and among the members of this body . . . there must be solidarity of interests and reciprocal communication of life."

Pius XI, 1934

"Now from this Pauline visualization of the Church there follow certain inevitable conclusions," argues Archbishop J. F. Rummel in addressing the National Council of Catholic Women. "The first is the necessity of solidarity among its members, involving mutual dependence and mutual responsibility. No member can subsist alone and no member can repudiate a definite sense of proportionate responsibilities for the welfare of others or for the perfection of the whole body. There is no room for individualism in the Mystical Body. Individualism shrivels up men's souls and robs them of the glorious opportunity of sharing in the full life of the Church and enjoying the exhilarating sensation of passing forward the stream of life blood and energy to other members of the

1935 Mystical Body." The picture the Archbishop here paints is the current

Pope Pius XI

pattern of American Catholicism in its social relationships, as one or other further quotation may illustrate. "In an age when men seem to have lost the appreciation of Christianity as a divine life," wrote Archbishop J. G. Murray in 1936, " . . . it seems providential that the Mystical Body has become the basis for the spiritual reconstruction of society." Archbishop S. A. Stritch handed on the same message when addressing a gigantic Catholic Action rally in Milwaukee, 1937:

Saint Paul expresses this social unity with the metaphor of the Mystical

Body of Christ in which we all are members, each doing his own function for the welfare of the whole. *Here we have a formula for which men these days are groping.* We may say that the exaggerated and unfortunate systems proposed are a very part of the groping.

Corporate Worship, Corporate Working. This grounding of society, as it were, on the exemplar of the Mystical Body, the upbuilding of an order of things on the principles, the preferences, and the love of Christ, a program to which the ringing name of Christocracy has been given, how is it to be done? or how is it to be *begun?* The answer is phrased with limpid clearness in a recent utterance of the Cardinal Archbishop of Quebec, Rodrigue Villeneuve, in addressing himself to Catholics in the United States:

> In our day, when every effort is being made to instil a religious spirit in society, it would be a lamentable mistake to give predominant place, above liturgy, to various organizations and pious works, whose supernatural efficacy depends entirely on how much they are imbued with a liturgical sense. And therefore, among the many activities of Catholic Action, the liturgical apostolate should be given the first place.[1]

The Apostolic Delegate, the Holy Father's personal representative in the United States, Archbishop Giovanni Cicognani, in 1934 analyzed the papal program of Catholic Action as comprising:

1. A striving after personal sanctification;
2. More frequent *participation in public worship;*
3. Applying the *zeal thereby aroused* to Christian reform;
4. Through channels of hierarchic guidance.

Some months later, addressing the Catholic Charities Conference, in Peoria, Archbishop Cicognani gave us a masterly exposition of the relations between corporate worship and Catholic social action. He says in part:

> The Holy Sacrifice of the Mass, and Holy Communion, which is an integral part of that Sacrifice, are the only true life that we possess. Upon that nourishment depend both the entire life of the individual Christian and the corporate life of the Church in the body of her faithful here on earth. The Christian has no life of his own. . . .
> From the beginning of the Church even to this day it is in the

---

[1] Cf. *Liturgical Arts,* XI (1937), 1, p. 6.

Eucharist that God makes Himself known: that God and man meet. . . . In earliest times, the clergy and faithful were comparatively few in number. Only one Mass was celebrated in each church. Bread and wine were offered by the faithful for the Holy Sacrifice; and every one brought gifts to be distributed later to the clergy and to the poor. This offering was considered obligatory, for it was held necessary to provide for all the needy of the Christian community. The rich and poor met alike as brothers of Christ. . . . They knew themselves to be incorporated into Our Lord: and as He made Himself one with them and gave Himself for all, so they would fire the world with love and, by His Gospel, make themselves one with another.[2]

Lay Liturgists, Lay Workers. And the laity, the Catholic Actionists, so to speak, how are they reacting to the papal and episcopal leadership? Shall we mention the *Liturgy Manual* of the National Catholic Alumni Federation? It is the belief of this body of lay leaders that in fostering corporate worship they have an "opportunity to engage in an essential form of Catholic Action more important in its ultimate consequences than any . . . merely economic and material plan." With similar direct-   1935 ness the National Council of Catholic Women voiced their corporate program "for the extension of the Mystic Body of Christ," to encourage the nation-wide adoption of courses in worship and plainsong by all Catholic colleges and high schools, and to second eagerly all efforts to promote active lay participation in worship. The Catholic youth move-   1936 ment, as led by the Sodality of the Blessed Virgin, has for several years subscribed to Father Lord's statement: "We may almost say that devotion to the Mass and the appreciation of Catholic Liturgy are at the very basis of Catholic Action." Note the significant resolutions passed by the   1932 Catholic college men and women at the Cleveland Eucharistic Congress of 1935:

"*Resolved:* 1. That the University and College Men and Women become active leaders of Catholic Action;

"2. That the students and graduates attend daily Mass;

"3. That Catholic men and women participate regularly in the Holy Sacrifice by receiving Holy Communion;

"4. That the Liturgical Movement be encouraged and promoted by the University and College students;

---

[2] A. G. Cicognani, *Addresses and Sermons* (New York: Benziger, 1938), pp. 197 sqq.; quoted by permission.

"5. That the students and graduates foster a greater appreciation of public worship or communal prayer."

Sociology and Catholic Action. A phenomenon no one can fail to take into account in any survey of our current Catholic life is the *Catholic Worker* group. Dorothy Day, converted Communist, and editor of the paper of that name, has dedicated the movement to "bringing the doctrine of the Mystical Body to the man in the street," and in this effort she has stated she considers nothing more serviceable than the liturgy. Bishop J. H. Schlarmann (Peoria) not long ago called liturgy "the finest possible course in Sociology and Catholic Action." Indeed, corporate worship is nowadays serving as a bridge, leading those interested in worship into sociology and sociologists into the sphere of corporate worship. Note this neat juxtaposition: there appeared almost simultaneously two books, *Christian Social Reconstruction*[3] by Dom Virgil Michel, O.S.B., and *Fire on the Earth*[4] by Paul Hanley Furfey. Well, the former book, which is the most systematic American commentary on the great encyclical on reconstruction, is by the late editor of *Orate Fratres,* our leading *liturgical* review; the latter work, by an author of years' standing in *sociology,* becomes a book in praise of the liturgical movement, which the author characterizes as "the rallying point for those who are enthusiastic about the new social charity." "Catholic Action will be successful in its efforts only in proportion as the liturgy is grasped and lived by its promoters," is the theme running through Confrey's *Catholic Action, a Text-Book for Colleges and Study Clubs.*[5] Even the sociologies being written for high-school use focus attention on the motivation of corporate worship and the Mystical Body, as clearly evidenced by Confrey's *Social Studies*[6] and, to a less extent, Ross' *Rudiments of Sociology.*[7]

"All One Person." The whole realm of social, including racial, economic, and religio-political activity of American Catholicism is being grounded on the notion of this endless upbuilding of Christ's Mystical Body. One sector of the far-flung line that is winning singularly beneficent victories is that of racial relationships, based on the recognition and application of the truth that

1934

Gal. iii,29

[3]Milwaukee: Bruce, 1937.
[4]New York: Macmillan, 1936, p. 53.
[5]New York: Benziger, 1935, p. 47.
[6]New York: Benziger, 1934.
[7]Milwaukee: Bruce, 1934.

> there is not Gentile and Jew . . .
> barbarian, Scythian,
> slave, freeman,
> but Christ is all and in all. Col. iii,10,11

Again, to a generation of laymen that had grown impersonally business-like and "efficient" in institutionalized charity, are being recalled the salutary lessons of *The Saints and Social Work,* and the motives of a personal love of the poor set before us once again: "To love our neighbor is to love God; for He is part of the Mystical Body of Christ. Too often we regard the words of our Lord,

> As long as ye did it to one of these, My least brethren,
> ye did it to Me, Matt. xxv,40

as a mere metaphor, whereas these words are really an accurate expression of the consequences of the union of the poor with Christ in the Mystical Body."[8]

A Glorious Church, a Glorious Land. This Church, the Mystical Eph. v,27 Body as growing up in our own land, is the Church of yesterday, that of the pioneers and missionaries adventuring for Christ on the frontiers of each age's expanding civilization. It is, moreover, the Church of the Middle Ages, of the catacombs, of the Apostles. The Christ that won the love of Paul on the road to Damascus long ago is the same that inflamed St. Ambrose and St. Augustine. Benedict of Nursia knew no other, nor Francis of Assisi, nor Dominic, nor Xavier, nor Vincent de Paul. The martyrs Agnes and Cecilia flung away their lives for the same Lover of Men who captured the affections of Scholastica, Clare and Catherine, Theresa of Avila, and Thérèse of Lisieux. In the narrow rounds of collegiate duties, or in the wider schools of life, the Christian of the twentieth century is called upon in turn to collaborate with the same peerless Leader in making himself and all others, as far as possible, flawless copies and expressions of Christ. The motivating force now is that same love of Christ which Cyprian described long ago in the last lines of his treatise *That Idols Are Not Gods:*

> It is with Christ that we journey, and we walk with our steps in His footprints: He it is who is our Guide and the burning Flame which

---

[8] M. E. Walsh, *The Saints and Social Work* (Silver Spring, Md.: Preservation of the Faith Press, 1937), p. 3.

illumines our paths; Pioneer of Salvation, He it is who draws us toward heaven, toward the Father, and promises success to those who seek in faith. We shall one day be that which He is in glory, if by faithful imitation of His example, we become true Christians, other Christs.[9]

Toward this country, land of our birth, fed in its traditions so largely on the "post-Christian" gospel, and threatened with paroxysms of accumulated poison, what is our obligation in bringing America under the saving and unifying headship of Christ? Bishop O'Hara (Kansas City) once put the question thus in a pastoral to his flock:

> It is reported that on Saturday evening, November 13th, of this year [1937], 3,000 Communists at Madison Square Garden in New York, with clenched fists raised in the Communist salute, "pledged their complete devotion to the Leninist struggle for socialism, for a Soviet America." These represent in America the forces which within the past eighteen months have destroyed or desecrated every church or altar under the power of loyalist Spain. As against their spirit of class hatred we shall gather in the spirit of Him who said: "Love your enemies, and do good to them that hate you." As against materialist atheism, we shall strive to serve God "in spirit and truth." As against a Soviet America, or any other form of dictatorship, we shall pray God for the perpetuation of the spirit of traditional American democracy, and for a renewal of a Christian sense of social justice and social charity. The Sacramental Presence of Jesus Christ on our altars is the symbol and cause of the unity of the Christian people who form the Mystical Body of Christ.

Matt. v,44
John iv,24

The Church is ready for the rescue; we must march with it, conscious of our Christing at baptism, our Christ-strength from confirmation, fed Christ-ful in the daily Eucharist; the call is to us armies of Christocrats recruited in our corporate worship. America's manhood in homes and schools and factories, in council chambers, legislative halls and executive mansions, Christocracy must reach, permeate, consolidate.

Summary. Action corresponds to being, as the axiom runs. The Catholic is embodied in a holy, corporate mode of being. To this state corresponds the duty nowadays called Catholic Action, which, motivated by corporate worship, corporately works out the peaceful revolution of bringing modern life under the headship of Christ.

---

[9]The translation is quoted from C. Marmion, *Christ, the Life of the Soul.*

Twentieth-Century Source Material

(One of the keenest observers of the present scene is Christopher Dawson, from whose book, RELIGION IN THE MODERN STATE, we quote.)

It is often objected that Christianity fails to find a remedy for our modern difficulties and that it has no clear-cut solutions for the political and economic problems of the present age. And this is in a sense true, inasmuch as it is not the business of Christianity to solve political and social problems except insofar as these problems become moral or religious. There is no Christian economic system that can be compared with the Capitalistic system or with the Communist economics. There is not even a Christian State in the absolute sense, there are only States that are more or less Christian and all more or less different from one another.

This is not to say, as Protestants used to say, that religion is a matter for the individual conscience and not a social matter at all. Christianity is anti-individualistic — as anti-individualistic as Communism itself. It is not merely a social religion, it is in its very essence a society, and it is only in the life of this One Body that the individual human being can attain his true end. But this society is not a State or an economic organization. It is the society of the world to come, the Bride of God, and the Mystical Body of Christ. Consequently Christian sociology is also theology. It is the theory of this divine society through which and through which alone the true destiny of the human race can be realized. All other societies are partial and relative ones — they exist to serve the temporary needs of humanity and to organize and protect the natural foundations on which the supernatural structure of the one absolute society is built up. As soon as they make themselves the absolute ends of human life they become *counter-churches,* representative of that City of Man which to the end of time makes war upon the City of God. — Quoted by permission of Sheed and Ward.

Topics for Further Discussion:

"There is no time or place better suited for the education of youth in Catholic Action than the schools and colleges." — *Pius XI* to Brazilian Hierarchy, 1936.

" 'Two things equal to a third are equal to each other.' . . . Incorporated into Christ, we are concorporated with each other." — *Bishop R. A. Kearney* (Auxiliary, Brooklyn), 1935.

"Once the Christian feels . . . the joy of incorporation into the Mystical

Body . . . then almost spontaneously . . . he will strive to impart the blessing he has received." — *Bishop J. A. Duffy* (Buffalo), 1935.

"Catholic peoples are wont to help one another mutually . . . practising the law of charity and brotherhood which joins us all in one Mystical Body of Christ." — Opening words, *Letter of Spanish Bishops*, 1937.

Readings:

Pope Pius XI, *On the Reconstruction of the Social Order on Christian Principles*, edit. *Catholic Mind*, June 8, 1931.

—— *On Atheistic Communism*, edit. *Catholic Mind*, April 22, 1937.

—— *The Present Position of the Catholic Church in the German Empire*, edit. *Catholic Mind*, May 8, 1937.

B. Confrey, *Catholic Action, A Text-Book for Colleges and High Schools* (New York: Benziger, 1935); "On What Is Catholic Action Based?" pp. 46–68; *passim*.

L. Civardi, *A Manual of Catholic Action* (New York: Sheed and Ward, 1936); A. G. Cicognani, Preface, pp. xvii–xxiii; *passim*.

R. J. S. Hoffman, *Restoration* (New York: Sheed and Ward, 1934); "Restoration and the Great Adventure," pp. 181–205.

J. LaFarge, *Interracial Justice* (New York: America Press, 1937); "A Catholic Interracial Program," pp. 172–187.

G. Michonneau, *Revolution in a City Parish* (Oxford: Blackfriars, 1949), "A Living, Apostolic Liturgy," pp. 25–46.

O. von Nell-Breuning, *Reorganization of Social Economy* (Milwaukee: Bruce, 1937; enl. ed.); "The Mystical Body of Christ," pp. 253, 254; "The Well-Springs of Love," pp. 339, 340.

H. Perrin, *Priest-Workman in Germany* (New York: Sheed and Ward, 1947), "Dreams and Plans," pp. 195, 196.

J. F. T. Prince, *Creative Revolution* (Milwaukee: Bruce, 1937); "Catholic Revolution," pp. 98, 99.

Restore the Sunday (Loveland: Grailville, 1949), *passim*.

M. Ward, *Insurrection vs. Resurrection* (New York: Sheed and Ward, 1937); "Epilogue," pp. 538–551.

—— *France Pagan?* (New York: Sheed and Ward, 1949), III, Impressions.

Chapter XXVII

IN RETROSPECT

Whose is the adoption and the glory . . .
and the liturgy and the promises
(Rom. ix,4).

B Y PRESENTING Catholicism from the point of view of its
worship, this book has sought to give the reader a clearer realization of his or her position in the Christian scheme of life. This
point of view is inspirational; for, in the very fact of having been baptized,
Catholics are absorbed in a super-world, endowed with super-life, become
in a real sense, super-men. In exploring these truths the mind is lifted to
hitherto unsuspected heights, which afford the vision of new wonders in
man's own nature, in the Church, and in the eternal kingship of Christ.
Indeed, it may be said that even a glimpse is had of the enchanting
beauties of the eternal mansions of God.

Lifted Up in Christ. A deep sense of how much human nature is
ennobled by being elevated to the divine life in and through Christ
should be one of the most abiding and transcendent lessons of this study.
Another most important conviction, which should be built into the Catholic's everyday consciousness as a result of this course, is a sense of
fellowship, of corporate being, so to speak, with Christ and His members.
Christian *worship* is social and corporate, that of the members with the
Head: "No man goeth to the Father save through Me"; Christian *work*   John xiv,6
is likewise corporate, that of the members with the Head: "Without Me
ye can do nothing." When these truths are pondered, and their vital   John xv,5
consequences little by little drawn out in the diversities of life, they should
produce a twofold modification of one's appreciation of Christianity.
Toward Christ a new bond is formed in the deepened knowledge of His
mediatorial character, and in the realization of a sharing in His life and
eternal priesthood. Respecting the neighbor, there is a far loftier estimate

of social obligations toward actual or potential fellow members of the Mystical Body. Contact with religion in its holiest rites, sacrifice, and sacraments has its enduring gains from the unifying concepts of Christ-life and Christ-work. In fine, in the light of the new knowledge, a synthesis results in which the close-knit solidarity of all things under the scepter of Christ is perceived as never before.

From the first page onward our never-failing Scriptural guide has been the Apostle of the Gentiles, from whose inspired writings have been drawn all our proofs. He now furnishes us with the apt phrases set out above, in which we can sum up, and, as it were, outline the leading ideas of the whole book.

No Longer I That Live. After a preparatory comparison of the "catechism religion" of childhood with maturer understanding of the same, we began with the stupendous fact that the Christian through Christ, the second Adam, has been lifted up by *adoption* into the family of God. We are made to share, as St. Peter puts it, in the very nature of God. We are made *to live,* to return to the language of St. Paul, *with the life of Christ* living within us. In fact, in the eyes of God, all other life save this co-life with Christ is as death. We who were formerly dead in sin have been *brought to life in Christ.* Commenting on those words, "It is no longer I that live; it is Christ that liveth in me," an English author writes:

Gal. ii,20

> As if he [Paul] would say (for he is speaking only of the life of grace), I have life in the eyes of God only so far as the life that I have is the life of Christ, only insofar as I *am* Christ. God looks for Christ in me, and I am alive — I am what He created me to be — in proportion as He sees Christ in me.[1]

A comparison of the new life acquired in Christ with the old integrity lost in Adam led us to estimate more truly, if still inadequately,

> what is the breadth and length and height and depth —
> to know the charity of Christ that surpasseth knowledge,
> *that ye be filled unto all the fulness of God.*

Col. iii,19

Ye Did It to Me. As a further step, the contemplation of Christianity as a Christocentric universe proves to be a theme rich in abiding values.

---

[1] R. H. J. Steuart, *The Inward Vision* (New York: Longmans, Green, 1933), pp. 56, 57.

What consequences may not follow from the general realization of the truth that to be a Christian means to be one with Christ? What a many-sided revelation of Christianity as a whole, of my place in that union, and of the endless *social implications* of this living solidarity!

> Herein there is not gentile and Jew . . .
> barbarian, Scythian, slave, freeman,
> but Christ is all and in all.   Col. iii,11

Once upon a time the living of this truth had such direct and transforming effects on Christians everywhere and in all their mutual associations, that the world in amazement cried: "See how these Christians love one another!" To such an extent nowadays "has the love of many grown cold," that a scoffing cynic parodies the ancient tribute, "See how *these*   Matt. xxiv,12 Christians tear one another!" In the widespread disillusionment and dis-belief of our age, Catholicism will flourish and extend its beneficent influence only in proportion as it renews itself in this sense of social union and love. It is a sad commentary on the needs of the age that the motto of the present Pope should have to read: "In justice there is peace."

Corporate Worship a Dictate of Nature. It is profitable at times to give oneself an account of ideas so long taken for granted that they are as it were relegated to the storerooms of the subconscious mind. In this way the *concept of worship* was re-examined early in the course. It was seen to be one of those primal impulses of human nature, as native to man as the air we breathe, and as necessary. It belongs to the very creaturehood of man, so to speak, to "seek after God," to adore Him   Acts xvii,27 as the Creator, to thank Him as our Benefactor, to petition Him as Father, and to appease Him as Judge. These spontaneous motions of the mind and heart are voiced in external acts of worship (called in their ensemble liturgy), and quite naturally they tend to become public and social. "There can be no religion," says St. Augustine, "there can be no   *Contra Faustum,* religion true or false, without external ceremonial."   xix,11

Priestly Mediation. What characterizes Christian worship in con-trast to all others is its manner of approach toward God. The pagan and the Jew go direct to God; the Catholic approaches Him only *through a*

> *Mediator* standing between God and man,
> himself a man, Jesus Christ.   I Tim. ii,5

Instead of being an intermediary who interposes Himself between God and man, Christ is found to be a real and vital connecting bond, linking the human with the divine.

> Amen, Amen, I say to you:
> ye shall see the Heaven opened
> and angels of God ascending and descending
> upon the Son of Man.

John i,51

To Preserve, Not to Destroy. How admirably Christianity in its worship *hallows* and *purifies* and *preserves* all that is good in man's native religious impulses was seen in broad outline. From the dawn of recorded history man was everywhere seen to seek to set up permanent relationships between himself and the Creator. To this end he organized social and public worship, set up priesthoods, devised elaborate rituals, composed fixed prayers, and instituted all the other offices of religion. He early explored the many possible ways of expressing devotion through varieties of vocalization, of posture, through the use of natural symbols, and in the manifold creation of sacred art-forms. Further, he felt prompted to consecrate to God all the crises of natural life, birth, adolescence, marriage, sickness, death, interment, with religious usages proper to each case. Lastly, he sought to sanctify the ebb and flow of time by observing annual and seasonal religious commemorations of various kinds. By common consent men were agreed that the *paramount expression of the religious sentiment* is the public giving to God of a gift in token of personal and social dedication to Him, and this act is called *sacrifice*. To this natural groping toward God, how eminently Christianity is the all-satisfying solution! Its hierarchical priesthood, its inexhaustible wealth of ceremonial, its almost limitless use of nature and art in its worship, its sevenfold sacramental system — all are utilized in lending adornment and beauty to its crowning excellence, the day-by-day re-enactment of the Christian Sacrifice, which is no other than the supreme Oblation by which the race was ransomed.

"Do This in Memory of Me." The august rites of this *Christian Sacrifice* naturally bulked large in the preceding chapters. Thus, we saw how these were carried out in primitive Christianity, and in the early Middle Ages. This is another valuable aspect of human and Christian solidarity. In Christ, and only "in Him all things hold together." The

Col. i,17

analysis of the Christian's sacrificial calendar showed us the function of this detailed unfolding and commentary on the life of Christ in the upbuilding of a Christian character. In the case of Christ, the Christian theory of life is presented as the Way and the Truth and the Life: in the case of the perfect Christians, the Blessed Virgin Mary and the saints, the theory is shown as reduced to practice. This endless procession of Christ-in-His-brethren walking before us in triumph, little by little engenders an unwavering conviction that we, too, have been

> fitted for our portion
> of the inheritance
> of the saints in light.   Col. i,12

Our Eucharistic Age. The vicissitudes of twenty centuries have brought, as we saw, certain *changes in Christian piety* in relation to even such a central mystery as the Holy Eucharist. Thus, while in the fullest possession of a sacrificial consciousness, the earlier Christians regarded the Eucharist chiefly as a *means* of sacrifice and of personal union with God through the actual reception of Communion. This attitude having been in a measure obscured by historical developments, a new attitude of adoration and worship of the Eucharist itself, of the Eucharist as an *end*, one might say, came largely to occupy the center of Christian piety. In the earlier period the Eucharist made the Sacrifice possible, and was the bond of union with Christ and among the members of the Mystical Body; but there was lacking all that wealth of conscious devotion directed to the Real Presence. In subsequent ages Christ in the Eucharist was reserved in tabernacles, was visited and adored and borne in processions; but Christ as the food and drink of the Father's Table had but a rare opportunity to delight men with His sweetness. Our cursory survey of the guiding factors in these developments awakened a sense of gratitude in us, that it is our good fortune to live in the twentieth century. We are entering upon an age which preserves the gains of the worship of the Real Presence, and is learning to combine them with the ancient sense of fellowship in sacrificial oblation and sacrificial banquet. Additional grounds for gratitude were seen on surveying the reforms now in quiet progress for the fuller and more intimate participation of the laity in the sublimest offices of worship.

Fountains of Life. The study of the *sacraments* was approached by

way of the respective *rites of administration*. This method of approach was found to yield new and deeper knowledge of these *life-giving streams*. "The Sacraments," says Archbishop Goodier, "to him who believes in the indwelling of Jesus Christ, are very much more than the mere ceremonial which is seen from without. They are the ingrafting into the body, they are the joints of the limbs; they are the channels through which the blood of Jesus Christ flows down into the members."[2] Abundantly providing for every necessity of life and tenderly anticipating every wish, the sacraments lift us to the plane whereon the divine life is communicated to us

> through His power
> which is at work in us,

and the Apostle has it,

> He [God] is able to accomplish
> far beyond all that we ask or understand.   Eph. iii,20

Even in the recreant

> where sin hath been multiplied,
> grace hath abounded yet more.   Rom. v,2

These great sacramental graces the Christian knows he can obtain *only* in the sacraments. Therefore he "frequents," as he says, the sacraments as the most manifest evidence of the practice of his religion.

Christocrats. The force of the Christ-life within produces in its gradual unfolding a sense of strength, an exigency of motion and activity, an impelling desire to use these faculties for Christ-work. This is the Christian life in operation, to *"work out* our salvation," our own and   Phil. ii,12 our neighbor's. This means, above all else, allowing Christ to dominate our lives, to have full sway over our thoughts, aspirations, and activities. St. Paul called this "making the life of Jesus manifest in our bodies."   II Cor. iv,10 And the timely bearing of all this in the reconstruction of the social order now being undertaken was reviewed in words of Pius XII's new encyclical letter of 1947.

There, in a word, is the immediate term of the Christian life, Christ,

> the Alpha and the Omega
> the Beginning and the End.   Apoc. xxi,6

---

[2] A. Goodier, *The Inner Life of the Catholic* (New York: Longmans, Green, 1933), p. 53.

Christians in the world, no less than those called to the sublime consecration of the priesthood or cloister, are Christ's soldiers, His ambassadors, His collaborators, His members in which He is to reach
Eph. i,23   fulfillment.

Col. i,28

> Christ within you, your hope of glory,
> Him we proclaim.

This fellowship, in which each one "is rooted and built up in Him," we
call our holy Mother, the Church, and Catholics love her with a filial love.

Conscience, it is true, demands that we yield the Church obedience, but
love anticipates conscience by prompt and ready service. Salvation, indeed, requires allegiance to the Church unto death, but fellowship inspires
a sense of responsibility and of common interests and active leadership
for the cause of Christ. "This is the very definition of a Christian," says
Cardinal Newman, "one who looks for Christ; not who looks for gain
or distinction, or power, or pleasure, or comfort, but who looks for the
Saviour, the Lord Jesus Christ."

> I count all things loss
> by reason of the excellence of the knowledge of Christ.
> For His sake I have suffered the loss of all things
>   and count them but refuse
>   in order that I may gain Christ
>   and be found in Him . . .
>   so that I may know Him,
> what the power of His resurrection,
> what fellowship in His sufferings,
> and become one with Him in His death,
> in the hope that I may attain to the resurrection from the dead . . .

Phil. iii,9–14   to attain the reward of God's heavenly call in Christ Jesus.

Outline of Course

"Whose is the adoption"
Chapters I to III
  Adult Catholicism; the Mystical Body, Super-nature, or grace.

"and the liturgy"
Chapters IV to XXV
  Christ's Priesthood; natural impulse to worship; this, as elevated by

Christ; worship as a social bond; the ecclesiastical year; the altar and vestments; a papal Mass in the early Middle Ages; the relation of the frequency of Communion to the general sacrificial consciousness; historical and ritual study of the present Roman Mass; modern modes of active lay participation in worship; the Breviary: the seven sacraments in relation to Christ-life in the Mystical Body; the Christian's "falling asleep"; sacramentals.

"and the promises"
Chapters XXVI, XXVII
    Christ-work, and its rewards; summary.

Twentieth-Century Source Material

(Monsignor Fulton J. Sheen is an eloquent herald of the doctrines this book propounds: with his permission we conclude by quoting):

. . . Communism, as it has been defined, is not peculiar to Russia alone. We see there the mobilization of souls under an *economic* disguise where one hundred and sixty millions of God's creatures destined for eternal Life are dehumanized and reduced to the state of ants, whose sole business in life is to build up the great ant-hill of the Classless Class; we see it in Mexico with a *political* disguise where treason is synonymous with the worship of the Crucified; we see in with a *racial* mask in Germany where the State would crush the religion of Him who rose from the dead, and would return to the barbarism of gods who are still rotting in their graves. In all three instances men are bludgeoned into living their lives without God; they are beaten and hammered into the new pattern of the collective, where barbarism filters through the sieve of the State and where the gods of economics are supreme. . . .

Because Communism does insist on the social and communal it can never be opposed by any system of ideas, or by any loud shouting about rugged individualism; it can be stopped only by something social and communal. Because it mobilizes souls for economic ends and crushes the spiritual element in man, it can only be stopped by some force which mobilizes souls for eternal ends and preserves the honor of a man. In a word, Communism can be met only by that historical form of Christianity which has been excluded from Western Civilization for 300 years and which is now returning from exile, namely the Church. . . .

What is the Mystical Body of Christ which alone can save the soul of civilization? The Mystical Body of Christ is the Church. In order to understand its role in the world let it be recalled that when Our Blessed Lord was born of the Virgin Mother over 1,900 years ago, under the floor of the world in the village of Bethlehem, the political, economic and social conditions of His time were very much like our own. Politically there was militarism with practically the whole world under the eagle of Rome; economically there was heavy taxation. Hence the burning question: Was it lawful to pay tribute to Caesar? Socially there was a legalism, an externalism, a Pharisaism, or what we call Puritanism.

The interesting and instructive fact is, that He who set out to regenerate a world said nothing whatever about militarism, about finances, about economics; He said nothing about armaments; He even said nothing about the horrors of war. And yet He did something for all these things. How? Not by making religion a purely individual affair, for how could a million men love God without loving one another, since things that are equal to the same thing are equal to each other. Rather did He lay plans to infuse the world with a new society, a new kingdom, a new organism which would be the social prolongation and extension of the Divine Life He brought to earth. . . .

As He took a human body from the womb of His Blessed Mother, overshadowed by the Holy Spirit, so now He took His Mystical Body or the Church from the womb of humanity, overshadowed by that same Holy Spirit. Through this Body, Christ at the right hand of the Father, continues to do the same three things He did with His physical body, namely, to teach, govern and to sanctify. . . .

The Eucharist is the lymph of the Mystical Body. Like a mighty river it swells and sweeps through the Church in every part of the world, breaking its secret of salvation to every individual Catholic, whispering its wondrous message of love for the healing of wounds to this one, dipping the chalice of its wine for the increase of joy to that one, thus making them all one because nourished by the same Bread. Such is the meaning of the words of St. Paul: "WE, being many, are one body, for we all partake of one Bread." What a beautiful foundation for the social order, for international peace, for brotherly love, for we are all one in Christ Jesus Our Lord! . . .

The Communion rail is, for that reason, the greatest Democracy on the face of the earth; it is even a greater Leveller than Death, for there the distinction between the rich and poor, the learned and unlearned, disappears; there the millionaire must take the paten from the common laborer; the employer must kneel at the same board as the employee; the University Professor must eat the same Bread as the simple Irish woman who knows only how to tell her beads. The dividing wall between nationalities is broken down and rebuilt into that spiritual Kingdom where all are one, because One Lord, one Faith, one Baptism, one Bread. Every prayer is said in the great context of that brotherhood, where every selfish act of the rich and every envious deed of the poor, is envisaged as a hindrance to the unity of that Body. Hence we say if you want to be a real Communist then be a communicant and bring your hearts to the anvil of Divine Life, and have them all forged into unity by the Eucharistic Flames of the Sacred Heart, where we call one another, not the atomic name of "Comrade" but the spiritual name of "Brother."

Do you say that the Eucharist as a solution for world troubles is too idealistic; do you condemn it because it is impractical? Certainly it is impractical, but that is precisely why it will succeed. . . . There is only one way left to effect social and economic reconstruction, and that is by spiritual and moral regeneration through the Eucharist and the Sacrifice of the Mass.

That is the impractical way Our Lord chose to redeem and transform the world. Extremely impractical it was to put down economical and political justices by dying on a cross, which was the first Mass; impractical indeed it was to win a victory over the hardened hearts of men by going down to defeat; impractical indeed it was to save a selfish world by the Love which ended in the Sacrifice of the Cross. . . .

Appendix

THE EUCHARISTIC FAST

Motu Proprio of His Holiness Pope Pius XII

"Sacram Communionem"

Early in 1953 (January 6) we proclaimed the Apostolic Constitution "Christus Dominus," with which we mitigated the severity of the laws regarding Eucharistic fasting, so that the faithful may receive Holy Communion more frequently and more easily satisfy the precept of hearing Holy Mass on feast days.

To this end we granted to the Bishops of the dioceses the faculty of permitting the celebration of Mass and the distribution of Holy Communion in the evening, as long as certain conditions were observed.

We reduced the time of fasting to be observed before Mass or Holy Communion, celebrated or received in the afternoon, to three hours for solids and one hour for non-alcoholic liquids.

The Bishops expressed their deep gratitude to us for these concessions which had produced such abundant fruits, and many have begged us unceasingly to authorise them to allow the celebration of Holy Mass in the afternoon every day, in view of the great benefit the faithful would draw from this.

They have also begged us to establish a similar time for fasting to be observed before Mass or Holy Communion celebrated or received in the morning.

We, understanding the considerable changes which have taken place in the organisation of work and of public offices and throughout social life, have thought it opportune to grant the insistent demands of the Bishops and we have therefore decreed:

1. The Bishops, except for Vicars General who are not provided with special mandate, may permit the celebration of Holy Mass in the after-

noon each day, as long as this is required for the spiritual good of a considerable number of faithful.

2. Priests and the faithful are bound to abstain for three hours from solid foods and alcoholic beverages, for one hour from non-alcoholic beverages, before Mass or Holy Communion respectively. Water does not break the fast.

3. From now on, also those who celebrate Mass or receive Holy Communion at midnight or in the small hours of the morning must observe the times of fasting as given in No. 2.

4. The sick, even if they are not confined to bed, may take non-alcoholic beverages and genuine medicines, both liquid and solid, before Mass or Holy Communion respectively, without time limit.

However, we fervently exhort the priests and the faithful who are in a position to do so to observe the old and venerated form of Eucharistic fasting before Mass and Holy Communion.

May all those who take advantages of these concessions, then, repay the benefits received by shining examples of Christian lives and principally by works of penance and charity.

The rulings of this Motu Proprio will come into force on March 25, 1957, the Feast of the Annunciation of the Blessed Virgin Mary.

All contrary rulings, even if worthy of special mention, are hereby abrogated.

Given in Rome, at St. Peter's, on March 19, the Feast of St. Joseph, Patron of the Universal Church, 1957, nineteenth year of our Pontificate.

SELECT RECENT PUBLICATIONS

(On which supplementary reading and term papers may be based)

P. F. Ansen, *Churches: Their Plan and Furnishing* (Milwaukee: Bruce, 1948).

The Assisi Papers: Addresses Given at Assisi-Rome (Collegeville: Lit. Press, 1957).

Baptism Is Social, Monks of Conception (Conception: Abbey Press, 1956).

J. Beguirztain, S.J.–J. H. Collins, S.J., *The Eucharistic Apostolate of St. Ignatius Loyola* (Boston: Loyola House, 1956).

L. Bouyer, C. O., *Liturgical Piety* (Notre Dame Univ. Press, 1955).

——— *The Paschal Mystery* (Chicago: Regnery, 1950).

M. Britt, O.S.B., *The Hymns of the Breviary and Missal* (New York: Benziger, 1948).

Sr. M. Gabriel Burke, O.S.F., *Liturgy at Holy Cross in Church and School* (St. Louis: Pio Decimo, 1952).

F. Cabrol, O.S.B., *Liturgical Prayer: Its History and Spirit* (Westminster: Newman, 1950).

Candlemas: Suggestions for the Christian Observance of Candlemas in the Parish (Loveland: Grailville, 1950).

Sr. M. Cecilia, O.S.B., *Companion to the Missal* (Milwaukee: Bruce, 1954).

H. E. Collins, *The Church Edifice and Its Appointments* (Westminster: Newman, 1946).

J. Coventry, S.J., *The Breaking of Bread: A Short History of the Mass* (New York: Sheed and Ward, 1950). Pictures by J. Gillick, S.J.

C. R. A. Cunliffe, ed., *English in the Liturgy: A Symposium* (London: Burns, Oates, and Washbourne, 1956).

J. Danielou, S.J., *The Bible and the Liturgy* (Notre Dame Univ. Press, 1956).

Sr. Laurentia Digges, *Transfigured World:* Design, Theme and Symbol in Worship (New York: Farrar, Strauss and Cudahy, 1957).

Directives For the Building of a Church. By the Liturgical Commission of the German Hierarchy (Collegeville: Lit. Press, 1950).

Directoire pour la pastorale de la messe, Committee of Cardinals and Archbishops of France (Paris: CPL, 1956).

G. Ellard, S.J., *The Mass in Transition* (Milwaukee: Bruce, 1956).

*First Liturgical Institute, Valparaiso University (Valparaiso: Univ. Press, 1950).

J. Gelineau, S.J., *Twenty-Four Psalms and a Canticle* (Toledo: Greg. Institute, 1957).

R. Guardini, *The Church and the Catholic* and *The Spirit of the Liturgy* (New York: Sheed and Ward, 1953).

—— *Meditations Before Mass* (Westminster: Newman, 1955).

M. B. Hellriegel, *How to Make the Church Year a Living Reality* (St. Louis: Pio Decimo, 1956).

I. Herwegen, *Liturgy's Inner Beauty* (Collegeville: Lit. Press, 1955).

C. Howell, S.J., *Of Sacraments and Sacrifice* (Collegeville: Lit. Press, 1952).

P. Hume, *Catholic Church Music:* A Pastoral Guide for the Choir Loft (New York: Dodd, Mead and Co., 1956).

J. A. Jungmann, S.J., *The Eucharistic Prayer* [Canon] (Chicago: Fides, 1956).

—— *The Mass of the Roman Rite* (*Missarum Sollemnia*) (New York: Benziger, I [1951], II [1955]).

—— *The Sacrifice of the Church:* the Meaning of the Mass (Collegeville: Lit. Press, 1957).

J. Kearney, *The Meaning of the Mass* (London: Burns, Oates, and Washbourne, 1948).

T. Klauser, *A Brief History of the Liturgy* (Collegeville: Lit. Press, 1953).

**E. B. Koenker, *The Liturgical Renaissance in the Roman Catholic Church* (Univ. of Chicago Press, 1954).

J. Kramp, S.J., *Live the Mass* (St. Paul: Cat. Guild, 1954).

G. Lefebvre, O.S.B., *Catholic Liturgy* (St. Louis: Herder, 1954).

H. de Lubac, S.J., *Catholicism* (New York: Longmans, 1949).

—— *The Splendor of the Church* (New York: Sheed and Ward, 1956).

---

*Books marked with an asterisk (*) are outstanding works in this field by non-Catholic scholars.

Sr. M. Marietta, S.N.J.M., *Singing the Liturgy:* A Practical Means of Christian Living (Milwaukee: Bruce, 1955).

P. Marx, O.S.B., *Virgil Michel and the Liturgical Movement* (Collegeville: Lit. Press, 1957).

E. Masure, *The Christian Sacrifice* (New York: Kenedy, 1948).

T. Merton (O.C.), *Bread in the Wilderness* (New York: New Directions, 1953).

G. Michonneau, *Revolution in a City Parish* (Oxford: Blackfriars, 1949).

*B. Minchin, *The Celebration of the Eucharist Facing the People* (Bristol: Bedminster Vicarage, 1954).

J. L. Murphy, *The Mass and Liturgical Reform* (Milwaukee: Bruce, 1956).

P. Murray, O.S.B., *The Canon of the Mass:* A New Translation (Dublin: The Furrow, 1955).

E. E. Nemmers, *Twenty Centuries of Catholic Church Music* (Milwaukee: Bruce, 1949).

M. R. Newland, *We and Our Children:* Molding the Child in Christian Living (New York: Kenedy, 1954).

J. B. O'Connell, *Church Building and Furnishing* (Notre Dame Univ. Press, 1955).

E. V. O'Hara, *The Participation of the Faithful in the Apostolate and in the Liturgy* (Kansas City, 1951).

P. F. Palmer, S.J., *Sacrament and Worship* (Westminster: Newman, 1955).

P. Parsch, O.S.A., *The Breviary Explained* (St. Louis: Herder, 1953).

———— *The Church's Year of Grace* (Collegeville: Lit. Press) (II, III available, I, IV in preparation).

M. Perkins, *Beginning at Home:* The Challenge of Christian Parenthood (Collegeville: Lit. Press, 1955).

T. Plassmann, O.F.M., *From Sunday to Sunday* (Paterson: Guild Press, 1948).

Promised in Christ (Loveland: Grailville, 1954).

J. Putz, S.J., *My Mass* (Westminster: Newman, 1948).

A. M. Roguet, O.P., *Christ Acts Through the Sacraments* (Collegeville: Lit. Press, 1954).

A. de Sauvboeuf, *Our Children and the Mass:* How to Make it Live for Them (Chicago: Fides, 1956).

F. J. Sheed, *Theology and Sanity* (New York: Sheed and Ward, 1946).

T. W. Smiddy, *A Manual for the Extraordinary Minister of Confirmation* (Milwaukee: Bruce, 1949).

G. D. Smith, ed., *The Teaching of the Catholic Church* (New York: Macmillan, 1949), 2 v.

G. W. Smith, transl., *Christian Worship:* Encyclical Letter, Mediator Dei, *On the Sacred Liturgy* (London: CTS, 1948).

*J. H. Srawley, *The Early History of the Liturgy* (Cambridge: Univ. Press, 1947).

—— *The Liturgical Movement: Its Origin and Growth* (For the Alcuin Club, London, Mowbray, 1954).

B. Steuart, O.S.B., *The Development of Christian Worship* (New York: Longmans, 1953).

B. Strittmatter, O.S.B., *Sacred Latin Hymns* (Latrobe: Archabbey Press, 1948).

A. Vonier, O.S.B., ed., *A Key to the Doctrine of the Eucharist* (Westminster: Newman, 1950).

G. Webb, *The Liturgical Altar* (Westminster: Newman, 1949).

F. X. Weiser, S.J., *Religious Customs in the Family:* the Radiation of the Liturgy into Christian Homes (Collegeville: Lit. Press, 1956).

P. T. Weller, *The Roman Ritual,* I, Sacraments (Milwaukee: Bruce, 1950); II, Christian Burial, etc. (1952); III, The Blessings (1946).

H. R. Williamson, *The Great Prayer* [Canon] (New York: Macmillan, 1956).

M. Zundel, *The Splendour of the Liturgy* (New York: Sheed and Ward, 1956).

INDEX